16 Years 2025-2010

ICSE

CHAPTERWISE TOPICWISE QUESTION BANK

Geography

Class 10

16 Years 2025-2010

ICSE

CHAPTERWISE TOPICWISE QUESTION BANK

Geography

Class 10

Author

Shivani Dogra

arihant

SUCCESS AND NOTHING LESS

arihant
SUCCESS AND NOTHING LESS

ARIHANT PRAKASHAN
(School Division Series)

卐 ADMINISTRATIVE & PRODUCTION OFFICES

Regd. Office
'Ramchhaya' 4577/15, Agarwal Road, Darya Ganj, New Delhi -110002
Tele: 011- 47630600, 43518550

Head Office
Kalindi, TP Nagar, Meerut (UP) - 250002, Tel: 0121-7156203, 7156204

卐 SALES & SUPPORT OFFICES

Agra, Ahmedabad, Bengaluru, Bareilly, Chennai, Delhi, Guwahati, Hyderabad, Jaipur, Jhansi, Kolkata, Lucknow, Nagpur & Pune.

卐 **PO No :** TXT-XX-XXXXXXX-X-XX

Published By Arihant Publications (India) Ltd.

For further information about the books published by Arihant, log on to www.arihantbooks.com
or e-mail at info@arihantbooks.com

卐 **PRICE** ₹230.00

Follow us on

Achieving 99+
Marks in Board Exams

Achieving 99+ marks in board exams is definitely an ambitious goal, but with the right approach and these 7 tips from toppers, you can definitely increase your chances of success!

Here are the 7 Topper Tips to ace your board exams:

1. Master the art of consistency

Consistency builds understanding and confidence, both crucial for excelling in exams.

2. Build a winning study strategy

Create a personalised timetable that prioritises subjects based on your strengths and weaknesses.

3. Befriend the syllabus

Focus on high-weightage topics and prioritise mastering core concepts before moving on to advanced ones.

4. Embrace active learning

Explain concepts to yourself or in study groups to solidify understanding.

5. Conquer the past

Solve Past years' papers and Sample Papers under timed conditions to practice time management and understand paper pattern.

6. Seek help, when needed!

Don't hesitate to clarify doubts with teachers, tutors, or study groups. Asking questions strengthens your understanding and prevents confusion.

7. Prioritise well-being

Eat nutritious meals, get enough sleep, have regular exercise, and practice stress management techniques like meditation, to stay calm and focused during exams.

These tips are just a starting point, and you can personalise them to fit your learning style and preferences.

Description of

Newly Added Features

01

The Climate of India

TREND ANALYSIS 3 YEARS

Average No. of Questions Across all Sets

	Types of Questions	2023	2020	2019
TOPIC 01 Distribution of Temperature	1 Mark	1	–	–
	2 Marks	1	1	1
	3 Marks	3	1	2

Trend Analysis

At the start of each chapter, Trend Analysis is given to indicate the types of Questions asked from different topics of the chapter. This feature helps students to know the importance of different topics of the given chapter from exam point of view and helps them to prepare accordingly.

1. Name the seasons of India and mention the duration of each season. *(ICSE 2023)*

Other Similar Questions

Or Name the different seasons in India stating the months when they are experienced.

Or Mention the four seasons that prevail in India stating the months for each.

Other Similar Questions

Other Similar Questions are given with selected questions that can be asked in different formats but their answers remain same. This feature help students to identify and answer the question correctly.

2. Discuss the relationship between the two Houses of

Ans. The Parliament exercises control over the
Some of them are

(i) **Adjournment Motion** To bring matters of urgent public importance, the Parliament can bring Adjournment Motion.

(ii) **Censure Motion** It can bring Censure

Various Administrative or Executive Power of the Union Parliament

- Adjournment Motion
- Censure Motion
- Monetary Control

Heading Boxes

Heading Boxes are given in those questions whose answers are divided into different headings. This feature will help students to remember the answer through headings only.

3. "Though an expensive mode of transport, airways is gaining popularity in India." Explain giving two reasons.

HINT *Dear students, this question simply asks you to write advantages of air transports.*

Ans. Through an expensive mode of transport airways is gaining popularity because India is a vast country where distances are large, and the terrain and the climatic conditions are so diverse and airways have following advantages

Hint

Hint provides a clue to the students about what the question is asking to write in the answer. This feature help students to write the answer correctly in sync with the question.

3. (i) Name the type of climate experienced by India. *(ICSE Specimen 2023)*

(ii) Mention *any two* factors responsible for it.

Ans. (i) The type of climate experienced by India is Tropical monsoon type of climate.

(ii) Two factors responsible for such a type of climate are

(a) India lies in the tropical belt.

(b) Its climate is deeply influenced by the monsoon winds.

Additional Info

Other factors responsible for Tropical monsoon type of climate are

- The presence of the Himalayas which do not allow the cold wind of Asia to reach the temperate Northern parts of India.

Additional Info

Additional Info is given in selected questions with the purpose to give extra information about the concept asked in the question.

Dream, Believe, Achieve

Insights from ICSE Toppers

"Board exams are way easier than you think. It's easy to score if you study regularly for even an hour. Consistency is key,"

DIVYANSH AGARWAL
ICSE Topper (99.40%)

He dedicated time to solving topic-wise papers from the last 10 years, providing valuable practice before his final revision. A planned approach and schedule help to prepare and cover the syllabus better.

ANONDEE SAHA
ICSE Topper (99.6%)

Before the boards, my school had given all students a month to study and I tried my best to study 8-9 hours every day. I relied on revising the syllabus of each subject at least twice during this period and went through past years' question papers and extra questions that my teachers had sent.

For excelling in the boards I would like to advice students to study regularly from DAY 1. They, should refer to previous years, Board question papers and should always have a positive attitude and should be confident. But not overconfident

MUSKAN PATHAN
ICSE Topper (99.4%)

"I studied everything independently, which gave me a better understanding of what topics I needed to improve. I studied only 1.5 to 2 hours daily but stayed consistent and regular,"

MIHIKA SANJANWALA
ICSE Topper (99%)

NILOTMA SINGH
ICSE Topper (99.6%)

"I had started preparing, chapter by chapter, right from the beginning of the academic session as we had weekly tests on every topic that was covered in class. However, the hard-core preparation started only in late November 2022 which was about three months prior to the board examination.,"

Previous Years Papers guide me to a great extent as they helped me understand the scope and area of the questions that could be asked. The specimen papers were extremely helpful as we had undergone a change in examination pattern this year.

"While my primary schooling in Shanghai (China) taught me to be a global citizen, my higher secondary schooling at Greenwood High (Bannerghatta) elevated my inquisitiveness and curiosity on various subjects,"

"Personally, POMODORO technique, a time-management method based on 25-minute stretches of focused work broken by five-minute breaks, helped me immensely not only to organise myself better but also to cover a vast syllabus with the least fatigue,"

SHIVANI NEELAMRAJU
ICSE Topper (99.40%)

Please Note that all the information is collected from different websites.

Contents

Most Important Topics

from each Chapter

On the basis of analysis of last 4 Years' Board Examination Papers, we have identified Important Topics from each chapter.

Chapter Name	Important Topics	Weightage in Last 4 Years' Boards			
		2025	2024	2023	2020
The Climate of India	Distribution of Temperature	7M	3M	12M	5M
	Monsoon and its Mechanism	4M	8M	8M	8M
Soils in India and Natural Vegetation of India	Soil	12M	11M	22M	12M
	Natural Vegetation	11M	11M	17M	10M
Water Resources	Irrigation	5M	8M	5M	8M
	Water Conservation	6M	3M	3M	-
Minerals and Energy Resources	Minerals	1M	3M	23M	2M
	Energy Resources	11M	6M	11M	3M
Agriculture in India	Indian Agriculture	4M	5M	10M	2M
	Major Crops Grown in India	7M	6M	16M	5M
Manufacturing Industries and Waste Management	Industries	12M	11M	18M	10M
	Waste Management	11M	11M	19M	7M
Transport	Modes of Transport	11M	8M	-	2M
	Major Ports in India	-	2M	13M	10M

Latest Syllabus

Geography Class X

There will be one paper of two hours duration carrying 80 marks and Internal Assessment of 20 marks.

The Paper will consist of two parts, Part I and Part II.

PART I (compulsory) will consist of two questions. Question 1 will be based on Topographical Map. Question 2 will be based on outline Map of India.

PART II Candidates will be expected to answer any five questions. Candidates will be expected to make the fullest use of sketches, diagrams, graphs and charts in their answers. Questions set may require answers involving the interpretation of photographs of geographical interest.

PART I MAP WORK

1. *Interpretation of Topographical Maps*

a. Locating features with the help of a four-figure or a six-figure grid reference.

b. Definition of contour and contour interval. Identification of landforms marked by contours (steep slope, gentle slope, hill, valley, ridge / water divide, escarpment), triangulated height, spot height, bench mark, relative height/ depth.

c. Interpretation of colour tints and conventional symbols used on a topographical survey of India map.

d. Identification and definition of types of scale given on the map.
Measuring distances and calculating area using the scale given therein.

e. Marking directions between different locations, using eight cardinal points.

f. Identify: Site of prominent villages and/or towns, types of land use / land cover and means of communication with the help of the index given at the bottom of the sheet.

g. Identification of drainage (direction of flow and pattern) and settlement patterns.

h. Identification of natural and man-made features.

2. *Map of India*

On an outline map of India, candidates will be required to locate, mark and name the following

Mountains, Peaks and Plateaus: Himalayas, Karakoram, Aravali, Vindhyas, Satpura, Western and Eastern Ghats, Nilgiris, Garo, Khasi, Jaintia, Mount Godwin Austin (K2), Mount Kanchenjunga. Deccan Plateau, Chota Nagpur Plateau.

Plains: Gangetic Plains and Coastal plains – (Konkan, Kanara, Malabar, Coromandel, Northern Circars).

Desert: Thar (The Great Indian Desert)

Rivers: Indus, Ravi, Beas, Chenab, Jhelum, Satluj, Ganga, Yamuna, Ghaghra, Gomti, Gandak, Kosi, Chambal, Betwa, Son, Damodar, Brahmaputra, Narmada, Tapti, Mahanadi, Godavari, Krishna, Cauveri, Tungabhadra.

Water Bodies : Gulf of Kutch, Gulf of Khambhat, Gulf of Mannar, Palk Strait, Andaman Sea, Chilika Lake, Wular Lake.

Passes: Karakoram, Nathu-La Passes.

Latitude and Longitudes: Tropic of Cancer, Standard Meridian (82° 30'E).

Direction of Winds: South-West Monsoons (Arabian Sea and Bay of Bengal Branches), North-East Monsoons and Western Disturbances.

Distribution of Minerals: Oil-Mumbai High (Offshore Oil Field) and Digboi. Iron – Singhbhum, Coal – Jharia.

Soil Distribution : Alluvial, Laterite, Black and Red Soil.

Cities : Delhi, Mumbai, Kolkata, Chennai, Hyderabad, Bengaluru, Kochi, Chandigarh, Srinagar, Visakhapatnam, Allahabad.

Population : Distribution of Population (Dense and sparse).

PART II GEOGRAPHY OF INDIA

3. Location, Extent and Physical features

- Position and Extent of India. (through Map only).
- The physical features of India – mountains, plateaus, plains and rivers (through Map only).

4. Climate

- Distribution of Temperature, Rainfall, Winds in Summer and Winter and factors affecting the climate of the area.
- Monsoon and its mechanism. Seasons –March to May – Summer; June to September – Monsoon; October to November - Retreating Monsoon; December to February –Winter.

5. Soil Resources

- Types of soil (alluvial, black, red and laterite) distribution, composition and characteristics such as colour, texture, minerals and crops associated.
- Soil Erosion – causes, prevention and conservation.

6. Natural Vegetation

- Importance of forests.
- Types of vegetation (tropical evergreen, tropical deciduous, tropical desert, littoral and mountain), distribution and correlation with their environment.
- Forest conservation.

7. Water Resources

- Sources (Surface water and ground water).
- Need for conservation and conservation practices (Rain water harvesting and its importance).
- Irrigation: Importance and methods.

8. Mineral and Energy Resources

- Iron ore, Manganese, Copper, Bauxite – uses and their distribution.
- Conventional Sources: Coal, Petroleum, Natural gas (distribution, advantages and disadvantages) Hydel power (Bhakra Nangal Dam and Hirakud).
- Non-conventional Sources: Solar, wind, tidal, geo-thermal, nuclear and bio-gas (generation and advantages).

9. Agriculture

- Indian Agriculture – Importance, problems and reforms.
- Types of farming in India: Subsistence and commercial: shifting, intensive, extensive, plantation and mixed.
- Agricultural seasons (rabi, kharif, zaid).
- Climatic conditions, soil requirements, methods of cultivation, processing and distribution of the following crops
  - rice, wheat, millets and pulses.
  - sugarcane, oilseeds (groundnut, mustard and soybean).
  - cotton, jute, tea and coffee.

10. Manufacturing Industries

- Importance and classification.
- Agro-based Industry - Sugar, Textile (Cotton and Silk).
- Mineral-based Industry – Iron & Steel (TISCO, Bhilai, Rourkela, Visakhapatnam) Petro-Chemical and Electronics.

11. Transport

- Importance and Modes – Roadways, Railways, Airways and Waterways – Advantages and disadvantages.

12. Waste Management

- Impact of waste accumulation - spoilage of landscape, pollution, health hazards, effect on terrestrial, aquatic (fresh water and marine) life.
- Need for waste management.
- Methods of safe disposal - segregation, dumping and composting.
- Need and methods for reducing, reusing and recycling waste.

Analysis of Pupil Performance: ICSE Geography

Topics found difficult/confusing by candidates

The document 'Analysis of Pupils' Performance, 2019' in ICSE Class 10 Examination, is prepared by Research Development and Consultancy Division (RDCD) of the Council for the Indian School Certificate Examination (CISCE).

The purpose of this document is to provide feedback to schools in terms of strengths and weaknesses of the candidates in handling the examination.

TOPICS FOUND DIFFICULT BY STUDENTS

- Toposheet: six figure reference, reason for presence of causeway, main means of irrigation and transport and significance of water body found in 2221.
- Map pointing: area of laterite soil in North, Gangetic plain and Digboi.
- Identifying the type of wind, calculation of total annual rainfall and reasoning related to factors affecting climate of India.
- Identifying vegetation belt in Nilgiri Hills, reasons for deepening of river bed helping in preventing soil erosion, benefits of modern means of irrigation, how transport helps in industrial growth, usefulness of segregation of waste before disposal.
- Man-made and natural features.
- Identifying most important settlement.
- Physical characteristic of laterite soil.
- Soil formed by weathering of basic lava rocks.
- Conditions for littoral forests.
- Mixed farming.
- Cropping seasons.
- Mining areas of minerals.
- Climatic requirement of crops.
- Cottage industry and cotton textile industry.
- Location of petro-chemical industries.

SUGGESTIONS FOR STUDENTS

- Study the chapters thoroughly. Avoid selective studies.
- Prepare tables/charts/notes etc. to revise before examination.
- Study the subject for acquiring knowledge and understanding of the subject and not for marks alone.
- Understand the concepts instead of merely cramming the concepts.
- Practice topographic sheet and map-based questions regularly.
- Concentrate on acquiring accuracy in map pointing by practicing it regularly.
- Master the technique to take note of key words.
- Learn to answer critical and analytical questions.
- Read books, newspapers and periodicals regularly.
- Solve past years' question papers.
- Read the instructions given on the question paper attentively.
- Use the 15 minutes reading time judiciously to make a proper choice of questions by reading the requirements of the question carefully.
- Choose the questions in which you are sure of answering all the parts.
- Do not answer extra questions unnecessarily. Concentrate on the questions you need to attempt.
- Read through the paper on completion to avoid mistakes.

01

The Climate of India

TREND ANALYSIS 3 YEARS

Average No. of Questions Across all Sets

Topic	Types of Questions	2023	2020	2019
TOPIC 01 Distribution of Temperature	1 Mark	1	–	–
	2 Marks	1	1	1
	3 Marks	3	1	2
TOPIC 02 Monsoon and its Mechanism	1 Mark	2	–	–
	2 Marks	3	1	2
	3 Marks	–	2	–

The climate prevailing over India can be described as the Tropical Monsoon type of climate.

Distribution of Temperature

- The regions to the North of the **Tropic of Cancer** 23 ½° N have continental type of climate *i.e.,* very hot in summer and cold in winter.
- The regions to the South of the Tropic of Cancer 23 ½° N which are nearer to the equator, have a range of 25°C to 27°C average temperature during the entire year.
- The Indian coastline has an equable or maritime type of climate due to the moderating effect of the sea.

Some Facts about Variation of Temperature

Some facts about places having temperature variation are given below

- **Kanyakumari** experiences equable climate because it is located at the tip of the Indian subcontinent where the Bay of Bengal and the Arabian Sea and Indian Ocean meet, moderating the climate making it equable or maritime.
- **Jaipur** has a higher annual range of temperature than **Mumbai** because Jaipur lies in the interiors far away from the sea, so experiences higher temperature whereas Mumbai lies on the Western coast, so experiences moderate type of temperature.

- **Kanpur** has extreme temperature conditions because, it is located in the interiors therefore, it is very hot in summers and very cold in winters.
- **Kochi** is warmer than **Mumbai** even though both lie on the Western coast of India because Kochi is situated closer to the equator and get adequate sunshine throughout the year.
- **Kanpur** has a higher range of temperature than **Chennai** because Kanpur is to the North of Tropic of Cancer and experiences a continental type of climate, i.e, very hot during summer and very cold during winter. While Chennai, experiences equable maritime or oceanic type of climate.
- The annual range of temperature is more at **Agra** than **Mumbai** because, continental Agra is situated in the interiors, it experiences extreme type of climate and has more variations in temperature. Mumbai experiences maritime or equable type of climate hence, the annual range of temperature is less.
- **Agra's** temperature in January is higher than **Darjeeling** in spite of having same latitudinal locations. It is so because Darjeeling is situated in the mountains at a higher altitude where the temperature is less than plain areas where Agra is located.
- The South facing slopes of the **Garo**, **Khasi**, **Jaintia Hills** or Himalayas or Shivaliks are warmer than the North facing slopes of these hills or mountains. It is so because all these hills are in the Northern hemisphere and have an East-West alignment. The South facing slopes get more direct rays as the Sun rays strike at a steeper angle than the North facing slopes and hence, they are less intense.
- Even in Summer **Shimla** is cooler than **Delhi** because Shimla is situated at a higher altitude where the atmosphere is cooler. Delhi is in the plains where atmosphere gets heated up fast.
- The Himalayan mountains act as a natural barrier against the cold winds coming from North thus, protecting the Northern plains from freezing.

Rainfall Distribution

- The climate of India is strongly influenced by monsoon winds.
- The North-Eastern and some parts of Western India receive 400 cm of rainfall annually.
- In the interior of the Deccan plateau and East of the Sahyadris, the rainfall is low.
- The rest of the India receives moderate rainfall. Snowfall is restricted to the Himalayan regions.

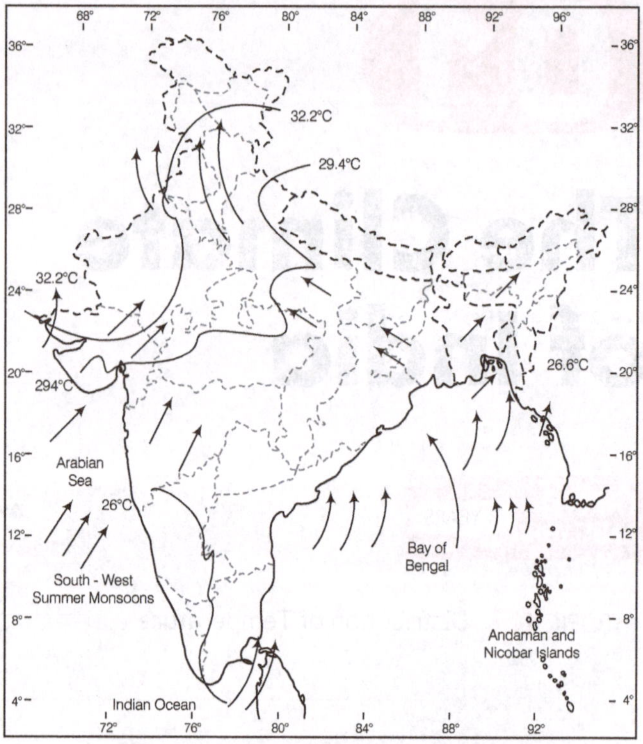

South-West Monsoons (June - September)

India has a wide distribution of rainfall which is highly variable from year to year. Areas of high rainfall are liable to be affected by floods while areas of low rainfall are drought prone.

Some Facts about Variation of Rainfall

Some facts about places having rainfall variation are given below

- **Central Maharashtra** gets less rainfall than **coastal Maharashtra** because Central Maharashtra lies in the rain shadow zone of the Western Ghats.
- **Kolkata** receives heavier rain then **Lucknow** because it lies close to East Coast from where the Bay of Bengal branch of South-West monsoon enters India. The rainfall goes on decreasing as the branch proceeds Westwards.
- The summer monsoon winds blow over the Arabian Sea from the South-West because one of the branch of the South-West monsoon is the Arabian Sea branch which strike the Western Coast of India in **Kerala** on 1st June. It gives very heavy rainfall. The duration and amount of rainfall goes on decreasing as Arabian Sea branch moves Northward.
- Thar is a desert because it gets scanty rainfall and it lies in the rain shadow area of Aravalli hills.

- The **Ganga Plains** get the monsoon rain much later than the West coast of India because the Arabian Sea branch of the South-West monsoon enters India from West coast. Then it moves upwards from Deccan Plateau towards Ganga Plains in North.
- **Kerala** has the longest rainy season because Kerala lies on the South-West coast from where the Arabian Sea branch of the South-West monsoon enters India.
- The **Konkan Coast** experiences orographic rainfall because orographic rainfall is mainly caused by the presence of a relief barrier. The Konkan coast lies on the Windward side of the Western Ghats which obstructs the onshore Arabian Sea branch of the South-West monsoon winds. Thus, causing heavy rainfall on the Konkan coast.
- **Western Rajasthan** receives no rain from the Arabian Sea branch of the South-West monsoon winds because these winds run parallel to the Aravalli ranges and do not cross it to give rainfall in Western Rajasthan. Also the temperature is so high that monsoon winds become dry and do not shed any moisture there.
- **Patna** receives heavier rain than **Delhi** because it lies to the East of Delhi and receives rainfall from the Bay of Bengal branch of South-West monsoon. The moisture of the branch decreases from East to West.
- The annual rainfall in Rajasthan is less than 25 cm because it lies in the rain shadow area of the Aravalli ranges. The Bay of Bengal branch of South-West monsoon is almost exhausted by the time it reaches Rajasthan while the Arabian Sea branch blows parallel to the Aravalli ranges.

Winds in Summer and Winter

- The summer months experience rising temperature and falling air pressure in the Northern part of India.
- The local wind **Loo** is the striking feature of the hot weather season, which is a gusty, hot, dry wind blowing during the day over the North and North-Western India.
- Winter season is influenced by the North-East trade winds, which blow from land to sea.
- The Northern plains act as the inflow gate of cyclonic disturbances from the West and the North-West.

Factors Affecting the Climate of India

The factors affecting the climate of India are as follows

Latitude

India's climate has characteristics of tropical as well as sub-tropical (interoperate) climates as Tropic of Cancer divides India into tropical and sub-tropical regions.

Northern Mountain Ranges

India has mountains to the North, which prevent the cold winds from Central Asia from entering into Indian sub-continent. These mountains also act as barrier to South- West monsoonal winds and responsible for monsoonal rainfall.

Pressure and Winds

India lies in the region of North Easterly winds, which originate from the subtropical high pressure belt of the Northern Himalayas. The Western disturbances experienced in the North and North Western parts of India are brought by Westerly jet stream.

Altitude

Generally, with increase in height, temperature decreases that's why Agra and Darjeeling are located in same latitude, but due to altitude or elevation differences the weather conditions differ.

Distance from the Sea

As we move far from sea, climate becomes extreme. Areas near sea experience moderate climate. That's why Delhi experience extreme summers and extreme winters, but Mumbai experience almost same weather conditions throughout the year. Areas near to sea experience moderate type of temperature throughout the year while areas in the interiors experience extreme temperatures.

Western Disturbances

During winters North-West and Northern part of India experience rainfall and snowfall from Western disturbances cyclonic depression which originates over mediterranean sea and move eastwards.

The Western disturbances cause snowfall in Western Himalayas which feed the glaciers. This rainfall is highly beneficial to 'Rabi crops' specially wheat in Punjab. During winter months, this rainfall is good for all rabi crops.

Upper Air Circulation

Jet streams blowing in upper tropopause also affects the climate of India. Westerly jet stream blows in region of South of Himalayas throughout the year except summer. In summer, these jet stream blows in and an easterly jet stream blows over Peninsular India.

Monsoon and its Mechanism

- India has a tropical monsoon type of climate.
- The differential heating and cooling of land and water creates low pressure on the landmass of India while the seas around experience high pressure comparatively.

- The position of the **Inter Tropical Convergence Zone (ITCZ)** shifts in summer over the Ganga plain, which attracts winds from Indian ocean and known as South-West monsoon.
- During winter, the position of ITCZ shifts over the Indian ocean which attracts winds from Indian sub-continent and known as North-East monsoon.

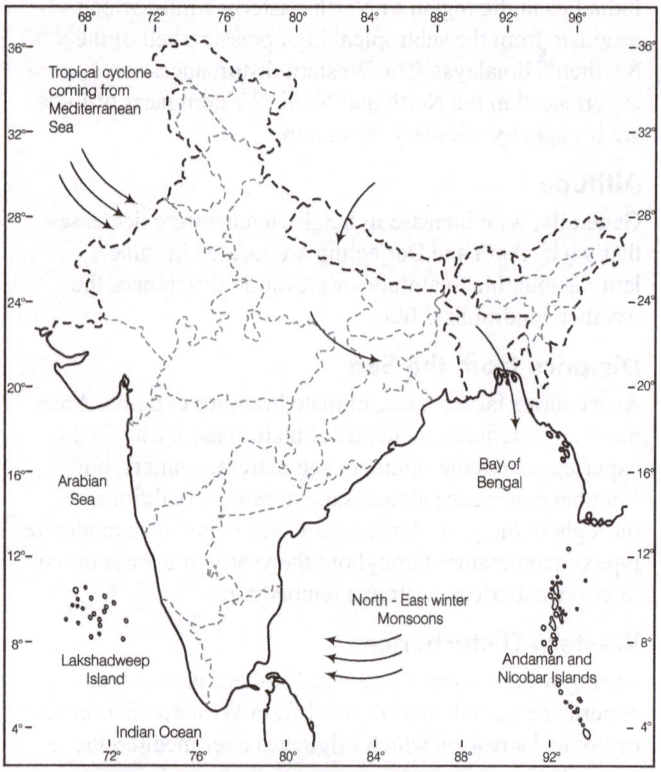

North-East Monsoons (December-March)

Factors responsible for having monsoonal type climate in India are

(i) **Location** Location plays an important role in having monsoon type climate in India. During summer location of ITCZ shifts over Ganga plains which attracts monsoon winds.

(ii) **Indian Ocean** Monsoon wind blow toward India from Indian ocean get moisture from ocean and bring rainfall in South Asia.

(iii) **Mountains** The Himalayan mountains located in North acts as barrier for monsoon winds. Winds collide with mountain and cause rainfall in the Southern part of Himalayas. Apart from Himalayas Western ghats also acts as barrier and cause rainfall in Western slopes. Similarly Garo, Khasi and Jayantia hills of North-East are also responsible for monsoonal rainfall in North-East India.

Characteristics of Indian Monsoon

Indian Monsoon has following characteristics

(i) **Uneven Distribution of Rainfall** Monsoon winds cause uneven rainfall over India. Some areas like Western slopes of Western ghats and North-East India receive heavy rainfall where as some areas receive less rainfall.

(ii) **Heavy Rainfall in Short Duration** Monsoon rainfall occurs in short time *i.e.* summers only.

(iii) **Erratic and Unpredictable Nature of Monsoon** Monsoonal rainfall varies every year. One year it may cause heavy rainfall and another year it may cause less rainfall.

(iv) **Relief or Topography** Mainly influences the Monsoon Rainfall. For example, Western slopes of Western ghats receive heavy rainfall and its Eastern slopes get less rainfall. This topographic influence can also be seen in North-East where Garo, Khasi and Jayantia hills cause heavy rainfall.

(v) The monsoonal rainfall has a decline trend with increasing distance from the sea. That's why Patna receives more rainfall than Delhi.

Seasons of India

Indian Meteorological Department of India, has identified four seasons in India

1. Hot Dry Season (March-May)

India's mainland experiences scroaching heat during these months and hence low pressure prevails over this region, while high pressure prevails over surrounding seas.

This season is also known for localised thunderstorms which brings light rain often accompanied by hail. These thunderstorms are known as **Kaal Baisakhi** in West Bengal, Assam (Good for tea cultivation).

In Kerala and Karnataka, when summer season is towards the end, pre-monsoon showers are experienced. These showers are known as **mango showers** or **April rains** as they help in the early ripening of mangoes. In South India (Karnataka) another pre-monsoon showers called 'cherry blossoms' are beneficial for coffee plantation.

Characteristics of hot dry season are as follows

(i) This season is marked by dry weather and excessive heat.

(ii) The whole of tropical India, South of Himalayas, experiences very high temperatures.

(iii) The range of temperature is very high in the interior.

(iv) The range of temperature is low over the coastal regions as they experience equable climate.

(v) In this season, the Sun shines directly above the Tropic of Cancer.

2. Rainy Season or the Season of South-West Monsoon (June-September)

- During these months, areas with low pressure attract the South-East trade winds coming from the Southern Hemisphere.
- After deflection at the equator, they cross towards the Indian sub-continent and get moisture from the Arabian Sea. The winds are named as South-West monsoon because they come to India from the South-West direction. **Kerala** is the **first state** which experiences onset of monsoon.
- Due to the triangular shape of the Peninsular India, the monsoon winds divide into two branches i.e. Arabian sea branch and Bay of Bengal branch.
- Arabian sea branch of Indian monsoon brings moisture from Arabian sea and cause rainfall from windward side of Western ghats and Western part of India.
- Bay of Bengal branch of Indian monsoon brings moisture from Bay of Bengal and cause rainfall over North-East India and Indo-Gangetic plains.
- The Arabian sea and the Bay of Bengal branch of monsoon merge over the North-Western part of Ganga plain Delhi, Western Uttar Pradesh, Punjab, Haryana, Eastern Rajasthan get rainfall in the end of the June and first week of July.
- Aravalli range is situated in the parallel to the direction of Arabian sea branch of monsoon that's why Rajasthan get no or less monsoon rainfall.

3. Season of the Retreating Monsoon or North-East Monsoon (October-November)

The retreat of the monsoon is marked by clear skies and rise in temperature. The low pressure conditions over North-Western India get transferred to the Bay of Bengal by early November, which causes the occurrence of **cyclonic depression**. Cyclonic depressions, generally cross the Eastern coast of India causing heavy and widespread rainfall.

Difference between South-West Monsoon and North-East Monsoon

South-West Monsoon	North-East Monsoon
These winds blow from sea to land.	These winds blow from land to sea.
In this season oppressive heat and humidity is felt, which is known as 'October Heat'.	In this season pleasant weather with low temperature, low humidity and clear skies are experienced.
These winds have two branches i.e. the Arabian Sea and Bay of Bengal branch.	These winds have only one branch.
These winds blow from June to September	These winds blow from December to February.
These winds bring rainfall to almost entire India.	These winds bring rainfall to coromandel coast.

4. The Cold Season (December-February)

- A feature of the cold weather season over the Northern Plains is the inflow of cyclonic disturbances from the West and the North-West. It is the dry season due to influence of North-East trade winds which blow from land to sea.
- The winter rainfall in North-West India is the main feature of the cold season. This light rainfall is very useful for the rabi crop, especially wheat. The variation in the winter temperatures North of the Tropic of Cancer, which goes on decreasing as one moves North and South of the Tropic of Cancer, which goes on increasing as one moves towards South with an average of 20°C.

PYQs Previous Years' Questions

1 Mark Questions

Multiple Choice Questions

1. Choose the correct option.
……… is a hot and dry local wind that blow in North India during pre-monsoon period. *(ICSE Specimen 2023)*
(a) Western Disturbance
(b) Loo
(c) Kal Baisakhi
(d) Cherry Blossom

Ans. (b) Loo

2. Which of the following area receives rain from the North-East monsoon ? *(ICSE 2023)*
(a) Konkan coast (b) Ganga basin
(c) Coromandel coast (d) Malabar coast

Ans. (c) Coromandel coast

3. Which state in India is the first to experience the onset of the monsoons and the last to see it retreat? *(ICSE Specimen Semester I 2021)*
(a) Andaman & Nicobar (c) Kerala
(b) Maharashtra (d) Tamil Nadu

Ans. (c) Kerala

4. Which of the following is good for Tea and Jute cultivation? *(ICSE Specimen Semester I 2021)*
(a) Kalbaisakhi
(b) Loo
(c) Western Disturbance
(d) Monsoon showers

Ans. (a) Kalbaisakhi

5. Which of the following factor is responsible for the rises in the temperature of mainland of India in the month of March? *(ICSE Specimen Semester I 2021)*
(a) Southward migration of the Sun from the equator
(b) Northward migration of the Sun from the equator
(c) The pressure belts shift.
(d) The land breeze blows towards the sea

Ans. (b) Northward migration of the Sun from the equator

6. Why has Thar developed into a desert? *(ICSE Specimen Semester I 2021)*
(a) It has no cloud cover.
(b) It is near the sea.
(c) It is on the windward side of Western Ghats.
(d) Aravalli is parallel to SW Monsoon wind.

Ans. (d) Aravalli is parallel to SW Monsoon wind.

7. Name the type of climate experienced in India. *(ICSE Specimen Semester I 2021, ICSE 2012)*
(a) Tropical cyclonic type
(b) Tropical monsoon type
(c) Temperate monsoon type
(d) Subtropical monsoon

Ans. (b) Tropical monsoon type

8. Give reason for the following.
There is heavy rainfall in the Western coastal plains *(ICSE Specimen Semester I 2021)*
(a) Presence of Aravali mountain range in Western India.
(b) The Eastern coastal plains have no intercepting barrier.
(c) Presence of Deccan Plateau.
(d) Presence of Western Ghats.

Ans. (d) Presence of Western Ghats.

9. Give reason for the following.
In June, Bhopal is warmer than Kolkata *(ICSE Specimen Semester I 2021)*
(a) due to its continental location.
(b) due to Kolkata's proximity to the sea.
(c) due to Bhopal is closer to the Tropic of Cancer.
(d) due to Himalayan hill station Darjeeling, is closer to Kolkata than it is to Bhopal.

Ans. (c) due to Bhopal is closer to the Tropic of Cancer.

10. Western disturbance provide rain to which of the following States? *(ICSE Semester I 2021)*
(a) Punjab (b) Sikkim
(c) West Bengal (d) Maharashtra

Ans. (a) Punjab

11. Which of the following cause rain to Coromandel Coast? *(ICSE Semester I 2021)*
(a) Retreating monsoons
(b) Kalbaisakhi
(c) Western disturbance
(d) South-West monsoons

Ans. (a) Retreating monsoons

12. Westerly depression are active in India during which of the following months? *(Semester I 2021)*
(a) Between September and November
(b) Between December and January
(c) Between June and September
(d) Between March and May

Ans. (b) Between December and January

13. Why is the Central part of Deccan Plateau a dry area? *(ICSE Semester I 2021)*

(a) It is away from the sea
(b) There is no barrier in the path of rain bearing wind
(c) It is due to Jet Streams
(d) It is a rain shadow area of Western Ghats

Ans. (d) It is a rain shadow area of Western Ghats

14. Why does Patna get more rain than Agra during the summer monsoon season? *(ICSE Semester I 2021)*

(a) Patna lies on windward side.
(b) Patna is on Western side, so Arabian Sea branch brings more rain to it than to Agra.
(c) Patna is on Eastern side, so Bay of Bengal branch brings more rain to it than to Agra.
(d) Patna gets rain throughout the year.

Ans. (c) Patna is on Eastern side, so Bay of Bengal branch brings more rain to it than to Agra.

15. Which of the statement is not correct for Indian monsoon? *(ICSE Semester I 2021)*

(a) It is erratic in nature.
(b) It is seasonal in nature.
(c) Most of the rain is in winter time.
(d) Most of the rain is geographic or relief type.

Ans. (c) Most of the rain is in winter time.

Very Short Answer Questions

1. Name the type of climate prevailing over India. *(ICSE 2012)*

Ans. The Tropical monsoon is a type of climate which prevails over India.

2. Mention any two factors responsible for the Tropical monsoon climate. *(ICSE 2012)*

Ans. Following two factors are responsible for the Tropical monsoon climate

(i) Shifting of ITCZ over Ganga plain in summer season.
(ii) Presence of the Himalayas as a barrier against monsoonal winds.

3. Give a reason for the following. *(ICSE 2007)*

Western coastal plains receive more rainfall than the Eastern coastal plains.

Ans. Western coastal plains receive more rainfall because the Western Ghats check the rain bringing South-West monsoon winds to cause heavy rainfall.

2 Marks Questions

1. Name the seasons of India and mention the duration of each season. *(ICSE 2023)*

Other Similar Questions

Or Name the different seasons in India stating the months when they are experienced.

Or Mention the four seasons that prevail in India stating the months for each.

Ans. There are total four seasons in India namely

(a) Spring – February to March
(b) Summer – April to June
(c) Monsoon – July to Mid-September
(d) Autumn – September end to November

2. Why maximum rainfall in India occurs after the summer season? *(ICSE 2023)*

Ans. Maximum rain occurs in India after the summer season due to the impact of warm weather, there is a lot of water loss due to sweating by humans and transpiration by plants due to excessive heat. This increases the amount of moisture and humidity in the atmosphere which ultimately results in rainfall.

3. (i) Name the type of climate experienced by India. *(ICSE Specimen 2023)*

(ii) Mention *any two* factors responsible for it.

Ans. (i) The type of climate experienced by India is Tropical monsoon type of climate.

(ii) Two factors responsible for such a type of climate are

(a) India lies in the tropical belt.
(b) Its climate is deeply influenced by the monsoon winds.

Additional Info

Other factors responsible for Tropical monsoon type of climate are

- The presence of the Himalayas which do not allow the cold wind of Asia to reach the temperate Northern parts of India.
- The Himalayas also trap the monsoon winds, forcing them to shed their moisture within the subcontinent.

4. With the help of a suitable example, explain how relief features affect the rainfall of a place. ***(ISCE Specimen 2023)***

Ans. Relief features affect the rainfall of a place. For example, rainfall can be affected by mountains because mountains act as a barrier in the path of rain bearing winds and force them to shed their moisture over there. When these rain bearing winds reach the upper part of the mountains they cool down, causing moist air to condense and fall out as rainfall.

5. Study the following data and answer the questions that follow: ***(ICSE Semester I 2021)***

MONTH	JAN	FEB	MAR	APR	MAY	JUN	JULY	AUG	SEP	OCT	NOV	DEC
TEMP (°C)	23.1	24.8	26.3	20.3	12	12.8	33.1	32.1	30.3	29.3	28.7	26.1
RAIN (cm)	15.3	10.1	0.3	0.1	1.3	4.5	6.1	10.2	10.3	20.1	16.8	19.0

(i) What is the annual range of temperature experienced by the station?

(a) 20°C (b) 10°C (c) 16°C (d) 21°C

(ii) Which according to the given data is the driest month?

(a) March (b) April (c) May (d) June

Ans. (i) (d) Annual range of temp = Max tempt - Minimum

33.1°C – 12°C = 21.1°C tempt

(ii) (b) April

6. (i) Name one state in the North-Western part of India that receives rainfall during winter. ***(ICSE 2020)***

(ii) What is the source of this rainfall?

Ans. (i) Punjab in North-Western part of India receives rainfall in winter.

(ii) The North-Western plains of India experience winter rainfall due to the invasion of the Western disturbances rising from the Mediterranean sea, led by the Westerly jetstream. As the Western disturbances are associated with the cyclonic winds, they bring rainfall.

7. Give a reason for each of the following. ***(ICSE 2020)***

(i) Tamil Nadu has more rainy months than Kerala, yet, Kerala receives more rainfall than Tamil Nadu.

Ans. (i) Tamil Nadu has more rainy months than Kerala because it receives rainfall from both South- West monsoon winds and North-West monsoon winds (during winters), but Kerala receives rainfall only from South-West monsoon winds.

The South-West Monsoon winds first strike Kerala and give abundant rainfall there. Thus, Kerala gets more rainfall than Tamil Nadu.

8. (i) What type of wind is 'Monsoon'? What is its direction during summer? ***(ICSE 2019)***

(ii) Mention two characteristics of the Indian monsoon.

Ans. (i) Monsoon is a seasonal wind system that reverses during a year which strongly influence climate of India. The South-West Moonsoon winds blow from June to September. The direction of these winds in summer is from South-West to North-East. These winds tend to carry moisture with them and cause rain in the entire country.

(ii) Two characteristics of monsoon in India are as follows

(a) A large part of the country receives rainfall mainly in the summer from the South-West Monsoon winds. Very little rain is caused in winter from the North-East winter monsoons.

(b) Erratic and unpredictable nature of monsoon causes heavy or very little rainfall in some years.

Examiner's Comment

- Many candidates gave vague answers. Some candidates wrote the meaning of the term monsoon instead of the type of wind Monsoon is. As regards the direction, some candidates wrote sea to land instead of South West direction.
- Some candidates wrote factors affecting monsoon instead of characteristics of the Indian monsoon.

Suggestions for Students

- Explain about the monsoon, its mechanism, types, origin and its direction.
- Make a clear comparison between monsoon winds and the land and sea breeze.
- Discuss the concept of Ferrel's Law to make the students understand the wind direction over the Indian territory.
- Explain the difference between factors affecting monsoons and characteristics of monsoons.

9. With reference to the summer season in India, answer the following questions. *(ICSE 2019)*

(i) Mention the duration of the summer season in India.

(ii) What is the atmospheric pressure condition during summer season over the central part of India?

Ans. (i) The months of March, April and May are the summer months in India when the Sun moves from over the equator towards the Tropic of Cancer (Northward movement) and the global heat belt shifts Northward. By 21st June, it is directly overhead the Tropic of Cancer.

(ii) India has a unique pressure and wind system. The atmospheric pressure conditions in Central India is low in summer as the region experiences high temperature and heat waves during summer.

10. Define *(ICSE Specimen 2018)*

(i) Western Disturbances

(ii) Mango Showers

Ans. (i) Western Disturbance is an inflow of cyclonic disturbances from the West and the North-West, which originate over the Mediterranean Sea and Western Asia. The frequency of these disturbance is 4 to 6 days per month between December and January. This causes rainfall in North and North-West India.

(ii) Mango showers are local winds which occur in South India States of Kerala and Karnataka during April-May. These winds carry little rain which help in blooming of coffee and cherries as well as ripening of mangoes.

11. How is the winter rainfall of the North-West part of India different from the winter rainfall of the South-East of India? *(ICSE 2018)*

Ans. The differences between winter rainfall of the North-West part of India and winter rainfall of the South-East part of India are

Winter Rainfall of North-West Part of India	Winter Rainfall of South-East Part of India
The North-West India receives winter rainfall from low pressure systems, called the Western disturbances.	The South-East of India receives rainfall in winter due to North-East monsoons.
Western disturbances travel Eastward across Iran and Pakistan from Mediterranean Sea and Gulf of Persia and reach India during the winter season. They cause much rainfall over plain areas of North-West regions of India.	During winter season several cyclonic storms develop in Bay of Bengal which moves from the North-East causing substantial rainfall on the coast of Tamil Nadu and Southern tip of Andhra Pradesh and Tamil Nadu.

Examiner's Comment

- Most of the candidates were able to answer this question. Some candidates gave a long explanation of the answer without breaking it into points.

Suggestions for Students

- Write the differences in a tabular form, point wise and with the basis for distinction.

12. (i) Name a state that is the first to experience the onset of the monsoon. *(ICSE 2018)*

(ii) How does the 'Mango shower' influence the state of Karnataka?

Ans. (i) Kerala is the first state in India to experience of the onset of the monsoon from Arabian Sea branch of monsoon. After the South-West monsoon gains momentum, it crosses the Western Ghats and downpours in all other states in India.

(ii) Mango shower also called as April rains, or summer showers or mango rains are so called because they help in early ripening of mangoes in Karnataka and parts of Tamil Nadu.

13. (i) Why is the annual range of temperature more at Agra than at Mumbai? *(ICSE Specimen 2017)*

(ii) Name a region in India which receives rainfall both in summer and winter.

Ans. (i) Agra has an extreme climate as it is in the interior of the country. This means it has cold winters and hot summers. Mumbai has a maritime climate, which means that it has very little difference between the summers and the winters, as it is situated near the sea. Thus the annual range of temperature is more at Agra than at Mumbai.

(ii) Tamil Nadu has rain during the monsoon season due to the South - West monsoon, which blows towards the Northern Hemisphere. Again, Tamil Nadu receives rainfall in the winter due to the retreating South-West monsoon.

14. State the agricultural *benefits* derived from ***(ICSE 2017)***

(i) The Westerly depressions in Punjab.

(ii) The 'Kalbaisakhi' in Assam.

Ans. (i) The Westerly depression in Punjab causes rain during winter. This is good for rabi crop. Rabi crops are sown at the start of winter and harvested in spring or at the start of summer. Rabi crops mainly wheat in Punjab get sufficient precipitation during winter months due to the Western temperate cyclone or Westerly depression.

(ii) The 'Kalbaisakhi' wind usually blows in North-West direction. These winds are accompanied by thunderstorms and bring heavy rainfall. This rain in the month of April/May is good for tea crop in Assam and West Bengal.

15. Name the following. ***(ICSE 2016)***

(i) The winds that bring heavy rain to Cherrapunjee.

(ii) The local wind that bring a light rainfall to South India and is good for tea and coffee crops.

Ans. (i) The South-West Monsoon wind of Bay of Bengal branch provides heavy rainfall to Cherrapunjee.

(ii) 'Cherry Blossom' are the local wind of South India that bring a light rainfall and are good for tea and coffee crops.

16. Explain two factors that affect the climate of India giving a suitable example for each. ***(ICSE 2015)***

Ans. The two factors that affect the climate of India are

(i) **Tropic of Cancer** (23½° N) dividing the country into two halves—North Temperate Zone and South Tropical Zone.

Example North of Tropic of Cancer experience extreme type of climate, while the Southern Peninsula, enclosed on three sides by the Arabian Sea, Indian Ocean and Bay of Bengal, experiences moderate climate.

(ii) **Great Himalayan Range** separating the Indian subcontinent from the rest of Asia, thus, preventing the bitter cold winds from the Central Asia from entering the country.

Example The Himalayan range intercepts the rain-bearing South-West monsoon winds, forcing them to shed their moisture, resulting in heavy rainfall in the North-East and Indo-Gangetic Plain.

17. State two differences between the rainfalls that occur from June to September and that from December to February in North India. ***(ICSE 2015)***

Ans. Two differences between the rainfalls that occur from June to September (South-West Monsoon) and that from December to February (North-East Monsoon) in North India are

(i) South-West monsoon is characterised by a clear burst of Monsoon, while the North-East Monsoon has no clearly defined onset.

(ii) The South-West monsoon causes rainfall in most of the country except in Tamil Nadu, while Tamil Nadu and Southern tip of Andhra Pradesh get heavy rainfall during North-East monsoon.

18. Mention the different sources of rain in Punjab and Tamil Nadu during the winter season. ***(ICSE 2014)***

Ans. Punjab gets rainfall by temperate cyclones or Western disturbances whereas Tamil Nadu gets rainfall by the North-East monsoon winds.

19. State the benefits that are derived from the local winds that blow in summer in the following states. ***(ICSE 2014)***

(i) Kerala (ii) West Bengal

Ans. (i) Local winds or Mango showers in Kerala help in blooming of coffee and cherries as well as ripening of mangoes.

(ii) Local winds in West Bengal is called Kalbaisakhi. This is good for the growth of jute in West Bengal.

20. Name any two types of cyclonic systems that affect India and two areas that receive rainfall from these systems. ***(ICSE 2013)***

Ans. Two cyclonic systems by which India is affected, are as follows

(i) **Temperate Cyclones** Regions affected are North-West India (Punjab, Haryana).

(ii) **Tropical Cyclones** Regions affected are Eastern coast of India (Andhra Pradesh, Tamil Nadu, Odisha and West Bengal).

21. What is the direction of the summer monsoon? Why? ***(ICSE 2012)***

Ans. The direction of the summer monsoon is from the South-West to North-East, because after crossing equator, monsoonal winds get deflected towards their rights in the Northern Hemisphere.

22. 'Rainfall in India is orographic in nature'. Give an example with reference to the distribution of rainfall and the effect of relief on its distribution. *(ICSE 2011)*

Ans. Orographic rainfall is a type of rainfall in which moisture containing winds uplift with the help of mountain and shed its moisture on the windward side of mountain. When these winds reach the leeward side, winds have no or less moisture. For example, Western Ghats which lie parallel to the Western coast are in a suitable direction to check the rain bearing monsoon winds. The Western slope of the Western Ghats that faces the winds receives heavy rainfall (*i.e.* more than 200 cm). The leeward side of the Western Ghats is not able to do so as the winds have lost their moisture and are descending on that slope. This region receives low rainfall.

23. Mumbai receives rainfall in the summer season, while Chennai receives rainfall from October to December. Why? *(ICSE 2009)*

Ans. Mumbai receives rainfall in the summer season because it receives rainfall from South-West monsoon, whereas Chennai receives rainfall in the winter season from the North-East monsoon.

24. Name the source of winter rain in Tamil Nadu. How does Tamil Nadu benefit from it? *(ICSE 2008)*

Ans. North-East monsoon which takes moisture from Bay of Bengal is the source of winter rain in Tamil Nadu. Tamil Nadu benefits from it, because it is best suited for rice and coffee cultivation.

25. What type of climate is experienced in the Northern plains of India? State one main characteristic of this type of climate. *(ICSE 2007)*

Ans. Northern plains of India experience continental type of climate. Its main characteristic is high range of temperature *i.e.,* it is extremely hot in summer and extremely cold in winter.

26. State the climatic significance of the Himalayas to the people of South Asia. *(ICSE 2005)*

Ans. The Himalayas act as a barrier to the South Asian people from the cold winds blowing from Central Asia and thus acts as a climatic divide. They also act as a barrier to prevent the monsoon winds moving further towards North.

27. Name the area in India which receives rainfall from the Western disturbances. State the importance of this rainfall. *(ICSE 2005)*

Ans. North-West of India receives rainfall from the Western disturbances, which is very important for the cultivation of wheat and barley.

28. Why are there great variations in the climate of the Indian sub-continent? *(ICSE 2002)*

Ans. India's vast longitudinal and latitudinal extent and various topographical features are the reasons for great variations in the climate of the Indian sub-continent.

29. Name any two local winds, which blow in India and write briefly about each. *(ICSE 2002)*

Ans. The two local winds which blow in India are

(i) The Loo are hot, dry and dusty winds blowing during May and June in the Northern plains.

(ii) In West Bengal, localised thunderstorms accompanied with violent winds, torrential downpours and sometimes hail also occur. These winds are called Kalbaisakhi.

30. Explain why? *(ICSE 2001)*

(i) Mumbai is warmer than Kanpur in December.

(ii) Account for the winter rain in Northern India.

Ans. (i) Mumbai has the moderating influence of the sea, which makes it warmer, whereas Kanpur is very far from the sea and has a continental type of climate.

(ii) The Westerly disturbances originating in the Mediterranean Sea are responsible for the winter rain in Northern India.

3 Marks Questions

1. Give a geographical reason for each of the following. *(ICSE 2023)*

(i) The Malabar coast receives heavy rainfall in the month of July, but the Coromandel coast during this time remains comparatively dry.

(ii) Punjab receives rainfall in winter season.

(iii) Mumbai is warmer than Delhi in the month of December.

Ans. (i) Malabar coast receive heavy rainfall from the Arabian Sea branch of South-West monsoon during June to October as it lies in the windward side of Western Ghats. On the other hand, Coromandel coast gets very low rainfall from South-West monsoon as it lies in the leeward side of Western Ghats.

(ii) The cyclones originating in the Mediterranean Sea during the winter gradually shifts towards the East and reaches India. This causes winter rainfall in Northern plains, especially in the Punjab region.

(iii) Mumbai is warmer than Delhi in the month of December because it has an equable climate or marin time climate due to coastal location, while Delhi is an inland town and have continental type of climate which mean great annual range of temperature. The presence of land and sea breezes keep the nights warm at Mumbai.

2. Study the climate date of Station X and answer the questions that follow. *(ICSE 2023)*

Month	Jan	Feb	Mar	April	May	June	July	Aug	Sept	Oct	Nov	Dec
Temp. °C	21.0	21.9	24.3	27.2	28.0	26.4	26.1	25.4	26.0	26.0	23.8	21.2
Rainfall (cms.)	5.1	2.8	1.2	1.7	3.9	4.6	8.4	11.4	11.9	31.6	34.5	14.8

(i) Calculate the annual range of temperature of Station X.

(ii) Name the wind that brings most of the rainfall to this station.

(iii) On which coast of India is Station X located ?

Ans. (i) The annual range of temperature of Station X is 28.0 – 21.0 = 7°C

(ii) North-East monsoon

(iii) Tamil Nadu

3. Give a geographical reason for each of the following. *(ICSE Specimen 2023)*

(i) Annual range of temperature is higher in Delhi than Mumbai.

(ii) Mango showers are beneficial local winds.

(iii) The North-East monsoons bring almost no rain to most parts of India.

Ans. (i) Annual range of temperature is higher in Delhi than Mumbai. It is due to fact that Delhi is located in the interior part of India where the moderating influence of the sea is absent. On the other hand, Mumbai lies closer to the sea which gives moderating effect to the area.

(ii) The mango showers are beneficial local winds because they bring the required rainfall which helps in the ripening of mangoes and is important for the tea and coffee plantations.

(iii) The North-East Monsoon winds are dry winds as they blow from land to the sea. Thus, they bring almost no rain to most parts of India.

4. Study the climatic data and answer the following questions : *(ICSE Specimen 2023)*

	Jan	Feb	Mar	April	May	June	July	Aug	Sept	Oct	Nov	Dec
Temp. °C	23.8	25.0	27.7	28.3	30.2	30.3	30.4	30.3	30.0	25.5	25.5	24.2
Rainfall (cms.)	0	0	1.1	1.5	2.1	45.3	46.4	45.4	43.3	20.1	3.0	1

(i) Calculate the annual range of temperature.

(ii) What is the total rainfall during the monsoon season?

(iii) On which coast is the station located? Give a reason for your answer.

Ans. (i) The annual range of temperature of this region is 6.6° C.

(ii) The total rainfall during the monsoon season is 209.2 cm.

(iii) It is located on the West coast of India because there is low annual range of temperature due to moderating influence of the nearby sea.

5. (i) What do you understand by the term 'Burst of Monsoon'? Name the state that experiences the 'Burst of Monsoon'. *(ICSE 2020)*

(ii) Even though India gets abundant rainfall during the rainy season, yet, some places experience drought. Explain giving suitable examples.

(iii) Why is Shimla colder than Delhi during summer?

Ans (i) Around the time of the arrival of the monsoons, the normal rainfall increases suddenly and continues constantly for several days. This is known as the 'burst of monsoon'. This branch is responsible for giving Meghalaya the highest rainfall in the world.

(ii) Even though India gets abundant rainfall during the rainy season, yet some places experience drought because rainfall is uncertain and unreliable. Distribution of rainfall in the country is uneven. While some states receive abundant rainfall during monsoon, whereas some states face drought like condition due to scanty rainfall e.g. Rajasthan and Haryana.

(iii) Shimla is colder than Delhi in summer because Shimla is situated at a higher altitude where the atmosphere is cooler. Delhi is in the plains where atmosphere gets heated up fast.

6. Study the climatic data given below and answer the questions that follow: *(ICSE 2020)*

Months	**JAN**	**FEB**	**MAR**	**APR**	**MAY**	**JUN**	**JUL**	**AUG**	**SEP**	**OCT**	**NOV**	**DEC**
Temp. in °C	8.4	11.5	21.6	28.3	35.1	38.5	41.0	38.0	30.8	29.2	15.6	10.2
Rainfall in cms.	1.5	0.9	0.5	–	–	12.5	17.8	17.8	12.5	12.5	6.2	2.1

(i) Calculate the annual range of temperature.

(ii) State whether the station is located in the coastal area or in the continental interior.

(iii) Name the wind that brings most of the rainfall to this area.

Ans. (i) The annual range of temperature is 41.0- 8.4 = 32.6°C.

(ii) The station is located in the continental interior due to having long range of temperature.

(iii) The wind that brings most of the rainfall to this area is South-West monsoon winds as most of the rainfall occur from June to September which is a period of South-West monsoon season.

7. Give a reason for each of the following. *(ICSE 2019)*

(i) Goa receives heavier rainfall than Puducherry.

(ii) Mawsynram receives the highest average annual rainfall.

(iii) Mangaluru is cooler than Delhi in summer season.

Ans. (i) Goa is situated in the West coast of India where it gets rainfall from the South-West monsoon which brings heavy rainfall in summer (from June to September). While Puducherry is situated in the Eastern Ghats where South-West monsoon does not give much rain therefore Goa gets heavier rainfall than Puducherry.

(ii) Mawsynram lies on the windward side of Khasi hills. The place is enclosed by hills on all the three sides due to which it gives a funnel shaped location to Mawsynram. The monsoon winds get trapped in this region causing heavy rainfall again and again thereby making it the highest average annual rainfall place.

(iii) Mangaluru is cooler than Delhi because it lies on the Western Coast of India and therefore has moderating influence of sea in summer whereas Delhi is located in interior of India and has continental type of climate (extremely hot in summer and extremely cold in winter).

Examiner's Comment

- Many candidates were unable to write why Goa gets more rain than Puducherry. Some candidates explained either about Goa or Puducherry.
- A number of candidates were able to give the correct reason for Mawsynram receiving the heaviest rainfall. Some candidates, however, did not write the key words and key points such as, windward side/Garo-Khasi hills/clouds trapped due to position of hills, etc.
- Most candidates were able to write the correct reason for Mangaluru being cooler than Delhi in summer season. However, some candidates, instead of coastal location and interior location gave the difference in altitude as the reason. A few candidates wrote only about one city.

Suggestions for Students

- Train the students to explain about both the cities in their answers in questions where two cities are mentioned.
- Give sufficient practice to the students in answering questions based on climatic data.

8. Study the data of distribution of temperature and rain for Station X and answer the questions that follow. ***(ICSE 2019)***

Month	JAN	FEB	MAR	APR	MAY	JUN	JUL	AUG	SEP	OCT	NOV	DEC
Tem.°C	10	11	23	35	39	42	40	33	30	25	13	11
Rainfall cm	2	1	0	5	15	62	71	81	59	12	10	3

(i) Is Station X in the coastal area or in the interior of the country?

(ii) Calculate the total annual rainfall for Station X.

(iii) Name the wind that brings most of the rainfall to Station X.

Ans. (i) The Station X is the interior area of the country as the variation of temperature between minimum and maximum is very high.

(ii) The total annual rainfall is 321 cm.

(iii) As Station X is located in the interior part of India it receives rainfall from South-West monsoon winds.

9. Give a reason for each of the following. ***(ICSE 2018)***

(i) Kanyakumari experiences equable climate.

(ii) Central Maharashtra gets less rainfall than coastal area of Maharashtra. ***(ICSE 2013)***

(iii) Jaipur has a higher annual range of temperature than Mumbai. ***(ICSE 2009)***

Ans. (i) Kanyakumari is located at the tip of the Indian subcontinent where the Bay of Bengal Indian Ocean and the Arabian Sea meet which moderate the climate, making it equable or maritime.

(ii) Central Maharashtra gets less rainfall than coastal area of Maharashtra because Central Maharashtra lies in the rain shadow zone of the Western Ghats. On the other side, coastal area of Maharashtra is humid, means water vapours are present and moist wind comes from sea, therefore it gets heavy rainfall.

(iii) Jaipur lies in the interiors far away from the sea, so it experiences higher temperature whereas Mumbai lies on the Western coast, so, it experiences moderate type of temperature.

10. Write three differences between summer monsoon and retreating monsoon season. ***(ICSE 2018)***

Ans. Three difference between summer monsoon and retreating monsoon are

Summer Monsoon	Retreating Monsoon
These monsoon winds or monsoon winds blow from June to September.	These winds blow from October and November.
These monsoon covers the whole India and gives heavy rainfall.	These monsoon covers little regions of India but the coastal areas of Tamil Nadu receives maximum rainfall.
The direction of the wind is from the South-West direction.	The direction of the wind is from the North-East direction.

11. Give a geographical reason for each of the following. ***(ICSE Specimen 2018)***

(i) Chennai has more rainy months but less rainfall than Kochi.

Ans. (i) Chennai has more rainy months but less rainfall than Kochi because Chennai is a rainshadow area.

12. Study the climatic data given below and answer the questions that follow: ***(ICSE Specimen 2018)***

Month	Jan	Feb	Mar	Apr	May	Jun	Jul	Aug	Sep	Oct	Nov	Dec
Temp. °C	23.1	24.8	26.5	29.3	32	32.8	33.1	32.1	30.5	29.3	28.7	26.1
Rainfall cm	15.3	10.1	0.3	0.1	1.3	4.5	6.1	10.2	10.5	20.1	16.8	19.0

(i) Calculate the annual range of temperature.

(ii) Calculate the total rainfall during the monsoon season.

(iii) On which coast does the station lie? Give a reason to justify your answer.

Ans. (i) Annual range of temperature $= 33.1°C - 23.1°C = 10.0°C$

(ii) Total rainfall during the monsoon season

= Rainfall received between June to September

$\therefore$ $4.5 + 6.1 + 10.2 + 10.5 = 31.3$ cm

(iii) The station lies on East coast, because the station is receiving most of its rain in October and November.

13. (i) Explain in what way are retreating monsoon winds different from North East Monsoon winds. ***(ICSE Specimen 2017)***

(ii) Give two reasons why Arabian Sea branch of the South-West monsoon does not shed any moisture in Western Rajasthan?

Ans. (i) The retreating monsoon winds are different from North-East Monsoon winds in the following ways

- North-East monsoon wind blow during winter season while retreating monsoon occur during October and November.
- North-East monsoon wind bring rainfall over the coastal region of Tamil Nadu while the retreating monsoon is marked by clear skies and rise in temperature and caused the formation of tropical cyclones in Bay of Bengal region.
- North-East wind blow from land are cold and dry but the retreating wind are cool and moist due to the local influence

(ii) Arabian Sea branch of the South-West monsoon does not shed any moisture in Western Rajasthan due to following two reasons

(a) The Aravali range's alignment is parallel to the rain-bearing South-West monsoon winds and as such they do not offer any obstruction. Furthermore, these hills are very low.

(b) The moisture-laden winds of the Arabian Sea branch of the South-West monsoon passing over Rajasthan do not saturate as the heat in the desert region increases their capacity to hold moisture.

14. Study the climatic data of two cities of India provided below and answer the questions that follow ***(ICSE Specimen 2017)***

Month	Jan	Feb	Mar	Apr	May	Jun	Jul	Aug	Sep	Oct	Nov	Dec
Station A												
Temp. (°C)	24.5	26.0	28.0	30.0	32. 0	32.5	30.7	30.0	29.7	28.0	26.0	24.6
Rainfall (cm)	2.8	0.7	0.7	1.5	4.5	5.1	9.5	11.3	12.4	28.1	34.5	13.6
Station B												
Temp. (°C)	24.4	24.4	26.7	28.3	30.0	28.9	27.2	27.2	27.2	28.3	27.2	25.0
Rainfall (cm)	0.25	0.25	0.45	1.25	1.75	50.2	61.0	37.0	27.0	4.75	1.00	0.75

(i) Calculate the annual range of temperature of Station A.

(ii) What is the total rainfall experienced by Station B?

(iii) On which coast is Station A situated? Name the rains that bring rainfall to this region.

Ans. (i) The annual range of temperature of Station A is 8°C.

(ii) Total rainfall experienced by Station B is 185.65 cm.

(iii) Station A is situated on the Eastern coast. The retreating South-West monsoon brings rainfall to this region.

15. Give a reason for each of the following ***(ICSE 2017)***

(i) Kolkata receives heavier rain than Lucknow.

(ii) The summer monsoon winds blows over the Arabian Sea from the South-West.

(iii) Thar is a desert.

Ans. (i) Kolkata receives heavier rain than Lucknow because the Bay of the Bengal branch of the South-West Monsoon advances North-Eastward, after picking moisture from the Bay of Bengal. The Lower Ganga Valley receives the rainfall first and upper Ganga later on. Kolkata is in lower Ganga Valley. The rainfall goes on decreasing as it proceeds through the Ganga Valley.

The Monsoons move Westward and get drier as the distance from the sea is increasing. Thus, Kolkata receives more rainfall than Lucknow, which is in Upper Ganga Valley.

(ii) The summer monsoon winds blows over the Arabian Sea from the South West because one of the branch of the South-West monsoon is the Arabian Sea branch. The Arabian Sea branch strike the Western Coast of India in Kerala on 1st June. It gives very heavy rainfall. The duration and amount of rainfall goes on decreasing as Arabian Sea branch moves i.e. Northward. The whole of the Arabian Sea branch is used up by the entire country.

(iii) Thar is a desert because the soil of the Thar Desert remains dry for most of the year having a scanty rainfall. The Aravalli range lies parallel to the South-West monsoon wind branch of Arabian Sea which fail to obstruct the wind and wind blow away which give birth to the desert region. There are very few local tree species. The sand in the desert is highly mobile due to strong winds.

16. Study the climatic data given below and answer the questions that follow. ***(ICSE 2017)***

Month	JAN	FEB	MAR	APR	MAY	JUN	JUL	AUG	SEP	OCT	NOV	DEC
Temp. °C	12.0	25.5	26.3	27.1	30.0	36.2	36.0	35.9	30.3	28.4	21.0	16.6
Rainfall cm	1.5	0.1	0.0	1.4	1.1	21.0	25.0	27.2	24.0	9.4	1.5	0.4

(i) What is the annual range temperature of the station?

(ii) What is the total annual rainfall experienced by the station?

(iii) Why would it be correct to presume that the station lies in the interior and not on the coast?

Ans. (i) The annual range temperature of the station is 24.2.

(ii) The total annual rainfall experienced by the station is 112.6 cm.

(iii) The Western coast gets its heaviest rainfall during June by South-West monsoon, while Eastern coast gets its maximum rainfall in winter. But in the given table there is no heavy rainfall either in summer or in winter. Thus, it is correct to presume that the station lies in the interior and not on the coast and the annual range temperature also differ a lot.

17. Study the climatic data of Station *X* given below and answer the questions that follow. ***(ICSE 2016)***

Month	Jan	Feb	Mar	Apr	May	Jun	Jul	Aug	Sep	Oct	Nov	Dec
Temp °C	24.5	25.7	27.7	28.4	30.0	32.5	31.0	30.2	29.8	28.0	25.9	24.7
Rainfall cm	4.3	1.6	1.7	2.4	2.8	4.6	8.6	11.4	11.8	30.6	35.0	13.9

(i) Calculate the total annual rainfall experienced by the station.

(ii) What is the annual range of temperature?

(iii) On which coast of India does the station lie? Give a reason for your answer.

Ans. (i) The total annual rainfall experienced by the station is 128.7 cm by adding the rainfall from January to December.

(ii) The annual range of temperature varies 8°C.

(iii) The given Station *X* lie on the Eastern coast of India as it receives more rainfall during retreating monsoon season.

18. Give a geographic reason for each of the following. ***(ICSE 2015)***

(i) Kerala has the longest rainy season.

(ii) The Konkan coast experiences orographic rainfall.

(iii) The city of Kanpur in Uttar Pradesh has a higher range of temperature than that of Chennai in Tamil Nadu.

Ans. (i) Kerala has the longest rainy season because Kerala is surrounded by water bodies i.e. Arabian sea on West. So when monsoons blow they bring rainfall from the Arabian sea and strikes on the Western Ghats. It also receive rain from the retreating monsoon and it is also prone to storm surge and torrential downpour as a result of cyclones. This results in frequent and long rain in Kerala.

(ii) The Konkan coast experiences orographic rainfall because it is located on the windward side of mountain range. As the moisture laden winds are blocked by mountains they cool, condense and fall as rain on the windward side of the mountain.

(iii) Kanpur city in Uttar Pradesh has a higher range of temperature than that of Chennai in Tamil Nadu because Kanpur is to the North of Tropic of Cancer and experiences a continental type of climate, i.e. very hot during summer and very cold during winter. While Chennai is situated on coastline hence experiences equable/maritime or oceanic type climate, which is neither too hot nor too cold.

19. Mention a geographical reason for each of the following *(ICSE 2014)*

(i) Patna receives heavier rain than Delhi.

(ii) Western Rajasthan receives no rain from the Arabian Sea branch of the South-West monsoon winds.

(iii) Mangalore is not cold even in the month of December.

Ans. (i) It is because Patna receives rainfall from the South-West monsoon winds (i.e. Bay of Bengal current), but when these winds move towards West their moisture content gradually decreases thus, causing less rain in Delhi.

(ii) Western Rajasthan lies in the shadow of the Aravalli hills and the wind runs parallel to these hills without any obstacles, thus, causing no rain in Western Rajasthan.

(iii) Mangalore lies on the Western coastal plains, where the influence of the sea moderates the climate. Hence, it is not cold even in the month of December.

20. Give reasons for the following. *(ICSE 2013)*

(i) When the Malabar coast is receiving heavy rainfall in July, the Tamil Nadu coast is comparatively dry.

(ii) The Northern Plains of India have a continental type of climate.

Ans. (i) The reason for this is that Tamil Nadu lies in rain shadow region of Arabian Sea branch and the Bay of Bengal is parallel to the coast.

(ii) Continental type of climate occurs in Northern Plains of India because it is away from the moderating influence of the sea.

21. Study the climatic data given below and answer the questions that follow *(ICSE 2013)*

Months	Jan	Feb	Mar	Apr	May	Jun	Jul	Aug	Sep	Oct	Nov	Dec
Temperature in °C	23.1	24.8	26.5	29.3	32	32.8	33.1	32.1	30.5	29.3	28.7	26.1
Rainfall in cm	15.3	10.1	0.3	0.1	1.3	4.5	6.1	10.2	10.5	20.1	16.8	19.0

(i) Calculate the annual rainfall experienced by the station.

(ii) Suggest a name of this station, giving a reason for your answer.

(iii) Name the season during which the rainfall is highest.

Ans. (i) Annual rainfall experienced by the station is 114.3 cm.

(ii) Chennai is the name of the station as it is receiving most of its rain in the winter season. Also, there is not much variation in the temperature, indicating a coastal location.

(iii) Rainfall is highest in winter season.

22. Give geographical reasons for the following. *(ICSE 2012)*

(i) The Northern Plains of India do not freeze in winter.

(ii) Kochi has a lesser annual range of temperature than Agra.

Ans. (i) The presence of Himalayas does not allow the cold winds from Central Asia to enter India. So that, Northern plains of India do not freeze in winter.

(ii) Kochi is located on the sea coast and its temperature is moderated by the sea, whereas Agra is far away from the sea. Therefore, Kochi has a lesser annual range of temperature than Agra.

23. Study the climate data given below and answer the questions that follow. *(ICSE 2012)*

Months	Jan	Feb	Mar	Apr	May	Jun	Jul	Aug	Sep	Oct	Nov	Dec
Temperature in °C	23.8	25.0	27.7	28.3	30.2	30.3	30.4	30.3	30.0	30.3	25.5	24.2
Rainfall in cm	0	0	1.1	1.5	2.1	45.3	46.5	45.4	43.3	20.1	3.0	0.1

(i) Calculate the mean annual temperature.
(ii) What is the total rainfall during the monsoon season?
(iii) Does the station have a maritime or a continental climate? Give a reason for your answer.

Ans. (i) Mean annual temperature is 28.0°C.
(ii) Total rainfall during the monsoon season (June to October) is 200.6 cm.
(iii) The station has a maritime type of climate because it has less temperature variation (from 30.4°C to 23.8°C).

24. Give a reason to explain why? *(ICSE 2011)*

(i) The coastal areas of India do not experience a significant variation in temperature between summer and winter months.
(ii) The annual rainfall in Rajasthan is less than 25 cm .
(iii) The Coromandel coast gets most of its rain during the winter season.

Ans. (i) The coastal areas of India do not experience temperature variation due to moderating influence of the sea.
(ii) The annual rainfall in Rajasthan is low because it lies in the rain shadow of the Aravalli hills for the Bay of Bengal branch of the South-West monsoon and the Arabian Sea branch of the monsoon runs parallel to the Aravalli hills, thus, not giving any rain to Rajasthan.
(iii) Coromandel coast gets its rain during the winter season due to the retreating monsoon, which takes moisture from Bay of Bengal and strikes at the coast.

25. Study the climatic data given below and answer the questions that follow. *(ICSE 2011)*

Months	Jan	Feb	Mar	Apr	May	Jun	Jul	Aug	Sep	Oct	Nov	Dec
Temperature in °C	24.5	25.7	27.5	20.4	30.0	32.5	31.0	30.2	29.8	28.0	25.9	24.7
Rainfall in cm	4.6	1.8	1.3	1.8	3.8	4.5	8.7	11.3	11.9	30.6	35.0	13.9

(i) Name the driest month.
(ii) Calculate the annual rainfall experienced by the station.
(iii) What is the annual range of temperature?

Ans. (i) March is the driest month.
(ii) 129.2 cm is the annual rainfall experienced by the station.
(iii) The annual range of temperature is 20.4 to 32.5° C.

26. Give reasons for the following. *(ICSE 2010)*

(i) The latitudinal extent of India is responsible for the variation in the climatic conditions which prevail in the country.

Ans. (i) India's latitudinal extent is from 8°4′ N to 37°6′ N. This vast latitudinal extent is responsible for the climate change and controls the climate all over India. This covers two Climatic Zones, the Temperate Zone (Northern part of India with a Continental Climate) and the Tropical Zone (Southern part of India with a Tropical Climate).

27. Study the climatic data provided below and answer the questions that follow. *(ICSE 2010)*

Months	Jan	Feb	Mar	Apr	May	Jun	Jul	Aug	Sep	Oct	Nov	Dec
Station A												
Temperature in (°C)	21.0	22.6	26.3	29.2	29.7	27.5	25.1	24.5	24.8	25.5	22.5	20.5
Rainfall in cm	0.1	0.1	0.5	1.5	2.7	11.4	16.7	9.0	13.4	9.0	2.7	0.3
Station B												
Temperature in (°C)	24.4	24.4	26.7	28.3	30.0	28.9	27.2	27.2	27.2	28.3	27.2	25.0
Rainfall in cm	0.2	0.3	0.3	1.7	1.9	50.2	61.0	37.0	27.0	4.8	1.4	0.3

(i) Calculate the annual range of temperature of Station B.

(ii) Calculate the annual rainfall of station A.

(iii) Presuming that both the stations are located in West India, state giving a reason as to, which of the two lies on the windward side of the Western Ghats.

Ans. (i) The annual range of temperature of Station B is 24.4° to 30°C and difference between maximum and minimum annual temperature is 5.6°C (30.0-24.4)

(ii) The annual rainfall of station A is 67.4 cm.

(iii) Station 'B' is at the windward side of the Western Ghats as it is getting 50.2 and 61 cm of rainfall in the months of June and July, whereas station 'A' gets only 11.4 and 16.7 cm of rainfall in the same months, which shows that it lies on the leeward side of the mountain.

28. Given below is the climatic data of a station. Study the table and answer the questions that follow. *(ICSE 2009)*

Months	J	F	M	A	M	J	J	A	S	O	N	D
Temperature in (°C)	24.5	25.7	27.7	20.4	30.0	32.5	31.0	30.2	29.8	28.0	25.9	24.7
Rainfall in (cm)	4.6	1.3	1.3	1.8	3.8	4.5	8.7	11.3	11.9	30.6	35.0	13.9

(i) Calculate the annual rainfall experienced by the station.

(ii) What is the annual range of temperature?

(iii) Name the wettest month.

Ans. (i) 128.7 cm is annual rainfall experienced by the station.

(ii) The annual range of temperature is 20.4° to 32.5° C and difference between maximum and minimum annual temperature is 12.1°C (32.5-20.4).

(iii) The wettest month is November.

29. Give a reason for each of the following. *(ICSE 2008)*

(i) Patna gets a heavier rainfall than Varanasi.

(ii) India has varied climatic conditions.

Ans. (i) It is because Patna receives rainfall from the South-West monsoon winds (Bay of Bengal current), but when these winds move towards Varanasi, which lies to the West, their moisture content decreases, causing less rainfall there.

(ii) India has varied climatic conditions due to its large latitudinal and longitudinal extent and also distance of its various areas from the sea and their variable altitudes.

30. Study the climatic data provided below and answer the questions that follow. *(ICSE 2008)*

Station	Months	J	F	M	A	M	J	J	A	S	O	N	D
A	Temperature in (°C)	24.4	25.4	26.7	29.3	30.0	29.9	29.8	27.8	26.9	25.3	25.1	24.8
	Rainfall in cm	0.1	0.1	0.5	0.6	3.8	26.6	29.6	30.5	26.5	11.9	1.1	0.2
B	Temperature in (°C)	8.1	8.9	15.6	20.1	25.2	24.3	24.1	22.7	20.6	18.4	14.1	9.6
	Rainfall in cm	0.4	0.3	0.3	1.1	1.3	3.2	7.7	10.3	5.8	0.7	0.4	0.3

(i) Calculate the annual range of temperature of station A. Suggest a reason why the range is a small one.
(ii) Which of the two stations has the lower temperature? Why?
(iii) Calculate the annual rainfall of station B.

Ans. (i) The annual range of temperature of station A is 24.4° to 30.0° C and difference between the maximum and minimum temperature is 5.6° C (30-24.4). The difference of annual range of temperature is less. Probably the station is close to the sea.

(ii) Station B has the lower average temperature because this station experiences winter season, whereas there is no definite winter season in station A.

(iii) The annual rainfall of station B is 31.8 cm.

31. Given below is the climatic data of a station. Study the table and answer the questions that follow. *(ICSE 2007)*

Months	Jan	Feb	Mar	Apr	May	Jun	Jul	Aug	Sep	Oct	Nov	Dec
Temperature in (°C)	13.7	16.6	21.6	25.5	33.2	33.5	30.8	29.8	29.2	25.5	19.6	15.2
Rainfall in cm	2.5	2.0	1.5	0.9	1.5	7.5	17.8	18.5	12.5	1.0	0.2	1.5

(i) Calculate the annual range of temperature.
(ii) What is the total rainfall experienced by the station?
(iii) Which is the driest month?

Ans. (i) Annual range of temperature is 13.7° to 33.5° C and difference between and maximum and minimum temperature is 19.8° C (33.5-13.7).

(ii) 67.4 cm is the total rainfall.

(iii) November is the driest month.

32. Study the table given below and answer the question. *(ICSE 2005)*

Station	Months	Jan	Feb	Mar	Apr	May	Jun	Jul	Aug	Sep	Oct	Nov	Dec
A	Temperature in (°C)	12.7	15.1	22.1	31.8	37.2	39.1	37.3	33.4	28.0	26.7	16.1	13.6
	Rainfall in cm	2.1	2.3	1.0	0.9	1.5	5.6	18.3	18.9	15.1	0.6	0.3	1.8
B	Temperature in (°C)	23.1	24.8	26.5	29.3	32.0	32.8	33.1	32.1	30.5	29.3	28.7	26.1
	Rainfall in cm	15.3	10.1	0.3	0.1	1.3	4.5	6.1	10.2	10.5	20.1	16.8	19.0

(i) Calculate the annual rainfall in station A.
(ii) What is the annual range of temperature in station B?
(iii) Name the winds that bring most of the rainfall to station B. State one reason for your answer.

Ans. (i) 68.4 cm is the annual rainfall in station A.

(ii) The annual range of temperature in station B is 23.1° to 33.1° C and difference between maximum and minimum annual temperature is 10° C (33.1-23.1).

(iii) North-East winds bring most of the rainfall to station B. It receives maximum rainfall in winter season.

33. Study the data and answer the following questions. *(ICSE 2004)*

Station	Months	Jan	Feb	Mar	Apr	May	Jun	Jul	Aug	Sep	Oct	Nov	Dec
A	Temperature in (°C)	16.8	19.2	26.6	29.8	33.3	33.9	31.3	29	20.1	27	20.1	14.9
	Rainfall in (°C)	0.5	0.6	0.3	0.3	1.0	3.1	10.8	13.1	5.7	0.8	0.3	0.2
B	Temperature in (°C)	24.5	25.7	27.7	30.4	33	32.5	31	30.2	29.8	28	25.9	24.7
	Rainfall in cm	4.6	1.3	1.3	1.8	3.8	4.5	8.7	11.3	11.9	30.6	35.0	13.9

(i) Calculate the annual rainfall for station B.
(ii) Which of the two stations is located away from the sea? Give a reason to justify your answer.
(iii) Calculate the annual range of temperature for station A.
(iv) Which is the driest month in station A as shown in the table?

Ans. (i) 128.7 cm is the annual rainfall for station B.
(ii) Station A is located away from the sea because the annual temperature variation is high and the annual rainfall is low.
(iii) The annual range of temperature of station A is 14.9° C to 33.9° C and difference between maximum and minimum temperature is 19° C (33.9-14.9).
(iv) December is the driest month in station A.

34. Study the climatic data given below and answer the questions that follow. *(ICSE 2004)*

Station	Months	Jan	Feb	Mar	Apr	May	Jun	Jul	Aug	Sep	Oct	Nov	Dec
A	Temperature in (°C)	14.4	16.7	23.3	30.0	33.3	33.3	30.0	29.9	28.9	25.6	19.4	15.6
	Rainfall in (°C)	2.5	1.5	1.3	1.0	1.8	7.4	19.3	17.8	11.9	1.3	0.2	1.0
B	Temperature in (°C)	24.4	24.4	26.7	28.3	30.0	28.9	27.2	27.2	27.2	27.8	27.2	25.0
	Rainfall in (°C)	0.2	0.2	0.0	0.0	1.8	50.6	61.0	36.9	24.8	4.8	1.0	0.0

(i) Calculate the annual rainfall for station A.
(ii) What is the annual range of temperature at station B?
(iii) In which hemisphere do you think station A lies?
(iv) Which of these stations has an equable climate?

Ans. (i) Annual rainfall for station A is 67 cm.
(ii) The annual range of temperature of station B is 24.4° to 30.0° C and difference between maximum and minimum annual temperature is 5.6° C (30.0-24.4).
(iii) Station A lies in the Northern Hemisphere because the temperatures are high during April to September and low during November, December and January.
(iv) Station B has an equable climate because its temperature variation is lower than that of station A.

35. Answer the following question. *(ICSE 2001)*

(i) Name the place in India which receives the heaviest rainfall.
(ii) Name the states where Mawsynram is located.
(iii) Name the winds which are responsible for this heavy rainfall.

Ans. (i) Mawsynram receives the heaviest rainfall in India.
(ii) Mawsynram is located in Meghalaya.
(iii) South-West monsoon wind of Bay of Bengal branch is responsible for heavy rainfall.

CHAPTER TEST

01 Multiple Choice Questions

1 What type of climate does India experience ?

(a) Equatorial (b) Temperate
(c) Polar (d) Tropical monsoon

2 A local wind that blows in North-Western part of country and causes heat strokes.

(a) Kalbaisakhi (b) Loo
(c) EL Nino (d) Jet Streams

3 'Cherry Blossom' showers in Kerala helps in the growth of

(a) Coffee and Tea (b) Coconut
(c) Wheat (d) Mangroves

4 What type of wind is monsoon ?

(a) Natural (b) Regular
(c) Irregular (d) Periodic

5 The wettest place on the Earth is ....

(a) Mawsynram (b) Hyderabad
(c) Mumbai (c) Chennai

6 Which physical feature of India protects India from cold Siberian winds from entering the Indian region ?

(a) Indian ocean (b) Arabian Sea
(c) Bay of Bengal (d) Himalayas

Answers

1. (d) | 2. (b) | 3. (a) | 4. (d) | 5. (a) | 6. (d)

10 Marks Questions

7 (i) Why does Kanyakumari experience an equable climate?

(ii) Name the states that receive rainfall during the winter and its source.

(iii) What do you understand by the term ' Burst of Monsoon '. Name the state that experience burst of monsoon.

8 (i) Why there is a great variation in the climate of the Indian sub-continent ?

(ii) Give two important characteristics of South-West monsoon rainfall.

(iii) Mumbai receives rainfall in summer season, while Chennai receives rainfall from October to December. Why ?

(iv) Name the cyclonic systems that affect India and two areas that receive rainfall from these systems.

9 (i) Name two local winds, which blow in India and write briefly about each.

(ii) 'The Rainfall in India is orographic in nature'. Give example to the distribution of rainfall and effect of relief on its distribution.

(iii) What is the source of winter rain in the state of Tamil Nadu? How does it benefit the State ?

(iv) What are the climatic significance of the 'Great Himalayas' of the Indian sub-continent?

10 (i) Explain the term.

(a) Kalbaisakhi (b) Temperate cyclone

(ii) State the benefits derived from local winds that blows in Summer in states of

(a) Kerala (b) West Bengal

(iii) What is the importance of summer monsoon rainfall in India ?

(iv) Study the data of distribution of temperature and rain for station '*x*' and answer the question that follows.

Month	Temp.°C	Rainfall cm.
Jan	10	3
Feb	11	1
Mar	23	1
April	35	4
May	39	15
June	42	60
July	40	72
Aug	33	82
Sept	30	50
Oct	25	13
Nov	13	9
Dec	11	2

(a) Is station *x* is located in the coastal area or in the interior of the country ?

(b) Calculate the total annual rainfall for station *x*.

(c) Name the wind that brings most of the rainfall to station '*x*'.

02

Soils in India and Natural Vegetation of India

TREND ANALYSIS 3 YEARS

Average No. of Questions Across all Sets

	Types of Questions	2023	2020	2019
TOPIC 01 Soil	1 Mark	2	–	–
	2 Marks	4	3	1
	3 Marks	4	2	2
TOPIC 02 Natural Vegetation	1 Mark	2	–	–
	2 Marks	3	2	2
	3 Marks	3	2	2

Soil

Soil is the loose material, which forms the thin surface of the Earth. Soil supports plants, animals as well as human life. Soil is important as man depends on it for food. Agricultural production depends on the fertility of soil because, if the soils are fertile, production is more and such areas support a high density of population.

Formation of Soil

The formation of soil depends upon various factors such as the parent rock material, relief, climate and vegetation. Animals and man also play an important role in formation of soil. Soil forms under natural conditions. It is a mixture of minerals, organic and inorganic matter. Thus, soil is renewable natural resource. The process of soil formation is called **pedogenesis**.

Types of Soil

India has a large variety of soil groups distinctly different from each other by way of origin, colour, texture, fertility and chemical composition due to physiographic, climatic and structural diversities.

In-situ Soils

These are the soils which are found at the places where they are formed by the disintegration and weathering of rocks. Example of in-situ soils are laterite soils, black soils, red soils, etc.

Transported Soils

These are soils which are found at the places where they got transported by agents of erosion. Example of transported soils are alluvial soils.

The Indian Council of Agricultural Research (ICAR) set-up an All India Soil Survey Committee in 1953, which divided Indian soils into the major groups of Alluvial soils, Black soils, Red soils and Laterite and Lateritic soils.

Alluvial Soils

These originate from the transported alluvium brought by the rivers and they support the maximum share of agricultural products and a major part of the population.

Characteristics of Alluvial soils are

Colour and Textures These soils vary from **light** to **dark** in colour. In upper course of river alluvium is more coarse than lower course of river.

Minerals They are rich in potash and humus, but deficient in phosphorus and nitrogen and also very fertile, give better response to irrigation and manuring.

Crops They are good for both Rabi and Kharif crops. Rice, wheat, jute, sugarcane, millets, pulses etc, are common crops grown in alluvial soils.

Distribution The areas, where they found are the Indo-Gangetic plains, Brahmaputra plain and the deltas of Godavari, Krishna and Cauvery.

These soils can be divided into two types

(i) **Young Khadar Soils** These soils are newer alluvium of sandy pale brown composition found in the lower areas or valley bottoms, which are flooded every year.

(ii) **Old Bhangar Soils** These soils consist of older alluvium and are of clayey composition and dark in colour. These soils are coarse in nature and contain *kankars*, pebbles and gravels.

Black Soils

Black soils are formed by the weathering and erosion of volcanic origin rocks. These are also known as **regur** or **black cotton** soils as cotton is important crop grown in black soils of India.

Characteristics of Black soils are

Colour and Textures This soil is deep black, medium black or dark brown in colour. They retain moisture and become sticky when wet and get cracked when dry. Due to this characteristic it is also known as **self-ploughed soil.** Thus, these are very useful in areas where irrigation is not possible.

Minerals These soils are rich in lime, iron, potash, magnesium carbonates and calcium. They are deficient in phosphates, nitrogen, humus and organic matter.

Crops High fertility and retentivity of moisture, the black soils are widely used for several important crops like cotton, sugarcane, wheat, tobacco, rice, jowar, millets, oilseeds like linseed and sunflower and fruits and vegetables.

Distribution They are found in most parts of the Deccan plateau region (Maharashtra, Madhya Pradesh, Gujarat, Telangana, Andhra Pradesh) where volcanic rocks of Deccan trap are found. As it is mainly found in these moderate rainfall and temperate regions, thus this soil does not get leached.

Red Soils

These soils are formed due to weathering of ancient crystalline and metamorphic rocks. Red colour is due to the presence of high iron content.

Characteristics of Red soils are

Colour and Textures The colour varies from **chocolate brown** to **yellow** as percentage of iron varies. This soil is more sandy and less clayey. Soil aggregates (kankars) are absent in the soils.

Minerals These are rich in potash and iron, but lack in lime, magnesia, phosphate, nitrogen and humus.

Crops They are suitable for cultivation of wheat, rice, cotton, sugarcane, pulses, tobacco and oilseeds. These soils become productive with the use of suitable fertilisers and irrigation.

Distribution They are found in parts of Jharkhand, Chhattisgarh, Odisha, Andhra Pradesh, Karnataka, Tamil Nadu and Eastern Rajasthan.

Laterite Soils

These soils are formed by leaching under conditions of high temperature and heavy rainfall with alternate wet and dry periods.

Characteristics of Laterite soils are

Colour and Textures Leaching is the process by which the nutrients of the top soils are washed away, thereby making the top soil infertile. They are **red** in colour due to the presence of iron ore.

Minerals Laterite soils are rich in iron and aluminium compounds, but poor in lime and silica due to leaching. They are acidic in nature and not capable of retaining moisture.

Crops They are suitable for cultivation of tea, coffee, rubber and coconut.

Distribution These are found on the higher reaches of Western Ghats and Eastern Ghats, Karnataka, Tamil Nadu, Andhra Pradesh and parts of Odisha and Kerala as well as in Meghalaya and Assam.

Composition of Soil

Soil is a mixture of inorganic materials, minerals and organic materials.

Inorganic Components

The soil is made up of three main substances Silica, Clay and Chalk.

(i) **Silica** is present in the soil, in the form of small crystalline grains. It is derived from the disintegration of rocks.

(ii) **Clay** is a mixture of silicates and many other minerals such as iron, calcium, sodium, potassium and aluminium. It retains moisture.

(iii) **Chalk** is also known as calcium carbonate. It provides the most essential element for plant growth, which is calcium.

Organic Components

These determine the fertility of the soil. They are derived from the decay of living matter. The ultimate form of organic matter is **humus**. It is not a mineral. It is organic matter because it is formed by the decomposition of plant and animal remains. It helps the soil to retain moisture. It imparts a dark colour to the soil. It also helps the plant to draw the nutrients from the soil essential for its growth.

Soil Profile

The soil mainly consists of two layers *i.e.*, **Topsoil** and **Subsoil**. Topsoil forms the layer where the plant growth takes place; hence fertile topsoil yields good crops. It also contains bacteria, worms and insects which are important for the fertility of the soil.

The formation of soil is a very slow and long process, but it can be washed away in a very short period. Therefore, conservation of the topsoil is very important as its loss would affect the economy of the country as well as the life of people.

Subsoil is formed by the weathering of the parent rock. It also contains a part of organic matter and moisture, but it is not very productive. For good crops, it would have to be converted to soil, which is a very slow process.

Soil Erosion

It is the removal of topsoil by different agents of weathering such as wind, water, etc.

Causes of Soil Erosion

(i) Wind

The broad flat lands are subject to a windy dry season for part of the year which results in soil erosion by wind. The upper soil surface becomes loose and susceptible to wind erosion due to lack of moisture.

(ii) Men, Plants and Animals

Man's activities like construction work, ploughing and cutting of trees cause soil erosion. Overgrazing by animals and uprooting of plants also result in dismantling the soil.

(iii) Running Water

The prime factor of soil erosion is running water. Indirectly, soil erosion helps in soil forming because from wherever the soil is removed, it is deposited elsewhere. However, it disturbs the agricultural pattern and should be prevented.

Ways of Soil Erosion by Running water

There are several ways in which soil erosion takes place due to running water

(a) **Splash Erosion** In this, the soil disintegrates under the impact of heavy drops of rain or hailstones as in case on convectional rainfall.

(b) **Sheet Erosion** In this, due to heavy rains, a surface film of water carries away the even surface layer of the topsoil as it moves. For example, Himalayan foothills and the North-Eastern parts of the Peninsular India.

(c) **Gully Erosion or Rill Erosion** In the absence of any vegetation, the flow of storm water flows with force downhill, developing into a channel flow, cutting steep sided valleys as it runs off. Gullies change the agricultural land into bad land, where no cultivation is possible. For example, Chambal ravines.

(iv) Overgrazing

Due to overgrazing by animals, wind erosion occurs as in the absence of vegetation, soil is directly exposed to the wind.

Soil Conservation

Soil conservation is an effort, made by man to prevent soil erosion to retain the fertility of soil. Soil is our most precious resource. It is important to our national economy, as productive soil ensures prosperity in agriculture, industrial development and general economic development.

Methods for Prevention of Soil Erosion

Several measures have been adopted by the Government to prevent soil erosion. Some of the measures by which soil erosion can be prevented are as follows

Adopting Sustainative Farming Techniques

Contour bunding, terrace farming, cover cropping, mixed farming, crop ratation etc are some of the sustainative farming techniques by which we can conserve soil.

To Check Overgrazing

Overgrazing of forests and grassland by animal grazing, especially by goats and sheep should be checked. Separate grazing grounds should be provided.

Constructing Dams and Barrages

Much of the soil erosion by floods can be checked by constructing dams or barrages over such rivers. This would check the speed of water and thereby save soil from erosion.

Afforestation

The best way to prevent soil erosion is to increase area under forests. Indiscriminate felling of trees must stop.

Natural Vegetation of India

The natural vegetation of India depends mainly on rain and relief. The main types of natural vegetation found in India are

Importance of Forests

Forest play an important role in human life and maintaining ecosystem.

Forests have following importances

(i) **Maintain Ecosystem** Forests are primary producers they are at the beginning of food chain. Thus, they support all wildlife.

(ii) **Act as Climate Control** Forests control the climate of a region. They moderate the temperature and help in bringing rain as well as purifying air.

(iii) **Prevent Soil Erosion** Roots of the trees hold soils and prevent it from erosion.

(iv) **Provide Food and Shelter** Forest provide food and shelter not only to wildlife but also to human beings. Many tribes are dependent on forest for their livelihood.

(v) **Industrial and Medicinal Use** Forest are valuable for timber, furniture, medicines, etc.

Types of Vegetation in India

1. Tropical Evergreen Forests

Climatic Conditions These are found in areas where the annual temperature is 25°C to 27°C and rainfall is more than 200 cm.

Distribution These are found on hill slopes of Western Ghats (parts of Maharashtra), Karnataka and Kerala, the Eastern Himalayas (Terai region) and North-East India : Lushai, Khasi, Jayantia and Garo known as **Assam hills** and also in Andaman and Nicobar islands.

Correlation with the Environment These forests are economically less important because they are dense and inaccessible and found in mixed stand. However, rosewood, gurjan and sheesham are used for furniture making. The species of trees in these forests are rosewood, sheesham, gurjan, toon, bamboo, jamun and cane.

2. Tropical Deciduous Forests

Climatic Conditions These are found in the areas where average temperature is about 27°C with average rainfall between 150 cm to 200 cm.

Distribution These forests are found in Bihar, Uttar Pradesh, Odisha, Madhya Pradesh, Manipur, Tripura, Mizoram, Assam and parts of Andaman and Nicobar islands.

Correlation with the Environment The trees of this vegetation have adapted the dry season. The trees shed their leaves for about 1-2 months during spring and summer due to lack of adequate moisture in environment. The main species of deciduous trees are sal, teak, sandalwood, mahua, kheir, palas, mango, neem, jackfruit, semul and myrobalan.

3. Desert and Semi-Desert Vegetation

Climatic Conditions It is found in the area of average temperature of 25°C to 27°C and with a rainfall of less than 25 cm.

Distribution It is found mainly in Kutch, Saurashtra, South-West Punjab, Rajasthan and dry parts of the Deccan. Scrub and thorn forests are found in the North-Western part of country, Rajasthan, Western Haryana, Kutch and Western Punjab.

Correlation with the Environment The trees of this vegetation have adapted the dry climatic condition. As due to lack of moisture the trees growing here have very small leaves and long plant roots penetrating deep into the soil and spreading in a radial pattern in search of water.

Leaves are small and thick to minimise loss of water. Vegetation mainly consists of babul (acacia - arabica) which is used for medicinal purposes.

4. Mountain Forests

Climatic Conditions These are found in the areas of average temperature less than 20°C or cool areas at an altitude of 1500 m to 3300 m and get 150 cm to 250 cm rainfall.

Distribution These are found in the temperate zone of the Himalayas, from Kashmir to Assam at varying altitude, as well as in the Nilgiri and Annamalai hills at an elevation 1000 m to 1500 m.

Correlation with the Environment There is difference in nature of vegetation of these forests found in lower slopes and upper slopes (above 1500 m). At higher altitudes, temperature falls and precipitation increases. Therefore, in these forests vegetation tends to become evergreen.

The species of trees found here are chirpine (important for resin and turpentine) silver fir (important for making paper, matches, packing cases, etc) eucalyptus, deodar (important for making railway sleepers and construction purposes) oaks, laurel, bamboo, poplass birch, walnuts and elm.

5. Tidal or Mangrove or Littoral Forests

Climatic Conditions These are found in and around deltas with average temperature of about 26°C to 29°C and get heavy rainfall more than 200 cm.

Distribution Tidal forests occupy a large area of the Sunderban delta, Eastern coast, Mahanadi delta, Godavari, Krishna and in the Andaman islands.

Correlation with the Environment These forests are quite sensitive, thus the proper ratio of both the fresh and saline water is necessary for them and if there is a deficit or excess in any of the two, it may cause damage to the vegetation.

The species of trees found here are sundari, (important for making boats and boxes) gurjan and hintal.

Deforestation

Deforestation refers to the indiscriminate felling of trees or destruction of natural vegetation for human purpose.

Reasons for Deforestation

- It is the consequence of indiscriminate cutting down of the trees due to **jhooming** (slash and burn) practices to clear the forests for cultivation and construction purposes.
- The uncontrolled cutting down of trees by timber merchants for the purpose of trade.
- Due to rapid population growth and the demand for more food, forest have been cleared.

Forest Conservation

To revitalise our forest cover, systematic preventive measures have been taken.

These are as follows

Van Mahotsava Programme

It was started in 1950 and under this, all government organisations are supposed to plant trees in the months of July and August.

Afforestation

Afforestation refers to the plantation of trees in the areas which were under no trees earlier. This programme has been proposed to plant trees in Rajasthan, Western Uttar Pradesh and Kutch desert to prevent soil erosion.

Reafforestation

To resolve the deflection of forest, the Government of India has started a programme under which two saplings are planted for every felled tree.

PYQs Previous Years' Questions

1 Mark Questions

Multiple Choice Questions

1. Which is the most widespread soil of India ? *(ICSE 2023)*

   (a) Red soil (b) Alluvial soil
   (c) Laterite soil (d) Black soil

Ans. (b) Alluvial soil

2. Which type of forest is found mostly in the coastal areas of India ? *(ICSE 2023)*

   (a) Tropical Evergreen Forest
   (b) Tropical Desert Forest
   (c) Littoral Forest
   (d) Tropical Deciduous Forest

Ans. (a) Tropical Evergreen Forest

3. Which are the most widespread forests of India? *(ICSE Specimen 2023)*

   (a) Tropical Rain Forests
   (b) Tropical Thorn Forest
   (c) Tropical Deciduous Forests
   (d) Littoral Forests

Ans. (c) Tropical Deciduous Forests

4. What are the chief characteristics of Deciduous forests? *(ICSE Specimen Semester I 2021)*

   (a) These regions receive a moderate rainfall.
   (b) The trees shed their leaves in the dry season.
   (c) The trees are found in pure stand.
   (d) All of the above

Ans. (a) These regions receive a moderate rainfall.

5. Gully erosion is common in the *(ICSE Specimen 2023)*

   (a) Chambal basin (b) Ganga basin
   (c) Rajasthan (d) Hilly region

Ans. (c) Rajasthan

6. What is the main reason for the red colour of Red soil? *(ICSE Specimen Semester I 2021)*

   (a) Abundance of magnesium
   (b) Accumulated humus
   (c) Presence of ferric oxides
   (d) Abundance of phosphates

Ans. (c) Presence of ferric oxides

7. Afforestation prevent soil erosion because *(ICSE Specimen Semester I 2021)*

   (a) it reduces pollution.
   (b) it protects the soil from being exposed.
   (c) the roots of the trees bind the soil particles.
   (d) trees produce fruits.

Ans. (c) the roots of the trees bind the soil particles.

8. Where are the various forest conservation methods that can be undertaken? *(ICSE Specimen Semester I 2021)*

   (a) Afforestation and stopping indiscriminate felling of trees.
   (b) Large scale of deforestation and overgrazing.
   (c) Allowing animals to graze in farm land.
   (d) Maintaining records of forest areas.

Ans. (a) Afforestation and stopping indiscriminate felling of trees.

9. What is Social Forestry? *(ICSE Specimen Semester I 2021)*

   (a) The management and protection of forests and afforestation on barren lands with the purpose of helping in the social development.
   (b) The practice of growing trees on farm lands.
   (c) Growing trees by social workers
   (d) Forest used for social gathering.

Ans. (a) The management and protection of forests and afforestation on barren lands with the purpose of helping in the social development.

10. In which vegetation belt multiple layer of trees is found? *(ICSE SQP 2021)*

   (a) Tropical Deciduous (b) Tropical Evergreen
   (c) Thorn and scrub forest (d) Tidal forest

Ans. (b) Tropical Evergreen

11. Why are Sundarbans so called? *(ICSE SQP 2021)*

   (a) The abundance of breathing roots
   (b) A beautiful forest
   (c) The abundance of Sundari trees
   (d) Ban of cutting of trees

Ans. (c) The abundance of Sundari trees

12. What is the other name of Littoral forests? *(ICSE SQP 2021)*

   (a) Rain forests
   (b) Monsoon forests
   (c) Tidal forests
   (d) Scrub lands

Ans. (c) Tidal forests

13. Which of the following factor is responsible for acidic nature of Laterite soil? *(ICSE Specimen Semester I 2021)*

   (a) As it is friable in nature.
   (b) As it can retain moisture.
   (c) As the bases leached down from the top soil.
   (d) All the above are correct.

Ans. (c) As the bases leached down from the top soil.

14. Name the process of removal of soluble mineral salts, especially the bases and silica from horizon A or the top soil by percolating rain water. *(ICSE Specimen Semester I 2021)*

(a) Pedogenesis (b) Leaching
(c) Lithification (d) Conglomeration

Ans. (b) Leaching

15. Study the map and answer the following questions. *(ICSE Specimen Semester I 2021)*

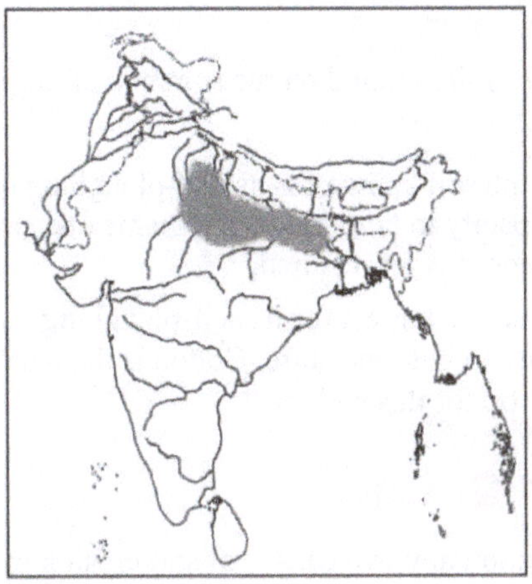

(i) Which soil is found in the shaded region?

(a) Black soil (b) Alluvial soil
(c) Red soil (d) Laterite soil

Ans. (b) Alluvial soil

(ii) How is this type of soil formed?

Ans. It is formed by the deposition of silt brought down by rivers. It is also formed by weathering of alluvium.

16. Which of the following features is not associated with Thorn and Scrub Forest? *(ICSE Specimen Semester I 2021)*

(a) Xerophyte or Drought resistant
(b) Evergreen and Multilayered
(c) Long roots going deep in the ground
(d) Leaves turned into spines

Ans. (b) Evergreen and Multilayered

17. Why is laterite soil used in Goa and Kerala for the construction of houses? *(ICSE Semester I 2021)*

(a) It become hard when dry
(b) This soil is generally coarse in texture and poors in nature
(c) It has more of clay contest in it
(d) It looks beautiful when used in buildings

Ans (a) It become hard when dry

18. Why are the foothills of Himalayas prime to excessive soil erosion? *(ICSE Semester I 2021)*

(a) Absence of crop cover
(b) Too much of development of transportation
(c) Large scale deforestation in past
(d) Tourists are spreading pollutants in rivers

Ans (c) Large scale deforestation in past

19. The productive functions of forests include *(ICSE Semester I 2021)*

(a) habitat for the wildlife
(b) control the water flow
(c) provide various products such as timber, fuel, wood, leaves, etc
(d) producing oxygen

Ans (c) provide various products such as timber, fuel, wood, leaves, etc

20. Which of the following pairs is correctly matched? *(ICSE Semester I 2021)*

(a) Babool – Tropical Evergreen Forest
(b) Sandalwood – Tropical Deciduous Forest
(c) Cinchona – Mountain Forest
(d) Sal – Tidal Forest

Ans (b) Sandalwood – Tropical Deciduous Forest

21. Name the type of Natural Vegetation that is found in the windward side of the Western Ghats. *(ICSE Semester I 2021)*

(a) Tropical Evergreen
(b) Tropical Deciduous
(c) Mangrove Forest
(d) Mountain Forest

Ans (a) Tropical Evergreen

22. Which of the following is not a characteristic of desert vegetation? *(ICSE Semester I 2021)*

(a) Short named growth of vegetation
(b) Thick fleshy stems
(c) Broad leaves
(d) Long and deep roots

Ans (c) Broad leaves

23. Why do we need forest conservation? *(ICSE Semester I 2021)*

(a) Forests provide food for growing population
(b) Forests helps in earning foreign exchange
(c) Forests help in maintaining ecological balance
(d) Forests look beautiful

Ans (c) Forests help in maintaining ecological balance

24. During which month do we celebrate Van Mahotsav every year in India? *(ICSE Semester I 2021)*

(a) In December to February time period
(b) In July to September time period
(c) In March to May time period
(d) In November to January time period

Ans (b) In July to September time period

25. What is the term used in describe the growing of trees in various parts of the country? *(ICSE Semester I 2021)*

(a) Re-afforestation (b) Deforestation
(c) Accuracy (d) Afforestation

Ans (d) Afforestation

Very Short Answer Questions

1. Under what rainfall conditions are the tropical rainforests found? *(ICSE 2003)*

Ans Tropical rainforests are found in areas where annual rainfall is more than 200 cm.

2. What are two main characteristics of the trees found in Tropical Evergreen Forests? *(ICSE 2002)*

Ans Two characteristics of the trees in Tropical Evergreen Forests are as follows

(i) They do not shed their leaves throughout the year.
(ii) These are hard, fine-grained and durable.

3. Name one state in India which mostly has red soils. *(ICSE 2002)*

Ans Tamil Nadu is a state in India, which mostly has red soils.

4. Mention two characteristics of red soils. *(ICSE 2002)*

Ans Two characteristics of red soils are as follows :

(i) They are red in colour due to high iron content.
(ii) Their colour may vary from yellow to brown as percentage of iron varies.

5. Name the vegetation type found in saline environment under tidal influence. *(ICSE 2001)*

Ans Mangrove forest is the vegetation type found in saline environment under tidal influence.

6. Name the most important tree associated with type of vegetation you have named above. *(ICSE 2001)*

Ans Sundari is the most important tree associated with mangrove vegetation.

7. How does the soil of the Ganga-Yamuna plain differ from that of central Maharashtra? *(ICSE 2000)*

Ans Ganga-Yamuna plain is made up of alluvial soil, which is transported by rivers whereas central Maharashtra is made up of black regur soil which is made up of weathered volcanic rocks.

8. Which soil is found suitable for coffee cultivation in Karnataka ? *(ICSE 2000)*

Ans Laterite soil is suitable for coffee cultivation in Karnataka.

9. Name the type of soil found on the summit of the Eastern Ghats. *(ICSE 2000)*

Ans Laterite soil is found on the summits of the Eastern Ghats.

10. Name the soil known for its self-ploughing quality and capacity to hold moisture. Name one cash crop for which it is most suited. *(ICSE 2000)*

Ans Black soil is known for its self-ploughing quality and capacity to hold moisture. Cotton is the most suited cash crop for this soil.

2 Marks Questions

1. (i) Mention any two causes of soil erosion in India. *(ICSE 2023)*

(ii) Name two soil conservation methods that may be practiced in arid (dry) regions.

Ans. (i) Rainfall deforestation and flooding are two main causes of soil erosion in India.

(ii) Contour barriers and terrace farming are two soil conservation methods that may be practiced in arid (dry) regions.

2. Mention two characteristics of Black soil. *(ICSE 2023)*

Ans. Two characteristics of black soil are

(i) The soil is rich in potash/calcium/magnesium but less in nitrogen/phosphate content.
(ii) It is generally soft when wet but gets hard on drying.

3. State two ways in which forests help in protecting the environment. *(ICSE 2023)*

Ans. Forests help in protecting the environment in the following ways

(i) Forests contribute in preserving soil, and supporting wildlife that leads to protection of environment.
(ii) Forests play an important role in the global water cycle, moving water across the Earth by releasing water vapour and capturing rainfall.

4. Mention two ways in which Tropical desert vegetation has adapted to its environment. ***(ICSE 2023)***

Other Similar Questions

Or How do trees in the tropical desert forest adapt themselves to the dry climate?

Or Which region of India has desert vegetation? How are they adapted to climate?

Ans. Trees in the Tropical desert forests have long roots which go out deep in search of water. The leaves of plants are waxy, small and thick to reduce transpiration. Thus, trees in the tropical desert forests are able to adapt themselves to the dry climate.

5. Differentiate between alluvial and laterite soil. ***(ICSE Specimen 2023)***

Ans. Differences between alluvial soil and laterite soil are given below

Alluvial Soil	Laterite Soil
Alluvial soil is very fertile as it is rich in mineral nutrients like potash and lime.	Laterite soil is red in colour due to presence of iron oxide. It is of coarse texture, soft and friable.
Alluvial soil is formed due to the deposition of alluvium from the river.	Laterite soil is formed due to leaching in wet and hot area.

6. Name the following. ***(ICSE Specimen 2023)***

(i) This soil is sticky when wet and cracks when dry.

(ii) This soil is mainly used for making bricks.

(iii) This soil is classified into khadar and bhangar.

(iv) When heavy rainfall washes away the topmost layer of the soil.

Ans. (i) Black soil (ii) Laterite soil

(ii) Alluvial soil (iv) Soil erosion

7. Mention *any two* characteristics of Tropical Evergreen Forests. ***(ICSE Specimen 2023)***

Ans. Two characteristics of Tropical Evergreen Forests are as follows

(i) These are the dense, multi-layered forests that comprise several kinds of fauna and flora.

(ii) These forests are found in the region having heavy rainfall.

8. Name the forest which is found in the delta of the river Ganga. Name *two* trees which are found here.

Ans. Mangrove forests are found in the delta of the river Ganga.

- Trees found in these forests are sundari, palms, keora, agar, and coconut.

9. With reference to methods of prevention of soil erosion answer the following. ***(ICSE Semester I 2021)***

(i) Name the method used to prevent soil erosion by running water.

(a) Terrace farming

(b) Strip cropping

(c) Shelter belts

(d) Leaving the land fallow

Ans (a) Terrace farming

(ii) Name the method used to prevent soil erosion by wind.

(a) Contour ploughing (b) Strip cropping

(c) Plugging of gullies (d) Use of fertiliser

Ans (b) Strip cropping

10. (i) Name the soil that is found in Central Deccan Plateau. ***(ICSE Semester I 2021)***

(a) Black soil (b) Alluvial soil

(c) Red soil (d) Laterite soil

(ii) How is the soil named by you (i) above formed?

(a) Formed by the deposition of silt brought down by river.

(b) Formed by the weathering of laterite rocks.

(c) Formed by the weathering of metamorphic rocks.

Ans (i) (a) Black soil

(ii) (c) Formed by the weathering of metamorphic rocks.

11. Name the soil that possess the following characteristics ***(ICSE Semester I 2021)***

(i) Soil is generally confined to river basins

(a) Black soil (b) Alluvial soil

(c) Red soil (d) Laterite soil

(ii) Soil that becomes infertile because of desilication

(a) Black soil (b) Alluvial soil

(c) Red soil (d) Laterite soil

Ans (i) (b) Alluvial soil (ii) (d) Laterite soil

12. (i) Name the parent rock that contributes to the formation of red soil. ***(ICSE 2020)***

(ii) How does this soil get its 'red' colour?

Ans (i) Metamorphic rocks and old crystalline rocks are the most common parent materials that contribute to the formation of red soil.

(ii) The colour of the soil is red due to iron oxide content in it.

13. Name the following. ***(ICSE 2020)***

(i) A soil that occurs in-situ and is good for cotton crop.

(ii) Soil that is formed due to high temperature and heavy rainfall.

Ans (i) Black soil is the soil that occurs in-situ and is good for cotton crop. It is due to high temperature and heavy rainfall.

(ii) Laterite soil is formed due to high temperature and heavy rainfall.

14. State two ways by which forests help in protecting the environment. ***(ICSE 2020)***

Ans Two ways by which forests help in protecting the environment are

(i) After oceans, forests are the world's largest storehouses of carbon. These absorb harmful greenhouse gases that produce climate change.

(ii) It provide habitats to the lot of wild animals and birds.

15. With reference to Tropical Deciduous Forests, answer the following questions. ***(ICSE 2020)***

(i) Name two states where it is found.

(ii) Name two important trees found in this forest.

Ans (i) Tropical Deciduous Forests are found in Madhya Pradesh and Uttar Pradesh.

(ii) Teak and Sal are important trees found in these forests.

16. (i) Name the Indian soil which is formed due to the weathering of basic igneous rocks. ***(ICSE 2020)***

(ii) Name two states of India where this type of soil is found.

Ans (i) Black soil has been formed by weathering of the parent rock material found in Deccan Plateau i.e. igneous rocks and is called regur soil.

(ii) It is found in the Deccan trap (Basalt lava region) and covers the plateau areas of Saurastrian Gujarat, Maharashtra, Malwa of Madhya Pradesh, parts of Andhra Pradesh, Northern Karnataka, parts of Tamil Nadu, Chhattisgarh and also along the valleys of the Godavari and Krishna rivers.

17. Name the following. ***(ICSE 2019)***

(i) An important transported soil of India.

(ii) Soil that is rich in iron oxide.

Ans (i) Alluvial soil is an important transported soil of India.

(ii) Red and yellow soils are rich in iron oxide.

18. Give two reasons to explain as to why we need to conserve our forest resources. ***(ICSE 2019)***

Ans We need to conserve forest resources because

(i) Forests are an important part of the Earth's climate. It is primarily because of the presence of a variety of plants which due to their high density produce massive amount of oxygen and enables other organisms to breathe.

(ii) Forests provide home to diverse animals and plant species which not only provide biodiversity on the Earth, but each species has an important role in the ecosystem.

Additional Info

The other reasons to conserve forest resources are

- Forests help to balance the impact of carbon emissions.
- They help to regulate global temperature.
- They also support the various biogeochemical cycles.

19. (i) Mention two conditions required for the growth of Littoral Forest. ***(ICSE 2019)***

(ii) State one characteristic feature of the forest found in the Nilgiri Hills.

Ans (i) Littoral forests are specialised tropical type of vegetation that grows in coastal areas where the saline sea water encroaches at the time of high tides and fresh water of rivers continuously mixes with the saline water. So, these can survive in salty as well as in fresh water. These forests occur in areas receiving 100 to 150 cm rainfall and have temperatures ranging between 25°C to 27°C.

(ii) Forests found in the Nilgiri Hills are also known as monsoon forests. These forests spread over the region receiving rainfall between 70 to 200 cm.

Examiner's Comment

- Instead of writing two conditions required for the growth of littoral forest, some candidates wrote the characteristics of the forest.
- Feature of the forest found in the Nilgiri Hills was answered correctly by many candidates. Some candidates, however, could not identify/recall the vegetation type.

Suggestions for Students

- Explain the difference between conditions for growth of all types of natural vegetation belts found in India and their characteristics.
- Learn the names of the trees found in each vegetation belt of India.

20. Give two points of difference between Black and Alluvial soil. *(ICSE Specimen 2018)*

Ans. Two difference between alluvial soil and black cotton soil are

Black Soil	Alluvial Soil
Black cotton soil are fine grained in texture with more than 60% clay. They do not contain gravel or sand.	Alluvial soils are coarse in nature and contain kankar, pebbles and gravels.
Black soils are less fertile in uplands.	Alluvial soils are very fertile on the whole.

21. Name the process by which Laterite Soil is formed. Give a reason as to why the soil is not suitable for agriculture? *(ICSE Specimen 2018)*

Other Similar Questions

Or Explain the formation of Laterite soil. Mention one disadvantage of this soil.

Or Why is Laterite soil unsuitable for the cultivation of crops?

Ans. Laterite soil is formed by leaching in the region of high temperature and heavy rainfall. This soil is not suitable for agriculture because it is acidic in nature and cannot retain moisture.

22. State the climatic conditions required for the growth of Tropical Deciduous Forests. *(ICSE Specimen 2018)*

Ans. Tropical deciduous Forests are also known as monsoon forests as these spread over the region receiving rainfall between 70 to 200 cm. The average annual relative humidity is about 60%-75% and mean annual temperature is about 27°C.

23. Mention two benefits of forests. *(ICSE Specimen 2018)*

Ans. Two benefits of forests are

(i) They provide timber, medicinal plants etc.

(ii) They help in purifying air and giving rain.

24. (i) Why does alluvial soil differ in texture? *(ICSE 2018)*

(ii) State two cash crops that grow well in alluvial soil.

Ans (i) Alluvial soil differs in texture, as it is formed by the deposition of sediments by rivers. The alluvial soil which gets deposited in the upper reaches of the river is coarse and dry, while extremely fine and moist alluvial soil is deposited at lower reaches of the river.

(ii) Sugarcane and jute are major cash crops which grows well in this soil.

25. With reference to black soil, answer the following. *(ICSE 2018)*

(i) Name one important crop which grows in this soil.

(ii) Give one chemical property of this soil.

Ans. (i) The important crop which grows in this soil is cotton.

(ii) The chemical property of the black soil is that it is rich in calcium, potassium and magnesium.

26. (i) Name an area in India where Tropical Monsoon Forest is found. *(ICSE 2018)*

(ii) How is this forest of great commercial value to India?

Ans. (i) The Tropical Monsoon Forest is found in the Andaman and Nicobar Islands, the Western Ghats and the Coastline of Peninsular India and also in Assam region of North-East India.

(ii) The Tropical Monsoon Forests contain several tree species of great commercial significance. For example, teak, Indian rosewood, etc.

27. With reference to littoral forest, answer the following questions. *(ICSE 2018)*

(i) Why do the trees in this forest grow aerial roots?

(ii) Name one area in India where this forest is found.

Ans. (i) Littoral forests refer to trees that grow at shore region. In such regions, soil is accumulated with salt and cannot be aerated as normal soils, so trees grow upwards. Such roots are called as aerial roots and they are adventitious in nature.

(ii) Littoral forests or tidal forests are found in delta regions and along the marshy coasts. Sunderbans in West Bengal is one of the areas in India where littoral forests are found.

Examiner's Comment

- Many candidates were unable to write the correct answer as they considered Littoral as the name of a tree and not as a type of vegetation.
- A few candidates, instead of naming an area, named a state.

Suggestion for Students

- Explain the characteristic features of Littoral vegetation, different trees, uses of the trees and regions where this vegetation is found.

28. How is black soil formed? *(ICSE Specimen 2017)*

Ans. Black soil is formed by the breaking-up of volcanic rocks mainly basalt. It is black in colour and is also known as regur soil.

29. (i) Name the transported soil most widely found in India.

(ii) How is this soil formed?

Ans. (i) Alluvial soil is the transported soil, which is widely spread in Northern plains of India.

(ii) Transported soils are carried down as silt by rivers and deposited in the lower areas of the plains when floods occur.

30. What is the most commercially important vegetation belt in India? ***(ICSE Specimen 2017)***

Other Similar Questions

Or Name the forest which is commercially most important vegetation in India.

Or Name the economically most important vegetation belt of India.

Ans. Tropical Deciduous Forests are the most commercially important vegetation belt in India.

31. Name an area in India in which each of the following processes take place. ***(ICSE 2017)***

(i) Sheet erosion (ii) Gully erosion

Ans. (i) **Sheet erosion** – Himalayan foothills, over the North-Eastern parts of the Peninsula.

(ii) **Gully erosion** – Chambal riverine

32. Name the tree as per its characteristics given below. ***(ICSE 2017)***

(i) The wood is hard and suitable for ship building.

(ii) The stilt roots are underwater during high tide.

Ans. (i) Sundari (ii) Mangrove vegetation

33. Mention two steps that could be taken to prevent soil erosion. ***(ICSE 2016)***

Ans. The contour bunding and afforestation are the two important measures to prevent soil erosion.

34. Mention two similarities between red soil and laterite soil. ***(ICSE 2016)***

Ans. The two similarities between red soil and laterite soil are as follows

(i) Both the soils contains iron oxide hence are red in colour.

(ii) Both the soils are mainly found in highland region.

35. (i) Name the forests which grow on the wind ward slope of the Western Ghats. ***(ICSE 2016)***

(ii) Why do such forests grow in this region?

Ans. (i) Tropical evergreen forests grow on the wind ward slope of the Western Ghats.

(ii) Such forests grow in this region because of the favourable climatic condition such as rainfall is more than 250 cm, average annual temperature is between 25°C and 27°C and humidity exceeds 77%, prevails here.

36. State the characteristic of each of the soils named below that makes them most suitable for crop cultivation ***(ICSE 2015)***

(i) Black soil (ii) Red soil

Ans Characteristics of the soils which make them most suitable for crop cultivation are

(i) **Black soil** Black soil retain moisture and become sticky when wet. This property of retaining moisture and releasing it when required during dry period is very useful crops of lava tracts of Maharashtra, this soil is most suitable for cotton cultivation.

(ii) **Red soil** Red soils are rich in potash and iron and with application of proper fertilisers this soil becomes suitable for crops like wheat, rice, millets and sugarcane.

37. State the geographic term for each of the following processes. ***(ICSE 2015)***

(i) The process by which soluble minerals dissolve in rainwater and percolate to the bottom, leaving the top soil infertile.

(ii) The process by which rainwater, flowing in definite paths, removes the top soil, thus causing deep cuts to the surface of the land.

Ans (i) Leaching. (ii) Gully erosion/Rill erosion

38. State two characteristics of Tropical Deciduous Forests. ***(ICSE 2015)***

Ans Following are the two characteristics of Tropical Deciduous Forests

(i) They are found in the areas of average temperature of about 27°C.

(ii) These forests shed their leaves for about 6-8 weeks during the month of March/April.

39. Mention two differences between alluvial soils and red soils. ***(ICSE 2014, 2005)***

Ans. Differences between alluvial soils and red soils are as follows

Alluvial Soils	Red Soils
Transported soil and deposited by rivers.	In-situ soil made by weathering of old crystalline rocks.
Rich in potash and lime.	Red in colour due to its high iron content.

40. Write two reasons why monsoon deciduous forests are commercially more valuable than other types of forest. *(ICSE 2014)*

Ans. Monsoon deciduous forests are commercially more valuable because

(i) they yield valuable timber and other forest products.

(ii) they are not very dense, therefore, are easily accessible for commercial use.

41. State two differences between bhangar and khadar. *(ICSE 2013, 2008)*

Ans. The two differences between bhangar and khadar are as follows

Bhangar	Khadar
It is old alluvium soil.	It is new alluvium soil.
It is less fertile.	It is more fertile.

42. Mention two main characteristics of tropical rainforests. *(ICSE 2013)*

Ans. The two main characteristics of tropical rainforests are as follows

(i) Trees are dense and evergreen and do not shed leaves in any particular season.

(ii) The thick ground cover has climbers and epiphytes.

43. Mention two differences in the alluvial soils of the Northern plains and the Alluvial soils on the coastal plains of India. *(ICSE 2012)*

Ans. The two differences in the Alluvial soils of the Northern plains and the alluvial soils on the coastal plains of India are

(i) The alluvial soil of the Northern plains is lighter in colour than that on the coastal plains.

(ii) The alluvial soil of the Northern plains is more porous and less clayey than that on the coastal plains.

44. Give two characteristics of tidal forests. *(ICSE 2012)*

Ans. Two characteristics of tidal forests are as follows

(i) They have breathing roots, which act as respiratory organs.

(ii) Trunks of these trees are supported by stilt like roots, helping the plants to survive in the shifting mud of coastal regions.

45. Name two states in India where regur soil is found. In what way does regur soil help agriculture? *(ICSE 2011)*

Ans Regur soil is found in Gujarat and Maharashtra. It is moisture retentive and rich in iron, potash, lime, calcium, magnesium and humus, which is very helpful for agriculture.

46. Mention two main characteristics of laterite soils. *(ICSE 2011, 2007)*

Ans. Two characteristics of laterite soils are as follows

(i) They lack in nutrition due to leaching.

(ii) They are not moisture retentive and coarse in texture.

47. What are 'Tidal forests'? Name two typical trees found there. *(ICSE 2011)*

Ans. The forests that grow in delta regions of Ganga, Godavari, Mahanadi, Krishna and Cauvery are called 'tidal forests'. Sundari and hintal are two typical trees found here.

48. Name the soil which *(ICSE 2010)*

(i) covers the summits of the Eastern Ghats.

(ii) makes up the delta of the river Ganga.

(iii) is the most suitable for the cultivation of cotton.

(iv) is sticky when wet and cracks when dry.

Ans. (i) Laterite soil

(ii) Alluvial soil

(iii) Black or Regur soil

(iv) Black or Regur soil

49. How does reafforestation help in soil conservation? *(ICSE 2010)*

Ans. Reafforestation is planting of two saplings in place of one felling tree, in areas which are deforested, thus saving the soil from erosion caused by both water and wind.

50. Name the soil which is formed due to high temperature and heavy rainfall with alternate wet and dry periods. Name two states where this type of soil is found. *(ICSE 2010, 2009, 2003)*

Ans. Laterite soil is formed due to high temperature and heavy rainfall with alternate wet and dry periods. This type of soil is found in Karnataka and Odisha.

51. Give one difference between the following *(ICSE 2008)*

(i) Sheet erosion and Wind erosion

Ans. (i) Sheet erosion occurs by water due to heavy rain washing away the even top surface of the soil, while wind erosion occurs on extensive flat lands due to blowing of wind during the dry season.

52. Name an area of black soil in India. Mention any two crops grown in this soil. ***(ICSE 2007)***

Ans. The Deccan plateau is an area of black soil in India. Cotton and tobacco are two crops grown in this soil.

53. Why is laterite soil unsuitable for the cultivation of crops? Name an area in India where this soil is found. ***(ICSE 2005)***

Ans. Laterite soil is unsuitable for cultivation of crops because it is acidic in nature and it is unable to retain moisture. This soil is found mainly on the summits of the Western and Eastern Ghats.

54. Define leaching. In which region, South of the Tropic of Cancer, can one find soil formed by leaching? ***(ICSE 2003)***

Ans. The process in which the nutrients of the topsoil are washed away, thereby making the topsoil infertile, is called leaching. The regions where this soil can be found are the summits of the Western and Eastern Ghats.

55. Mention two advantages of black soils. ***(ICSE 2002)***

Ans. The two advantages of black soils are as follows

(i) It retains moisture and is highly fertile.

(ii) It contains lime, alumina, iron, potash, magnesium carbonates and calcium, which are very useful for cultivation of crops like cotton, sugarcane, etc.

56. Name of one region in India for each of the following

(i) Tropical evergreen forest ***(ICSE 2001)***

(ii) Thorn and scrub forest

Ans. (i) Western Ghats

(ii) Rajasthan, Haryana, Kutch of Gujarat and Western Punjab.

3 Marks Questions

1. Name the soil ***(ICSE 2023)***

(a) That is found on the summits of Eastern and Western Ghats.

(b) That is suitable for dry farming.

(c) That varies in texture.

Ans. (a) Laterite soil

(b) Black soil

(c) Alluvial soil

2. Give a geographical reason for each of the following. ***(ICSE 2023)***

(i) Terrace farming is an ideal soil conservation method for hilly areas.

(ii) Khadar soils are preferred over Bhangar soils.

(iii) Foothills of Himalayas have been affected by soil erosion.

Ans. (i) Terrace farming is an ideal soil conservation method for hilly areas as it prevents rain from washing away soil, hence preventing soil erosion.

In terrace farming, a terrace is a piece of the sloped plane that is cut into a series of successively receding platforms, that resemble steps.

(ii) Khadar soil is preferred to Bhangar because it is more fertile as it is replenished every year by floods.

(iii) The foothills of Himalayas are prone to severe erosion because of the topography as well as inherent soil properties such as coarse texture, poor water holding capacity, surface stoniness, etc.

3. (i) In which natural vegetation belt is Sundari tree found ? ***(ICSE 2023)***

(ii) Why is the Tropical Deciduous Forest commercially the most exploited forest belt of India ?

Ans. (i) The Sundari trees are the dominant varieties of mangrove trees present in the Indian subcontinent that are found abundantly in the Sundarban delta situated near West Bengal.

(ii) The Tropical Deciduous Forest commercially the most exploited forest due to following reasons

- They are extensively used to make the furniture on a large scale.
- It is also used in transportation and building components.

4. (i) Name one region in India where Tropical Evergreen Forest is found. ***(ICSE 2023)***

(ii) Mention the temperature and rainfall conditions found suitable for its growth.

Ans. (i) Western Ghats

(ii) The Tropical Evergreen Forests require a condition of 200 cm of rainfall and a temperature of 15-30 degrees celsius for their growth.

5. Give geographical reasons for the following:
(i) Black soil is a residual soil. *(ICSE Specimen 2023)*
(ii) Red soils are generally infertile.
(iii) Alluvial soil differs in texture.

Ans. (i) Black soil is a residual soil. It is due to the fact that black soils are formed from basalt rocks of Deccan trap which weathered at the same place and not being transported anywhere else.
(ii) Red soils are generally infertile. It is due to fact that they are usually poor in nutrients and humus. These are also difficult to cultivate because of its low water holding capacity.
(iii) Alluvial soil differs in texture. It is due to the fact that it has been formed due to erosional, transportation and depositional activities of the Himalayan Rivers. The upper reaches of river valley have coarse soil while lower reaches of river valley have fine soil.

6. What is soil conservation? Mention any two measures taken to conserve soil. *(ICSE Specimen 2023)*

Ans. Soil conservation means prevention of soil loss from erosion or prevention of reduced fertility of soil caused by over-use, acidification, salinisation or other types of soil contamination.

Two measures taken to conserve soil are as follows
- Plant trees on barren lands to limit erosion of soil.
- Add mulch and rocks to prevent the plants and grass underneath to prevent soil erosion.

7. Give geographical reasons for the following
(i) Xerophytic plants have long roots.
(ii) Forests prevent floods. *(ICSE Specimen 2023)*

Ans. (i) Xerophytic plants have long roots in order to gather water that is deep down under the surface of the earth.
(ii) Forests prevent flood because they soak up excess rainwater, prevent run-offs and damage from flooding.

8. With reference to Alluvial soil, answer the following.
(i) What are the two types of Alluvial soil? *(ICSE 2020)*
(ii) Name an area where Alluvial soil is found.
(iii) Name two crops that grow well in this soil.

Ans (i) Alluvial soil can be classified into two groups on the basis of its age which are
- **Khadar** It is light in colour and is made up of newer deposits.
- **Bhangar** It is the older alluvium and is composed of lime nodules or kankar and its composition is clayey.

(ii) The entire Northern Plains including parts of Arunachal Pradesh, Assam, Bihar (almost entirely), Chandigarh, Delhi (almost entirely), Haryana, Himachal Pradesh, Madhya Pradesh, Punjab, Rajasthan, Uttarakhand, Uttar Pradesh and West Bengal are made of alluvial soil.
(iii) Two cash crops which grow well in Alluvial soil are sugarcane and cotton.

9. (i) Define the term 'Residual' soil. *(ICSE 2020)*
(ii) Name two crops that are grown on laterite soil.
(iii) Name two important agents of soil erosion.

Ans. (i) Residual soil can be defined as a soil material which is the result of weathering and decomposition of rocks that has not been transported from its original place.
(ii) The two crops that are grown on laterite soil are tea and rubber.
(iii) The agents of soil erosion are the same as of other types of erosion i.e. water, ice, wind and gravity.

10. Briefly explain the following. *(ICSE 2020)*
(i) Why are Tropical Evergreen Forests called "Evergreen"?
(ii) Why is afforestation essential in the cities that have iron and steel industries?
(iii) How do forests act as a source of income for the people?

Ans. (i) The regions of Tropical Evergreen Forests receive heavy rainfall throughout the year. As there is no particular dry season, the trees do not shed their leaves at the same time. Thus, the forests always appear green. This is the reason due to which they are called Evergreen forests.
(ii) Afforestation is essential in and around iron and steel industries because it provides a clean environment as trees take up carbon dioxide and give out oxygen.
(iii) Forests provide important sources of income to many rural people. Forest products such as bushes and fuel wood are gathered and traded at local and regional markets. Forests also provide the raw materials for artisan and processing activities.

11. Give a reason for each of the following. *(ICSE 2020)*

(i) Tropical Evergreen Forests occur on the windward side of Western Ghats.

(ii) It is very difficult to move through tidal forests.

Ans. (i) The Tropical Evergreen forests grow on the windward side of the Western Ghats because this region receives heavy rainfall above 250 cm annual.

(ii) In the Tidal forests, they are usually found in the backwaters of the seas or estuaries where one or many rivers can join together and enter into the sea. They are muddy due to the soil erosion and the silt carried by the rivers and their tributaries downstream which causes difficulty in moving through tidal forest.

12. Give a geographical reason for each of the following.

(i) Terrace farming is an ideal soil conservation method for hilly regions. *(ICSE 2019)*

(ii) Dry farming is preferred in areas with red soil.

(iii) Wind is a common agent of soil erosion in arid regions.

Ans. (i) Terrace farming is an ideal soil conservation method for hilly regions as in this farming technique, Step-like terraces are built on slopes. They prevent water run off from rushing downhill and carrying away the soil.

(ii) Red soil is found in the low rainfall areas of India. Thus, dry farming is done in this soil because this farming does not need much water.

(iii) Wind erosion is active in arid and semi-arid areas which are devoid of vegetative cover. Soil erosion by wind is performed through wind picking up soil particles and carrying them away; and through abrasion. Soil erosion by wind is common in Rajasthan and the adjoining areas of Haryana, Punjab and Gujarat.

Examiner's Comment

- Some candidates, wrote a lengthy explanation but with key words were missing. Some candidates related it to wind erosion. A few candidates simply wrote the meaning of terrace farming instead of explaining its relevance for hilly areas.
- Several candidates, instead of explaining the characteristics of red soil, wrote the meaning of dry farming.
- This question was attempted correctly by majority of the candidates.

13. Briefly answer the following. *(ICSE 2019)*

(i) Mention one way in which man is responsible for soil erosion.

(ii) How can deepening of the river bed help in preventing soil erosion?

(iii) Mention a physical characteristic of laterite soil.

Ans. (i) Faulty practice of farming like faulty ways of ploughing, shifting cultivation, etc done by man is responsible for soil erosion.

(ii) Deepening of the river bed help in preventing soil erosion as by deepening of river beds, the bed could hold more water during heavy rainy season and water would get more space to flow easily without breaching the embankment and near by areas.

(iii) The laterite soil is compact, reddish or yellowish-red in colour and turns black on exposure to the Sun.

14. (i) Give two reasons to explain as to why the Tropical Evergreen Forests are difficult to exploit for commercial purpose. *(ICSE 2019)*

(ii) Name any two trees found in Tropical Evergreen Forests.

Ans. (i) Two reasons for difficulty in exploiting Tropical Evergreen Forests for commercial purpose are as follows

- Tropical Evergreen Forests do not occur in pure stands i.e. main canopy do not consist of single species.
- The forests are dark and dense, so it is difficult for commercial exploitation.

(ii) Mahogany, rubber ebony, rosewood, etc are found in tropical evergreen forests.

15. Briefly explain each of the following. *(ICSE 2019)*

(i) The trees in the Tropical Desert Forest have stunted growth.

(ii) There is a gradual increase in the forest cover in India in recent times.

(iii) The trees in Monsoon Deciduous Forests, shed their leaves for about 6-8 weeks during March and April.

Ans. (i) These forests have stunted growth because they receive low or scanty rainfall, due to low humidity and high temperature.

(ii) There is a gradual increase in the forest cover in India in recent times due to the work of central government in the direction to increase the forest cover areas in the country by formulating different policies and programmes.

(iii) As deciduous plants lose their leaves to conserve water or to better survive winter weather conditions, they must regrow new foliage during the next suitable growing seasons. Thus, they shed their leaves for about 6-8 weeks during March and April after which new leaves grow on them.

16. Mention two measures to conserve soil in the hilly terrain. *(ICSE Specimen 2018)*

Ans. (i) Two measures to conserve soil in the hilly terrain are

- By doing contour ploughing.
- By constructing steps along the hilly areas by cutting the rock layers to reduce the flow of rivers.

17. Give a geographical reason for each of the following.

(i) Khadar is more fertile than Bhangar.
(ii) Red soil is acidic in nature.
(iii) The foothills of the Himalayas are prone to excessive soil erosion. *(ICSE Specimen 2018)*

Ans. (i) Khadar soil is more fertile than Bhangar because Khadar soils are replenished every year by floods.

(ii) Red soil is acidic due to the nature of parent rocks. They are poor in lime, magnesia, phosphates, nitrogen and humus.

(iii) The foothills of the Himalayas are prone to excessive soil erosion because the vegetation over there is very less.There are not many plant or tree roots to hold the soil in place, which makes the foothills of the Himalayas prone to excessive soil erosion.

18. Name an area where Tidal forests are found. *(ICSE Specimen 2018)*

Ans. Tidal forests are found in deltas Ganga, Mahanadi, Godavari, Krishna and Kaveri.

19. Give a reason for each of the following.

(i) The forest area has greatly depleted in India.
(ii) The Tropical Evergreen forests are found on the western slope of the Western Ghats.
(iii) Acacia has long roots. *(ICSE Specimen 2018)*

Ans. (i) The forest area has greatly depleted in India due to cutting of forests for urbanisation.

(ii) The Tropical Evergreen forests are found on the Western slope of the Western Ghats because in this reason annual rainfall is over 200 cm with a short dry season.

(iii) Acacia has long roots to survive in an environment with little water. It has long roots to reach sources of water which is available in deep underground.

20. Give one geographical reason for each of the following. *(ICSE 2018)*

(i) Red soil requires irrigation.
(ii) Afforestation prevents soil from getting eroded.
(iii) Laterite soil is red in colour.

Ans. (i) Red soil is a type of soil that develops in a warm, temperate, moist-climate and generally derived from crystalline rock. That is why red soil requires irrigation.

(ii) Trees reduce the rate of erosion by protecting the soil from the impact of rain and also binding soil to sloping land with their roots. Thus, afforestation prevents soil from getting eroded.

(iii) Laterite soil is made up of high level of iron oxides in the form of minerals like goethite and haematite. Thus, it appears red in colour.

Examiner's Comment

- Most of the candidates laid stress on Dry farming. Very few candidates wrote on porous soil and low moisture retention.
- Most candidates gave correct reason for afforestation prevents soil from getting eroded.
- The reason for laterite soils being red in colour was given by some candidates as presence of iron.

21. (i) What is soil erosion? *(ICSE 2018)*
(ii) Mention two causes of soil erosion in India.

Ans. (i) Soil erosion is a displacement of the upper layer of soil by the dynamic activity of erosion agents like water, ice, snow, wind, plants, animals and humans.

(ii) The two causes of soil erosion in India are

- **Running Water** It is the prime factor of soil erosion as it disturbs the agricultural pattern.
- **Deforestation** Removal of forest cover which functions as a binder of the top layer of the soil with increasing land demand have resulted in enhancing extent of soil erosion.

22. (i) Name a state in India where thorn and scrub forest is found. *(ICSE 2018)*
(ii) Give two ways by which the trees that are found here have adapted to the climate.

Ans. (i) The thorn and scrubs forests are found in regions where the rainfall is less than 70 cm. Rajasthan, Punjab, Haryana and Deccan are the major states where thorn and scrub forests are found.

(ii) The thorn and scrub forest trees have long tapering roots which go deep to tap water. The trees are stunted as there is no enough rain for tree growth. The thorny branches reduce loss of water by transpiration. The fleshy leaves prevent loss of water by evaporation. The wax on the leaves closes pores. Therefore, the thorn trees and scrubs can survive in the arid climate.

23. (i) Give two ways in which forests are important. *(ICSE 2018)*

(ii) Mention one forest conservation method followed in India.

Ans. (i) The two ways in which forests are important are

- **Forests Help us Breathe** They release oxygen and absorb the carbon dioxide.
- **People Lives in Forests** Some 300 million people live in forests worldwide and their survival depends almost on the forests.

(ii) To conserve the forest in India, one can follow the method of regulating and planing the cutting of trees and checking over forest clearance for agricultural habitation purpose.

24. (i) Name the soil found on the summits of Eastern Ghats. *(ICSE Specimen 2017)*

(ii) How is this soil formed?

(iii) Why is this soil not suitable for cultivation?

Ans. (i) Laterite soil is found on the summits of Eastern Ghats.

(ii) Laterite soil is formed due to high temperature and heavy rainfall with alternating wet and dry periods.

(iii) This soil is not suitable for cultivation because

- It is acidic and not moisture retentive.
- It lacks nitrogen and potassium and is coarse and crumbly.

25. (i) What is ment by soil erosion? *(ICSE Specimen 2017)*

(ii) How is it caused?

(iii) Give two methods adopted by the government to conserve soil.

Ans. (i) The denudation of the soil cover and its subsequent washing down is described as soil erosion.

(ii) Soil erosion is caused by different agents of weathering, running water and wind faulty methods of agriculture, irresponsible activity by men (cutting down trees, excessive construction work etc).

(iii) Several measures have been adopted by the government to prevent soil erosion, which include

- Afforestation.
- Improved techniques of agriculture.

26. (i) State two characteristic features of Tropical Evergreen Forests. *(ICSE Specimen 2017)*

(ii) Name an important tree of Tropical Evergreen Forest and state its use.

Ans. (i) Characteristic features of Tropical Evergreen Forests are

- These forests are found in hot and humid areas of India, where the rainfall is over 200 cm and average temperature is about 24°C.
- Trees are over 60 m high and there is no fixed time for trees to shed their leaves. So, the forests appear green all the year round.

(ii) An important tree of tropical evergreen forest is Mahogany which is used for making furniture.

27. (i) State two characteristic features of vegetation found in tropical deserts.

(ii) Give an example of the desert vegetation and state its uses. *(ICSE Specimen 2017)*

Ans. (i) Important features of vegetation found in tropical desert are as follows

- Trees are scattered and have long roots penetrating deep into soil in order to get moisture.
- The stems of the vegetation are succulent to conserve water and leaves are mostly thick and small to minimise evaporation.

(ii) One important tree found in tropical deserts is Babul. Its bark is used for tanning purposes and is also used in medicines.

28. State a method of soil conservation in the *(ICSE 2017)*

(i) Arid and Semi-arid Region

(ii) River valleys prone to flood

Ans. Methods of Soil Conservation are

(i) **Soil conservation in Arid and Semi -arid region** Methods of soil conservation in the overgrazing of forests and grassland by animal grazing especially by goats and sheep should be checked, separate grazing grounds should be provided. Belts of trees and shrubs should be planted to check the velocity of wind and thus prevent wind erosion.

(ii) **River valleys prone to flood** Soil erosion by floods can be checked by constructing dams or barrages over such rivers which are responsible for flood.

29. Name the soil which *(ICSE 2017)*

(i) is good for cultivation of sugarcane.
(ii) is acidic in nature.
(iii) occurs ex-situ.

Ans. (i) Black soil is good for cultivation of sugarcane.
(ii) Black soil is acidic in nature.
(iii) Alluvial soil occurs ex-situ.

30. Explain why the forest cover in India is shrinking? *(ICSE 2017)*

Ans. The forest cover in India is shrinking as a consequences of indiscriminate cutting down of the trees.

This deforestation has brought complete deterioration of flora and fauna of our country. The main reasons of deforestation are

(i) It is a consequence of indiscriminate cutting down of the trees due to Jhooming (or slash and burn) practices to clear the forests for cultivation and construction purposes.

(ii) There is uncontrolled and unauthorised cutting down of trees by unscrupulous timber merchants for the purpose of trade.

31. Name the natural vegetation found in the following regions *(ICSE 2017)*

(i) The Western slopes of the Western Ghats
(ii) The Nilgiris
(iii) Western Rajasthan

Ans. (i) Tropical Evergreen Forest
(ii) Mountain Forests
(iii) Desert and semi-desert vegetation and scrub and thorn forests

32. Distinguish between agro forestry and social forestry. *(ICSE Specimen 2017)*

Ans. Agro forestry is a land use management system, in which trees or shrubs are grown around or among crops or pasture land. It combines agriculture and forestry technology to create more diversive, productive, profitable and sustainable land use system.

Social forestry means, the management and protection of forests and afforestation on barren lands with the purpose of helping in environmental, social and rural development.

33. Give a geographical reason for each of the following.

(i) Alluvial soil differs in texture. *(ICSE 2016)*
(ii) Black soil does not get leached.

Ans. (i) Alluvial soil differs in texture because they are formed by the silt deposited by rivers. Hence, known as Khadar (new alluvium) and Bhangar (old alluvium).

(ii) Black soil does not get leached because black soil in India found mainly in Deccan Trap which has moderate rainfall and moderate temperature.

34. Define the following. *(ICSE 2016)*

(i) Sheet erosion (ii) In-situ soils

Ans. (i) Sheet erosion is the removal of top layer of soil due to heavy rains as water carries away the top surface layer of soil.

(ii) In-situ soils are those soils which are formed in their original position by breaking up of parent rocks. They include black soil, red soil, etc.

35. To which type of forest do the following trees belong?

(i) Hintal and Sundari *(ICSE 2016)*
(ii) Rosewood and Ebony (iii) Deodar and Chir Pine

Ans.

	Trees	Forests
(i)	Hintal and Sundari	Littoral or Tidal Forest
(ii)	Rosewood and Ebony	Tropical Evergreen or Rain Forest
(iii)	Deodar and Chir Pine	Montane Forest

36. Define the following. *(ICSE 2015)*

(i) Pedogenesis (ii) Humus (iii) Bhangar

Ans. (i) Pedogenesis is the science and study of the processes that lead to the formation of soil.

(ii) The decomposed form of plant remains, animal manure and dead animals is called humus.

(iii) Bhangar is the soil that consists of older alluvium of clayey composition and is dark in colour. These soils are coarse in nature and contain *kankar* (lime nodules), pebbles and gravels.

37. Give a geographic reason for each of the following. *(ICSE 2015)*

(i) Alluvial soil is extremely fertile.
(ii) Need for soil conservation. *(ICSE 2014)*
(iii) Reafforestation should be practised extensively.

Ans. (i) Alluvial soil is extremely fertile because it is rich in potash and humus, and respond very well to irrigation and manuring. They are good for both *rabi* and *kharif* crops.

(ii) Soil is our most precious resource. Conserving soil is important to our national economy as productive soil ensures prosperity in agriculture, industrial development and general economic development.

(iii) Reafforestation should be practiced extensively because forests are our national heritage, providing us vast varieties of flora and fauna. Reafforestation also helps in controlling soil erosion and denudation in catchment areas like rivers, lakes and reservoirs.

38. Identify the tree as per its characteristics mentioned below. *(ICSE 2015)*

(i) It yields wood that is hard and scented and is usually found in high altitudes.

(ii) It is generally found in deltaic regions and is used to make boats.

(iii) The furniture made from the wood of this tree is generally the most expensive.

Ans. (i) Deodar (ii) Sundari (iii) Sandalwood

39. Differentiate between Afforestation and Deforestataion. State a disadvantage of Deforestation. *(ICSE 2015, 2003)*

Ans. The differences between Afforestation and Deforestation are

Afforestation	Deforestation
Afforestation has a beneficial effect on the environment.	Deforestation has a detrimental effect on the environment.
The main reason for Afforestation is to control carbon footprint and to ensure the sustainability of the natural environment.	Deforestation is a result of industrialisation, globalisation and urbanisation.
Afforestation can ensure balance and survival for all life on Earth.	Deforestation, if left unchecked, leads to global warming, rising sea levels and encroachment or possible extinction of wildlife.

40. Give a geographical reason for the following. *(ICSE 2014)*

(i) Different regions in India having different kinds of soil.

(ii) Black soil being suitable for growth of cotton.

Ans. (i) Different regions in India have different kinds of soil because they have different parent materials and climatic conditions.

(ii) Black soil is suitable for cotton cultivation because it is moisture retentive and highly fertile.

41. Name the soil which *(ICSE 2014)*

(i) is good for the cultivation of cashew nuts.

(ii) covers almost all of West Bengal.

(iii) is a result of leaching.

Ans (i) Laterite soil is good for the cultivation of cashew nuts.

(ii) West Bengal is part of Indo-Gangetic plain which is rich in alluvial soil.

(iii) Laterite soil is formed as a result of leaching.

42. Give one important use of each of the following types of trees. *(ICSE 2014)*

(i) Sundari (ii) Sandalwood

(iii) Rosewood

Ans. (i) Sundari wood is suited for making boats.

(ii) Sandalwood is used for making medicine, handicrafts and perfume.

(iii) Rosewood is used for making expensive furniture.

43. Name the natural vegetation largely found in the following regions *(ICSE 2014)*

(i) The delta of the Ganga river

(ii) The windward side of the Western Ghats

(iii) The Deccan plateau

Ans. (i) Tidal Forests.

(ii) Tropical Evergreen Forests.

(iii) Deciduous Monsoon Forests and scrub/Thorn forests

44. Differentiate between Transported soil and In-situ soil, quoting a suitable example for each. *(ICSE 2013)*

Ans.

Transported Soil (ex-situ)	In-situ Soil
A soil, which is carried by rivers or wind from elsewhere to the place of rest. *e.g.,* Alluvial soil	A soil, which remains at the place where it has been formed due to decomposition of rocks. *e.g.,* Black soil.

45. With reference to red soils in India, answer the following questions. *(ICSE 2013)*

(i) Name two states where it is found.

(ii) State two advantages of this type of soil.

(iii) Mention two important crops grown in this soil.

Ans. (i) Tamil Nadu and Karnataka are two states where red soil is found.

(ii) The two advantages of red soil are as follows
(a) It has high iron oxide content and potash.
(b) It is porous and easily crumbles.
(iii) Rice and millets are two important crops grown in this soil.

46. Name the tree, the timber of which could be used for the following *(ICSE 2013)*
(i) A soft and white timber used for making toys and matchboxes.
(ii) A hard durable timber used for ship building and furniture making.
(iii) A sweet smelling timber, which yields an oil, used for handicrafts.

Ans. (i) Semul (ii) Teak (iii) Sandalwood

47. (i) Name one region in India for each of the following *(ICSE 2013)*
(a) Tidal forest (b) Thorn and scrub
(ii) Explain why thorn and scrub forests are found in the above mentioned region.

Ans. (i) (a) Tidal forest—Ganga delta.
(b) Thorn and scrub forest—North-West parts of India.
(ii) Thorn and scrub forests are found in the above region because these areas get less than 70 cm of rainfall and average temperature of 25°C to 27°C.

48. Give geographical reasons for the following. *(ICSE 2012)*
(i) Laterite soil is not suitable for cultivation.
(ii) Red soil is red in colour.

Ans. (i) Laterite soil is lacking in fertility due to the leaching away of nutrients, also it is not moisture retentive.
(ii) Red soil is red in colour due to presence of iron.

49. Mention three reasons, why forests must be conserved. *(ICSE 2012)*

Ans. Forests must be conserved because
(i) They check soil erosion.
(ii) They help maintaining the ecological balance of the region.
(iii) They help in preventing floods.

50. Name any three trees found in Monsoon Deciduous Forests and state one use of each of these trees. *(ICSE 2012)*

Ans. Sal, teak and myrobalan are three trees found in Monsoon Deciduous Forest.
Their uses are as follows
(i) Sal is useful for railway sleepers.
(ii) Teak is used for house construction and furniture.
(iii) Myrobalan provide material for tanning leather.

51. State the difference between Alluvial soils found in the lower courses and the upper courses of rivers. *(ICSE 2011)*

Ans. Alluvial soil found in the lower courses of rivers is fine in texture, moist and rich in humus whereas Alluvial soil found in the upper courses is drier, porous and sandy as well as being coarser in texture.

52. Name two important agents of erosion. For each, state one method of controlling the erosion caused. *(ICSE 2011, 2007)*

Ans. Wind and running water are two important agents of erosion. Erosion by wind can be controlled by planting a shelter belt of tress and shrubs perpendicular to the wind direction. Erosion by running water can be controlled by terracing and contour ploughing.

53. Name the type of forests found in the Western part of the Western Ghats. Give two reasons why these forests are so named? *(ICSE 2011)*

Ans. Tropical Evergreen Forests are found in the Western part of the Western Ghats. These forests are called evergreen because they do not have any particular season to shed leaves and thus, remain green throughout the year. The second reason is that they grow in the tropical region of India and thus, are named 'tropical'.

54. Mention three methods for the conservation and development of forests in India. *(ICSE 2011)*

Ans. Three methods for the conservation and development of forests in India are as follows
(i) Checking indiscriminate deforestation
(ii) Afforestation by planting trees.
(iii) Banning the practice of shifting cultivation by tribals and reafforestation.

55. Give reasons for the following. *(ICSE 2010)*
(i) Black soil is largely found in the Deccan trap region.
(ii) Soil erosion by wind is common in arid regions.

Ans. (i) The reason is that it is 'in-situ' and formed by the weathering of lava origin rocks spread over large areas of the Deccan trap region.
(ii) The arid regions receive no rainfall or very scanty rainfall and are also devoid of vegetation cover. In the absence of vegetation, soil becomes loose and easy to move by high velocity winds.

56. Explain the following term *(ICSE 2009)*

(i) Transported soil

Ans. (i) When soil is carried from the place of its origin to another place by degrading agents, it is called transported soil.

57. Give a reason as to why

(i) Large tracts in Maharashtra are covered with black soil.

(ii) Man is largely responsible for soil erosion. *(ICSE 2008)*

Ans. (i) Large tracts of Maharashtra come under the Deccan trap region which was formed by weathering of volcanic lava origin rocks.

(ii) Deforestation for habitation, wrong method of farming and overgrazing by domesticated animals make man responsible for soil erosion.

58. Why is this soil agriculturally important? *(ICSE 2007)*

Ans. It is agriculturally important due to the presence of high content of potash and humus which is good for the cultivation of rice, wheat, sugarcane, cotton, oilseeds and jute.

59. How is red soil formed? State two reasons for the low productivity of red soil. *(ICSE 2006)*

Ans. Red soil is formed by weathering of old crystalline and metamorphic rocks.

Reasons for its low productivity are

(i) It is not moisture retentive.

(ii) It is deficient in various minerals and humus.

60. Differentiate between sheet erosion and gully erosion. *(ICSE 2005)*

Ans. Differences between sheet erosion and gully erosion are as follows

Sheet Erosion	Gully Erosion
Torrential downpour of rain in hilly regions causes this erosion.	It is caused by running water down the slope and gushes in distinct path forming rills.
It is harmful because it removes the fertile topsoil.	It cuts up agricultural land and makes it unfit for cultivation.

61. With reference to the red soils in India, answer the following *(ICSE 2000)*

(i) Name two states, where it is found.

(ii) State two advantages of the above named soil.

Ans. (i) Tamil Nadu, Chhattisgarh

(ii) The two advantages of red soil are

(a) Red soil has better drainage capacity compared to other soils and the soil is porous, fine grained and fertile in nature.

(b) Red soils also have higher iron, lime content and aluminium.

CHAPTER TEST

01 Mark Questions

1 Which of the following soil is transported soil ?

(a) Black Soil (b) Alluvial Soil
(c) Red Soil (d) Laterite Soil

2 ……… is the most suitable soil for the cultivation of cotton .

(a) Alluvial soil (b) Red soil
(c) Black soil (d) Laterite soil

3 Name the vegetation type found in Saline environment under Tidal influence.

(a) Tropical evergreen rainforest
(b) Mangrove vegetation
(c) Desert vegetation
(d) Mountain forests

4 Which soil in found suitable for coffee cultivation in India ?

(a) Black Soil (b) Alluvial Soil
(c) Laterite Soil (d) Red Soil

5 Which of the following term is used to refer growing of trees in various parts of the country?

(a) Re-afforestation (b) De-forestation
(c) Afforestation (d) De-afforestation

Answers

1. (b) | 2. (c) | 3. (b) | 4. (c) | 5. (c)

10 Marks Questions

6 (i) (a) Name the parent rock that contributes to the formation of red Soil.

(b) How does this soil gets its 'red' colour ?

(ii) State two ways by which forests help in protecting the environment.

(iii) What is soil conservation ? How does reafforestation help in soil conservation ?

(iv) Give a Geographical reason for each of the following.

(a) Red soil is acidic in nature.

(b) Khadar is more fertile than Bhangar.

(c) Foothills of Himalayas are very much prone to excessive soil erosion.

7 (i) Name the area associated with Black soil.

(ii) (a) Mention any two crops that grows in this soil.

(b) Give a geographical reason for both statements

(i) Red soil requires irrigation.

(ii) Afforestation prevents soil from getting eroded.

(iii) Name the soil which is

(a) good for cultivation of cotton

(b) good for the cultivation of sugarcane.

(c) occurs ex-situ.

(iv) Give a geographical reason for each of the following

(a) Why alluvial soil differs in nature?

(b) Alluvial plain region is very fertile.

(c) Black soil is largely found in deccan trap region.

8 Explain the terms

(i) (a) Humus

(b) In -situ

(ii) How is black soil agriculturally important ?

(iii) Why re-afforestation should be promoted extensively ?

(iv) How does Soil erosion takes place ? Suggest measures.

9 (i) Why do littoral forest grows aerial roots ?

(ii) Name the tree as per the details given below.

(a) The hard wood that is suitable for ship building.

(b) The stilt roots are underwater during high tides.

(iii) (a) Name the state where tidal forest are found.

(b) Name the state in India where thorn and scrub forests are found extensively.

(c) How are thorny forest adapt to the climate ?

(iv) Name the type of forest found in the Western part of Western Ghats. Give reasons why these forests are named so?

03

Water Resources

TREND ANALYSIS 3 YEARS

Average No. of Questions Across all Sets

	Types of Questions	2023	2020	2019
TOPIC 01 Irrigation	1 Mark	–	–	1
	2 Marks	1	1	2
	3 Marks	1	2	1
TOPIC 02 Water Conservation	1 Mark	–	–	1
	2 Marks	–	–	–
	3 Marks	1	–	–

Water resources are used in various ways including domestic, agriculture, irrigation, fisheries, hydropower, industrial production, recreation, navigation, environmental protection as well as the disposal and treatment of sewage and industrial effluents.

97% of water on the Earth is **salt water** and only 3% is **freshwater**. Slightly over 2/3rd of this is frozen in glacier and polar ice caps. The remaining unfrozen freshwater is found mainly as groundwater with only a small fraction present above ground in the form of lakes and rivers or in the air in the form of water vapour.

Water Resources in India

Water resources are of utmost importance in our country. In India, agriculture is the main occupation of the people. The dense population, which is increasing rapidly, needs to be provided food.

Agricultural production can be increased by following better farming techniques, with the use of fertilisers and High Yield Varieties (HYV) of seeds. This is not possible unless an adequate amount of water is available.

Therefore, irrigation is absolutely essential in India, where water resources are available in the form of surface water and groundwater.

Sources of Water

The main sources of water are

(i) **Groundwater** The part of rainwater that seeps through the cracks and crevices into the ground is called groundwater. About 60% of groundwater is used up for agriculture.

(ii) **Surface Water** The total water available from precipitation in a year in India is about 4000 cubic km. Out of this, 1150 cubic km flows away as surface runoff. Most of it exists in the form of rivers, lakes, ponds and tanks. The three main rivers **Indus**, **Ganga** and **Brahmaputra**, which supply about 60% of the surface water of India.

Water Requirement and its Utilisation

Although India's agriculture totally depends on the monsoon system, uneven distribution of water requires planning for water utilisation. Multi-purpose projects were established in order to tackle the problem of drought and supply of water for agriculture.

Some of them are

(i) **Bhakra Nangal Project** This is on the river **Sutlej**, which is a tributary of the river Indus. The main purpose of this project is to supply water to Sirhind and Western Yamuna canal as well as flood control in the river Sutlej. It also generates electric power for supply to the Northern grid.

(ii) **Damodar Valley Project** This consists of four dams on the **Damodar** river. It was designed to tackle the devastating floods by Damodar river. The dams are used to supply water for irrigation.

(iii) **Hirakud Dam** This is one of the longest dams in India on the river **Mahanadi**. Hence, it is also called the 'Mahanadi Valley Project'. It was designed to regulate the flow of water during floods.

Advantages of Multi-Purpose Projects

(i) Multi-purpose projects can help in the reduction of seasonal flooding of rivers.

(ii) Stored water can be used for various purposes such as domestic, industrial or for irrigation.

(iii) Multi-purpose projects are also used for generation of hydroelectricity.

(iv) Multi-purpose projects provide livelihood to fishermen as fisheries can be developed in the reservoir.

(v) Stored water can be provided to areas having water scarcity through canals.

Disadvantages of Multi-Purpose Projects

(i) After a long period, multi-purpose projects can create problem of sedimentation of the bottom of the reservoir.

(ii) Thousands of people living in the reservoir area are displaced due to the construction of multi-purpose projects.

(iii) Over-irrigation has created the problem of **salinisation of soil** because cropping pattern of many regions has changed to water extensive and commercial crops.

(iv) Multi-purpose projects also create problem of environmental degradation as they submerge the existing vegetation and soil leading to its decomposition over a period of time.

Irrigation

It is the process of supplying water to crops by artificial means such as canals, wells, tanks and other sources like rivers, ponds or underground water.

Importance of Irrigation

Irrigation is essential for agriculture. The primary reasons for irrigation in India are as follows

(i) The monsoons are uncertain. So, irrigation is necessary to protect crops from drought as a result of uncertain rainfall.

(ii) There is unequal distribution of rain throughout India. So, irrigation is necessary for agriculture in areas having less rainfall.

(iii) Unequal pattern of soil composition necessitates irrigation facilities.

(iv) Majority of the population is engaged in agriculture. Hence, extensive irrigation is necessary for more production of crops.

(v) Rainwater flows down very quickly along the slopes of hillsides. So, irrigation is necessary to grow crops in such areas.

Importance of Irrigation in Punjab and Rajasthan

Punjab is the major wheat producing state in India. Rainfall in the state is irregular, particularly in the Rabi season, when wheat is grown. Thus, irrigation works are required extensively in Punjab. This is done through an extensive network of canals.

Rajasthan receives scanty rainfall as it is in the Western part of India and the South-West monsoon has lost most of its moisture before arriving there. So here also irrigation is important, which is done through canals.

Traditional Methods of Irrigation

Originally, the traditional methods of irrigation used were tanks, wells and canals. Some new methods which were more efficient were developed. These are

Furrow Irrigation

This is used where crops are grown in rows by forming furrows in between rows of crops through which water flows.

Strip Irrigation

Here the fields of crops are divided into strips of different sizes depending on the slope and the quantity of water available. This method is cheap and requires less labour.

Basin Irrigation

This is only suitable for horticulture and not for crops, as a raised platform is formed around the trees or bushes to store water.

These trees are connected to each other through drains for ensuring that the water reaches each tree.

Modern Methods of Irrigation

Sprinkler Irrigation

It is a type of overhead irrigation and has been in use for about 20 years. In this type of irrigation, sprinklers are installed in the fields and supplied with water through hoses from the source of water. The method is best for conserving water as there is no wastage of water and it is not exposed to the Sun.

Drip Irrigation

In drip irrigation, water is taken directly to the roots of the plants or trees. A plastic tube is used which has small holes through which water keeps on dripping steadily.

Bamboo Irrigation System

In **Meghalaya**, the state of North-East India, a 200 year old system of tapping stream water by using bamboo pipes is prevalent. About 20 litres of water enters the bamboo pipe system per minute and is transported over hundreds of metres to the plants requiring water. This is useful in hilly terrain and can be employed as a modern method as it conserves water.

Problems Faced by India in Irrigation Systems

Following problems are faced by irrigation systems in India

(i) Irrigation by canals, the best and most economical, is not possible in South India because of the rocky and uneven terrain.

(ii) Irrigation infrastructure is lacking in large parts of India which are totally dependent on monsoon rains.

(iii) Over-exploitation of groundwater in some states has resulted in the depletion of the groundwater table.

(iv) There is a need of more multi-purpose projects, but due to large scale opposition by the local residents, various projects have been delayed or discontinued.

Water Conservation

It means prevention and control of the depletion and degradation of water and making the best use of available water resources for the present and future needs.

Steps necessary for water conservation are

(i) Developing water saving technology.

(ii) Preventing water pollution.

(iii) Promoting watershed development, rainwater harvesting, water recycling and reuse.

Need for Conservation of Water/ Causes of Water Scarcity in India

- India gets 4% of the global precipitation, but still suffers from water scarcity. Over-exploitation, excessive use and uneven distribution of water make water conservation necessary.
- Domestic and industrial usage, seepage of chemicals, pesticides and fertilisers used in agriculture cause water scarcity.
- A large and growing population is another reason of water scarcity. Industrialisation also exerts pressure on our existing water resources.

Measures to Handle Present Water Crisis

To overcome from the present water crisis the government should take measures

- Change the principles and practices of water resources management programmes.
- Evaluate and monitor water resources.
- Improve trans-boundary cooperation between states.
- Use freshwater, coastal and marine environments for better water management.
- Support innovative and participatory approaches by individuals and companies.

Conservation Practice: Rainwater Harvesting

Rainwater is the ultimate source of freshwater. Harvesting of rainwater is the activity of direct collection of rainwater. Rainwater can be stored for direct use or can be used to recharge groundwater aquifers.

Objectives of Rainwater Harvesting

1. Recharging the groundwater and raising its level.
2. Preventing rainwater from being wasted.
3. Avoid the flood like situations.
4. Reduce groundwater salinity.
5. Meet the increasing demand of water.

Types of Rainwater Harvesting Practised in India

(i) **Rooftop Rainwater Harvesting** These are common in semi-arid and arid regions of India, especially in Rajasthan and Gujarat, where water is stored in an underground tank or *tankas*.

(ii) **Kuls** In hilly and mountainous regions people built diversion channels like *'guls'* or *'kuls'*. It is common in Western Himalayas and largely used for irrigation.

(iii) **Johads and Khadins** In arid and semi-arid regions, agricultural fields were converted into rain fed storage structures that allowed the water to moisten the soil. This is known as *khadins* in **Jaisalmer** and *johads* in other parts of **Rajasthan**.

Importance of Rainwater Harvesting

The main importance of rainwater harvesting is as follows

(i) It meets the demand and increases the availability of water during the dry season.

(ii) It reduces the dependence on groundwater.

(iii) It improves the quality of groundwater by reducing salinity.

(iv) It is cost effective and easily affordable.

(v) It provides drinking water to those areas where potable water is not available.

PYQs Previous Years' Questions

1 Mark Questions

Multiple Choice Questions

1. Hirakud dam is based on which of the following rivers ? *(ICSE 2023)*

(a) River Godavari (b) River Mahanadi
(c) River Krishna (d) River Narmada

Ans. (b) River Mahanadi

2. Which of the following is a ground water source ? *(ICSE 2023)*

(a) Pond (b) Lake
(c) Spring (d) River

Ans. (c) Spring

3. Which is the most advanced and efficient method of irrigation? *(ICSE Specimen Semester I 2021)*

(a) Canal irrigation (b) Well irrigation
(c) Drip irrigation (d) Tank irrigation

Ans. (c) Drip irrigation

4. What is the meaning of irrigation? *(ICSE Specimen Semester I 2021)*

(a) The water received by rainfall
(b) The man-made arrangements of supplying water to the fields
(c) The storage of rain water
(d) Growing of crops

Ans. (b) The man-made arrangements of supplying water to the fields

5. Which of the following is a type of canal found in India? *(ICSE Specimen Semester I 2021)*

(a) Perennial Canal (b) River Canal
(c) Artificial Canal (d) Ground Canal

Ans. (a) Perennial Canal

6. Sprinkler irrigation is efficient but is still not a very commonly used method of irrigation by the Indian farmers. Why? *(ICSE Specimen Semester I 2021)*

(a) There is no loss of water by seepage
(b) It is an expensive method of irrigation
(c) There is no loss of water by evaporation
(d) Farmers are scared of getting wet

Ans. (b) It is an expensive method of irrigation

7. Why do the inundation canals have limited use? *(ICSE Specimen Semester I 2021)*

(a) They get water only when the rivers are in flood
(b) They are taken out from a perennial river
(c) They are constructed to store rain water
(d) It occupies lot of space.

Ans. (a) They get water only when the rivers are in flood

8. Match the following. *(ICSE Specimen Semester I 2021)*

(a)	Khatri	1.	Western Ghats
(b)	Johads	2.	Ladakh
(c)	Zings	3.	Western Himalayas
(d)	Surangam	4.	Central India

Codes

	A	B	C	D		A	B	C	D
(a)	1	2	3	4	(b)	1	3	4	2
(c)	4	2	1	3	(d)	3	4	2	1

Ans. (d)

9. Why is there a need to conserve water in India? *(ICSE Semester I 2021)*

(a) A lot of water is polluted

(b) No water is found below the land in India

(c) Water is in abundance in India

(d) We receive lot of rain in summer

Ans (a) A lot of water is polluted

10. What are the advantages of rain water harvesting? *(ICSE Semester I 2021)*

(a) Recharge of ground water and conservation of water

(b) Provide water through canals to the farms and its conservation

(c) It helps in harvesting of crops and its storage

(d) Provide water for multinational companies to produce packaged drinking water

Ans (a) Recharge of ground water and conservation of water

11. Why is canal irrigation more popular in Northern Plains? *(ICSE Semester I 2021)*

(a) The surface of land is almost flat and soft soil is easy to dig

(b) To supply water to a number of cities in the plain area

(c) Rocky surface of the plain help in their construction

(d) Rivers are seasonal and canals are needed

Ans (a) The surface of land is almost flat and soft soil is easy to dig

12. Which of the following pair is correctly matched? *(ICSE Semester I 2021)*

(a) Tube well – Karnataka

(b) Tank – Punjab

(c) Lined well – Uttar Pradesh

(d) Canal – Mizoram

Ans (c) Lined well – Uttar Pradesh

13. Which of the following is not a suitable condition for the development of tank irrigation? *(ICSE Semester I 2021)*

(a) Presence of natural depressions

(b) Permeable rock structure

(c) Plenty of rain in rainy period

(d) Hard substance rock structure

Ans (b) Permeable rock structure

14. What is the importance of 'drip irrigation'? *(ICSE Semester I 2021)*

(a) It is an ultra-modern system of irrigation

(b) It is cheaper than other sources

(c) It can irrigate more areas with less usage of water

(d) It is used by almost all farmers in India

Ans (c) It can irrigate more areas with less usage of water

Very Short Answer Questions

1. Give one geographical reason for the sprinkler irrigation being practiced in arid and semi-arid regions. *(ICSE 2018)*

Ans Sprinkler irrigation is practiced in arid and semi-arid regions because this type of irrigation does not involve any loss of water by seepage or evaporation, as water is supplied through pipes. It is not exposed to the Sun.

2. Give one reason for the following. *(ICSE 2016)*

Although expensive, yet sprinkler irrigation is gaining popularity in recent times.

Ans Although considered as expensive sprinkler irrigation is gaining popularity in recent times because there is no loss of water by seepage or evaporation.

3. In which part of the country, wells are the most important means of irrigation? *(ICSE 2002)*

Ans In Uttar Pradesh and Bihar wells are the most important means of irrigation.

4. Name any two states, in which tank irrigation is given more importance. *(ICSE 2001)*

Ans Andhra Pradesh and Tamil Nadu are two states, where tank irrigation is significant.

5. Irrigation through groundwater is still popular despite big river projects, why? *(ICSE 2000)*

Ans Groundwater irrigation is popular because abundance of water availability.

2 Marks Questions

1. (i) Where in India is tank irrigation most widely used ? *(ICSE Specimen 2023)*

(ii) Give one factor that has led to its popularity in the region mentioned by you.

(iii) Mention one advantage of using tank as a means of irrigation.

Ans. (i) The tank irrigation systems are widely found in the States of Tamil Nadu, Andhra Pradesh, Maharashtra, etc.

(ii) Tank irrigation is popular and preferred because of presence of hard rocks in Peninsular India, that makes it difficult to dig canals.

(iii) Tank water harvesting and irrigation offer a host of benefits such as replenishing groundwater levels, providing drinking water for rural communities and livestock, conserving top-soil and harbouring fish.

2. Mention *two* conditions necessary for the construction of wells. ***(ICSE Specimen 2023)***

Ans. Two conditions necessary for the construction of wells are

(i) Water level should be high in the area.

(ii) Soil should be loose.

3. Define ***(ICSE Specimen 2023)***

(i) Surface water (ii) Ground water

Ans. (i) Surface water is a form of water bodies which is flowing on the land, e.g. streams, lakes, rivers and ponds. It is an important natural resources used for many purposes like drinking, irrigation and theromo electric power industry.

(ii) Ground water is the water which seeps through the cracks and crevices under the surface of the land.

4. Mention one agricultural and one industrial problem solved by the Bhakra Nangal Dam. ***(ICSE 2020)***

Ans. Bhakra Nangal Dam solved the agricultural problem of soil erosion. It also solved the energy crisis of industries by providing regular electricity supply.

5. Mention any two methods of recharging ground water aquifers. ***(ICSE 2020)***

Ans. Two methods of recharging ground water aquifers are

- Constructing recharging wells.
- Constructing recharge pits and shafts.

6. (i) Name the most common means of irrigation used in India. ***(ICSE 2020)***

(ii) Give one reason for the popularity of this means of irrigation in our country.

Ans. (i) Canals are the most common source of irrigation used in India. In Punjab, Haryana, Delhi, Uttar Pradesh, Bihar and Northern Rajasthan, canals are used to irrigate the soil.

(ii) Reasons for the popularity of canal irrigation is

- As compared to conventional watering, higher productivity per hectare land is obtained due to canals.
- The canals constructed are permanent means of irrigation which can be used when there is fluctuation in rainfall.

7. "The modern means of irrigation are gaining popularity." ***(ICSE 2019)***

Give two reasons to justify this statement.

Ans The modern methods of irrigation are gaining popularity due to the following reasons

(i) In the conventional methods of irrigation a large quantity of water is wasted due to waterlogging and often results in gradual salinity of the soil. It does not happen in modern methods of irrigation such as drip irrigation method and sprinkler irrigation method.

(ii) Sprinkler irrigation method is suitable for arid and semi-arid region because it does not involve any loss of water by seepage or evaporation.

Examiner's Comment

- Many candidates, not being very clear on the modern means of irrigation, wrote about the traditional methods as well. Several candidates wrote about the need for irrigation instead of advantages of modern means. Some candidates wrote that modern means were becoming popular as they were cheaper.

Suggestions for Students

- Students, should know the difference between the traditional and modern means of irrigation along with the advantages and disadvantages of both the categories.

8. Mention two factors that favour the development of tube well irrigation in Punjab. ***(ICSE 2019)***

Ans Punjab state has extensive use of tubewells. The importance and reason for the development of tube wells as a source of irrigation in Punjab are as follows

(i) The level of water table is high in Punjab due to which tubewell irrigation is favourable.

(ii) The soil in Punjab is soft which makes it easier to dug holes required for tubewell irrigation.

9. Give two reasons why well irrigation is popular in North India? ***(ICSE Specimen 2018)***

Ans. Well irrigation is a popular method of irrigation due to the following reasons

(i) North India has wide spread deposition of alluvial soil which is suitable for well irrigation, so wells can be dug very easily in these areas.

(ii) By the use of pumps and tube wells, water can be lifted even from great depths.

10. There is plenty of rain in India during the rainy season, yet we need irrigation. Give two reasons to support this statement. *(ICSE 2018)*

Other Similar Questions

Or "Without irrigation, development of agriculture is difficult in India." Clarify the statement by giving two reasons.

Or Irrigation is indispensable for an agricultural country like India. Give two reasons to explain why artificial irrigation is essential?

Or State two reasons why irrigation is important to a country like India?

Ans. Yes, there is plenty of rain in India, yet we need irrigation because

(i) The rainfall is uncertain and unevenly distributed not all the place get same amount of rainfall.

(ii) It fluctuates every year i.e. there may be good rainfall in one year and there may be a drought in another year.

11. (i) Name three traditional means of irrigation. *(ICSE 2018)*

(ii) Give a reason why traditional means of irrigation are still important in most parts of India. *(ICSE 2018)*

Ans. (i) The three traditional means of irrigation are

- Basin Irrigation
- Strip Irrigation
- Furrow Irrigation

(ii) Traditional means of irrigation are still important in most parts of India because these are more sustainable as they are easy to use, due to which farmers use them extensively.

12. Give a reason for the significance of irrigation in

(i) Punjab (ii) Rajasthan *(ICSE 2017)*

Ans. (i) Punjab is the major wheat producing state in India. Rainfall in the state is irregular, particularly in the Rabi season, when wheat is grown. Thus, irrigation works are required extensively in Punjab. This is done through an extensive network of canals.

(ii) Rajasthan receives scanty rainfall as it is in the Western part of India and the South-West monsoon has lost most of its moisture before arriving there. So, here also irrigation is important, which is done through canals.

13. (i) Why are perennial canals more useful than inundation canals? *(ICSE Specimen 2017)*

(ii) Name one state where canal irrigation is popular.

Ans. (i) Perennial canals have water in them throughout the year as they draw out water from perennial sources, but inundation canals have water in them when excess water flows into them during the rainy season.

(ii) Canal irrigation is popular in Punjab.

14. Name two modern methods of irrigation. State one important reason for their growing popularity. *(ICSE 2015)*

Ans. The two modern methods of irrigation are

(i) Sprinkler irrigation (ii) Drip irrigation

The modern methods of irrigation are getting popular because they are best for conserving water and best suited for arid and semi-arid regions.

15. State the significance of rainwater harvesting. *(ICSE 2015)*

Ans. Rainwater harvesting increases the availability for water during dry season by increasing the levels of dried borewells and wells. It improves the quality of groundwater by reducing salinity. Harvesting rainwater does not lead to any type of pollution. It is cost effective and easily affordable.

16. Give two main reasons why water scarcity occurs in India. *(ICSE 2013)*

Ans. Water scarcity occurs in India due to the following reasons

(i) Monsoons are seasonal in nature.

(ii) Transformation of society into urban and industrial has increased the requirement of water.

17. Mention two advantages of rainwater harvesting. *(ICSE 2012)*

Ans. The advantages of rainwater harvesting are as follows

(i) It prevents water from being wasted.

(ii) It raises the groundwater table.

18. State one advantage and one disadvantage of large dam. *(ICSE 2005)*

Ans. One advantage of large dams is that they provide water for irrigation. One disadvantage of large dams is that they prevent the natural flow of river water, causing excessive sedimentation at the bottom of the reservoir created by the dam.

3 Marks Questions

1. Mention one advantage of canals and two disadvantages of tanks. *(ICSE Specimen 2023)*

Ans. One advantage of canals is that canals are fed by rain water received by rivers and the water is used for irrigation. Production of crops needing more water is also possible through canals.

Two disadvantages of tanks are as follows

- Tanks dry out in the summer and aren't very useful.
- Silting of the tank bed is a major issue that necessitates tank desilting at regular intervals.

2. Mention three ways by which you as an individual can reuse and conserve water. *(ICSE Specimen 2023)*

Ans. Three ways by which we as an individual can reuse and conserve water are as follows

- Water used to wash vegetables or boiling purpose can be reused in toilet flushes, mopping of rooms or to water your plants.
- Create a rain garden. A rain garden is a constructed area which collects rainwater from roofs, pipes and driveways, etc which can be reused in times of need.
- Make it a habit to use your half-filled bottle or glass to water the plants, or use it to wash utensils or any other household items.

3. (i) Name two states of India where canal irrigation is extensively used. *(ICSE 2020)*
(ii) Name the types of canals used in India.
(iii) Mention one point of difference between the types of canals mentioned by you.

Ans. (i) Canal irrigation is mostly followed in Uttar Pradesh, Andhra Pradesh, Punjab, Haryana, West Bengal and Bihar. In canal irrigation, Uttar Pradesh stands first followed by Punjab and Haryana.
(ii) Inundation canals and Perennial canals are used in India.
(iii) Inundation canals are taken out from the rivers without constructing dams, barrage and embankments.
On the other hand, perennial canals are taken out from the rivers or reservoirs by constructing dams or barrages.

4. (i) What geographical conditions make irrigation necessary in the country? *(ICSE 2020)*
(ii) How has irrigation changed the cropping pattern in India?
(iii) Why is there a scarcity of surface water in our country?

Ans (i) The physical and climatic diversity of India has made it necessary to have irrigation facility to provide water for both agricultural purpose.
(ii) Availability of adequate water for irrigation has changed the cropping pattern of various regions. In many regions, farmers have switched over to the cultivation of water intensive commercial crops such as jute, cotton and tea, rather than food grains such as bajra, wheat and ragi because of availability of water.
(iii) Water scarcity may be caused by climate change, such as altered weather patterns including droughts or floods, increased pollution and increased human demand and overuse of water. Water scarcity is being driven by two converging phenomena, growing freshwater use and depletion of usable freshwater resources.

5. Give a reason for each of the following. *(ICSE 2019)*
(i) Most of the South Indian states are not suitable for development of canal irrigation.
(ii) There is an urgent need for water conservation in India.
(iii) Development of irrigation is essential for the growth of the agriculture sector of India.

Ans (i) Most of the South Indian states are located over a rocky surface. The digging of canals in rocky and uneven areas is difficult and uneconomic. Thus, these states are not suitable for canal irrigation.
(ii) Conservation of water resources is essential in India due to following reasons

- To safeguard ourselves from health hazards as the quality of water is badly affected by discharge of urban wastes, industrial effluents, pesticides and fertilisers.
- The underground water has been exploited and the water table has been lowered.
- Uneven rainfall pattern and changing climate is making it essential to conserve water.

(iii) Development of irrigation is essential for the growth of the agriculture sector of India because the Indian agriculture mostly depends on monsoon rainfall which is inadequate and fluctuates every year. Thus, to minimise this dependence different methods of irrigation should be developed in the country.

6. Briefly explain the following terms. *(ICSE 2019)*

(i) Inundation canal
(ii) Rooftop rainwater harvesting
(iii) Surface water

Ans (i) Inundation canals are taken out from the rivers and do not have any kind of wine and barrages to regulate the flow of water from the rivers.

(ii) It is a system of catching rainwater where it falls. In this technique, the roof becomes the catchments and the rainwater is collected at the roof of the building. This method is less expensive and very effective and if implemented properly, helps in augmenting the groundwater level of the area.

(iii) Surface water is the water present in the water bodies which are found on the surface of the ground. For example, rivers, lakes, ponds, lagoons, backwater and so on.

Examiner's Comment

- Most candidates wrote the correct answer.
- Some candidates gave general answers such as, that rain water is collected.
- Some candidates wrote that surface water is the water found on the surface of the earth without giving any examples.

Suggestions for Students

- Clearly explain the two types of canals, their need along with the advantages and disadvantages of both types.
- Clarify to the students, the meaning of ground water or surface water, with examples.
- Teach the students the difference between rainwater harvesting and rooftop rainwater harvesting.

7. Give a reason for each of the following. *(ICSE Specimen 2018)*

(i) Inundation canals are being converted into Perennial canals.
(ii) Ground water reserves are depleting at a fast rate.
(iii) Drip irrigation reduces loss of water through evaporation.

Ans. (i) Inundation canals are converted into Perennial canals because

- The farmer depends upon flood water and dry up during the summer.
- While perennial canals can provide water throughout the year.

(ii) Ground water reserves are depleting at a fast rate due to following reasons

- Overexploitation of groundwater to satisfy the needs of growing population.
- Agricultural needs require a large amount of groundwater.

(iii) Drip method adheres highest water application efficiency and directly reaches the roots of plant, thus, conserving water.

8. Differentiate between surface water and groundwater. *(ICSE 2018)*

Ans The differences between surface and ground water are

Surface water	Ground water
The water found on the surface of the Earth is known as surface water.	The water that is located below the Earth's surface is referred to as ground water.
Due to less minerals it's also known as soft water.	Due to the minerals picked during the process of filtration via the rock, it is considered as hard water.
It is easier to extract surface water.	It is comparatively difficult to extract ground water.

9. Mention two reasons to explain as to why we are facing water scarcity in recent times.

Ans. We are facing water scarcity in recent times because of

- increasing in population and urbanisation.
- discharge of effluent and dumping of waste in water bodies.

10. (i) What is rainwater harvesting? *(ICSE 2018)*

(ii) What are the advantages of rainwater harvesting?
(iii) Name two water harvesting systems practiced in India.

Ans (i) Rainwater harvesting is the system of collecting rainwater directly and improving groundwater storage in aquifers.

(ii) For answer, refer to Q. 17 of 2 marks questions.

(iii) Two water harvesting systems practised in India are

- In Rajasthan and Gujarat, uses of *tankas* and *khadins* are done for storing water by people.
- In Himachal Pradesh, *guls* and *kuls* are used for storing water for irrigation.

11. Study the diagram below and answer the questions that follow. *(ICSE 2017)*

(i) Name the activity shown in the diagram.

(ii) Give two objectives of the activity.

Ans (i) The activity shown in the diagram is the rooftop rainwater harvesting method.

(ii) Two objectives of rainwater harvesting method are

- It is a simple scheme to replenish the groundwater and increase its level.
- The purpose is to utilise rainwater to its maximum and not to let it run off or go waste.

12. (i) State one advantage of tank irrigation. Where is it commonly used in India? *(ICSE Specimen 2017)*

(ii) What is a tube well? Why is it useful during drought conditions?

(iii) How is a new method like drip irrigation useful for the farmers?

Ans. (i) Tank irrigation allows the surplus water during monsoon to be stored and used later.
In India, it is commonly used in the Deccan Plateau region.

(ii) A tube well is a borewell dug deep in the ground by a drilling machine, from which water is pumped out using an electric motor or manually. It is useful during drought conditions because surface wells dry up.
Tube wells are deep, so they are useful during drought condition.

(iii) The new method of drip irrigation is a method in which water is given directly to the roots of the plants or trees. A plastic tube is used which has small holes through, which water keeps on dripping steadily. This method conserves water as there is no wastage of water.

13. (i) Why is the world in danger of facing a severe water shortage in the coming future? Give two reasons to support your answer. *(ICSE 2015)*

(ii) State one measure the government should adopt to handle the present water crisis.

Ans (i) The world is in danger of facing a severe water shortage in the coming future because

- Most of the surface water in rivers and lakes has been polluted by industrial waste, sewage and other effluents.
- Indiscriminate use of chemicals, fertilisers, pesticides, etc to increase agricultural production has led to increased groundwater pollution.

(ii) One measure the government should adopt to handle the present water crisis is rainwater harvesting to recycle and reuse water.

14. Give one geographical reason for each of the following statements. *(ICSE 2014)*

(i) Irrigation is necessary despite the monsoon.

(ii) Canal irrigation leads to the unproductivity of grounds around it.

Ans. (i) There is spatio-temporal variation in monsoon i.e. rainfall by monsoon is not same at every place and it fluctuates every year. So, irrigation is necessary.

(ii) The farm land around a canal faces the problem of waterlogging in case of unlined canals, as water soaks into the adjoining areas, turning them into swamps and making them unproductive.

15. Mention any three water harvesting systems practiced in India. *(ICSE 2011)*

Ans. Water harvesting systems practiced in India are as follows

(i) **Rooftop Rainwater Harvesting** These are common in semi-arid and arid regions of India especially in Rajasthan, where water is stored in an underground tank or *tankas*.

(ii) **Kuls** In hill and mountainous regions people built diversion channels like the *'guls'* or *'kuls'*. It is common in Western Himalayas and largely used for irrigation.

(iii) **Johads and Khadins** In arid and semi-arid regions agricultural fields were converted into rain fed storage structures that allowed the water to stain and moisten the soil. This is known as *khadins* in Jaisalm and *Johads* in other parts of Rajasthan.

17. Irrigation in India faces many problems. Name any two. *(ICSE 2000)*

Ans. The two problems of irrigation in India are as follows

(i) Irrigation by canals, the best and most economical, is not possible in South India because of the rocky and uneven terrain.

(ii) Irrigation infrastructure is lacking in large parts of India, which are totally dependent on the monsoon rains.

CHAPTER TEST

01 Mark Questions

1 Which of the following is a source of fresh water ?
(a) Glaciers (b) Lakes (c) Rivers (d) All of these

2 One should conserve the water because
(a) water is abundant in nature.
(b) there is high water pollution.
(c) it is a renewable resource.
(d) fresh water is a limited resource.

3 What does the term 'drip irrigation' means ?
(a) Irrigation through drones.
(b) Low rate dripping irrigation through drippers.
(c) Irrigation through canals
(d) None of the above

4 .... is an example of ground water source.
(a) River (b) Lake (c) Pond (d) Spring

5 The main purpose of rainwater harvesting is recharge of ....
(a) well (b) canal (c) pond (d) groundwater

6 The most common means of irrigation used in India is
(a) canals (b) rainwater harvesting
(c) ponds (d) drip irrigation

Answers

1. (d) | 2. (b) | 3. (b) | 4. (d) | 5. (d) | 6. (a)

10 Marks Questions

7 (i) What do you mean by Rain water harvesting ?
(ii) How is 'drip-irrigation' a better way than the regular method of irrigation ?
(iii) Define surface water and ground water.
(iv) Why there is a need to conserve water in India ?

8 (i) What are the major issues faced by irrigation process in India ?
(ii) Mention any two main objectives of rainwater harvesting in India ?
(iii) What are the different types of rain water harvesting in India ?
(iv) What are the major issues responsible for water scarcity in India ?

9 (i) What do you mean by water pollution ?
(ii) What is the sustainable use of water resources ? How it can be conserved for future generation ?
(iii) Which methods were used in arid and semi-arid regions for irrigation ? What are the major cause of irrigation concerns there ?
(d) What makes Tamil Nadu to stand out with regard to rainwater harvesting ?

4 (i) Describe the factors responsible for poor condition of Indian rivers. Suggest measures also.
(ii) What are the important and small efforts to save water on individual level?
(iii) Explain different methods of rain water harvesting in different regions of India.
(iv) How rainwater harvesting system is considered a viable alternative for both socio-economically and environmentally in a country like India ?

04

Minerals and Energy Resources

TREND ANALYSIS 3 YEARS

Average No. of Questions Across all Sets

	Category (Year)	2023	2020	2019
TOPIC 01 Minerals	1 Mark	3	–	–
	2 Marks	4	1	2
	3 Marks	4	–	–
TOPIC 02 Energy Resources	1 Mark	–	–	–
	2 Marks	1	–	1
	3 Marks	3	1	2

Minerals

India has a large number of economically useful minerals and they constitute 1/4th of the world's known mineral resources. A **mineral** is a compound formed by an inorganic process and has a definite chemical composition and physical properties. Minerals in India are found in two distinct forms

(i) Metallic (ii) Non-metallic

Metallic minerals are found in igneous rocks and contain metals. For example, iron-ore, manganese, nickel and copper.

Non-metallic minerals are found in sedimentary rocks and do not contain metal. For example, mica, limestone and gypsum.

Importance of Minerals

Importance of minerals can be understood from the points given below

(i) Their extraction, refinement and utilisation provide employment directly or indirectly to a large number of people.

(ii) They are the basic raw material for many industries.

(iii) They contribute to a large inflow of foreign currency to the country by their export or exports of products made using them.

Iron Ore

Iron is extracted from different forms of iron ore. It is the backbone of modern industries.

Types of Iron Ore

There are four varieties of iron ore

(i) **Magnetite** is also called blado ore. It contains 72% of pure iron and is the best quality of iron ore.

(ii) **Haematite** consists of 60% to 70% of pure iron.

(iii) **Limonite** is yellow or brown in colour, which contains 40% to 60% of pure iron.

(iv) **Siderite** contains only 10% to 40% of pure iron.

Uses of Iron Ore

- 90% of iron ore is used to make steel. Raw iron combined with other elements is used for construction, automobiles, railways machineries, etc.

- Black iron oxide is used as **pigments** in polishing compounds, medicine and magnetic inks.
- Low grade iron ore is used in manufacturing sponge iron.
- Iron blue is used in blueprints, inks, paints, enamels, crayons, linoleum, etc.

Distribution of Iron Ore in India

Major states producing iron ore in India are Odisha, Jharkhand, Goa, Madhya Pradesh, Karnataka, Maharashtra, Andhra Pradesh and Tamil Nadu. Some of these are

- **Odisha** is the largest iron ore producer. The districts of Sundergarh, Mayurbhanj, Keonjhar, Cuttack, Koraput, Badampur, Gurumahisani, Kirburu, Bohnai, Sulaipet and Umarkot are known for good quality of haematite.
- **Jharkhand** is also known for large haematite reserves. The major producer of iron-ore is Singhbhum district where **Noamundi mining field** is situated.
- **Karnataka** has the largest magnetite and haematite reserves. Important iron ore mines are at Kudremukh, Bellary, Hospet and Sandur.
- **Chhattisgarh** is one of the largest producers of iron ore in India.
- **Goa** Mines of Goa have recently started production. Now they produce 16% of India's iron ore.

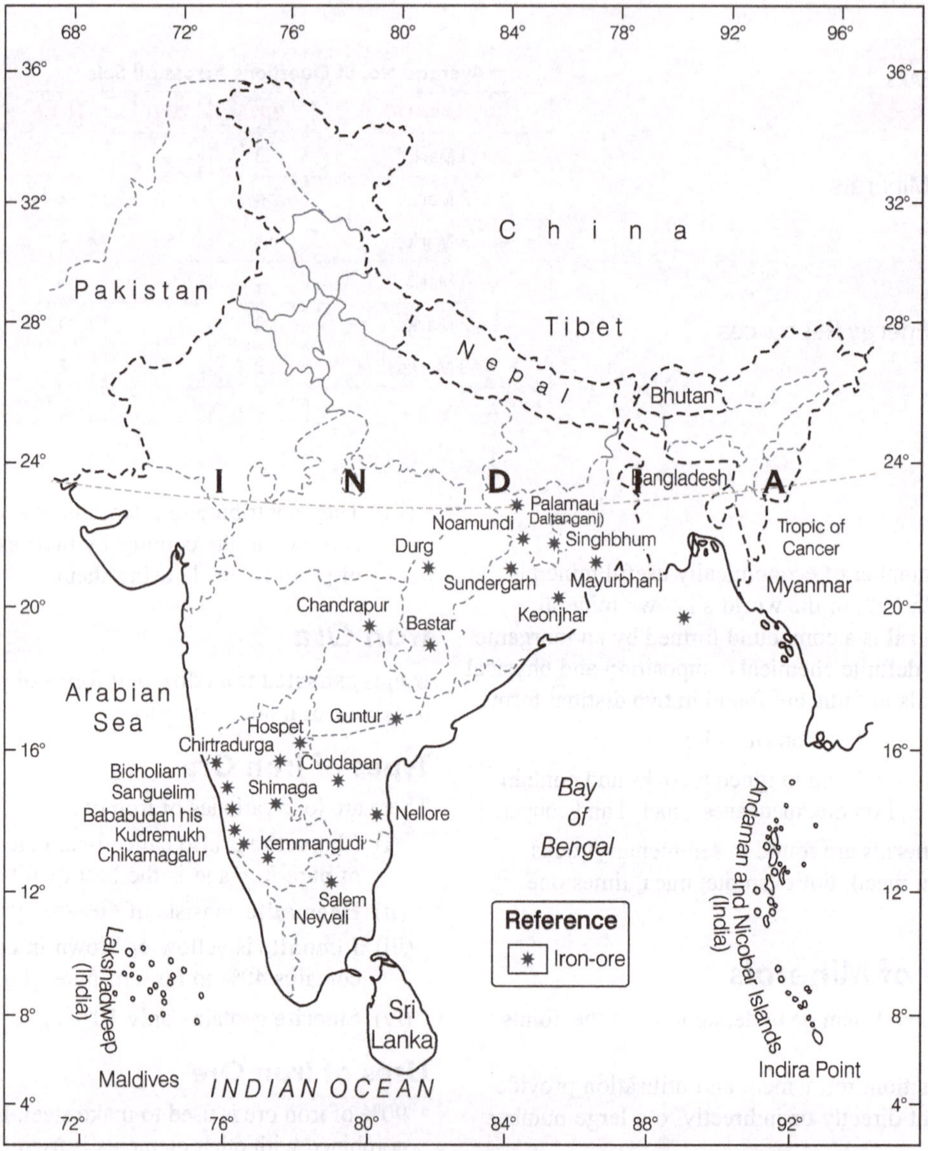

Distribution of Iron-ore

Manganese

India is third in manganese production in the world. It is a very useful mineral for making steel tough and also for manufacturing bleaching powder, insecticides, paints and batteries.

Uses of Manganese

- It is used to improve the quality of many **alloys**, e.g. iron and steel.
- It is used in industries for manufacturing bleaching powder and insecticides.
- It is used to manufacture coloured glass.
- It is also useful in plant growth as it reduces nitrates in green plants and algae.

Distribution of Manganese

- **Odisha** produces about 40% of India's manganese. Its important mines are situated in Sundergarh, Kalahandi, Koraput, Keonjhar, Bolangir and Mayurbhanj.Karnataka produces about 30% of India's manganese.
- **Maharashtra and Madhya Pradesh** The remaining manganese reserves are mostly concentrated in the Nagpur-Bhandara belt of Maharashtra and Balaghat-Chhindwara belt of Madhya Pradesh.

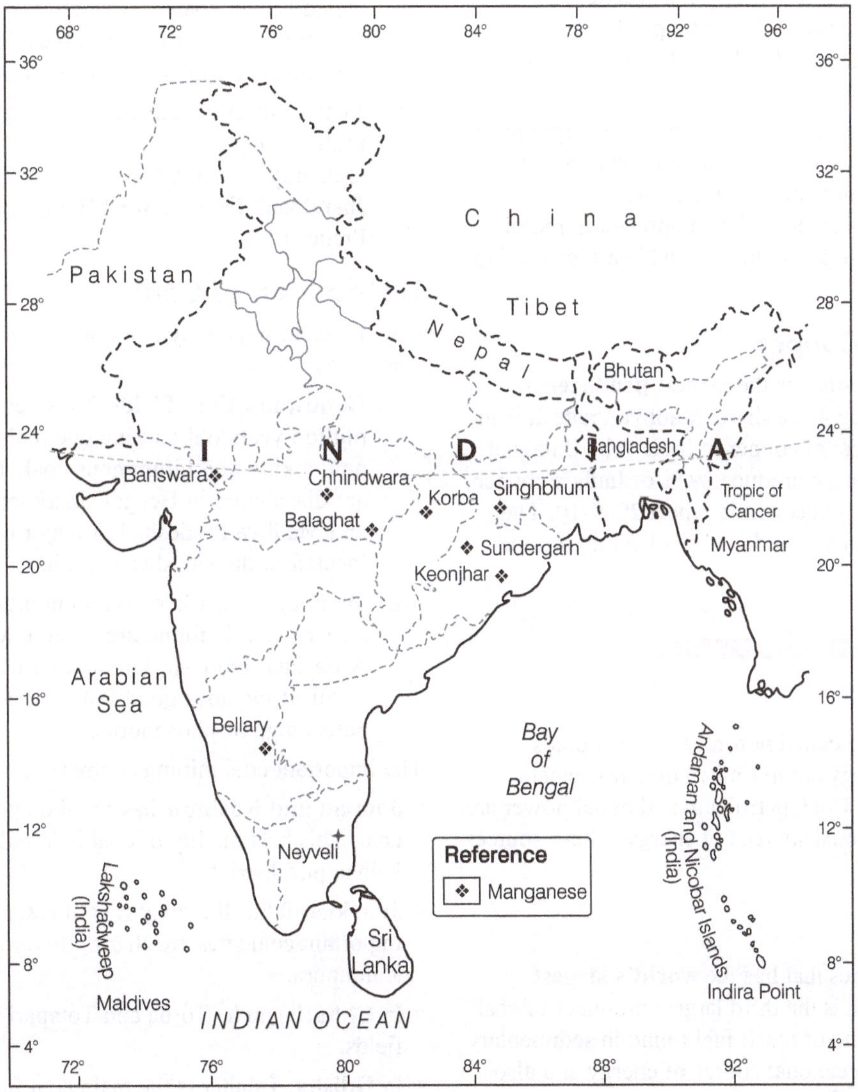

Distribution of Manganese

Copper

India is critically deficient in the reserves and production of copper. Its production is only about 0.2 % of the world's total production. But in total production it is still within the first 20 countries of the world and also one of its largest importers in line with China, Japan, South Korea and Germany.

Copper is an important mineral due to its excellent **electrical conductivity.** The excellent alloying properties of copper have made it invaluable when combined with other metals such as zinc (to form brass), tin (to form bronze), or nickel.

Uses of Copper

Presently copper is used in building construction, power generation and transmission, electronic product manufacturing, production of industrial machinery and transportation vehicles.

Copper wiring and plumbing are integral to any appliances, heating and cooling systems. Telecommunications links used every day in homes and businesses use copper extensively. Copper is an essential component in motors, wiring, radiators, connectors, brakes, and bearings used in cars and trucks.

Distribution of Copper

Khetri mines in Rajasthan is the **largest producer** of copper in India, having 48 % share. Madhya Pradesh is the second largest producer of copper in India. The Balaghat mines in Madhya Pradesh produce 29 % of India's copper production, according to economic report 2009-10. The Singbhum district of Jharkhand is also a leading producer of copper.

Conventional Sources of Energy

These sources are also called non-renewable sources. These sources of energy are in limited quantity except hydro-electric power. Coal, petroleum and hydel power are examples of conventional sources of energy. These sources are discussed below

Coal

India is one of countries that has the **world's largest deposits** of coal. India is the third largest producer of coal in the world. It is a kind of fossil fuel found in sedimentary rocks, which is a conventional source of energy and also inflammable organic substance. Coal is an important conventional source of energy despite the fact that many other sources of energy are available in India.

Types of Coal

There are four types of coal on the basis of carbon percentage

(i) **Anthracite Coal** It contains 80% of carbon and is the **best coal quality**. It is used mainly for domestic and industrial purposes. It is only found in Jammu and Kashmir in small quantity.

(ii) **Bituminous Coal** It contains 60-80% of carbon and is the most widely used coal. It is used for power generation, cement, manufacturing and steel industries. It is mostly found in Jharkhand, Odisha, West Bengal, Chhattisgarh and Madhya Pradesh.

(iii) **Lignite Coal** It contains 60% of carbon and is also called brown coal. It is inferior in quality and friable in nature i.e., it easily crumbles. It is found in Rajasthan, Tamil Nadu, Assam and Jammu Kashmir.

(iv) **Peat Coal** It contains 50-60% of carbon and it is the primary stage of the wood to coal transformation. It is mainly used for power generation. It is found in Jharkhand, Odisha, West Bengal and Madhya Pradesh.

Distribution of Coal

Coal fields in India may be divided into two main categories

(i) **Gondwana Coal Fields** These coal fields are 250 million years old and include mainly coking, non-coking and bituminous coal. These coal fields are distributed in Bengal, Jharkhand, Bihar, Odisha and Madhya Pradesh. 113 major coal fields are located in the Gondwana region.

(ii) **Tertiary Coal Fields** The important areas where tertiary coal is found are Assam, Meghalaya, Arunachal Pradesh, Jammu and Kashmir and Tamil Nadu. It includes good semi-coking coal with a high percentage of phosphorus.

The important coal mining centres are

- **Jammu and Kashmir** has small quantities of anthracite coal. This best quality of coal is found in Kalakot in Udhampur district.
- **Jharkhand** has the **largest coal reserves** in India and its important coal sites are Jharia, Bokaro, Giridih and Karanpura.
- In **Chhattisgarh**, Korba and Totapari are the main coal fields.
- In **Odisha**, Talcher is the main coal field.
- **West Bengal** contributes 18% of coal reserves in India and its main and oldest coal field is **Raniganj**.

- In **Madhya Pradesh**, the main coal fields are Singrauli and Sholapur.
- In **Maharashtra**, Wardha Valley and Mahapari are the important coal fields.

Drawbacks of Coal Found in India

Coal is a popular source of energy in India, but there are some drawbacks of coal found in India

(i) Distribution of coal is uneven *i.e.,* it is not distributed everywhere. It is limited in river valleys and areas of tertiary rocks.

(ii) Coal found in India has high ash content and low calorific value.

(iii) Reserves of high quality anthracite coal are small and only in Jammu and Kashmir.

(iv) Consumption of coal is high in India because, more low quality coal is used to obtain energy.

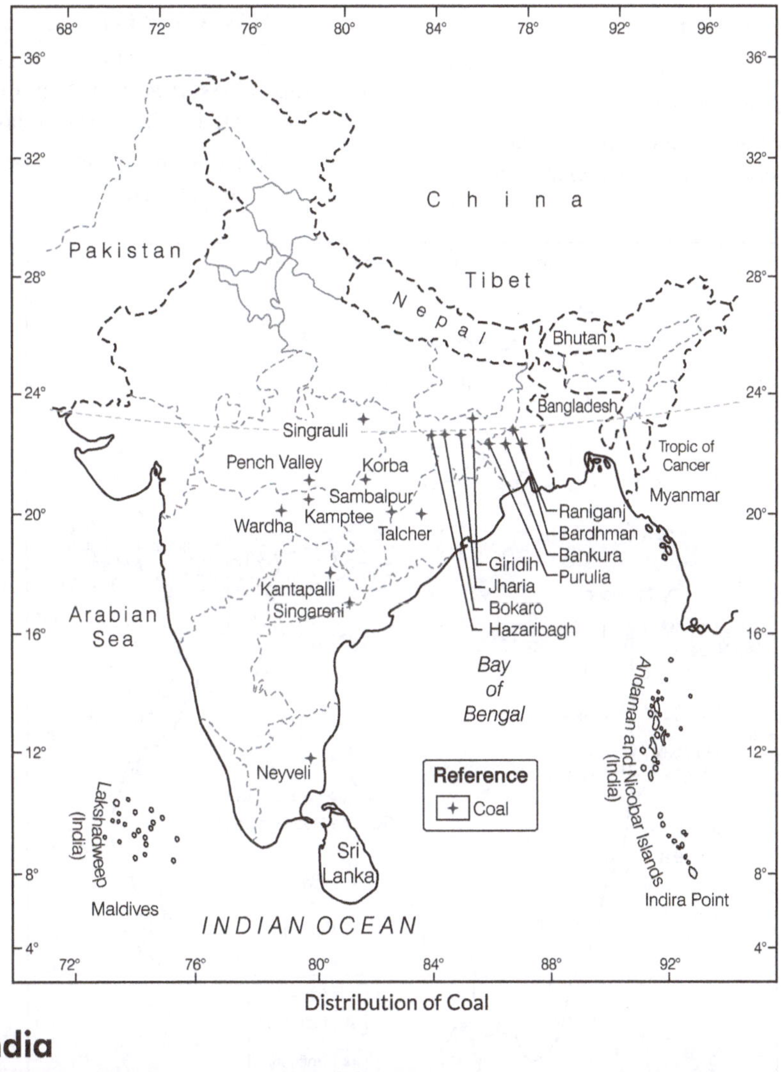

Distribution of Coal

Petroleum in India

Petroleum is a mixture of hydrocarbons which is obtained from sedimentary rocks. It is found in crude form and is known as **mineral oil**.

Petrol, kerosene, diesel oil, paraffin wax, vaseline and benzene are extracted and purified from mineral oil.

Uses of Petroleum

It is mainly used for energy in India. Petroleum is also a raw material for various industries such as fertiliser, plastics etc.

Importance of Petroleum

The importance of petroleum can be understood from the points given below

(i) Petroleum is the next major energy source in India after coal.
(ii) Transportation is easy and can be done through pipelines or tankers to areas where it is required.
(iii) It leaves no ash after combustion.
(iv) It supports many industries, mainly the petro-chemical, fertiliser and chemical industries.

Distribution of Petroleum

About 5% of the world's petroleum reserves exist in India.

The main areas of mineral oil deposits are

(i) **North-Eastern Region** Major oil fields are located in Upper Assam Valley, Nagaland and Arunachal Pradesh.

- **Assam** Digboi (oldest in India), Naharkatiya, Moran, Galeki, Rudrasagar and Hugrijan.
- **Arunachal Pradesh** Nigru oil field in Tirap district.
- **Nagaland** Borholla oil field close to the Assam-Nagaland border.

(ii) **Western Region** Major oilfields are located in Khambat basin, Gujarat plain and Mumbai coast.

- **Gujarat** Ankleshwar, Kalol, Navagam, Sanand and Lunej.
- **Offshore oil fields** Aliabet offshore oil field in Gujarat and Mumbai High near Mumbai coast.

(iii) **East Coastal Region** Major oilfields of this region are located in Krishna- Godavari and Kaveri basin.

- Maharashtra is largest petroleum producing state in India.

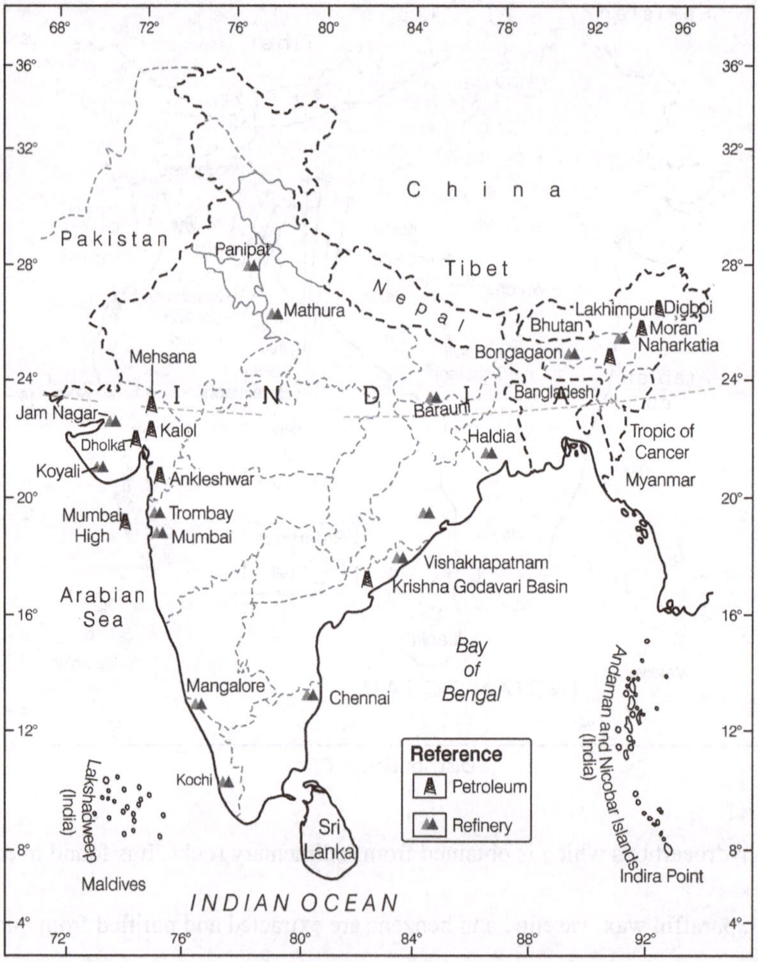

Distribution of Petroleum and Refinery

Natural Gas

Natural gas is a clean energy resource. Its formation is similar to the formation of petroleum. Natural gas was formed millions of years ago when plants and tiny sea animals were buried by sand and rock. Layers of mud, sand, rock, plant and animal matter continued to build up untill the pressure and heat turned them into oil and natural gas.

Compared to coal and petroleum products, it burns with a very low emission of harmful gases and other pollutants. It provides energy for running of petrochemical industry besides being used as fuel for cooking and automobiles.

Distribution of Natural Gas

- The offshore region of the **Krishna-Godavari basin** has the **largest amount of natural gas** currently available in India.
- Cauvery basin also has natural gas reserves.
- Much of India's natural gas reserves are found in the Bombay High basin and in Gujarat.
- Onshore reserves are located in Gujarat and the North-Eastern states (Assam and Tripura).
- To fulfil its natural gas needs, India imports some gas and feeds its various industries through pipelines.
- The 1700 km long Hazira-Vijaipur-Jagdishpur (HVJ) pipeline links Mumbai High and Bassein with the fertiliser, power and industrial complexes in West and North India.

Hydroelectric Power (Hydel Power)

Electricity generated by gravitational force of falling or flowing water is called Hydroelectricity. It is pollution free and commonly used all over India, as it is a renewable resource.

In India, 26% of electrical energy generated is contributed by hydro power. India is the 5th largest producer of hydroelectric (also called 'hydel' in short) power in the world and ranks third worldwide in the total number of dams.

Distribution of Hydroelectric Power

At present, maximum station capacity for a hydel power station is 2400 MW is at Nathpa Jhakri in Himachal Pradesh. The Tehri dam on Bhagirathi river near Tehri in Uttarakhand is the highest dam in India.

Hirakud dam on the Mahandi river, near Sambalpur, Odisha is the **longest dam** in the world and was the first hydel multipurpose project after independence.

The second largest hydro power plant is the Koyna Hydorelectric dam (capacity of 1,960 MW) situated at the Western Ghat of India.

Beside these, the Srisailam Dam across the Krishna river at Srisailam in Kurnool district of Andhra Pradesh, the Sardar Sarovar dam at the Narmada river near Navagam, Gujarat, the Bhakra-Nangal dam, a concrete gravity dam across the Sutlej river in Bilaspur, Himachal Pradesh and the Nagarjuna Sagar Dam at the Krishna river at Nagarjuna Sagar, Andhra Pradesh are other major leading hydel project in India under operation.

- **The Bhakra-Nangal Dam** It is a concrete gravity dam across the Sutlej river, in district Bilaspur, Himachal Pradesh. Its reservoir, known as the **Gobind Sagar**, stores upto 9.34 billion cubic metres of water, making it the second largest reservoir in India. It is enough to drain the whole of Chandigarh, parts of Haryana, Punjab and Delhi. Its total capacity of electric power generation is about 1325 MW.
- **Hirakud Dam** It is built across the Mahanadi river, about 15 km from Sambalpur, Odisha. Its total capacity of electric power generation is about 307.5 MW.

Advantages of Conventional Sources

Advantages of conventional sources are given below

(i) **High in Energy** Conventional sources of energy such as coal and oil tend to provide us with more energy per unit than do renewable energy sources such as solar or wind energy.

(ii) **Able to Move** Because they tend to come in solid, physical form such as lumps of coal or barrels of oil, conventional energy sources can usually easily be taken from place to place. This means that they can be convenient for people who live in areas that are not amenable to the harnessing of major renewable sources of energy (such as solar or wind energy).

(iii) **Profitable** It is profitable to mine coal, extract oil or construct natural gas pipelines.

(iv) **Cost Effective** Many conventional sources of energy (such as natural gas, for example) are very cheap.

(v) **Create Jobs** Extracting, transporting and refining conventional sources of energy – as well as creating the machinery for using them – create many jobs and thus can be one way of sustaining a country's economy.

Disadvantages of Conventional Sources

Disadvantages of conventional sources are given below

(i) **Time Consuming to Extract** Mining coal, searching for oil, and building drills and pipes to extract and transport natural gas, are all very time consuming processes.

(ii) **Contribution to Climate Change** Burning coal, oil and natural gas releases large amounts of carbon dioxide and carbon monoxide, which are major contributors to **global warming**. These chemicals destroy the ozone layer, make the oceans acidic and saturated with carbon, and make the air more difficult for animals to breathe and plants to flourish in.

By creating a 'mantle' of carbon rich air in the atmosphere. These chemicals trap the Sun's rays and make the atmosphere around the Earth much warmer. This is the so-called greenhouse effect because it makes the atmosphere like a giant warm greenhouse.

(iii) **Contribution to Acid Rain** Burning fossil fuels releases oxides (including sulfur oxide) which cause rain to become acidic. This is very harmful to wildlife and also erodes buildings.

(iv) **Dangerous for Humans** Conventional sources like fossil fuels can emit carbon monoxide. This is dangerous to humans and can cause respiratory problems and death if inhaled. It is especially dangerous because it is colourless and odorless and thus not detectable by the human eye or sense of smell.

(v) **Not Viable for Future Generations** Using these sources without taking steps to make our infrastructure, homes and factories ready to use renewable sources of energy could be said to be very selfish. Moreover, using up all the conventional sources of energy now, without leaving any for future generations, is unsustainable.

(vi) **Dirty** Many conventional sources of energy are quite dirty, leaving soot and dirt on furnishings in the home. When used in factories, they release soot and other dirty substances into the air which can coat buildings and pavements, and make cities feel dirty and grimy. One reason for the unsightliness of modern cities – which some people complain about – and the smog that can make them seem dark and overcast is the overuse of dirty, conventional sources of energy.

Non-Conventional Sources of Energy

Non-conventional or Renewable energy sources are automatically replenished by nature, i.e., Sun's rays, water, tides, wind, air etc. The abundant supply of renewable energy sources contrasts with the limited supply of non-renewable sources of energy.

If not replenished, non-renewable sources of energy will eventually get exhausted completely. However, there is no need to replenish renewable energy sources and they never get exhausted. These sources are

Solar Energy

Energy produced through sunlight is called solar energy. In this process, solar photovoltaic cells are exposed to sunlight and they generate electricity. Photovoltaic cells heating convert solar energy into electricity.

Advantages of Solar Energy

- Solar energy is renewable and inexhaustible source of energy.
- Large amount of free energy can be produced due to high availability of sunlight.
- It can be used in heating, drying and cooking.
- It saves fossil fuels and used to produce electricity.

Distribution of Solar Energy

Solar power installed capacity is concentrated in a few states in India. Such states are Gujarat, Rajasthan, Andhra Pradesh, Telangana and Tamil Nadu. They generate more than 67% of the total solar power available in India.

Wind Power

Wind energy is a renewable energy source. This kind of energy is generated by the motion of wind turbines. It involves the use of windmills to produce power for heating and lighting purposes. India has the fifth position in the worldwide installed capacity of wind power.

Advantages of Wind Power

- Wind energy is a clean source of energy.
- It is a sustainable form of energy.

- The generation machinery needs very little maintenance.
- Rural areas that are far away from other sources of power can use wind power for their heating and lighting needs.
- Due to the rise in global warming issues, most environmentalists and governments advocate the use of wind power.
- A wind farm can generate enough power to provide electricity for a whole village.

Distribution of Wind Power

Wind energy distribution is not uniform across India. Southern and Western states have maximum wind capacity installed due to highest wind density and velocity.

Tamil Nadu is the leading state in terms of wind installations with 34.2% share of the overall wind capacity installed in the country. It is followed by Maharashtra 19.3%, Gujarat 16.1%, Rajasthan 13.3% and Karnataka 11.3%.

Nuclear Energy

Nuclear energy is generated in equipment known as **nuclear reactors**. Inside the nuclear reactor, energy is generated by means of a chain reaction involving uranium atoms.

When the uranium atom is split, it releases heat energy. Thus, by splitting uranium atoms inside a nuclear reactor, we can generate energy that can be converted into electricity. Thorium is also are used to for generating nuclear power in India.

Advantages of Nuclear Energy

- A single uranium atom can generate much energy when it is split.
- When they are kept safe and secure, nuclear power plants are relatively clean sources of energy.
- Nuclear energy is a viable alternative to fossil fuel use. It is important to find such an alternative, as stocks of fossil fuels may get exhausted before the end of this century.
- The waste produced by nuclear power plants (depleted uranium) can be re-used. Reprocessing plants can turn this waste into useful materials used in aircraft production.

Distribution of Nuclear Energy

Currently India has 6780 MW of Nuclear power capacity distributed into 22 power plants across 6 places located mostly in Southern and Western parts of the country. The important states are Maharashtra (4 power plants), Rajasthan (6 power plants), Tamil Nadu (4 power plants), Karnataka (4 power plants), Uttar Pradesh (2 power plants) and Gujarat (2 power plants).

Tarapur is India's oldest power plant and It has 1400 MW capacity. Kota in Rajasthan has India's second largest nuclear power capacity at 1080 MW. India has another 3.7 GW of Nuclear Power Capacity under construction which may come into operation in the next 5 years.

Biogas

Biogas is primarily **methane** and **carbon dioxide**. It may have small amounts of hydrogen sulphide, moisture and other impurities. The gases methane, hydrogen and carbon monoxide can be combusted or oxidised with oxygen. This energy release allows biogas to be used as a fuel.

A family type biogas plant generates biogas from organic substances such as cattle –dung, and other bio-degradable materials such as biomass from farms, gardens, kitchens, night soil wastes etc. The plants using cattle dung are known as **Gobar gas plants** in rural India.

Uses of Biogas

It can be used for any heating purpose, such as cooking. It can also be used in a gas engine to convert the energy in the gas into electricity and heat.

Advantages of Biogas

- It provides clean gaseous fuel for cooking and lighting mainly in rural areas because it has a higher thermal efficiency as compared to kerosene, charcoal and dung cake.
- Biogas used for generation of electricity has the advantage of being a clean source of energy as it uses the methane in biogas for generating energy.
- Chemical fertilisers can be done away with since the digested slurry obtained from the biogas plants can be used as enriched bio-manure.
- It is good for the climate and for sanitation problems since toilets can be linked directly with biogas plants.
- In cities, it allows large sewage treatment plants to operate profitably and sell the biogas produced electricity to the grid.
- It improves the quality of manure and also prevents the loss of trees.

Distribution of Biogas

In India, the estimated production of biogas is about 20,757 lakh cubic metres in 2014-15. This is equivalent to 6.6 crore domestic LPG cylinders. This is equivalent to 5% of the total LPG consumption in the country today.

Biogas plants can be established municipal, cooperative and individual levels. In biogas production the state of Maharashtra is topmost. It is followed by Andhra Pradesh, Karnataka, Gujarat, Uttar Pradesh, West Bengal, Assam, Madhya Pradesh, Tamil Nadu and Odisha.

Advantages of Non- Conventional Energy Sources

There are many advantages of non- conventional energy sources which are as follows

(i) **Environment Friendly** Unlike fossil fuels (which are non-renewable energy sources and which release harmful substances such as CO_2 and CO when burned), non-conventional energy sources have a very low impact on the environment. In fact, most of them are environment friendly.

(ii) **Sustainable Energy** Because, crucially, they do not run out, non- conventional energy sources are sustainable. This makes them viable for use well into the future.

(iii) **Low Operating Cost** Once they have been set up, non-conventional energy apparatus such as wind farms and solar panels are very cost effective to operate and maintain. As such, they are good and cheap sources of energy.

PYQs Previous Years' Questions

1 Mark Questions

Multiple Choice Questions

1. Rourkela Steel Plant was built with the cooperation of .... *(ICSE Specimen 2023)*

(a) USSR (b) Germany
(c) Japan (d) France

Ans. (b) Germany

2. ...... is the oldest coalfield of India. *(ICSE Specimen 2023)*

(a) Raniganj (b) Jharia
(c) Bokaro (d) Karanpura

Ans. (a) Raniganj

3. Copper is alloyed with zinc to form *(ICSE 2023)*

(a) stainless steel (b) brass
(c) bronze (d) aluminium

Ans. (b) brass

Very Short Answer Questions

1. Name two leading states producing manganese. *(ICSE 2012)*

Ans. Odisha and Karnataka are two leading states in the production of manganese.

2. Mention one use of manganese. *(ICSE 2012)*

Ans. Manganese is used for manufacturing paints and glass.

2 Marks Questions

1. (i) Why is manganese an important raw material for iron and steel industry? *(ICSE Specimen 2023)*

(ii) Name one iron ore field in Odisha.

Ans. (i) Manganese is an important raw material for making iron and steel because it removes impurities from steel and makes it tough and hard.

(ii) One iron ore field in Odisha is Keonjhar.

2. Mention one advantage and one disadvantage of coal found in India. *(ICSE Specimen 2023)*

Ans. One advantage of coal is that coal is easy to burn and produces high energy upon combustion. One disadvantage of coal found in India is that coal generates carbon emission which is responsible for air pollution.

3. (i) Name the best quality of iron ore which has magnetic properties. *(ICSE Specimen 2023)*

(ii) Name an important coal field located in Paschim Bengal.

Ans. (i) Magnetite is the finest iron ore with a very high content of iron up to 70% and has magnetic properties.

(ii) Raniganj is the most important coalfield in Paschim Bengal.

4. Name two states where copper is found in India. Mention one use of it. *(ICSE Specimen 2023)*

Ans. Two states where copper is found in India are Jharkhand and Madhya Pradesh. One use of copper is that it is used in electrical industry.

5. (i) Give any one use of manganese. *(ICSE Specimen Semester II 2022)*

(ii) Why is copper used in electrical appliances?

Ans. (i) Manganese is used to improve the many alloys, e.g. iron and steel. For manufacturing one tonne of steel, 10 kg of manganese is used.

(ii) Copper is used in electrical appliances because it is a good conductor of heat.

6. Give two advantages of using natural gas over coal. *(ICSE Specimen Semester II 2022)*

Ans. Two advantages of using natural gas over coal are

(i) Natural gas is eco-friendly fuel than coal.

(ii) It has multiple uses like generating electric power, powering vehicles, fertilisers, etc.

7. What grade of iron-ore is mostly mined in India? Name two leading iron-ore producing states. *(ICSE Semester II 2022, 2011)*

Ans. Iron-ore like haematite and magnetite is mostly mined in India. Odisha and Jharkhand are the leading iron-ore producing states.

8. (i) Why is iron ore called the back bone of our modern industry? *(ICSE 2020)*

(ii) Mention two uses of iron ore.

Ans. (i) Iron ore is called as the backbone of the modern civilisation because it provides raw materials, all types of machinery to run other industries. This sector has helped in the generation of several small scale industries supporting power, transport and communication industries in India.

(ii) The two uses of iron ore are

(a) The primary use of iron ore (98%) is to make steel.

(b) The remaining 2% is used in various other applications such as for certain types of steels, magnets, auto parts and catalysts.

9. Name the following. *(ICSE 2019)*

(i) A metallic mineral for which the Balaghat district of Madhya Pradesh is famous.

Ans. (i) Manganese

10. Mention two advantages of using non-conventional sources of power. *(ICSE Specimen 2018)*

Ans. Two advantages of using non-conventional sources of power are

(i) They are renewable and inexhaustible source of energy.

(ii) They are available at low cost.

11. With reference to the Bhilai iron and steel plant.

(i) Name its foreign collaborator.

(ii) State the source from where it obtains iron ore and coal. *(ICSE Specimen 2018)*

Ans. (i) Bhilai iron and steel plant was established in 1953 in collaboration with the erstwhile USSR in Durg district of Chhattisgarh.

(ii) It obtains iron ore form Dalli-Rajhara range which is just 80 km South of Bhilai. It obtains coal from Korba and Kargati fields of Chhattisgrah. High quality coals are further brought from Jharia and Bokaro.

12. Give two reasons why the cotton textile industry has developed in Mumbai. *(ICSE 2018)*

Ans. The factors that favour the concentration of cotton textile mills in Mumbai are as follows

(i) Mumbai has proper network of roads and railways at facilitates easy transportation from mills.

(ii) It is a very important port that provides opportunity for import and export of cotton goods.

13. Give two advantages that non-conventional energy sources have over conventional energy sources. *(ICSE 2018)*

Ans. Two advantages that non-conventional energy sources have over conventional energy sources are

(i) They are environment friendly because they do not release harmful gases (like conventional sources do) while generating energy.

(ii) They are virtually inexhaustible and sustainable, unlike conventional sources, which are limited in quantity.

14. Give the names of four important types of iron ore found in India. *(ICSE 2017)*

Ans. Four important iron ore found in India are

(i) Magnetite (ii) Haematite

(iii) Limonite (iv) Siderite

15. Name the following. *(ICSE 2017)*

(i) An offshore oilfield in the Gulf of Cambay.

(ii) An oil refinery in Bihar.

Ans. (i) An offshore oilfield in the Gulf of Cambay is the Cambay Basin oilfield.

(ii) An oil refinery in Bihar is the Barauni Refinery.

16. Name the following. *(ICSE 2016)*

(i) An iron ore mine of Karnataka.

Ans. (i) An iron ore mine located in Karnataka is at Kudremukh.

17. Which are the two different varieties of coal used for domestic purposes and why? *(ICSE 2014)*

Ans. Anthracite and bituminous are two varities of coal used for domestic purposes because they are very high in carbon content and hence best suited as fuel.

18. What is lignite? Name the two areas where lignite is found in India. *(ICSE 2011)*

Ans. Lignite has about 60% of carbon content and is a poor quality of coal. It is found in Kashmir and Tamil Nadu.

19. Name one centre in each of the following states where iron is mined. *(ICSE 2010)*

(i) Odisha (ii) Jharkhand

Ans. (i) Keonjhar in Odisha

(ii) Singhbhum in Jharkhand

20. Which state is the largest producer of mineral oil? Name any two oil refineries of India. *(ICSE 2009)*

Ans. Maharashtra is the largest mineral oil producing state. Trombay refinery and Mathura refinery are the two oil refineries of India.

21. Name two states with large deposits of coal. Name the coal fields in the states that you have named. *(ICSE 2008)*

Ans. Jharkhand and West Bengal are two states with large deposits of coal. Raniganj (in West Bengal) and Jharia (in Jharkhand) are two coal fields in India.

22. Name an important coal producing state in India and a coal mine located in that state. *(ICSE 2007)*

Ans Jharkhand is an important coal producing state and Jharia is a coal mine in Jharkhand.

23. Name two states in India where manganese is found. *(ICSE 2006)*

Ans. Odisha and Madhya Pradesh are the leading producers of manganese.

24. Name two important oilfields in India. *(ICSE 2005)*

Ans. Mumbai and Ankleshwar are two important oilfields in India.

25. State two main drawbacks of the coal found in India. *(ICSE 2005)*

Ans. The two drawbacks of the coal found in India are

(i) Uneven distribution of coal.

(ii) It has high ash content and low calorific value.

3 Marks Questions

1. (i) State one important use of bauxite as a raw material. *(ICSE Specimen 2023)*

(ii) Name one state where bauxite is found.

(iii) Name an industry which uses limestone as raw material.

Ans. (i) Bauxite as a raw material is used for the extraction of aluminium.

(ii) Odisha is the largest producer of bauxite.

(iii) Limestone is used as raw material for manufacturing cement.

2. (i) Mention two main uses of petroleum.

(ii) Name one new and one old oilfield in India. *(ICSE Specimen 2023)*

Ans. (i) Two main uses of petroleum are as follows

(a) It is used as a fuel.

(b) It is used in the petro-chemical industry for manufacturing fertilisers and other chemicals.

(ii) One new oilfield in India is Mumbai High or khambat basin and one oil oilfield in India is Digboi in Assam.

3. Mention two advantages of using natural gas over petroleum. Name an area where natural gas is found. *(ICSE Specimen 2023)*

Ans. Two advantages of using natural gas over petroleum are as follows

- Natural gas is a cleaner fuel. It is less harmful to the environment then petroleum as it has less carbon dioxide emissions.
- It can easily stored and transferred through pipelines.

An area where natural gas is found is Mumbai.

4. What are the advantages of using bio gas?

Ans. Advantages of using bio gas are as follows

- Bio gas is eco-friendly.
- It produces organic fertilisers.
- It is available all the time and is cost effective.

5. (i) Name two states where coal is mined in abundance. *(ICSE 2023)*

(ii) Mention one advantage of using wind energy.

Ans. (i) Jharkhand and Odisha

(ii) The advantage of using wind energy is that it's an environmentally friendly fuel source and is a sustainable resource.

6. Name the following. *(ICSE 2023)*

(i) A mineral used to generate nuclear energy.

(ii) The non-conventional energy source that has the most widespread potential usage in India.

Ans. (i) Uranium

(ii) Solar energy

7. Give three disadvantages of using coal. *(ICSE Semester II 2022)*

Ans. Three disadvantages of using coal are as follows

(i) Coal emits deadly pollutants into the air including mercury, arsenic and sulphur dioxide.

(ii) The sulpur dioxide emitted by coal also causes acid rain.

(iii) Coal creates large amounts of greenhouse gases that contribute to global warming.

8. (i) Mention two advantages of nuclear power.

(ii) What is the advantage of using solar energy in place of the conventional sources of energy? *(ICSE Semester II 2022)*

Ans. (i) The advantages of nuclear power are

- It is one of the most low-carbon energy sources.
- It also has one of the smallest carbon footprints.
- It is reliable and cost-effective.

(ii) The advantages of using solar energy in place of the conventional source of energy are as follows

- Solar energy is a truly renewable energy source. It can be harnessed in all areas of the world and is available every day unlike conventional sources of energy such as coal.
- Solar energy has multiple usages. For example, we can generate electricity (photovoltaics) or heat (solar thermal). Solar energy can be used to produce electricity in areas without access to the energy grid, to distil water in regions with limited clean water supplies and to power satellites in space.

9. Answer the following *(ICSE Semester II 2022, 2018)*

(i) State one industrial use of copper.

(ii) Name the mineral that toughens steel and makes it rust-proof.

Ans. (i) Copper is used in electrical industry in the form of copper wires and numerous kinds of electrical equipment.

(ii) The mineral manganese is used in steel industries to make steel tough and rust-proof.

10. (i) Mention one disadvantage of using natural gas as a source of power. *(ICSE 2020)*

(ii) How is the residue from a Bio-gas plant put to use?

(iii) Why is the use of alternative sources of energy becoming essential in modern time?

Ans. (i) Natural gas is explosive and can cause a fire hazard if the pipeline bursts.

(ii) The residue left out in the biogas plant is slurry which is essentially used in the manure.

(iii) As the consumption of energy grows, the population depends more and more on fossil fuels such as coal, oil and gas day by day. Thus, there is a need to use alternative sources of energy.

11. Give a reason for each of the following. *(ICSE 2019)*

(i) Odisha has benefitted greatly from the Hirakud project.

(ii) Copper is used to make electric wires.

(iii) India's location is advantageous for the generation of solar power.

Ans. (i) Odisha is benefitted from Hirakud project as water from the Hirakud dam is used in various industries, e.g. in minerals processing and thermal power plants.

(ii) Copper is a good conductor of heat and electricity, so it is extremely useful in refrigeration, utensils and in wires.

(iii) India's location is advantageous for the generation of solar power as the country receives adequate solar radiation for 300 clear and sunny days. India is located North of Equator which helps to increase the amount of sunlight because sunlight falls directly on the equator.

Examiner's Comment

- Most candidates answered this subpart of the question correctly.
- This subpart of the question was attempted well by most candidates.
- Most candidates wrote the correct reason for the question; India's location is advantageous for the generation of solar power.

Suggestion for Students

- Write complete name of multipurpose projects.

12. Briefly answer the following. *(ICSE 2019)*

(i) Name a mineral used to generate nuclear power.

(ii) Why is petroleum often referred to as "liquid gold"?

Ans. (i) Uranium and thorium are the main atomic minerals which are mostly used in generating nuclear energy.

(ii) Petroleum is obtained in the form of liquid and has high price and value and is economically important for all countries world wide. Thus, it is often referred to as "liquid gold".

13. (i) Name one fossil fuel and mention an area where it is found. *(ICSE Specimen 2018)*

(ii) Give one disadvantage of using the fossil fuel mentioned.

Ans. (i) Coal is a fossil fuel which is found in Jharkhand.

(ii) One disadvantage of using the fossil fuel is that it pollutes the environment.

14. (i) Name two types of iron ore mined in India.

(ii) State two uses of copper.

Ans. (i) Two important types of iron ore mined in India are Magnetite and Haematite.

(ii) Two uses of copper are as follow

(a) It is used in electrical industry in the form of copper wires and other numerous kinds of electrical equipments.

(b) It is used in space programmes and telecommunications.

15. (i) Mention two advantages of setting up a small scale industry.

(ii) What is the difference between a public sector and a private sector industry?

Ans. (i) Two advantages of setting up a small scale industry are

(a) Small Scale industries require less capital in comparison to large scale industries. They can be started and run small entrepreneurs who have limited capital resources.

(b) The managment of small scale industry is easy and economical.

Additional Info

Other advantages of setting up small scale industry are

- Small-scale industries have the ability to generate a large number of job opportunities.
- Small-scale industries make productive use of locally available resources that would otherwise be wasted.
- Small businesses are more adaptable. They can quickly adjust to shifting market conditions and capitalize on new opportunities.

(ii) Differences between public sector and private sector industries are as follow

Public Sector	Private Sector
Owned and controlled by the government (State or Central).	Owned and controlled by private group of people or individual.
Its objective is to serve the citizens of the country.	Its objective is to earn profit.

16. State an important industrial use of *(ICSE 2017)*

(i) Manganese

(ii) Coal

(iii) Aluminium

Ans. An important use of

(i) **Manganese** It is the most important mineral for making steel.

(ii) **Coal** It is the main source of power generation in India.

(iii) **Aluminium** It used for packing in various forms such as cans, foils, tubes and bottle tops.

17. (i) Name any three types of coal found in India. *(ICSE 2016)*

(ii) Which type of coal is mostly used in iron and steel industries?

Ans. (i) Three types of coal found in India are

(a) Anthracite (b) Bituminous (c) Lignite

(ii) Anthracite coal is used for metallurgical processes in iron and steel industry.

18. Name the following. *(ICSE 2016)*

(i) Largest coal field of India.

(ii) Oldest oilfield of India.

(iii) Best variety of iron ore.

Ans. (i) Jharia is the largest coal field of India.

(ii) Digboi is the oldest oilfield of India.

(iii) Magnetite ore is the best variety of iron ore.

19. Name the following. *(ICSE 2015)*

(i) Largest oil refinery in the public sector.

(ii) State that is the largest producer of coal.

(iii) Best variety of iron ore.

Ans. (i) BPCL's Kochi refinery

(ii) Jharkhand

(iii) Magnetite

20. Give a geographic reason for each of the following. *(ICSE 2015)*

(i) Many port cities have their own oil refineries.

(ii) Petroleum is called a 'fossil fuel'.

(iii) Coal is called a versatile mineral.

Ans. (i) Many port cities have their own oil refineries because most of the petroleum India needs is imported through tankers coming to these ports.

(ii) Petroleum is called a fossil fuel because it is derived from plant and animal life buried in sedimentary rocks for millions of years.

(iii) Coal is called a versatile mineral because it forms the basic raw material for production of steel, other industrial products and for generation of power.

21. Which state is the leading producer of the following minerals? *(ICSE 2014)*

(i) Coal (ii) Oil (iii) Manganese

Ans. (i) Coal – Jharkhand

(ii) Oil – Rajasthan

(iii) Manganese – Madhya Pradesh

22. Give geographical reason for the following. *(ICSE 2012)*

(i) Anthracite is used for domestic purposes.

(ii) Oil refineries are located close to oil field or near ports.

(iii) The location of coal fields is an important factor in industrial development.

Ans. (i) Anthracite does not give more smoke and has above 90% of carbon. Hence, it is used for domestic purposes.

(ii) Most of the oil refineries are located close to the oil fields because of easy accessibility of crude oil to the refinery. Most of the crude petroleum is exported and imported to or from other countries respectively. That's why they are located near ports.

(iii) Coal is the basic source of power in industries and it is heavy and bulky, hence industries are located near coal fields.

23. Name two important industrial uses of manganese. *(ICSE 2011)*

Ans. Manganese is an important mineral. It is widely used in industrial areas for making alloy steel, manufacturing of bleaching powder, paints and other chemicals.

24. Name the following. *(ICSE 2009)*

(i) The oldest and the largest coal field in India.

(ii) Two raw materials derived from coal.

Ans. (i) Raniganj is the oldest and Jharia is the largest coal field in India.

(ii) Ammonia and benzol are two raw materials derived from coal.

25. Name the different types of iron-ore found in India. What is the best quality of iron ore? *(ICSE 2009)*

Ans. The various types of iron-ore found in India are

(i) Haematite

(ii) Magnetite

(iii) Limonite

Magnetite is the best quality of iron-ore.

26. Answer the following questions. *(ICSE 2008)*

(i) Mention two reasons why minerals are important.

(ii) Name one area in Odisha and one area in Chhattisgarh, where iron-ore is mined.

Ans. (i) Minerals are important because they are source of raw material to many industries and a source of power for the country.

(ii) Sundergarh and Mayurbhanj in Odisha and Palamau and Singhbum in Chhattisgarh are the areas where iron-ore is mined.

27. Name four types of coal. Which of these is the best for the industrial purposes? Justify your answer. *(ICSE 2006)*

Ans. The four types of coal are

(i) Anthracite coal

(ii) Lignite coal

(iii) Bituminous coal

(iv) Peat coal

Anthracite coal is the best for the industrial purposes because it contains 90% of carbon and has highest ignition value.

28. State the SAARC country which has the largest iron-ore reserves. Mention two states in the country named by you, where the reserves are abundant. *(ICSE 2005)*

Ans. India is one of the SAARC countries, which has the largest iron-ore reserves.

Odisha and Jharkhand are the leading producers of iron-ore in India.

CHAPTER TEST

01 Mark Questions

1 Gold, silver and platinum are examples of ....
(a) ferrous minerals
(b) non - ferrous minerals
(c) precious minerals
(c) non- metallic minerals

2 .... is considered as the finest iron ore.
(a) Magnetite (b) Hematite
(c) Limonite (c) Siderite

3 Which of the following types of coal has the best quality ?
(a) Bituminous (b) Lignite
(c) Anthracite (c) Peat

4 .... is the largest petroleum producing state in India .
(a) Odisha (b) Telangana
(c) Maharashtra (c) Rajasthan

5 .... is a clear energy resource.
(a) Natural Gas (b) Coal
(c) Diesel (c) Petroleum

Answers

1. (c) | 2. (a) | 3. (c) | 4. (c) | 5. (a)

10 Marks Questions

6 (i) What is conventional source of energy ? What are its advantage ?
(ii) Why is the iron ore called the backbone of our modern industry ?
(iii) Mention the importance and uses of Biogas.
(iv) What are the advantages of using natural gas over the other sources like petroleum or coal ?

7 (i) Define the term 'mineral' and mention its uses.
(ii) What are the uses of manganese ? Which state is the largest producer of it ?
(iii) How is energy an indispensable requirement of modern life ? Explain with examples .
(iv) Why there is a need to use non-conventional sources of energy in India ? Explain any three reasons.

8 (i) Mention any three iron-ore belts in India and give characteristics.
(ii) Mention the characteristics of ferrous group of minerals found in India .
(iii) How are 'gobar gas plants' beneficial to farmers?
(iv) Why should the use of cattle cake as fuel be discouraged?

9 (i) How do the minerals occur in sedimentary rocks ?
(ii) Which is the most abundantly available fossil fuel in India ? Name its four major forms of it.
(iii) What are the two main ways of generating electricity? How are they different from each other? Explain.
(iv) Briefly answer the following.
(a) Name a mineral that is used to generate nuclear power.
(b) Why copper is used to make wires?
(c) Why is petroleum often referred to as 'black gold'?

05

Agriculture in India

TREND ANALYSIS 3 YEARS

Average No. of Questions Across all Sets

Topic	Category (Year)	2023	2020	2019
TOPIC 01 Indian Agriculture	1 Mark	2	–	–
	2 Marks	4	1	1
	3 Marks	–	–	1
TOPIC 02 Major Crops Grown in India	1 Mark	2	–	–
	2 Marks	1	1	–
	3 Marks	4	1	1

Among all the economic activities, agriculture is human's most important economic activities. It is also known as **primary activity** because it is associated direct with land and nature. In India, agriculture has a significant history since the ages.

Indian Agriculture

India is an agricultural country. It ranks second largest in agricultural production. Almost 2/3rd of India's population depends upon agriculture.

Importance of Agriculture in India

Agriculture is important in India due to following reasons

(i) Agriculture provides food and fodder to a huge population of human beings and livestock.

(ii) About 2/3rd population of India is dependent of agriculture because it provide them livelihood.

(iii) Agricultural products supports various agro-based industries like cotton-textile, jute, sugar, paper, etc.

(iv) Agriculture contributes a major share in GDP of India.

(v) Various agro-products are responsible for major flow of foreign currencies in India. These products share a major parts of export commodities.

Problems of Indian Agriculture

There are several problems in Indian agriculture. These are discussed below

Small and Fragmented Landholdings The pressure of increasing population and the practice of dividing land equally among the heirs has caused excessive sub-division of farm holdings in subsequent generations. Consequently, the holdings are small and fragmented. The small size of holdings makes farming activity uneconomical and leads to social tension, violence and discontent.

Poor Quality of Seeds Due to enormous price of seeds, the poor farmers cannot afford good quality seeds.

Lack of Proper Use of Manure and Fertiliser Continuous use of a land leads to low fertility and there is no proper manure available for the farmers. Therefore, soil becomes depleted.

Traditional Upbringing Indians believe in traditional way of farming and produce only for their own needs. Thus, there is few improvements and the agriculture stays the subsistence type only.

Excess Load on Land The large population leads to illiteracy, ignorance about better methods of farming, etc.

Steps taken by Government to Solve the Problems of Indian Agriculture/Reforms

Some main steps taken by government to solve the problems of Indian agriculture are

(i) Government of India had set-up the **National Seeds Corporation of India** in 1963 to supply improved varieties of seeds to farmers.

(ii) Many states like Punjab, Haryana, Rajasthan and Maharashtra started reuniting lands of the farmers, which were fragmented before.

(iii) Farmers are being educated about protection of crops and use of biocides.

(iv) Government has taken many steps to increase crop productivity in the Five Year Plans. e.g., Green Revolution, Good Irrigation System, etc.

(v) Government is providing high incentives, especially in the form of heavy subsidies, for using chemical fertilisers.

Salient Features of Indian Agriculture

Salient features of Indian agriculture are as follows

(i) Indian agriculture has always been dependent on the arrival of monsoon, which is uncertain.

(ii) Indian agriculture has tropical, sub-tropical and temperate crops because of its vast relief, varying climatic conditions and different soils.

(iii) Preponderance of food crops is the most significant feature, because India has a huge population and needs to feed it.

Types of Farming

Indian agriculture can be divided into the following categories

Subsistence Farming

Subsistence farming is a type of agriculture in which farmers produce only for their own consumption and subsistence. The sizes of holdings are small and there is an extensive use of human labour. Farming technology tends to be primitive and of low yield.

Intensive Farming

- In India as well as in China, farmers are forced to use the small landholding to produce enough for their own consumption. The small surplus produce is used for exchange against other goods.
- These people work to obtain maximum yield from their lands and use animal waste as manure. This kind of cultivation is known as **intensive farming.**

Extensive Farming

- This kind of farming commonly practiced in areas where small amounts of labour and capital give high agricultural productivity. This is used in relatively large areas of land. It is mostly **mechanised,** as labour is very expensive and not easily available.
- This kind of farming is also implemented in farming of sheep and cattle, where crop cultivation is relatively less. It is practiced mainly in the terai regions of North India. Here, crops that are produced are sugarcane, rice and wheat.

Plantation Farming

- A plantation is usually a large estate in a tropical or sub-tropical region that is cultivated by unskilled or semi-skilled labour. It was started in India by the British in the 19th century. It involves growing and processing of a **single cash crop** meant for sale in the market.
- The important features of plantation farming are vast extensive estates, managerial ability, large capital, technically developed, good fertilisers, well-developed transport, etc.
- This farming also facilitates their workers by providing schools, houses, market places, hospitals and other facilities. In India, it is practiced in Assam, Darjeeling, Nilgiri and Anaimalai, etc.
- The important crops grown on plantations are tea, coffee, coconut, oil palm, spices, banana, cinchona and rubber. Many of these crops are developed as single cash crops on a vast scale and are exported.

Mixed Farming

Mixed farming is an agrarian system, that mixes arable farming with the rearing of livestock. Mixed farming has following characteristics

(i) It emphasises on advanced technology for ploughing, sowing and harvesting. It also uses high yielding varieties of seeds with proper use of chemical fertilisers.

(ii) **Rotation of crops** is done in this type of farming. Root crops are grown to maintain fertility of the lands. e.g., beets, turnip, beans and peas, etc. It practices raising of livestock like poultry, dairy farming, etc, with crop farming simultaneously.

(iii) Mixed farming reduces the dependancy on fertilisers as manures are provided by animal components. Rearing of livestock also adds upto the income of the farmers.

Note Mixed farming is the dominant system in developed countries of Europe, America as well as Russia. In India, it is not well-developed, because of land pressure of the large population and also lack of technology.

Commercial Farming

It is a system of farming, where food crops are grown especially for sale. In this farming, HYV seeds are used. Such crops are sugarcane, rice and wheat. It is practiced in Punjab, Haryana and Western Uttar Pradesh.

Agricultural Seasons

India has **three main crop seasons** which are most influenced by the changing seasons

(i) Kharif (ii) Rabi (iii) Zaid

Kharif Season

Kharif season starts with the sowing of seeds in onset of monsoon (June) and ends with the harvesting in the beginning of winter (November). Rice, maize, jowar, bajra, cotton, seasum, groundnut and some pulses like moong, urad are grown in this season.

Rabi Season

Rabi season starts with the sowing of seeds in beginning of winter (November) and ends with the harvesting in the beginning of summer (March). Wheat, barley, jowar, gram oilseeds and tobacco are important crop grown in this season.

Zaid Season

This is a short cropping season between Rabi and Zaid. Vegetables and fruits like watermelon, muskmelon, cucumber, etc are important crops grown in this season.

Major Crops Grown in India

In India, large varieties of crops can be grown due to the variation in soil and climatic conditions.

Food Crops

Rice, wheat, millets and pulses are major food crops grown in India.

Rice

Rice is the most important crop of India, because most of the population is dependent on it. It is tropical as well as a sub-tropical crop.

Regional Diversity

Rice is divided into three types by regional diversities which are as follows

(i) **Wet or Lowland Rice** is grown in well watered lands.

(ii) **Terraced Rice** is grown in hill slop areas.

(iii) **Dry or Upland Rice** is grown in the hilly areas because in these regions water supply is not as much as in the plains.

Climatic Conditions and Soil

Rice can be grown in 16°C to 32°C temperature range with 150 cm to 200 cm rainfall. Rice can be grown in deep fertile clay or friable loam.

Methods of Cultivation

Rice cultivation requires lot of manual labour because there are a series of processes involved in the cultivation of rice. These are as follows

(i) **Broadcasting Method** This method involves sowing the seeds by sprinkling them all over the field by hand. This method is generally used to sow inferior quality of seeds.

(ii) **Dibbling** It means dropping of seeds along with ploughing.

(iii) **Transplantation** It used where adequate labour is available, means shifting of grown seeds from nurseries to the paddy field. There are various advantages of transplantation. When grown seeds are re-sown in fields, weeds are removed. There is less wastage of seeds compared to other forms of sowing.

(iv) **Japanese Method of Rice Cultivation** This method includes the use of good quality seeds which are of the high yield variety. Seeds are sown in nursery and transplanted in rows. So, as to make weeding and fertilising easy.

Processing

The processing of rice include the following methods

- **Threshing** Rice is threshed and crushed by bullocks to separate the **kernel** from the seed. It is done in the rice fields in order to minimise the cost of transporation.
- **Winnowing** The process removing unwanted husk from the grain is called winnowing. It involve pouring the grain.

- **Milling** It is the process of removing the yellowish outer cover of the grain. The rice is then polished which makes it attractive, but lesser in nutrients.

Distribution

Rice is grown in the plains of North and North-Eastern India, coastal areas and deltaic region because it requires standing water so hill slopes are not suitable. **West Bengal** is **largest producer** of rice in India followed by Uttar Pradesh, Andhra Pradesh, Punjab, Odisha, Tamil Nadu, Bihar, Chhattisgarh, Karnataka.

Development of irrigation has resulted into the high production of rice in Punjab, Haryana and Western Uttar Pradesh. Here, it is grown as a cash crop.

Wheat

Wheat is a Rabi crop. India has the fourth position in the world in production of wheat after Russia, USA and China. It is the main crop of the North and North-West regions of the country. It is rich in proteins, vitamins and carbohydrates and provides a balanced diet. It is sown in winter and harvested in March to April.

Climatic Conditions and Soil

Temperature An average temperature of 10°C to 15°C is required at the time of sowing the seeds.

Rainfall It needs 50 to 100 cm rainfall during the growing season. But in areas where, rainfall is less than 50 cm, a good irrigation system is required.

Soils It grows in well-drained, fertile, loamy alluvial soil of clayey composition. It is mostly grown in **Indo-Gangetic plain**.

Methods of Cultivation

The main methods of cultivation of wheat are

- **Sowing** Sowing is done during October and November, while the harvesting is done during March and April. Seeds are sown by broadcasting, dibbling or drilling method. These are
  (i) **Broadcasting** means scattering of seeds by hand over the soil.
  (ii) **Drilling** is another method of sowing seeds at regular intervals through a bamboo shaft attached to the plough which makes furrows.
  (iii) **Dibbling** is the placing of seeds at cross mark made in the field with the help of matter as per the requirement of the crop in both the directions.
- **Harvesting** Wheat is harvested, when the leaves are coloured reddish brown. The plants are then kept in the Sun to dry and then taken to the thresher or trampled by bullocks to remove the chaff. Harvesting is done by sickle and now-a-days by machines. Hailstorms, frost and rain at the time of harvesting are harmful.
- **Processing** Wheat is processed into various grades of flour by cleaning, tempering, grinding, sifting (refining) and purifying. Then, flour is sold in the markets.

Distribution

Punjab, Haryana, Uttar Pradesh are leading producers of wheat in India. Bihar, West Bengal, Maharashtra, Madhya Pradesh are other states which produce wheat.

Pulses

Pulses are rabi crop. Pulses are used as dal and are important sources of protein specially for the vegetarians. Pulses are leguminous plants with root nodules. They have the capacity to rotate and use nitrogen in the soil and also fix it. Gram, tur, urad, moong, masoor, matar (peas) and moth are important pulses. It also serves as food for cattle.

Climatic Conditions and Soil

Temperature Mild, cool and comparatively dry. It needs 20°-25°C temperature.

Rainfall Pulses need 50-100 cm rainfall.

Soil It is best grown in loamy soil.

Methods of Cultivation

- **Sowing** Being a rabi crop, pulses are sown between September and November after maturing in about 5-6 months.
- **Harvesting** Pulses are harvested in February and April. It is pulled out and is kept in the open area to dry.
- **Processing** The processing of pulses is done in the following ways
  (i) Cleaning and Grading (ii) Pitting
  (iii) Pretreatments with Oil (iv) Conditioning
  (v) De-husking (vi) Polishing

Distribution

Madhya Pradesh is a leading state in the production of pulses in India followed by Uttar Pradesh, Rajasthan, Maharashtra and Karnataka.

Fibre Crops

Cotton

Cotton is an important cash crop which provide us fibre by which our clothes are made. **Ginning** is a process in which cotton fibre is separated from the raw material, which is in the form of cotton bolls. India grows both short staple cotton and long staple cotton.

Cotton is a labour intensive crop because its processes like picking and ginning are the main activities which are mostly done by hand.

Climatic Conditions and Soil

Cotton is a tropical crop which requires temperature ranging from 20°C to 30°C and rainfall ranging from 65 to 80 cm. Frost is not good for the growth of cotton plants. Black cotton soil is best suited for the crop.

Methods of Cultivation

- **Sowing** Cotton is sown in April-May (before onset of monsoon) and mainly as Kharif crop in case of long staple varieties and in September in case of short and medium staple varieties. It takes 6 to 8 months to mature. Bright and sunny days helps in ripening at bursting of cotton bolls.

  In Punjab and Haryana, it is sown as a Rabi crop while in peninsular India, it is grown as Kharif crop because of the fear of frost. The seeds are sown by the broadcasting method. Irrigation helps the crops to grow better.
- **Harvesting** In peninsular India, it is harvested between January and March, whereas in Northern India, it is harvested in December and January before the winter frost which is very harmful for the crop.
- **Processing** Picking and ginning are the main activities under processing of cotton which is mostly done by hand. The picking season normally continues for 3 months as the cotton bolls continue to mature. A lot of labour is required for picking process because it cannot be mechanised.

Distribution

Maharashtra is the largest producer of cotton in India. Gujarat, Madhya Pradesh, Tamil Nadu, Haryana, Punjab, Karnataka are other producers of cotton. Punjab and Haryana grows long staple in India.

Jute

Jute is another fibre crop grown in India. It provides coarse fibre for jute industry. It is also known as **Golden Fibre**. Fibre is obtain from raw material by the process of **retting**. It is a microbiological process which losses the bark of the jute plant and facilitates removal of the fibre from the stalk by submerging bundles of Jute in flowing water for 20-25 days and then dried in the Sun. Retting is done after harvesting.

Climatic Conditions and Soil

Hot and humid climate is a basic requirement for the growth of jute crops. It requires temperature between 25° C to 35° C and rainfall of 150 cm and above.

Well-drained alluvial loamy soil is considered best for the growth of jute.

Methods of Cultivation

- **Sowing** Jute is generally sown in February on lowlands and in March-June on upland. Sowing is mostly done by drilling or broadcasting method. **Weeding** is very important in the early stages of growth. Relatively higher yields are obtained from the crop sown during the winter season.
- **Harvesting** Jute plant is harvested from July to September. A delay in harvest also adds to yields, but usually produces coarse fibre. The plant are generally uprooted, if the area is flooded, otherwise it is cut to ground length. Some part of the crops is left behind in the fields to develop the seed.
- **Processing** Retting is used for processing jute. After harvesting the plant, it is tied into bundles. It is dried and stripped of unwanted leaves and is kept submerged in water for 2 to 3 weeks.

Distribution

West Bengal is largest producer of jute in India. It produces about 4/5th of total production. Assam, Bihar, Odisha, Tripura are other producers.

Other Crops

Tea

Tea is an important beverage crop of India. Plantations of tea was first introduced by the Britishers in India in 1840s in Brahmaputra valley.

Climatic Conditions and Soil

Tea requires a moderate temperature of 25° to 35°C and well distributed rainfall of 150 to 250 cm. Well-drained deep friable loamy soil which is acidic in nature is most suitable to the tea. Stagnant water is harmful to the tea plantations that's why it is grown on hilly slopes.

- It is grown by the method of **clonal planting** or by seeds in nursery. **Clonal planting** is a method where high yielding plants are cut and grown separately.
- Direct sunlight and strong winds are also harmful that's why shelter belts are planted to save tea bushes.
- Tea bushes are pruned at regular interval. This help in growth of more new leaves and also the height of the plant does not increase which help in picking leaves.

Methods of Cultivation

- **Sowing** The sowing of tea plants include following methods
  (i) **Transplantation Method** In this method, first the seeds are sown in small germination beds or nursery and are allowed to grow for 9 to 12 months into proper seedlings.
  (ii) **Clonal Planting** Under this method, tea plants can be grown from cuttings of a good high yielding mother plant instead of seeds. This method is called clone planting because the new plant has the qualities of the mother plant.
- **Harvesting** Tea planters start the **pruning** of the bush after two years. It is done in order to maintain the height and diameter of the tea plant limited to one metre. In India, tea is picked every ten days during the growing season at lower elevations and every fifteen days, at higher altitudes.
- **Processing** Processing of tea includes the following steps
  (i) Withering (ii) Rolling (iii) Fermentation
  (iv) Drying (*or Fixing*) (v) Sorting
  (vi) Blending (vii) Packing

Distribution

Assam is **largest producer** of tea in India. It contributes more than half of the production. West Bengal is another important producing state. In Southern India, tea is grown in Tamil Nadu, Kerala and Karnataka on Nilgiri and Anamalai hills.

Sugarcane

Sugarcane is important plantation crop which provide raw material to sugar industry. The yield per hectare is higher in the Southern states as compared to Northern states due to presence of black lava soil with high fertility and absence of loo during summer and frost during winter in the Southern states helps in better growth.

Climatic Conditions and Soil

Sugarcane can be grown either in tropical or sub-tropical region. It requires hot and humid climate with a temperature of 21° C to 27° C and an annual rainfall between 75 cm and 100 cm. It can be grown on variety of soils.

Methods of Cultivation

- **Sowing** Sugarcane is generally sown from January to April, in most part of the country. The field is prepared by ploughing and clearing all vegetation and also by **harrowing**. Heavy amount of manure is applied before planting as the crops exhaust the fertility of the soil.
- Sugarcane can be planted through the following methods
  (i) Sett Method (ii) Ratooning (iii) By Seeds
- **Harvesting** Harvesting is done with the use of a long curved knife before the cane begins to flower. Its harvesting and crushing period is from October-November till April.

  Sugarcane must be cut near the ground because the stem contains most of the sucrose content. Farmers in the Northern India cut sugarcane before the winter season due to frost which is bad for it.
- **Processing** The sugarcane must be processed within 48 hours of cutting to preserve its sugar content. This is the reason why most of the sugar factories are located near the sugarcane fields in order to save the transportation time.

Distribution

The major sugarcane producing states are Uttar Pradesh, Maharashtra, Karnataka, Tamil Nadu, Andhra Pradesh, Bihar, Punjab and Haryana.

Oilseeds

- Oilseeds are used to extract oil. They are most important commercial crops. India is one of the largest oilseed producing country in the world and has the **largest area under oilseeds** in the world. Important oilseeds grown in India are groundnut, mustard, rapeseed, seasame, linseed, soybean, sunflower and castor.
- Except linseed and castor all the oilseeds provide edible oil. The oil provided by these seeds are used for the production of soap, cosmetic and ointments and tanning of leather.
- **Soybean** Soybean is an important oilseed crop with high protein content, fibre polyunsaturated fats, vitamins and minerals.
- **Climatic Condition** Soybean grows well in warm and moist climate. It is Kharif crop. It requires well drained and fertile loam soil and 20°C-30°C temperature with 60-65cm of rainfall.
- **Distribution** Madhya Pradesh, Maharashtra, Rajasthan, Andhra Pradesh, Chhattisgarh, Gujarat, etc.

Groundnut

- **Climatic Conditions and soil** It is a kharif crop. It requires sandy loam and black soil. It needs 20°C-30°C temperature and 60-150cm of rainfall.
- **Distribution** Gujarat, Andhra Pradesh, Telangana, Maharashtra, Tamil Nadu and Karnataka are major producers of groundnut. **Gujarat** is the **largest producer** of groundnut.

Mustard

- **Climatic Conditions and soil** It is a Rabi crop. It requires sandy to clayey soils. It also grow well in alluvium loam soil. It needs 15°C–25°C temperature and 75 to 100cm of rainfall.
- **Distribution** It is cultivated in Rajasthan, Uttar Pradesh, Haryana, Madhya Pradesh and Gujarat.

Methods of Cultivation

- **Sowing** The seeds of the plant are sown in the month of June or July generally by the process of broadcasting or drilling. Its pods (seed vessels) grow underground and hence, they are called **groundnuts**. The plant bears flower on maturing. The flower stalk increases after self-pollination and move downwards.
- **Harvesting and Processing** The whole crop takes a time of about 4-5 months to be ready for harvesting. It is used as a rotation crop for millets and other crops as well. It is harvested in the months from October to December. The whole plant is removed from the soil, including its roots. After that, they are collected and dried in the Sun. They are shelled and seeds are collected and then sent to mills after packaging (in sacks).

Food Crops in India

Crops	Temperature	Rainfall	Soil	Method of Farming	Areas
Kharif (Rice)	Ranging from 16°C to 20°C at the time of ripening 18°C to 32°C.	150 cm to 200 cm (heavy).	Alluvial	Broadcasting, dibbling, drilling transplanting.	Northern plains, Eastern coastal plains, West Bengal, Uttar Pradesh, Andhra Pradesh, Punjab, Bihar, Jharkhand and Tamil Nadu.
Rabi (Wheat)	Need 10°C to 15°C to grow.	50 cm to 100 cm.	Alluvial soil and black soil	Broadcasting dibbling,drilling.	Uttar Pradesh, Punjab, Haryana, Madhya Pradesh, Bihar, Chhattisgarh and Rajasthan.
Zaid	26°C to 33°C range of temperature.	50 cm to 120 cm of rainfall.	Sandy and clayey deep regur soil.	Broadcasting method	Maharashtra, Karnataka, Andhra Pradesh, Madhya Pradesh, Uttar Pradesh, Jharkhand, Gujarat and Rajasthan.

Processing and Distribution of Food Crops

Crops	Processing	Areas
Rice	It is done by hand and called harvesting, then threshing and trampling.	Lower and middle Gangetic plain Brahmaputra valley East and West coastal regions Parts of Peninsular plateau.
Wheat	It is done by sickle or machine	Uttar Pradesh, Punjab, Haryana, Madhya Pradesh, Rajasthan, Bihar, Gujarat and Maharashtra.
Pulses	It is done by cleaning and grading, De husking and polishing	Madhya Pradesh, Uttar Pradesh, Himachal Pradesh, Rajasthan and Haryana.

Cash Crops of India

Crops	Temperature	Rainfall	Soil	Methods of Cultivation	**Distribution** (Areas)
Sugarcane	20°C to 30°C	70 cm to 100 cm	Alluvial and black soil	Stalk cutting of two to three joints.	Uttar Pradesh, Andhra Pradesh, Tamil Nadu, Haryana, Maharashtra and Karnataka.
Oilseeds	10°C to 25°C	25 cm to 100 cm (vary from crop to crop)	Alluvial, loams, black sandy soil	Broadcasting	Gujarat, Tamil Nadu, Andhra Pradesh, Karnataka, Punjab and Haryana.
Cotton	21°C to 27°C	80 cm to 120 cm	Black soil	Broadcasting and drilling	Gujarat, Maharashtra
Jute	29°C to 35°C	170 cm to 200 cm	Alluvial soil	Broadcasting, dibbling and drilling	West Bengal, Assam and Odisha.
Tea	12°C to 35°C	150 cm to 250 cm	Light loam soil	Sowing cutting	Assam and West Bengal.

PYQs Previous Years' Questions

1 Mark Questions (MCQ)

Multiple Choice Questions

1. Which of the following is not a problem of Indian agriculture ? *(ICSE 2023)*
   (a) Dependence on monsoon
   (b) Small land holdings
   (c) Two main cropping seasons
   (d) Use of traditional methods of farming

Ans. (c) Two main cropping seasons

2. Which of the following is a staple food grain of India ? *(ICSE 2023)*
   (a) Wheat (b) Rice
   (c) Gram (d) Arhar

Ans. (b) Rice

3. Cultivation of crops and raising of animals is a feature of .... *(ICSE Specimen 2023)*
   (a) intensive farming (b) plantation farming
   (c) mixed farming (d) commercial farming

Ans. (c) mixed farming

4. .... crops are associated with laterite soil. *(ICSE Specimen 2023)*
   (a) Wheat and rice (b) Sugarcane and rice
   (c) Maize and bajra (d) Tea and coffee

Ans. (d) Tea and coffee

5. Which of the following soils is most suitable for the cultivation of cotton and sugarcane? *(ICSE Specimen Semester I 2021)*
   (a) Laterite soil (b) Black soil
   (c) Red soil (d) Alluvial Soil

Ans. (b) Black soil

Very short Answer Questions

1. Distinguish between intensive commercial farming and extensive commercial farming. *(ICSE 2013, 2003)*

Ans. The differences between intensive commercial farming and extensive commercial farming are

Intensive Commercial Farming	Extensive Commercial Farming
It requires more use of fertiliser and labour.	It requires less use of fertiliser and labour.
It is predominated by food crops.	It is predominated by cash crops.

2. (i) With the reference to rice cultivation, name two leading states in the production of rice. *(ICSE 2013)*
   (ii) Give two advantages of growing rice in nurseries.

Ans. (i) West Bengal and Uttar Pradesh are two leading states in the production of rice.
(ii) The advantages of growing rice in nurseries are
   (a) When re-sowing in the fields, weeds are removed.
   (b) There is less wastage of seeds compared to other forms of sowing.

3. What is the importance of agriculture in India? Mention two factors. *(ICSE 2012)*

Ans. Two factors which contribute to the importance of agriculture in India are
(i) It provides a livelihood for almost two-third of the population.
(ii) It forms the backbone of the Indian economy by providing food and fodder, as well as raw material for agro-based industries.

4. Name a state which produces short staple cotton. Which climatic and soil conditions favour the cultivation of cotton in the state mentioned? *(ICSE 2012)*

Ans. Punjab produces short staple cotton. The climatic conditions favouring the cultivation of cotton are a mild, cool and dry climate with no frost. The soil here is alluvial and light, which suits this crop.

5. State two geographical requirements for the growth of wheat in India. *(ICSE 2011)*

Ans. Temperature ranging 15°C to 25°C at sowing time and 50 to 100 cm annual rainfall are the two geographical requirements for the growth of wheat in India.

6. Give geographical reasons for the followings. *(ICSE 2010)*
   (i) Tea bushes are pruned at regular intervals.
   (ii) Oil cake is a useful residue.

Ans. (i) Pruning is the method in which the branches of tea bush are cut off. This method encourages the growth of new shoots with softer leaves and to keep it about 1.2 m high, so that the leaves can be picked up easily.
(ii) Oil cake is useful as manure and can be used as fodder for cattle.

7. Study the given picture and answer the following questions. *(ICSE 2010)*

(i) Name the crop which is being planted. Give one benefit of this method of planting crop.

(ii) Mention the climatic conditions which favour the cultivation of the crop being planted.

Ans. (i) Rice is being planted using the transplantation method. One benefit is that weeds are removed at the time of transplantation.

(ii) The two geographical conditions which suit the cultivation of rice are

(a) Temperature must be 16ºC to 32ºC and rainfall varies from 150 cm to 200 cm.

(b) Plain lands or gentle slopes are suitable for the production of rice because stagnancy of water is must for the cultivation of rice.

8. Name the state in India which leads cotton cultivation. Mention two climatic factors which affect the cotton cultivation adversely. *(ICSE 2010)*

Ans. Maharashtra leads in cotton cultivation. Frost and excess at the time of ripening of cotton bolls affect cotton cultivation adversely.

9. Explain the two important characteristics of plantation farming. Name one important plantation crop. *(ICSE 2009)*

Ans. Two important characteristics of plantation farming are

(i) Size of estate is large.

(ii) Monoculture is common *i.e.*, one crop dominates the farm.

10. Which state is the leading producer of jute? Give any two factors responsible for this. *(ICSE 2009)*

Ans. West Bengal is the leading producer of jute. The state has deposited alluvial soil and receives 170 cm to 200 cm of rainfall, which favours jute plantation.

11. Answer the following questions. *(ICSE 2008)*

(i) When are Kharif crops sown and harvested?

(ii) Name the cash crop which is also a Kharif crop.

Ans. (i) Kharif crops are sown in June and July with the arrival of the monsoon rains .They are harvested in October and November.

(ii) Cotton is a cash crop and also a Kharif crop in Peninsular India.

12. India is the second largest producer of tea. State the climatic factors necessary for its growth. *(ICSE 2008)*

Ans. Tea needs 10°C to 35°C range of temperature with 150 cm to 250 cm annual rainfall.

13. Explain, why wheat is grown as a Rabi crop? *(ICSE 2007, 2005)*

Ans. Wheat is grown as a Rabi crop, because it is grown in winter, requiring low temperature and less rainfall.

14. Mention two differences between shifting agriculture and plantation agriculture. *(ICSE 2006)*

Ans. Two differences between shifting agriculture and plantation agriculture are

Shifting Agriculture	Plantation Agriculture
Subsistence type of agriculture.	Commercial type of agriculture.
Needs less capital.	Needs huge capital.

15. Describe any two main features of subsistence agriculture. *(ICSE 2005)*

Ans Two main features of subsistence agriculture are as follows

(i) Farmer produces for their needs only.

(ii) Farms are mainly small and only the farmer's family works on it to cultivate food crops such as rice, wheat, pulses, etc.

16. Why is tea considered a labour intensive crop? Name two states in India where tea is widely grown. *(ICSE 2004)*

Ans. Tea cultivation requires a number of activities like sowing, running and plucking by hand which need a large number of skilled and unskilled workers thus, making it a labour intensive crop. Assam and West Bengal are two states where tea is widely grown.

17. Name an area of wheat cultivation in India and state why it is suitable for the cultivation of wheat. (Mention two reasons) *(ICSE 2003)*

Ans. Haryana is an area of wheat cultivation in India. It is suitable for the cultivation of wheat because

(i) wheat requires rainfall around 50 cm–100 cm and the above area fulfils the requirement.

(ii) wheat needs a temperature range of 10° to 15°C at sowing time and higher temperature at harvesting time. Haryana fulfils this temperature requirement.

18. Which state is the largest producer of sugarcane in India ? Mention the climatic conditions, needed for the cultivation of this crop. *(ICSE 2002)*

Ans. Uttar Pradesh is the largest producer of sugarcane in India. It requires hot and humid climate with a temperature of 21° C to 27° C and an annual rainfall between 75 cm and 100 cm.

19. Name one area in India, where jute is cultivated widely. *(ICSE 2002)*

Ans. In West Bengal, jute is cultivated widely.

20. Mention why there is a concentration of this crop in the area mentioned by you. *(ICSE 2002)*

Ans. Favourable climatic conditions like temperature and rainfall coupled with cheap abundant labour make suitable conditions for the growing of the crop here.

21. Mention a leading beverage crop of India. *(ICSE 2002)*

Ans. Tea is a leading beverage crop of India.

22. What is a Rabi crop? Is wheat a Rabi or Kharif crop? In which state of India is the largest amount of wheat grown? *(ICSE 2001)*

Ans. Rabi crop is sown in winter and harvested in March and April.

Wheat is a Rabi crop. Uttar Pradesh is the leading wheat producing state of India, accounting for about 34% of the total production in India.

23. State two important characteristics of Indian agriculture. *(ICSE 2001)*

Ans. Important characteristics of Indian agriculture are as follows

(i) Preponderance of food crops

(ii) Dependency upon monsoon

24. What is 'oil cake'? Name any two non-edible oilseeds grown in India. *(ICSE 2001)*

Ans. Oil cake is the solid residue that is left after oil from oilseeds has been extracted.

Castor and linseed are non-edible oilseeds grown in India.

25. What are tea's requirements in terms of soil and rainfall? *(ICSE 2000)*

Ans In tea production well-drained, deep, friable loamy soil is required. Tea needs a range of 10°C to 35°C temperature with 150 cm to 250 cm rainfall.

26. Name one crop each with which the following processes are associated *(ICSE 2000)*

(i) Retting (ii) Ginning

Ans. (i) Jute (ii) Cotton

27. After oil extraction, what other uses can the oilseeds be put to? *(ICSE 2000)*

Ans. After oil extraction, the oilseeds can be made into oil cakes and fed to cattle.

2 Marks Questions

1. Differentiate between intensive farming and extensive farming. *(ICSE 2023, ICSE Specimen 2023)*

Or Differentiate between intensive and extensive farming.

Or Differentiate between subsistence farming and commercial farming. *(ICSE Specimen 2017)*

Ans. Refer to Q. 1 of very short answer questions.

2. Give a reason for each of the following. *(ICSE 2023)*

(i) Agriculture sector in India needs the support of irrigation.

(ii) Well irrigation is a popular means of irrigation in Northern India.

Ans. (i) Irrigation is important to a country like India for its agricultural sector because rainfall here is seasonal in nature. It is limited to four months of a year.

(ii) Well irrigation is a popular means of irrigation in Northern India due to following reasons

(a) The ground water level is within easy reach in Northern India.

(b) It has sufficient availability of sweet ground water.

3. Distinguish between Inundation canal and Perennial canal. *(ICSE 2023)*

Ans. The differences between inundation and perennial canals are

Inundation canal	Perennial canal
The supply of water is uncertain.	The water supply is certain.
It irrigates only low-lying areas of land.	It irrigates all types of areas of land.

4. Mention two problems faced by the Indian farmers. *(ICSE 2023)*

Or Mention two problems of Indian agriculture. *(ICSE Specimen 2018)*

Or Mention any two problems of agriculture in India. *(ICSE Semester-II 2022, 2011)*

Ans. Two problems of agriculture are as follows

(i) Small and fragmented landholdings.

(ii) Poor quality of seeds.

5. Mention two ways in which agriculture sector is important for India. *(ICSE Specimen Semester II 2022)*

Ans. Two ways in which agriculture sector is important for India are

(i) Agriculture sector provides employment to vast section of the population of our country.

(ii) It provides food and food products like rice, wheat milk, etc to human population and fodder for livestock.

6. (i) Name two agriculture seasons of India.

(ii) Name one crop that grows in each of the season mentioned by you. *(ICSE Specimen Semester II 2022)*

Ans. (i) Two agriculture seasons are Rabi and Kharif.

(ii) Wheat is a Rabi crop and Rice is a Kharif crop.

7. Mention two points of difference between subsistence farming and commercial farming. *(ICSE 2020)*

Or Differentiate between subsistence farming and commercial farming. *(ICSE Specimen 2017)*

Ans. The differences between subsistence agriculture and commercial agriculture are

Subsistence Agriculture	Commercial Agriculture
Done with primitive methods.	Done with modern methods.
Fulfils the farmer's own requirements.	Done for selling the products in the market.

8. Explain briefly the following terms. *(ICSE 2020)*

(i) Ginning (ii) Ratooning

Ans. (i) **Ginning** It is the process of separation of seeds and fibre from the raw material known as 'lint'. It is known as 'roller gins' in India.

(ii) **Ratooning** It is a method of cultivation of sugarcane. In this method, during the first harvest, the sugarcane is cut leaving a little bit of the stalk in the soil with the roots. The stalk soon puts out new shoots or ratoons.

The second or any other successive crop obtained from the roots of the leftover crop is called ratoon.

9. Mention two steps taken by the government to boost agricultural production in India. *(ICSE 2019)*

Ans. Steps taken by government to boost agricultural production in India are

- Introduction of Green Revolution in India and use of High Yielding Varieties of seeds (HYVs).
- Providing subsidy to farmers by reducing the cost of agricultural inputs like seeds, electricity, irrigation facility at subsidised rates.

10. With reference to the cultivation of tea, answer the following. *(ICSE 2018)*

(i) Why is tea grown on hill slopes?

(ii) Why tea bushes have to be pruned at regular intervals? *(ICSE 2017, 2010)*

Ans. (i) Tea grows on hill slopes because tea plantation demands evenly distributed rainfall with no water-logging issues. The hill slopes provide an easy drainage of the rainwater. Moreover, the tea plants grow well in the loamy soil which is found mostly over the hill slopes.

(ii) For answer, refer to Q. 6 (i) of very short answer questions.

Examiner's Comment

- The answers given by majority of the candidates reflected lack of understanding of the topic.
- Most of the candidates were able to write the two geographical conditions which suit the cultivation of rice.

Suggestions for Students

- The students should learn the correct range of temperature and the rainfall requirement of crops.
- Practice reasoning-type questions.

11. With reference to rice cultivation answer the following. *(ICSE 2018)*

(i) Why does the cultivation of rice require a lot of manual labour?

(ii) Mention two geographical conditions which suit the cultivation of rice.

Ans. (i) Rice cultivation is a complex activity that requires a series of processes to achieve the finished product. Therefore, a lot of manual labour is required like for seed selection to post harvesting methods.

(ii) For answer, refer to Q. 7 (ii) of very short answer questions.

12. What is mixed farming? Mention *any one* benefit of mixed farming. ***(ICSE 2017, 2004)***

Ans. Mixed farming is a cultivation of arable crops and the rearing of livestock on the same farm.
Its advantage is that it reduces dependence on external impacts like fertilisers because the crop and animal components in the farm support each other.

13. Give the geographical requirements for the cultivation of sugarcane. ***(ICSE 2017)***

Ans. Sugarcane can be grown either in tropical or sub-tropical region. It requires hot and humid climate with a temperature of 21°C to 27°C and annual rainfall between 75 cm and 100 cm. It can be grown on a variety of soils.

14. Name two non-edible oilseeds grown in India. State one use of each. ***(ICSE Specimen 2017)***

Ans. Two non-edible oilseeds grown in India are
(a) **Linseed** It is used for manufacturing paints and varnishes.
(b) **Castor seed** It is used as a lubricant in various machines.

15. Mention any two reasons for the importance of agriculture in India. ***(ICSE 2016)***

Ans. For answer, refer to Q. 3 of very short answer questions.

16. With reference to rice cultivation answer the following. ***(ICSE 2016)***
(i) Why does rice grow well in a soil with a clay like subsoil?
(ii) What is the advantage of growing rice in nurseries before it is transplanted?

Ans. (i) Rice is grown well in a clay like subsoil because this soil can easily be puddled into mud and retains moisture.
(ii) Rice is grown in nurseries before it is transplanted because at the time of transplantation seeds are removed and there is less wastage of seeds as in broadcasting.

17. Differentiate between a Rabi crop and a Kharif crop. ***(ICSE 2015)***

Ans. Differences between a Rabi crop and a Kharif crop are as follows

Wheat (a Rabi crop)	**Rice** (a Kharif crop)
Wheat is the main crop of Rabi season.	Rice is the main crop of Kharif season.
It requires an average temperature of 10°C to 15°C and 50-100 cm rainfall.	It can be grown in 16°C to 32°C temperature range and 150-200 cm rainfall.
It grows in fertile, friable, loamy alluvial soil of clayey composition.	It needs deep fertile dry or friable loam.

18. State an important difference between the climatic requirements for growing cotton and jute. ***(ICSE 2015)***

Ans. An important difference between the climatic requirements for growing cotton and jute is given below
Cotton Cotton needs 20°C to 30°C temperature range with 65 cm to 80 cm rainfall.
Jute It requires 25°C to 35°C temperature and an amount of 170 cm to 200 cm of rainfall.

3 Marks Questions

1. (i) Give one advantage of transplantation method of sowing rice. ***(ICSE 2023)***
(ii) Name any two pulses grown in India.

Ans. (i) An advantage of transplantation method is that transplanting ensures a uniform plant stand and gives the rice crop a head start over emerging weeds.
(ii) Bengal Gram (Desi Chana) and Pigeon Peas (Arhar / Toor) are grown in India.

2. (i) What is meant by 'Retting'? ***(ICSE 2023)***
(ii) What kind of soil is required for the cultivation of tea ?
(iii) Why is pruning necessary for tea plant?

Ans. (i) The retting process is associated with jute. It is a microbiological process of separating fibers from the stalk. In this process, the stems of the plants get softened and rotten in water to remove the sticky substance.
(ii) The tea crop can be grown using the alluvial, mountain and laterite soils.
(iii) Regular pruning is essential for tea bushes to maintain the height and diameter of the plant.

3. With reference to rice cultivation answer the following. ***(ICSE Specimen 2023)***
(i) Name a state that produces the largest quantity of rice.
(ii) Mention any *two* geographical conditions necessary for its growth.
(iii) Which is the best method for its cultivation?

Ans. (i) West Bengal is the state that produces the largest quantity of rice.

(ii) Two geographical conditions for rice are

(a) It needs 18° C to 32° C temperature.

(b) It needs rainfall of 150 cm to 300 cm.

(iii) The best method of rice cultivation is transplantation. In this method, seeds are first sown in nursery and the seedlings are transplanted to the main field once they show 3-4 leaves.

4. (i) Mention two reasons why sugarcane cultivation is gaining importance in Peninsular India. ***(ICSE Specimen 2023)***

(ii) State one problem of sugarcane growers of Uttar Pradesh.

Ans. (i) Two reasons why sugarcane cultivation is gaining importance in peninsular India are as follows

(a) The tropical climate and black soil of Peninsular India result in higher yield per unit hectare of land.

(b) There is long crushing season for sugarcane crop in Peninsular India.

(ii) One problem of sugarcane growers of Uttar Pradesh is that they are depended on canal irrigation for water requirements. The canals are often non-perennial and so the supply of water is uncertain.

5. With reference to rice cultivation, answer the following. ***(ICSE Semester II 2022)***

(i) Name the soil found suitable for its growth.

(ii) Name the state that is the largest producer of this crop in India.

(iii) In which cropping season is it generally grown in India?

Ans. (i) The soil which is found suitable for the growth of rice is deep fertile clay or friable loam soil.

(ii) The state that is the largest producer of rice crop in India is West Bengal.

(iii) Rice is generally grown in India in Kharif cropping season.

6. (i) Name the state that is the largest producer of sugarcane in India. ***(ICSE Semester II 2022)***

(ii) Why more than two ratoon crops are not advisable for sugarcane farmers?

(iii) What is Zaid cropping season?

Ans. (i) Uttar Pradesh is the largest producer of sugarcane in India.

(ii) Due to following reasons, more than two ratoon of crops are not advisable for sugarcane farmers

- It yields thinner canes with lower sugar content.
- It increases risk of pest and diseases.

(iii) Zaid cropping season is a summer season which falls for a short time period between Kharif and rabi seasons. It mainly falls in March to June.

7. With reference to wheat cultivation answer the following.

(i) Name the soil found suitable for its growth.

(ii) Name the state that is the largest producer of this crop in India.

(iii) Why is this crop not grown in Southern parts of India? ***(ICSE Specimen Semester II 2022)***

Ans. (i) Well drained, fertile, loamy, alluvial soils of clayey type is best suitable for wheat crop.

(ii) Uttar Pradesh is the largest producer of wheat crop.

(iii) Wheat is not grown in Southern parts of India because these regions have very high temperature even in winters.

8. (i) Name the largest producer of tea in India.

(ii) What is ginning? ***(ICSE Specimen Semester II 2022)***

(iii) Why is pruning essential for tea crop?

Ans. (i) The largest producer of tea in India is Assam state.

(ii) Ginning is associated with cotton. Ginning is a process by which fibre is separated from the raw material. Earlier it was done by hands but now machines are also used for ginning.

(iii) Pruning is essential for tea leaves because it determines the productivity of tea bushes. Delay in pruning decreases the size and weight of growing tea shoots.

9. With reference to the wheat crop, answer the following questions. ***(ICSE 2020)***

(i) Name the state which is the leading producer of this crop in India.

(ii) Mention the climatic condition found suitable for the cultivation of this crop.

Ans. (i) Uttar Pradesh is the leading producer of wheat crop in India.

(ii) The climatic conditions for the cultivation of wheat are

- **Temperature** Wheat requires an average temperature of about 10°C to 15°C at the time of sowing. But higher temperature (20° C to 25° C) at the time of ripening and harvesting, though sudden rise of temperature is harmful.
- **Rainfall** Wheat requires rainfall of about 50 cm to 100 cm during growing period. Too much rainfall is harmful for wheat while the shortage of rain may dry the crop.

10. Study the picture given below and answer the questions that follow. ***(ICSE 2019)***

(i) Mention the climatic condition that is suitable for the cultivation of this crop.

(ii) Name the state that produces the largest amount of this crop.

(iii) In which cropping season is the crop grown in India?

Ans. (i) This crop is cotton. Cotton needs mild, cool and comparatively dry climate having temperature 21°C to 27°C and abundant sunshine is necessary during its growth period. A long period of 200 (frost free) days are essential for the plant to mature. Cotton plant need a moderate rainfall of 50 cm to 80 cm which should be well distributed throughout the year.

(ii) Gujarat is the largest producer of cotton.

(iii) Cotton is grown in India as a Kharif crop.

11. Give a geographical reason for each of the following. ***(ICSE 2019)***

(i) Cultivation of wheat is confined to the Northern part of India

(ii) Practicing mixed farming gives security to farmers.

(iii) Ratoon cropping is gaining popularity among sugarcane cultivators.

Ans. (i) Cultivation of wheat is confined to the Northern part of India because wheat requires an average temperature of about 10°C to 15°C at the time of sowing but higher temperature at the time of ripening and harvesting (20° C to 25° C). The winter temperature and rainfall of North India is more favourable for wheat production so it is confined to Northern part of India.

(ii) The practice of cultivation of crops as well as raising of animals/livestock simultaneously is popularly known as 'mixed farming'. Mixed farming is very helpful for the farmers because even if the crops fail they can rely on the rearing of animals for income.

(iii) Ratoon cropping is gaining popularity among sugarcane cultivators because in ratoon cropping, the crops are not required to be planted again. The ratoons have comparatively low maturation period, cheaper as planting of crops is not needed. As the successive crop goes on, its productivity decreases, therefore only one or two ratoon crops are generally harvested.

Examiner's Comment

- Some candidates related wheat cultivation being confined to North India to alluvial soil. They did not mention the correct geographical reason for cultivation of wheat confined to the northern part of India.
- Some candidates gave the meaning of mixed farming instead of its advantages.
- Some candidates did not mention the crop associated with Ratoon cropping.

Suggestions for Students

- Guide students to mention the name of the crop for those questions in which any term related to it is asked.
- Clearly explain terms such as ratooning, ginning, retting, etc.
- Train the students to write the answers to the point, using correct terms, in order to explain a concept.

12. Give the geographical requirement for the cultivation of coffee in Karnataka. ***(ICSE Specimen 2018)***

Ans. The geographical requirements for the cultivation of coffee in Karnataka are as following:

(i) It requires high temperature, ranging from 15ºC to 28ºC through the year.

(ii) Coffee plant requires a rainfall of about 150 to 250cm which should be well distributed all the year round.

(iii) Coffee plant grows well in deep, porous soil having high humus content and minerals like iron and calcium.

13. Give a geographic reason for each of the following.
(i) Millets are known as dry crops. ***(ICSE Specimen 2018)***
(ii) Pulses are grown as rotational crops.
(iii) Jute stems must be retted.

Ans. (i) Millets are important crops in the semiarid tropics of Asia and Africa. Millets are grown in regions of low rainfall and poor soil and thus, they are known as dry crops.
(ii) Pulses are grown as rotational crops because of their leguminous characteristics. This unique characteristic of pulses restores the soil fertility by fixing atmospheric nitrogen.
(iii) Retting is a processing technique of jute, under which the bundles of jute are immersed in soft running water for 2 or 3 weeks to remove fibre from the stalk.

14. Give a geographical reason for each of the following. ***(ICSE 2018)***
(i) Cotton is a labour intensive crop.
(ii) Jute is retted after it has been harvested.
(iii) The growing of pulses is important in India.

Ans. (i) Cotton is a labour intensive crop because its processes like picking and ginning are the main activities which are mostly done by hand.
(ii) Retting is a processing method of jute under which bundles of jute are immersed in soft running water for 2 to 3 weeks to remove fibre from the stalk. Therefore, jute is retted after harvesting.
(iii) The growing of pulses is important in India because pulses are rich in protein and found to be a main source of protein for vegetarian people.
It is also second most important Indian diet after cereals.

15. (i) Why is agriculture important in India? ***(ICSE 2018)***
(ii) Name the two main agricultural seasons in India.
(iii) What is mixed farming?

Ans. (i) For answer, refer to Q. 3 of very short answer questions.
(ii) The two main agricultural seasons in India are Rabi season and Kharif season.
(iii) Refer to Q. 12 of 2 marks questions.

16. Explain the following terms and name the crop with which each is associated ***(ICSE 2017)***
(i) Retting (ii) Ratooning
(iii) Ginning

Ans. (i) **Retting** It is a microbiological process in which the jute bundles are submerged in soft, clean water for 2-3 weeks. It loosens the outer bark and helps in removal of the fibre from the stalk. It is associated with Jute.
(ii) **Ratooning** Sugarcane Research Institute of Coimbatore introduced this method in which after the first crop the sugarcane is cut leaving the root intact in the soil. The lower part of the stem which is left in the soil is well fertilised and begins to grow again. Ratoon crop is the second or any other succession crop obtained from the root and leftover in the field after the first crop.
(iii) **Ginning** The process of to separate the seeds from the cotton fibre is known as ginning. Perfect ginning operation would be performed if the separation of fibres from seed was effected without the slightest injury to either seeds or to the fibre.

17. (i) What are the two main crop seasons of India? Give one example of a crop grown in each season. ***(ICSE Specimen 2017)***
(ii) State the method of cultivation of growing wheat.

Ans. (i) There are mainly two agricultural seasons in India, which are as follows
- Kharif (summer crop) - Rice is the main crop.
- Rabi (winter crop) - Wheat is the main crop.

(ii) Wheat is one of the most important foodgrains in India. Sowing of wheat is done after the rains, when the soil is moist. The fields are ploughed and the seeds are sown by broadcasting, dibbling or drilling. Harvesting is done before it is too hot, *i.e.,* in the months of March or April. Harvesting is done by sickle, although recently machines are being used in some areas.

18. (i) Which state in India is the largest producer of coffee? ***(ICSE Specimen 2017)***
(ii) State the climatic conditions that favour the cultivation of coffee.
(iii) Mention one problem faced by the sugarcane cultivators in India.

Ans. (i) Karnataka is the largest producer of coffee, as it produces nearly 60% of the total coffee production in India.

(ii) The climatic conditions that favour the cultivation of coffee are as follows
- Annual rainfall ranging from 125-200 cm well distributed throughout the year.
- Temperature between 15° C and 28° C throughout the year.
- The plants should be protected from direct sunlight and from hot dry winds.

(iii) One problem faced by sugarcane farmers is that it is a soil exhausting crop. So a large quantity of fertiliser is required which is very expensive.

19. Study the picture given below and answer the questions that follow. *(ICSE 2016)*

(i) Name one state, where this crop grows well.
(ii) Why are mostly women employed to harvest it?
(iii) Mention two geographical conditions suitable for the cultivation of this crop.

Ans. (i) The picture shown is of tea plantation is grown well in Assam and West Bengal.
(ii) Both men and women are employed in the field but women are employed mostly to harvest because womens are temperamentally suited to the job and men take care of loading, unloading, packaging, etc.
(iii) The geographical conditions suitable for the cultivation of this crop are ideal temperature for its growth is 25°C to 35°C and alternative cool and warm waves.

20. Explain briefly the following terms. *(ICSE 2016)*
(i) Shifting cultivation
(ii) Bud grafting
(iii) Oil cake

Ans. (i) Shifting cultivation is also known as jhum cultivation. In this region, people clear a patch of forested land by burning and crops are grown on it for 2-3 years until soil loses its fertility.
(ii) Bud grafting is done by inserting a strip of bank containing a bud from a high yield plant under the bark of a young seeding and leaving it till they become united after three to four weeks. Then, the old seedling stem is sown off and the grafted bud grows to form a new plant.
(iii) Oil cake is the solid residue that is left after oil from oilseeds that has been extracted. It is used as cattle feed or fertiliser.

21. Give the geographic term for each of the following. *(ICSE 2015)*
(i) Cultivation of sugarcane from the root stock of the cane which has been cut.
(ii) The residue left behind after the crushing of oil seeds.
(iii) The process by which latex is converted into a thick, spongy mass by adding acetic acid or formic acid.

Ans. Geographic term for each of the following
(i) Ratooning (ii) Oil cake
(iii) Coagulate

22. Give a geographic reason for each of the following. *(ICSE 2015)*
(i) Tea is cultivated on hill slopes.
(ii) The yield per hectare of sugarcane is higher in the Southern states.
(iii) Pulses are important food crops.

Ans (i) For answer, refer to 10 (i) of 2 marks questions.
(ii) Because of the presence of black lava soil with high fertility and absence of loo during summer and frost during winter in the Southern states helps in better growth.
(iii) Because pulses are a leguminous crops which increase the nitrogen content of the soil.

23. Mention three differences in the geographical conditions and cultivation of rice and wheat. *(ICSE 2014)*

Ans. For answer, refer to Q. 17 of 2 marks questions.

24. Give a geographical reason for each of the following. *(ICSE 2014)*
(i) Cotton grows widely in Maharashtra.
(ii) Clonal planting is the best method for tea propagation.
(iii) Oilseeds are an important commercial crop grown in India.

Ans. (i) Black soil is widely found in Maharashtra and is best suited for cotton.
(ii) It helps to produce superior quality, better yield and special flavour of the mother plants.
(iii) Oilseeds provide raw material to various industries which extract the oil for use.

25. Explain in brief the following. *(ICSE 2013)*

(i) Retting (ii) Ginning

(iii) Broadcasting

Ans. (i) For answer, refer to ans 16 (i) of 3 marks questions.

(ii) For answer, refer to ans 16 (iii) of 3 marks questions.

(iii) Broadcasting is the scattering of seeds by hand over the soil.

26. Explain the following terms. *(ICSE 2011)*

(i) Withering

(ii) Plantation Farming

(iii) Drilling

Ans. (i) Withering involves spreading tea leaves over withering racks and blowing air on them to reduce their moisture content and make them soft and flexible.

(ii) Plantation farming is a type of farming in which a single crop is grown on large estates which are scientifically managed. Crops are grown mainly for sale purpose.

(iii) Drilling is a method of sowing seeds at regular intervals through a bamboo shaft attached to the plough which makes furrows.

27. Answer the following questions with references to sugarcane *(ICSE 2010)*

(i) Mention two different ways in which it is propagated.

(ii) Why is a lot of labour required for its cultivation?

(iii) Why must the sugar mills be near the sugar fields?

Ans. (i) The sett method and ratooning are two different ways used to propagate sugarcane.

(ii) At the time of cultivation, furrows and cuttings are made and manuring is done two or three times. Thus, a lot of labour is required for sugarcane cultivation.

(iii) It is because, sugarcane contains sucrose and if it is not processed within 24hours the content of sucrose will start reducing, thus reducing the sugar output.

28. (i) The yield of sugarcane is higher in the Deccan. Give two reasons for this. *(ICSE 2009)*

(ii) Give one advantage and disadvantage of ratoon cropping.

Ans. (i) Two reasons for higher yield of sugarcane in the Deccan are

- Black lava soil with high fertility and water retention is favourable for this crop which is found in Deccan plateau.
- Absence of loo during summer and frost during winter in the Deccan helps in better growth.
- Due to this sugarcane can be grown throughout the year.

(ii) The advantage and disadvantage of ratoon croping are as follows

Advantage	Disadvantage
It is labour and time saving.	It yields thinner canes with lower sucrose content.

29. Answer the following questions. *(ICSE 2008)*

(i) What are the geographical conditions necessary for the cultivation of groundnuts?

(ii) What climatic conditions adversely affect the groundnuts crop?

(iii) Name two non-edible oilseeds grown.

Ans. (i) Groundnuts require tropical or sub-tropical climate with a temperature range of 20°C to 25°C and rainfall between 50 cm and 70 cm annually.

(ii) Continuous rain, stagnant water, frost or drought adversely affect groundnut crops.

(iii) Castor and linseed are two non-edible oilseeds grown.

30. State three important aspects of the Japanese method of rice cultivation. *(ICSE 2005)*

Ans. Important aspects of the Japanese method of rice cultivation are as follows

(i) Use of good quality seeds which are of the high yield variety.

(ii) Sowing the seeds in raised nursery beds.

(iii) Transplanting the seedlings in rows to make weeding and fertilising easier.

31. Give two reasons for pulses being grown extensively in India. Name any two pulses. *(ICSE 2005)*

Ans. Pulses are grown extensively in India because

(i) It forms a major part of the diet of vegetarians, supplying their requirement of proteins.

(ii) It is a leguminous crop which increases the nitrogen content of the soil. Two pulses are gram (chana) and tur (arhar).

32. Answer the following. **(ICSE 2005)**

(i) Name the most important fibre crop in West Bengal.

(ii) Describe two geographical conditions which favour the growth of this crop.

Ans. (i) Jute is the most important fibre crop in West Bengal.

(ii) It requires the following geographical conditions

(a) Temperature ranging from 24°C to 35°C.

(b) 170 cm to 200 cm of rainfall.

33. Name the state which is the largest producer of castor seed. State one important use each of its oil and oil cake. **(ICSE 2004)**

Ans. Gujarat is the largest producer of castor seed.

Important use of castor seed is as follows

- Its oil is useful as a lubricant in soap making and tanning of leather.
- Its oil cake is useful as a fertiliser.

34. Why is tea cultivated on hill slopes? What are the climatic conditions required for growing tea? **(ICSE 2001)**

Ans Tea is cultivated on hill slopes, because the tea plant cannot withstand waterlogging. The climatic conditions required for growing tea are temperature ranging from 10°C to 35°C and annual rainfall between 150 cm and 250 cm.

35. Answer the followings, in the context of the Indian agriculture. **(ICSE 2001)**

(i) Mention two features which reflect a shift from subsistence farming to commercial farming.

(ii) Give two reasons why the yield of Indian agriculture is low as compared to the world.

Ans. (i) The two features are

(a) Subsistence farming is generally dominated by wet paddy cultivation and crops other than paddy, whereas in commercial grain farming, wheat is the principal crop though other crops like – corn, barley and oats are also grown. This is now happening in India.

(b) In subsistence farming, farmers work with the help of family labour leading to intensive use of land whereas in commercial grain cultivation, entire operations of cultivation from ploughing to harvesting are mechanised. This is also gradually happening in India, particularly in Punjab.

(ii) The yield of Indian agriculture is low because of

(a) lack of modern techniques.

(b) small and fragmented land holdings.

36. State two characteristics of plantation agriculture. **(ICSE 2000)**

Ans. For answer, refer to Q. 9 of very short answer questions.

37. Which state of India is the leading producer of groundnut? Give three uses of groundnuts. **(ICSE 2000)**

Ans. Gujarat is the leading producer of groundnut in India.

Uses of groundnuts are as follows

(i) It is used for extracting oil.

(ii) It is used as food and after extraction of the oil as fodder.

(iii) It is used for making medicinal emulsions, soaps, etc.

CHAPTER TEST

01 Mark Questions

1. Which of the following states is the largest rice producer in India ?

(a) Uttar Pradesh (b) Bihar
(c) West Bengal (c) Odisha

2. .... is the largest cotton producing state of India.

(a) Jharkhand (b) Telangana
(c) Maharashtra (d) Gujarat

3. Which state is the largest producer of sugarcane in India ?

(a) Bihar (b) Uttar Pradesh
(c) Karnataka (d) Chhattisgarh

4. Wheat is a .... crop grown in India extensively.

(a) Rabi (b) Kharif
(c) Zaid (d) Cash

Answers

1. (c) | 2. (d) | 3. (b) | 4. (a)

10 Marks Questions

5. (i) What are Rabi crops ? Give examples.

(ii) When are kharif crops sown and harvested ?

(iii) India is the second largest producer of tea. What are the important factors required for its growth?

(iv) What are Cash crops ? what is its significance ?

6. (i) Distinguish between intensive commercial farming and extensive commercial farming .

(ii) What are the geographical requirements for the growth of wheat in India?

(iii) Mention the problems faced by agriculture sector in India.

(iv) Mention the suitable climatic conditions for the cultivation of cotton in India. Name the leading producer also.

7. (i) Differentiate between the subsistence farming and commercial farming.

(ii) Define the following terms mentioned below.

(a) Ratooning (b) Ginning

(iii) Why is agriculture an important - activity in India?

(iv) Give a geographical reason for each of the following.

(a) Cotton is grown well in black soil.

(b) The yield per hectare of sugarcane is higher in the Southern states.

(c) Clonal planting is the best method for tea propagation.

8. (i) Which state is the leading producer of groundnut in India ? Mention its uses.

(ii) State any two characteristics of Cash crops.

(iii) Amswer the following questions with reference to Sugarcane.

(a) Mention the two ways in which it is propagated.

(b) Why the sugar mills should be located near the sugarcane fields?

(c) Why there is a lot of requirement of labour for its cultivation ?

(iv) Explain the following terms.

(a) Retting

(b) Shifting cultivation

(c) Broadcasting

06

Manufacturing Industries and Waste Management

TREND ANALYSIS 3 YEARS

Average No. of Questions Across all Sets

Topic	Category (Year)	2023	2020	2019
TOPIC 01 Industries	1 Mark	2	–	–
	2 Marks	2	2	1
	3 Marks	4	2	2
TOPIC 02 Waste Management	1 Mark	1	–	–
	2 Marks	3	2	–
	3 Marks	4	1	2

Industries

The process of transformation of natural resources into a finished, ready to use product, utilising the full potential by processing of the resource is called **manufacturing**. Industries are places where these manufacturing processes take place. One of the apparent yardsticks of a country's economic development is the extent of its industrial development.

Importance of Manufacturing Industries

Importance of manufacturing industries is discussed below

- Manufacturing industries help in **modernising agriculture**; which forms the backbone of our economy.
- Apart from this, manufacturing industries also reduce the heavy dependence of people on agricultural income. This becomes possible because of creation of new jobs in secondary and tertiary sectors.
- Industrial development helps in eradication of unemployment and poverty.
- Export of manufactured goods expands trade and commerce and brings in much needed foreign exchange.
- A country with high level of manufacturing activities becomes prosperous.

Classification of Industries

Industries are classified on several basis. Some of them are as follows

On the Basis of Bulk and Raw Materials

(i) **Agro-based Industries** These types of industries use **agriculture products** as their raw material. Such as cotton is used in textile industries, sugarcane is used in sugar industries. These provide employment in rural areas. These industries mostly produce consumer goods like jam, sugar, etc.

(ii) **Mineral-based Industries** These types of industries use **minerals** as their raw material such as iron-ore is used in iron and steel industry, gypsum is used in cement industry. These industries provide employment to both rural and urban areas.

These industries produce goods to be used by other industries as well as consumer goods like iron and steel, heavy machinery, utensils, etc.

(iii) **Pastoral Based and Forest Based Industries** These industries use **animal and forest products** as their raw material. For example, shoe, paper, rubber, leather industries.

(iv) **Marine Based Industries** These types of industries use **marine or sea products** as their raw material. For example, fish processing industries.

On the Basis of their Role

(i) **Basic or Key Industries** These are the industries which supply their products as raw materials to another industries. For example, iron and steel industries, etc.

(ii) **Consumer Industries** These are the industries that produce goods for direct consumer use, For example, sugar, electronics, etc.

On the Basis of Investment

(i) **Small Scale Industries** These industries require less capital investment and labour force.

(ii) **Large Scale Industries** These industries require high amount of capital investment and labour force. For example, iron and steel industry, shipbuilding, automobile, etc.

On the Basis of Ownership

(i) **Public Sector** These industries are owned and operated by government agencies such as SAIL, BHEL, etc.

(ii) **Private Sector** These industries are owned and run by individuals such as Reliance petrochemicals.

(iii) **Joint Sector** These industries are owned and operated by both private and government agencies.

(iv) **Cooperative Sector** These industries are operated generally by the provider of raw material and seller of products. For example, sugar industries in Maharashtra and Amul in Gujarat.

On the Basis of Bulk and weight of Raw Material and Finished Goods

(i) **Heavy Industries** These industries uses heavy and bulky raw material and finished goods are also heavy and bulky. For example, iron and steel industries, etc.

(ii) **Light Industries** These industries use raw material and finished good is also light. For example, matches, toy handicraft industries, etc.

Agro-Based Industries

Agro based industries consists of the following

Textile Industries

Textiles is a vast term, which includes several fibres like cotton, jute, wool, silk, etc. Textile industries happened to be the **first manufacturing industries** in India.

Cotton Textile Industry

Cotton is one of the principal crops of the country. The cotton textile industry has an overwhelming presence in the Indian economy. A large number of cotton mills are situated in Maharashtra, Gujarat, Tamil Nadu and some other states.

Information about these mills statewise is given below

Maharashtra

Maharashtra is the most important cotton cloth producing state. That is why, it is called **Cottonopolis of India**. It generates about 40% of the mill cloth in India.

Reasons for Concentration of Textile Industries around Mumbai

(i) The rich hinterland and black soil or regur soil help in the growth of raw cotton.

(ii) Cheap power is available from the Tata Hydroelectric System.

(iii) Skilled and unskilled labour are available from the nearby areas.

(iv) The humid climate is ideal for the cotton yarn.

(v) Mumbai's location as an international port has helped making the import of long-staple cotton and machinery and export of finished goods possible.

(vi) Banking facilities are easily available as well.

(vii) Mumbai also has an advantage of an early start and has the oldest cotton industries.

Note Apart from Mumbai, the cotton mills in Maharashtra are situated in Sholapur, Pune, Kolhapur, Nagpur, Aurangabad and Jalgaon.

Gujarat

Gujarat is the second largest producer of cotton textiles in India. Ahmedabad is the largest centre, where cotton is readily available and where 73 out of the 118 mills of Gujarat are located. That is why, **Ahmedabad** is called the **Manchester of India**.

Reasons for Concentration of Textile Industries in Ahmedabad

(i) It has a humid climate which is ideal for cotton thread.

(ii) It has the advantage of being near both Kandla and Mumbai ports for export and import.

(iii) It is well connected by both road and rail to these ports.

(iv) Most of the mills produce cheap cloth, which find ready market among the poor masses of India.

(v) Cheap hydroelectric power is easily available.

Note Apart from Ahmedabad, textile centres in Gujarat are also situated in Vadodara, Surat, Rajkot, Porbandar, Moris and Bhavnagar.

Tamil Nadu

It is called the **Manchester of South India**. Mills here are small in size. Therefore, the production of cotton clothes is less. Tamil Nadu produces nearly 6% of the mill cloth of India. Most of the mills manufacture yarn for the handloom industry.

Other important centres are Madurai, Salem, Tirunelveli, Tiruchchirappalli, Tuticorin and Ramanathapuram. Further, Tamil Nadu accounts for nearly 1/3rd of the total yarn production of the country.

West Bengal

Kolkata is the most important textile centre in this state. Having a humid climate and an access to the coal from Raniganj with a local labour supply aids in the textile manufacturing process.

Uttar Pradesh

Most of the cotton mills have developed in the Western part of Uttar Pradesh. Kanpur is the largest centre. Moradabad, Lucknow, Modinagar, Etawah, Agra and Saharanpur are some other centres.

Note Other states known for their cotton industries are Andhra Pradesh, Kerala and Karnataka in the South. In the North, Punjab, Haryana and Rajasthan are important states in this regard.

Problems of Cotton Textile Industries

(i) **Scarcity of Raw Material** Most of the region grows short staple cotton in India. India has shortage of long staple cotton. Thus, long staple cotton is imported.

(ii) **Stiff Competition** Mill made textiles face stiff competition from the powerloom sector as well as synthetic products.

(iii) **Obsolete Machinery** After Independence, there were no changes in technology, which reduced the productivity further. Already 177 mills are going in loss and have been declared as sick.

(iv) **Low Productivity of Labour** In India, labour productivity is low as compared to other developed countries.

(v) **Problem of Availability** Production of cotton depends upon the cultivation of cotton crop which is seasonal. So it is not available throughout the year.

Silk Industries

- The art of rearing silkworms for silk production is called sericulture. The raw material is produced by silkworms reared on the mulberry bush. Silk industry is small scale industry and it does not require high capital investment and labour.
- Sericulture industry has two sectors i.e. **Mulberry** and **Non-Mulberry**. Mulberry sector produces 90% of natural silk. The areas of production are Karnataka, West Bengal, Jammu and Kashmir, Himachal Pradesh, Uttar Pradesh (Varanasi) and Tamil Nadu (Kanchipuram).
- **Karnataka** is **largest producer** of silk. It accounts for 70% of Indian silk. Mysore, Bangalore, Tumkur, Belgam, Kolar are important centres.
- Jammu and Kashmir silk production centres are in Anantnag, Baramula and Udhampur. **Srinagar** is the largest centre for silk manufacturing, as here automatic machinery is used.
- Non-mulberry silk such as **eri, muga** and **tassar** are produced in Assam, Bihar, Odisha, Meghalaya and Madhya Pradesh.
- Good quality of tassar silk is only produced in Madhya Pradesh and West Bengal. Muga silk also called pat in Assam is also used for ceremonial dress by local people.

Reasons for Concentration of Silk Industries in Karnataka

(i) Good climatic conditions i.e., temperature ranges from 16°C to 31°C.

(ii) Availability of mulberry plant.

(iii) Availability of soft water free from alkali salts and iron.

Problems of Silk Industry

- It is facing tough competition from artificial silk which is cheaper and needs less maintenance.
- The import of cheaper and better quality silk from China is proving to be very harmful for the Indian silk industry.
- The fluctuation in the prices of raw silk has an adverse effect on the silk industry.
- As compared to advanced countries like Japan, China, we do not have systematic testing and grading of silk.
- Latest and modern technology is required for increasing the production.

Sugar Industry

It is India's second largest agro-based industry. In the last five decades, India's sugar share has gone up from 5% to 13% in global sugar production. The sugar mills in India are uniquely positioned. Since, sugarcane production and processing in India has been practiced for many years.

There are various by-products which are produced during and after processes of sugar making. Some of them are

(i) **Molasses** It is a kind of dark brown syrup that drains from sugar during the process of manufacture. It is used in making alcohol, wine, fertiliser, etc.

(ii) **Bagasse** It is the rejected sugarcane left after being crushed and is important to make cardboards.

(iii) **Filter Mud** The precipitated impurities contained in the cane juice after removal by filtration, form a cake of varying moisture. Content called filter mud. It is used for making wax and shoe polish.

Factors Necessary for the Setting Up of Sugar Industry

- Sugarcane can be grown on a variety of soils, but alluvial clayey loams of the Indo-Gangetic plains are ideal for its growth. In South India it is grown on black soil, brown or reddish loams and laterites.
- Sugarcane needs an average temperature ranging from 20° C to 30° C. It needs a rainfall of about 75 cm to 120 cm. Sugarcane is a heavy and perishable raw material and therefore, it has to be crushed within 24 hours. That is why most of the mills are situated near farmlands.

Distribution of Sugar Industries in India

Sugar industries are distributed in all over India. Maharashtra is the leading producer of sugar in India followed by Uttar Pradesh, Bihar, Tamil Nadu, Karnataka, Punjab, Haryana, Andhra Pradesh, etc.

Northern India is a traditional producer of sugar in India. However, sugar mills of Southern India has shown growth in recent years and many states has emerged as leading states. Following reasons are responsible for this changing trend

(i) Crushing season is longer in Southern India.

(ii) Geographical conditions like temperature, rainfall and soil are more suitable to grow sugarcane in Peninsular India.

(iii) Sugar mills are managed by cooperatives so farmers get more profit as they are more efficient.

(iv) Content of sucrose is high in sugarcane grown in Peninsular India.

Problems Faced by the Sugar Industry

(i) **Low and Irregular Supply of Raw Material** The yield per hectare of sugarcane is very low as compared to other sugarcane producing areas in the world. This is because of irregular supply of raw material.

(ii) **Fluctuation in Sugarcane Output** This happens due to the erratic nature of monsoon. It is a seasonal crop.

(iii) **Old and Obsolete Machinery** Low production of sugar is also because of its traditional means of production. The machinery requires to be replaced with modern machinery.

(iv) **Small and Uneconomic Size of the Sugar Mills** Many of the sugar mills have a very small capacity of 1000 to 15000 tonnes per day.

(v) **Imbalanced Distribution of Sugar Mills** White favourable conditions for the sugar industry are found in South India, the concentration of the industry is in the North. Most of the mills are located in Uttar Pradesh and Maharashtra with 60% of the production coming from these two states. Also, as mills are situated far from the fields, the cost of transportation increases the cost of production.

Mineral Based Industry

Mineral based industries consist of the following

Iron and Steel Industry

The **first iron and steel industry** was established in India in 1873. The real development began after 1907, when the Tata Iron and Steel Company (TISCO) was set up at Jamshedpur. Most of the important industries such as automobile, locomotives, rail tracks, ship-building, machine tools and the manufacturing of defence equipment depend on the iron and steel industry. This industry determines the level of growth in the economy as industrialisation depends on it. Therefore, it is known as the **Basic Industry** or **backbone of Modern Industrial Economy**.

Types of Steel Plants

There are two types of steel plants which are as follows

Integrated Steel Plants The industrial units in which all the processes from providing raw materials to the conversion of steel rolling, etc, are all done at one place are called integrated steel plants.

Mini Steel Plants Mini steel plants use sponge-iron and scarp metal as raw material and melt it in electric furnaces and turned into steel. The steel is then made into various products. These plants produce mild steel, alloy steel and stainless steel.

There are 10 integrated steel plants and 173 mini steel-plants in the country. Presently, India is the 4th largest producer of steel in the world. The iron and steel industry is controlled by both private and public sectors but in India, the major industries of iron and steel are mostly in the public sector. This is because the privately owned firms cannot provide the large investments needed by this industry.

The mini steel plants require less investment so it is owned by private sector also. These plants use electric furnace instead of coal and use scrap metal so they also recycle the metals. These plants mostly cater to the local needs of the people and provide small utility goods.

Mini steel plant have following advantages

(i) Mini steel plants are **eco-friendly**. They are less polluted because they use scrap iron or sponge iron in a furnace.

(ii) These plant use electric arc furnace which conserve coal.

(iii) It requires **small capital investment.**

(iv) It caters to the local need of the market and cost of transport in their case is less.

Due to their advantages mini steel plants are becoming popular.

Major Iron and Steel Plants in India

Tata Steel Company

It is the **oldest** and **largest** steel industry of India. It is named after Jamshedji Tata. Its production was started in 1911. It is located at **Tata Nagar** near Jamshedpur in **Jharkhand**.

Favourable Factors

- It is near to the rivers Kharkai and Subarnarekha.
- It is near to the coalfields of Jharia.
- It is near to Sundergarh in Odisha and Singhbhum in Jharkhand for flux materials.
- The cheap labour is available.
- Due to well-developed road and rail link to major cities.
- It is near to the Kolkata port.

2. Rourkela Steel Plant

This plant was set up in collaboration with the German firm Krupps and Demag. It started its production in 1959. It is well known for its latest technology in steel making. It contributed special steels for vehicles related to Indian Space Satellite Programme.

Favourable Factors

- Iron ore is obtained from Sundergarh and Keonjhar districts of Odisha.
- Well-developed water facilities are available from river Brahmani.
- It is well connected to Kolkata through road and railways.

Problems Faced by Iron Steel Industries

(i) The iron and steel industry needs huge capital investment, which is difficult for a developing country like India.

(ii) The production of iron and steel always falls short as compared to demand and thus, it has to be imported.

(iii) The **lack of technology**, coupled with low investment towards any technological development has remained a major problem.

(iv) The per capita labour productivity in India is 90-100 tonnes/annum, which is the lowest in the world.

(v) **Strikes, energy crisis** and other factors result in low potential utilisation.

Iron and Steel Industries Summary

SN	Name	Foreign Collaborator	Location	State	Raw material available from	
					Material	**From**
1.	Tata Steel Ltd (Private sector)	None	Jamshedpur (East Singhbhum District)	Jharkhand	Iron ore	Singhbhum and Bonai
					Coal	Jharia
					Limestone	Mayurbhanj
					Manganese	Singhbhum and Sundargarh
					Water	Subernarekha and Kharkai rivers
					Labour	Odisha, Jharkhand, Bihar and Uttar Pradesh
2.	Rourkela Steel Plant (Sail management)	Germany (Krupps and Demag)	Sundergarh District	Odisha	Iron ore	Sundergarh and Keonjhar
					Coal	Jharia, Raniganj, Telcher, Noamundi and Korba
					Limestone	
					Manganese	Jharia and Raniganj
					Water	Birmitrapur
					Labour	Barajamda
						Brahmani river
					Power	Odisha, Jharkhand and West Bengal
						Hirakud Power Project

Petrochemicals

The chemicals and compounds which are derived from petroleum resources are called petrochemicals. Its products are replacing the traditional ones because

- petrochemicals are cost-effective and economically stable.
- petrochemicals are cheaper than traditional materials and produced on a mass scale.
- this industry mainly derives its raw materials from petroleum, LPG and coal. Benzene, polythene, PVC, nylon, terylene, ethylene and synthetic rubber form some of the products it produces. Their advantage is that, the products are cheaper and also durable.

Mumbai is the largest centre of petrochemical industries in India. Some units are also located in Auraiya (Uttar Pradesh) Jamnagar, Gandhar, Hazira (Gujarat) Nagothane, Ratnagiri (Maharashtra), Haldia (West Bengal) and Visakhapatnam (Andhra Pradesh), Mangalore (Karnataka).

Most of the petrochemical industries are located in the Western part of India especially in Mumbai and Gujarat because maximum refineries and oil fields are located in these two states which supply the raw material to petrochemical units. Easily availability of raw material and large scale production of cheaper products are reasons responsible for the development of petrochemical industries in India.

Electronics

The electronics industry covers a wide range of products from transistor sets to televisions, telephones, cellphones, telephone exchanges, radars, computers and other equipment required by the telecommunication and computer industry. **Bengaluru** has emerged as the **electronic capital of India**. Other important centres for electronic goods are Mumbai, Delhi, Hyderabad, Pune, Chennai, Kolkata, Lucknow and Coimbatore.

Space technology is a part of electronics industry. It requires satellites, digital technology and other electronic equipments. Electronics industry is also helpful in education, medicine and defence as lot of research can be carried because of it. Knowledge sharing and information exchange becomes easy through the use of electronic equipments. Therefore, this industry is expanding rapidly.

Waste Management

Need for Management

Waste must be recycled for the conservation of resources and protection of the environment. Management of waste adheres to the effective use of waste like recycling, replacement of plastic and synthetic bags, as well as optimum utilisation of water and non-renewable resources.

Need for Safe Waste Disposal

There is an urgent need for the safe waste disposal due to following reasons

- To control different types of pollution i.e. water, air, land, etc.
- To stop the spread of infectious diseases.
- It helps to prevent additional pollution which can improve public health.
- To recycle the hazardous waste for further production.

Methods of Safe Disposal of Waste

There are several ways of safe disposal of waste. These are as follows

- **Segregation** means demarcation of waste into biodegradable and non-biodegradable waste collected from residential areas, hotels, restaurants, office complex and commercial areas for disposal.
- **Dumping** means filling of land with waste.
- **Compositing** means treatment of organic waste over a period of time, which can be used as a manure.
- **Drainage-sewage Treatment** means cleaning of sewages and wastewater by filtering with chemical and biological technologies.
- Treatment of effluents before discharging through chemical mixing.
- Use of scrubbers means spraying of water to catch pollutants. Dry scrubbers are used for removing acid gases.
- Electrostatic precipitator is a device that removes chemicals from gas streams. These chemicals are also called fly ash. This device also removes particulates like cadmium, nickel and lead.
- **Incineration** is a process of controlled high temperature oxidation of primary organic compounds that release thermal energy and produce carbon dioxide and water.

Need and Methods for Reducing, Reusing and Recycling Waste Reducing Waste

We should avoid using non-biodegradable articles like polythene bags etc, by replacing them with biodegradable articles like jute bags, paper bags, etc. The judicious use of waste should be promoted which will lead to environment protection. We should also promote the use of Environment Friendly Technology. For example, bulbs can be replaced by CFLs.

Energy and raw materials should be used and reused. Unused pages of old notebook should reused. Similarly old clothes, toys, books that are no longer needed can be passed on to someone needy so that they can be reused. Solid wastes from the industry should be reused directly.

For example, fly ash can be used as a cement substitute. Reusing principles envisage the optimum utilisation of waste. Waste material must be recycled as and when necessary. The methods of waste recycling are paper recycling and plastic recycling.

Government Initiatives

Automobile fuel has been replaced by CNG (Compressed Natural Gas) in many cities for commercial vehicles. National Waste Management Council was set up for Solid Waste Management in 1990. Plastic bags are also replaced by cotton, paper and jute bags.

Social Initiatives

NGOs and civil society have come forward for making people aware about reduction of waste generation, recycling and waste management.

PYQs Previous Years' Questions

1 Marks Questions

Multiple Choice Questions

1. Which of the following method of waste disposal is harmful ? *(ICSE 2023)*
 (a) Composting (b) Segregation
 (c) Dumping (d) Vermicomposting

Ans. (c) Dumping

2. ....industries are also known as household industry. *(ICSE Specimen 2023)*
 (a) Basic (b) Co-operative
 (c) Cottage (d) None of these

Ans. (c) Cottage

3. Which of the following is a basic/key industry ? *(ICSE 2023)*
 (a) Iron and Steel Industry (b) Silk Industry
 (c) Electronic Industry (d) Cotton Textile Industry

Ans. (d) Cotton Textile Industry

2 Marks Questions

1. Why should waste management be practiced in every school ? *(ICSE 2023)*

Ans. The waste management should be practiced in every school as it encourages and make students learn and practice the proper waste disposal and management at individual level that can contributes in environment protection and reduction of pollution.

2. Mention one advantage and one disadvantage of dumping of waste. *(ICSE 2023)*

Ans. **Advantage** The main benefits of effective waste disposal include environmental protection from pollution or contamination.

Disadvantage Poor waste management contributes to climate change and air pollution and directly affects many ecosystems and species.

3. How are the industries important for India? *(ICSE 2023)*

Ans. The industries are important for India in following ways

(i) It provides greater opportunities for employment in small and large scale industries.

(ii) It reduce the heavy dependence of people on agricultural income by providing them jobs in secondary and tertiary sectors.

4. State the difference between agro based industry and forest based industry. Give one example for each type of industry.

Ans. Agro-based industries mostly produce consumer goods, e.g, sugar, jute, textile, etc.

Mineral-based industries produce both consumer and value-based goods, e.g., iron and steel, engineering industry, shipbuilding machine tools, etc.

5. (i) Explain the terms *(ICSE Specimen 2023)*
 (a) Ancillary Industry (b) Public Sector Industry

Ans. (a) **Ancillary Industry** Ancillary industry is an industry which has fixed investment in plant and machines that do not exceed 1 crore rupees. Ancillary industry manufactures parts, components, sub-assemblies, tools, intermediates, machines, etc.

(b) **Public Sector Industry** These are those industries which are owned and controlled by the Government (State or Central).

6. Give two reasons why we need to manage our waste? *(ICSE Specimen 2023)*

Ans. Two reasons for why we need to manage our waste are

(i) Hazardous waste can cause depletion of natural resources as they are corrosive and toxic in nature.

(ii) Being poisonous they can cause serious illness to human and animal health.

7. Why is there a need for waste management in India? *(ICSE Specimen Semester II 2022)*

Other Similar Questions

Or Why is there a need for waste management in large metropolitan cities?

Or Mention two reasons for the need of Waste management.

Ans. There is a need for waste management in India because

- High degree of growth in population and industrialisation has made pollution of environment a serious problem in many urban areas.
- The rapid increase in the number of vehicles on the road especially in metropolitan cities has degraded the quality of air severely. It leads to acid rain which adversely affects forests, freshwater, soil, killing insects as acid rain increases acidity in the soil, affects buildings, monuments, human health, plant growth, aquatic, species, etc.

8. Segregation considered a safe method of waste disposal. Explain. ***(ICSE Specimen Semester II 2022)***

Ans. Segregation is considered a safe method of waste disposal. It is due to the fact that in this method waste is segregated into different categories like dry and wet or biodegradable and non-biodegradable wastes and can dispose accordingly.

9. Differentiate between public sector and private sector industry giving suitable example for each from India. ***(ICSE Specimen Semester II 2022)***

Ans. Differences between public sector industry and private sector industry are

Public Sector	Private Sector
It is owned and controlled by the government (State or Central).	It is owned and controlled by private group of people or individual.
Example-Oil India, Railways, GAIL, BHEL.	Example-TISCO, Reliance, Wipro, Birla Mills.

10. Give two ways in which cotton textile industry is important for India. ***(ICSE Specimen Semester II 2022)***

Ans. Two ways in which cotton textile industry is important for India are

(i) It provides employment to huge section of population.

(ii) It brings lot of foreign exchange.

11. Give two ways in which petro-chemical industry is important for India? ***(ICSE Semester II 2022)***

Or Mention two reasons for the development of the petro-chemical industry in India. ***(ICSE 2010)***

Ans. The two major reasons for the development of the petro-chemical industry in India are as follows

(i) Raw material is easily available.

(ii) Cheaper products are produced on a large scale.

12. Why is composting considered a safe method of waste disposal? ***(ICSE Semester II 2022)***

Ans. Composting is considered a safe method of waste disposal because it is a natural degradation process in which biodegradable materials are decomposed by microbes and converted into manure. Composting offers a method of processing and recycling both garbage and sewage sludge in one operation. It recycles the nutrients and returns them to the soil as nutrients.

13. Give two reasons as to why Mumbai has developed into an important cotton textile centre? ***(ICSE 2020)***

Or Why has Mumbai a large number of cotton textile units? ***(ICSE 2002)***

Ans. The factors that favour the concentration of cotton textile mills in Mumbai are

(i) Mumbai has proper network of roads and railways that facilitates easy transportation from mills.

(ii) It has proper network of banks that provides credit for setting up of cotton mills.

14. (i) What are basic industries? ***(ICSE 2020)***

(ii) Give one example of a basic industry in India.

Ans. (i) Basic industries are those industries which supply their products or raw materials to manufacture other goods.

(ii) Iron and steel, copper smelting and aluminium smelting are the examples of basic industries.

15. Why should sewage be treated before disposal? ***(ICSE 2020)***

Ans. Sewage should be treated before its disposal because sewage water contains harmful substances. So, when sewage is discharged untreated into the water bodies, it becomes dangerous for aquatic plants and animals.

16. Mention any two problems faced by the cotton textile industry of India. ***(ICSE 2018, 16, 06, 04)***

Ans. The two problems faced by the cotton textile industry of India are

(i) Textile industry depends on cotton and its cultivation depends on seasons which creates a problem of availability.

(ii) Indian textile industry is not as modern as compared to those of developed countries. The technology is also obsolete type.

Additional Info

Some of the other problems faced by the cotton textile industry of India are

- There is a shortage of supply of raw materials which is imported from foreign countries, particularly of long-staple cotton.
- There is a tough competition for the cotton industry from the fiber industry.

17. Give two reasons as to why there is a need for safe waste disposal? ***(ICSE 2018)***

Ans. There is a need for safe waste disposal because of the following reasons

(i) It helps to prevent additional pollution which can improve public health.

(ii) Waste that is properly disposed off has a lesser chance of getting into the drinking water supply and thus causing illness.

18. How can waste be reused? Explain with help of an example. *(ICSE 2018)*

Ans. The best option to reduce solid waste altogether is to reuse as many items as possible. Reuse can mean purchasing non-disposable items or it can mean passing an item along to another person for confined use.

For example, instead of using paper towels to clean the house, one can use a washable rag, and instead of throwing out old clothes or toys pass them to needy people.

19. 'Though Uttar Pradesh has the largest number of sugar mills yet Maharashtra is the largest producer of sugar.' Give any two reasons to justify the statement. *(ICSE 2017)*

Or Mention two reasons why the sugar industry has grown in Maharashtra? *(ICSE 2018)*

Ans. Due to following reasons Maharashtra is the largest producer of sugar

(i) Sugar mills in Maharashtra are managed by cooperatives which are more efficient in production of sugar.

(ii) The soil, higher temperature, good amount of rainfall or irrigation and frost-free growing season are best-suited geographical condition which are found in Maharashtra. So sugarcane has high sucrose content.

20. Define the terms *(ICSE Specimen 2018)*

(i) Composting

(ii) Open dumping

Ans. (i) **Composting** It is a biological process in which micro-organisms, mainly fungi and bacteria, decompose biodegradable or organic waste in the presence of oxygen. Various wastes like leaves, twigs, grass, fruit peels and vegetable peels etc are dumped into a pit and then covered. The recycling produces compost and biogas. Compost is a rich source of organic matter. It plays an important role in sustaining soil fertility.

(ii) **Open dumping** It refers to uncovered areas that are used to dump solid waste of all kinds. The waste is untreated, uncovered and not segregated. It is the breeding ground for flies, rats and other insects that spread diseases. The rainwater runoff from these lumps contaminate nearby land, water and air thereby spreading disease.

21. Why is the jute industry concentrated in and around Paschim Banga? Give two reasons. *(ICSE Specimen 2017)*

Ans. The jute industry is concentrated in and around West Bengal because of

(a) proximity of the jute growing areas.

(b) availability of inexpensive water transport, supported by a good network of railways, roadways and waterways to facilitate movement of raw material to the mills.

22. Give two reasons why Ahmedabad in Gujarat is famous for cotton textile industry. *(ICSE Specimen 2017)*

Ans. Ahmedabad is famous for the cotton textile industry because of

(i) availability of raw cotton, which is grown in the nearby areas of Gujarat and Maharashtra

(ii) availability of transport including accessible port facilities.

23. (i) What is the most important requirement for heavy engineering industry in India? *(ICSE Specimen 2017)*

(ii) Name one important centre for ship building and aircraft construction.

Ans. (i) The most important requirement for heavy engineering industry in India is the huge capital investment required to set up a unit.

(ii) One important centre for ship building is Kochi (Cochin Shipyard) and one important centre for aircraft construction is Bengaluru.

24. (i) Name the countries having collaboration with Rourkela and Durgapur.

(ii) From where do these plants obtain their supply of coal and iron ore?

Ans. (i) The foreign collaborator for the Rourkela plant is Germany and for the Durgapur plant, it is Great Britain.

(ii) The Rourkela plant receives its supplies of coal from Raniganj, Jharia, Talcher, Noamundi and Korba. It receives its iron ore from Bonaigarh, Mayurbhanj, Keonjhar and Noamundi.

The Durgapur plant receives its supplies of coal from Raniganj and Jharia. It receives its iron ore from Singhbhum and Keonjhar.

25. (i) Why is rail transport more comfortable and popular in India? *(ICSE 2017)*

(ii) State any two problems faced by the railways.

Ans. (i) Rail transport is more comfortable and popular in India because it is cheaper than other forms of transport like road and air transport. Most of the roads in India are in poor condition and thus rail transport is more comfortable than road transport.

(ii) Two problems faced by the railways are as follows.

(a) There is tremendous pressure of traffic on them due to increasing population, urbanisation and industrialisation.

(b) They have become unsafe for travel due to poor maintenance of both tracks and rolling stock.

26. 'The iron and steel industry constitutes the backbone of modern industrial economy.' Give two reasons to justify the statement. ***(ICSE 2017)***

Ans. The iron and steel industry constitutes the back bone of modern industrial economy because of following reason

(i) Most of the important industries such as automobile, locomotives, rail tracks, shipbuilding, machine and tools and manufacture of defence equipment depend on iron and steel industry.

(ii) The production and consumption of iron and steel is one of the most significant measures of the level of industrialisation and economic growth of a country.

27. (i) Name an iron and steel Industry set up in Odisha with the help of a famous German firm. ***(ICSE 2017)***

(ii) From where does the industry named in (i) get its iron ore and manganese?

Ans. (i) The Rourkela Steel Plant was set up in Odisha with collaboration of the West German firm Krupps and Demag during the Second Five Year Plan. It started its production in 1959.

(ii) This iron and steel industry gets its iron ore from Sundargarh and Keonjhar district of Odisha and Manganese from Barajmda of Jharkhand.

28. Name two products of each of the following industries. ***(ICSE 2017)***

(i) Petrochemical industry (ii) Electronic industry

Ans. (i) Two products of petrochemical industry are polythene, PVC of plastic group, nylon and synthetic fibre.

(ii) Two products of electronic industry are personal computers and digital cameras.

29. Differentiate between mineral-based industry and agro-based industry giving one example for each. ***(ICSE 2017)***

Or With the help of an example, explain how agro based industry is different from mineral-based industry. ***(ICSE 2003)***

Ans. The difference between agro-based industries and mineral-based industries are

Agro-based Industries	Mineral-based Industries
Agro-based industries get raw materials from agriculture.	Mineral-based industries derive their raw material from minerals.
Agro-based industries provide employment in rural areas.	Mineral-based industries provide employment both in rural and urban areas.
Agro-based industries mostly produce consumer goods, e.g, sugar, jute, textile, etc.	Mineral-based industries produce both consumer and value based goods, e.g., Iron and steel, engineering industry, ship building, machine tools, etc.

30. Give a reason for each of the following. ***(ICSE 2016)***

(i) Products made from petrochemicals are growing in popularity.

(ii) The electronic industry contributes to the development of the country.

Ans. (i) Products made from petrochemicals are growing in popularity because they are cheaper and are durable.

(ii) The electronic industry contributes to the development of the country because it covers diverse areas such as space exploration, defence equipments, medical diagnosis, communication, information technology, etc.

31. (i) Why is the iron and steel industry called a basic industry? ***(ICSE 2015)***

(ii) Define a mini steel plant.

Ans. (i) The iron and steel industry is called a basic industry because most of the important industries such as automobiles, locomotives, rail tracks, ship building, machine and tools and manufacture of defense equipment depend on iron and steel industry.

(ii) A mini steel plant is a decentralised secondary unit. It uses scrap iron which is easily available in the country and is cheap. It does not use heavy capital investment. It does not cause pollution and produces special steel. It can be set up at any convenient place as it does not need huge infrastructure.

32. (i) What is understood by biodegradable waste? *(ICSE 2015)*

(ii) State one source of gaseous waste.

Ans. (i) Wastes which can be degraded by microorganisms and by natural processes are known as biodegradable wastes.

(ii) One source of gaseous waste is the release of carbon monoxide by automobiles.

33. The silk handloom industry is favourable in Mysore, give two reasons. *(ICSE 2014)*

Ans. The two reasons are as follows

(i) Availability of mulberry plant, which is the raw material for this industry.

(ii) Availability of Bombyx mori silkworm.

34. Give two reasons for the following. *(ICSE 2014)*

(i) Kolkata is an important cotton manufacturing centre even though West Bengal is not a leading producer of cotton.

Ans. (i) Kolkata has varied labour forces, excellent means of transport and easy power availability of coal from Raniganj and hence is an important centre.

35. Name two raw materials used in the petro-chemical industry and state two advantage or of petro-chemical products. *(ICSE 2014)*

Ans. Benzene and ethylene are two raw materials used in the petro-chemical industry.

Two advantages of petro-chemical products are as follows

(i) They are cheaper.

(ii) They are durable.

36. Answer the following questions *(ICSE 2013)*

(i) What is the significance of the electronics industry in recent times?

(ii) Name two cities that have leading software companies.

Ans. (i) The electronics industry is significant in recent times because it covers a wide range of fields and products including television, computers, transistors, cellular telecom, defence, railways, meteorological equipments, space research, medical equipments and software industry.

(ii) Bengaluru and Pune are two cities that have leading software companies.

37. Name an agro-based industry based in the following industrial centres. *(ICSE 2012)*

(i) Ahmedabad (ii) Mysore

Ans. Agro-based industries are as follows

(i) Cotton industry in Ahmedabad

(ii) Silk industry in Mysore

38. State two factors which favour the silk industry in Karnataka. *(ICSE 2012)*

Ans. Factors which favour the silk industry in Karnataka are as follows

(i) It has enough freshwater free from alkaline salts for the processing of silkworms.

(ii) Availability of mulberry plants is in abundance.

39. What are petro-chemicals? Name any two products made from petro-chemicals. *(ICSE 2012)*

Ans. The petro-chemicals are mainly chemicals derived from petroleum resources like coal, gas and petroleum.

Plastics and acrylic fibres are two products made from petro-chemicals.

40. What is sericulture? Name any two types of silk. *(ICSE 2010)*

Ans. Rearing of silkworms on mulberry leaves is called sericulture.

Tassar, eri and muga are the types of silk.

41. Which city is known as the Electronic Capital of India? Name any two major centres of electronic products. *(ICSE 2009)*

Ans. Bengaluru is the Electronic Capital of India.

Hyderabad and Pune are other major centres of electronic products.

42. Why is the silk industry considered as a small scale industry? Name the two types of silk produced in India. *(ICSE 2009)*

Ans. It does not involve much labour or capital. Hence, silk industry is considered as small scale industry.

Mulberry and non-mulberry are the two types of silk produced in India.

43. Mention two reasons for the importance of the electronic industry in India's development. *(ICSE 2009)*

Ans. The reasons for the importance of electronics industry in India's development are

(i) It covers a wide range of fields which are important for development like space research, software development, medical advancement, etc.

(ii) It provides job to large number of people who are well qualified thereby reducing educated unemployment.

44. What is a petrochemical industry? Mention two reasons why petro-chemical products are replacing traditional raw materials. ***(ICSE 2009)***

Or State two advantages of petro-chemical industry. ***(ICSE 2007)***

Ans. The petrochemical industry is concerned with the production and trade of petrochemicals. Its major part is constituted by the plastic industry. It is mainly comprise of synthetic fibre/yarn, polymers, etc.

The petro-chemical products are replacing traditional materials due to the following reasons

(i) These products are cost effective.

(ii) These are cheaper as compared to traditional products.

45. Give two reasons for the importance of the silk industry in India. ***(ICSE 2008)***

Ans. Reasons for the importance of the silk industry in India are as follows

(i) India is the fourth largest producer of the silk in the world.

(ii) Indian silk is of fine and good quality.

46. Give two reasons to show why the sugar industry has flourished in Uttar Pradesh and Bihar. ***(ICSE 2008)***

Or State two reasons for the concentration of the sugar industry in Uttar Pradesh. ***(ICSE 2007)***

Ans. The concentration of the sugar industry in Uttar Pradesh is because of the availability of fertile soil and abundant quantity of water.

47. Mention two ways in which the agro-based industries have affected the economy of India. ***(ICSE 2007)***

Ans. Agro-based industries have affected the economy of India in the following ways

(i) Most of the agricultural products are used by industries.

(ii) Products made by agro-based industries are exported which strengthens the economy.

48. Name four petro-chemical products. ***(ICSE 2007)***

Ans. PVC pipes, polythene bags, synthetic fibre and plastic products are four petro-chemical products.

49. Answer the following questions. ***(ICSE 2006)***

(i) State the importance of electronics in defence.

(ii) Mention one important requirement of the electronic industry.

Ans. (i) It can be used as making remote weapons, long distance transmissions, and tele-communication.

(ii) The electronic industry needs dust free, cool and a clean environment.

50. Give reasons, why? ***(ICSE 2005)***

(i) Maharashtra is favourable for textiles production.

Ans. (i) Maharashtra has rich black soils and a source of cheap electric power as well.

51. State four geographical factors which should be kept in mind while setting up an agro-based industry. ***(ICSE 2005)***

Ans. The geographical factors which should be considered before setting up an agro-based industry are as follows

(i) It should be set up near the source from where raw material is available.

(ii) The supply assurance of raw materials.

(iii) The market should be at close so to reduce the transportation cost.

(iv) Industry should not be of seasonal nature.

52. State the importance of electronics in the field of ***(ICSE 2005)***

(i) Space Technology

(ii) Entertainment

Ans. (i) India has launched several indigenously built satellites with the help of electronics industries.

(ii) Electronics has made wonders in entertainment like TV, radio, video, computers, etc.

53. With the help of an example each, differentiate between basic and consumer industries. ***(ICSE 2004)***

Ans.

Basic Industries	Consumer Industries
They are the industries on which other industries depend. *e.g.*, Iron and Steel Industry.	Industries which produce goods primarily for the direct consumption by the people. *e.g.*, Textile Industry.

54. 'The Khadi and Handloom sectors of the textile industry cannot be ignored.' Give two reasons justifying this statement. ***(ICSE 2004)***

Ans. Khadi and Handloom sectors of the textile industry are the basic cottage industries which provide employment, bring valuable foreign exchange and supplement the agriculture as well as farmers and hence cannot be ignored.

55. Name a state famous for each of the followings *(ICSE 2001)*
(i) Coal Industry
(ii) Mulberry Silk

Ans. (i) West Bengal is famous for coal industry.
(ii) Karnataka is famous for Mulberry silk.

3 Marks Questions

1. Briefly answer the following. *(ICSE 2023)*
(i) How is segregation of the waste helpful?
(ii) Mention one way in which we can reuse waste.
(iii) Mention one benefit of composting.

Ans. (i) Waste segregation facilitates the process of reuse, recycling and recovery of waste. Segregating waste can improve the recycling process.
(ii) We can reuse the waste by donating the items that are still in a good, usable condition to charities.
(iii) Composting enhances the soil nutrients such as nitrogen and phosphorus. It enhances the water retention capacity of the soil and increases the fertility of soil by adding humus.

2. (i) How is recycling of waste helpful? Give an example of recycling of waste. *(ICSE 2023)*
(ii) Mention any one initiative taken by the government to manage waste.

Ans. (i) Recycling helps in the protection of the environment, in reducing air, land, water and soil pollution and saving energy. For example, use reusable bags instead of plastic bags.
(ii) Swachh Bharat Mission is the initiative taken by the government to manage waste.

3. (i) What has made Mumbai an important centre for cotton textile production ? *(ICSE 2023)*
(ii) Why are the petrochemical products in great demand?

Ans. (i) Mumbai has become an important centre for cotton textile production due to following reasons
- The city has humid, warm climate which supports the growth of cotton.
- The availabilities of skilled labour, raw material, etc.

(ii) Petrochemical products are in great demand because they are cost effective, economically stable and cheaper as they are produced on a mass scale.

4. (i) Mention two problems faced by the sugar industry of India. *(ICSE 2023)*
(ii) Where is Tata Steel located?
(iii) Why is the silk industry losing the market in recent time?

Ans. (i) The two problems faced by sugar industry are
(b) Old and inefficient methods of production.
(c) Lack of efficient transportation.
(ii) Tata Steel is located in the city of Jamshedpur.
(iii) Silk industry is losing the market in recent times because domestic silk manufacturers are facing intense competition from China and India's share in the global market is declining gradually.

5. From where Tata Steel gets its supply of coal, iron ore and water supply? *(ICSE Specimen 2023)*

Ans. Tata steel gets its supply of coal from Jharia coal mines of Jharkhand, iron ore from Noamundi of Singhbhum region and Mayurbhanj and water supply from Subarnarekha River and Kharkai dam.

6. What is the significance of the electronics industry for education, entertainment and research? *(ICSE Specimen 2023)*

Ans. The significance of the electronics industry for education, entertainment and research can be seen through the following points
- Electronic industry, with mass scale integration process, has produced computers, servers, displays, televisions and cameras, telephones, etc. These devices help to capture and broadcast news, advertisements, cinema and educational programs etc, to a large section of the population over the country and overseas. Thus, these are changing the life style of the Indian masses.
- Various new technologies like smart boards, projectors, video clips, pictures, etc are used to make learning easy and fun for the students.
- Further, in this modern era online classes provided to the students by the use of various online applications have helped the students to continue their education from home.

7. Give reasons for the following. *(ICSE Specimen 2023)*
(i) We should avoid using plastics.
(ii) Radioactive wastes are hazardous.
(iii) Open dumping is not an environment friendly method of managing waste.

Ans. (i) Plastics are non-biodegradable substances that take several years to decompose. As we know that plastic does not decompose, it accumulates and causes environmental pollution.

(ii) Radioactive wastes are hazardous because radioactive wastes cause pollution and damage the environment and the high level products of nuclear wastes remain in the environment for several hundred years.

(iii) Open dumping is not an environment friendly method because the open pits spoil the sight of the area and become a breeding ground for mosquitoes, flies, insects, etc that are the carriers of harmful diseases. They give out foul odour. The burning of waste material in the open dumps pollutes the air.

8. How will you as an individual reduce and reuse waste at home? ***(ICSE Specimen 2023)***

Ans. In the following ways, we can reduce and reuse waste at home

(i) Avoid single-use food and drink containers and utensils.

(ii) Buy second-hand items and donate used goods.

(iii) Purchase products that come with less packaging and/or come in packaging that can be recycled.

9. With reference to Rourkela Steel Plant, answer the following. ***(ICSE Specimen Semester II 2022)***

(i) Where is it located?

(ii) Which country helped India to establish this steel plant?

(iii) From where does it get its iron ore requirement?

Ans. (i) Rourkela Steel Plant is located in the Sundergarh district of Odisha.

(ii) Germany helped India to establish Rourkela Steel Plant in the country in 1959 during the Second Five Year Plan.

(iii) This plant gets iron ore from Sundargarh and Keonjhar districts of Odisha.

10. (i) What are the benefits of using petrochemical products? ***(ICSE Specimen Semester II 2022)***

(ii) How has the electronic industry revolutionised the entertainment sector?

Ans. (i) Following are the benefits of using petrochemical products

- These products are made from petrochemicals thus have greater variety and are cheaper.
- These products are more durable and require less maintenance.

(ii) The electronic industry has revolutionised the entertainment sector by proving a wide range of products including transistor sets, televisions, telephone exchanges, telecommunication, and computers and so on.

11. With reference to Tata steel plant, answer the following questions. ***(ICSE Semester II 2022)***

(i) Where is it located?

(ii) From where does it get its coal requirement?

(iii) From where does it get its iron ore requirement?

Ans. (i) TATA steel plant is located at Tata Nagar near Jamshedpur in Jharkhand.

(ii) It gets its coal requirement from Jharia coalfield.

(iii) For answer, refer to Q.5 of 3 marks questions.

12. (i) Name any two by products of the sugar industry. ***(ICSE Semester II 2022)***

(ii) Why are the cotton textile industries mostly located in the coastal areas?

Ans. (i) There are various by-products which are produced during and after processes of sugar making. Some of them are

(a) **Molasses** It is a kind of dark brown syrup that drains from sugar during the process of manufacture. It is used in making alcohol, wine, fertiliser, etc.

(b) **Bagasse** It is the rejected sugarcane left after being crushed and is important to make cardboards.

(ii) The cotton textile industries are mostly located in the coastal areas because these areas have humid and dry atmosphere where processing of cotton becomes much easier. As the humidity or moisture in air increase the strength of cotton is also increases. That is why most of the mills are located the Western coast of India due to their suitable climate for growth and processing (spinning) of cotton fibre.

13. (i) Why should we resue water? ***(ICSE Semester II 2022)***

(ii) How can farm waste be made useful?

(iii) How is dumping of waste harmful?

Other Similar Questions

Or Open dumping is not an environmental friendly method of managing waste.

Or Mention three reason as to why the dumping of waste may be harmful.

Ans. (i) We should reuse water because through recycling water we protect water resources. This activity reduces water pollution discharges and develops a habit to minimise the water consumption unnecessarily.

(ii) In the following ways farm waste can be made useful
- Plant waste can produce biofuels such as biodiesel or ethanol.
- After the juice has been extracted from sugarcane, the stalk that is left is known as bagasse. Bagasse can be used to create plastics such as bowls, plates and other plastic containers.

(iii) Illegal dumping of waste is harmful because it damages the Environment. The chemicals and non-biodegradable materials in the waste affect the physical environment and the waterways by contaminating groundwater and soil. The wastes can also spread weeds and pests, therefore, affecting agriculture and wildlife.

14. Mention three ways to reduce waste generation at home. ***(ICSE Semester II 2022)***

Other Similar Questions

Or How will you as an individual reduce and reuse waste at home?

Or How can you as an individual contribute towards waste management?

Or What can an individual do to reduce waste at home?

Ans. Three ways to reduce waste generation at home are as follows

(i) Shop eco-friendly with reusable bags like jute bags instead of plastic bags.

(ii) Develop a habit of composting at home. Fruits and vegetable scraps, egg shells, coffee grounds, grass clippings, and leaves can all be composted.

(iii) By secondhand items and donate used goods. Purchase new items only when it is much needed.

15. (i) State two problems faced by the silk industry of India. ***(ICSE 2020)***

(ii) Mention the most important factor for location of sugar industries.

Ans. (i) The two problems faced by the silk industry of India are

(a) It is facing tough competition from artificial silk which is cheaper and needs less maintenance.

(b) The import of cheaper and better quality silk from China is proving to be very harmful for the Indian silk industry.

(ii) The favourable factors for location of sugar industries are
- Availability of raw inaterial i.e. sugarcane.
- Availability of capital.
- Availability of cheap labour.

16. Briefly answer the following. ***(ICSE 2020)***

(i) From where does the Rourkela Steel Plant obtain its supply of coal?

(ii) From where does the Tata Iron and Steel Plant obtain its supply of iron ore?

(iii) Name two cities that are important for the production of electronics.

Ans. (i) Rourkela Steel Plant obtain its supply of coal from Jharia, Talcher and Korba coal fields.

(ii) For answer, refer to Q.5 of 3 marks questions.

(iii) Bengaluru and Hyderabad are important for the production of electronics.

17. (i) How can recycling of waste help in reducing waste? Explain with suitable examples. ***(ICSE 2020)***

(ii) Mention one initiative taken by the government to manage waste.

(iii) How can you as an individual contribute towards waste management?

Ans. (i) Recycling of waste can help in reducing waste in many ways. For example, shoes, sandals and slippers can be made from old types, fly ash from power plants can be used as a substitute for cement, etc.

(ii) Initiatives taken by the government of India to manage waste are 'Swachh Bharat Mission', 'National Water Mission' and 'Waste to Energy'.

(iii) As an individual, I can contribute towards waste management by using three R's in my life i.e. Reducing, Reusing and Recycling wastes. Besides this, I would use segregation process for proper management of waste.

18. With reference to sugar industries, answer the following questions. ***(ICSE 2019)***

(i) Why should these industries be located close to the sugarcane growing areas?

(ii) Name two by-products of the sugar industry.

(iii) Mention one leading sugar producing state in North India and one in South India.

Ans. (i) Sugarcane must be crushed within 24 hours of harvesting as the sucrose content present in it, that is used to make sugar, keeps on decreasing in the sugarcane. Thus, industries should be located close to the sugarcane growing areas.

(ii) Molasses, bagasse and press mud are the by products of the sugar industry.

(iii) Leading sugar producing state in North India is Uttar Pradesh and leading sugar producing state in South India is Maharashtra.

19. Give a reason for each of the following. ***(ICSE 2019)***

(i) Ahmedabad is an important cotton textile producing centre in India.

(ii) Cottage industries are significant for our economy.

(iii) Petrochemical industries are usually located close to the oil refineries.

Ans. (i) Ahmedabad is situated in the heart of cotton growing area, hence the major raw material is easily available. The humid climate is ideal for spinning and weaving. The flat terrain and easy availability of land and cheap labour from densely populated states of Gujarat and Maharashtra are suitable for the establishment of the cotton mills here.

(ii) Cottage industries help in increasing employment and economic development of India. These improve the growth of the country by increasing urban and rural growth. These also create self employment and reduce unemployment. Thus, these industries are significant for economy.

(iii) Raw material for petrochemical industry includes petroleum, LPG, coal, etc. Thus, this industry is situated near oil refineries to obtain the raw materials Ethylene and Benzene.

Examiner's Comment

- Most of the candidates answered it correctly.
- Most of the candidates attempted it correctly.
- Some candidates could not relate the question to the availability of the raw material.

Suggestions for Students

- Instruct students to read the question carefully before answering.
- Train the students on the proper presentation of answers and advise them to follow the instructions given in the question paper.

20. (i) What can an individual do to reduce waste at home? ***(ICSE 2019)***

(ii) Why must segregation of waste be done before disposal?

(iii) How has composting proven to be a great help in managing waste?

Ans. (i) For answer, refer to Q.14 of 3 marks questions.

(ii) Segregation is important to be done before disposal because if the waste is not separated properly, it all gets mixed up in landfills. The danger of this is that they all leak after a period of time, resulting in contamination of groundwater. The toxic or non-biodegradable chemicals and e-waste must be treated separately. The waste must be collected in closed vans and vehicles of municipality.

(iii) Composting is a biological process in which micro-organisms, mainly fungi and bacteria, decompose biodegradable or organic waste in the presence of oxygen. Various wastes like leaves, twigs, grass, fruit peels and vegetable peels, etc are dumped into a pit and then covered. The recyling produces compost and biogas or gobar gas. Compost is a rich source of organic matter. It plays an important role in sustaining soil fertility.

21. Give a reason for each of the following. ***(ICSE 2019)***

(i) Trees must be planted in the industrial areas.

(ii) Chemical fertilisers must be replaced by organic manure.

(iii) Plastic and polythene products must be banned.

Ans. (i) Trees must be planted in the industrial areas due to following reasons

- Trees help reduce the heat produced by the industries.
- Trees perform transpiration and can affect the climate of a region considerably.
- Trees filter harmful dust and pollutants such as ozone, carbon monoxide and sulfur dioxide from the air we breathe.

(ii) Organic fertilisers are usually made from plant or animal waste, e.g. manure, compost bones and cotton seed meal, whereas chemical fertilisers are made from harmful chemicals. Organic fertilisers improve the structure of the soil and increase its ability to hold water and nutrients and overtime these fertilisers make soil and plants healthy and strong. Whereas chemical fertilisers are harmful when continuously used in farming. Thus, chemical fertilisers must be replaced by organic manure.

(iii) Plastic bags are a major contributor in plastic pollution. It is a kind of pollution which is deteriorating our environment. It is a threat to life on Earth.

Plastic and polythene bags cause land, air and water pollution. Plastic and polythenes do not degrade instead plastic gets broken down into small tiny pieces which are swept down and end up in the ocean which are then consumed by wildlife or keep on accumulating in the environment. Thus, plastic and polythene products must be banned.

22. Give a geographical reason for each of the following. ***(ICSE 2018)***

(i) Silk industry is doing particularly well in Karnataka.

(ii) Petrochemical products are gaining popularity in modern times.

(iii) The electronics industry is proving to be an asset for our country in the field of education.

Ans. (i) Silk industry is doing particularly well in Karnataka because of the temperature as it ranges from 16°C to 31°C and other favourable climatic conditions prevailing in Karnataka.

(ii) Petrochemical products are gaining popularity in modern times because products made from petrochemicals have greater variety and are cheaper. These products are more durable and requires less maintenance.

(iii) The electronics industry is an asset for India in the field of education because it encourages the education related electronic items like personal computers, calculators, GPS automotive, digital cameras, etc. The software industry has revolutionised education through providing digital platform for information exchange and knowledge sharing.

23. (i) What is meant by waste?

(ii) Mention two sources of waste. ***(ICSE Specimen 2018)***

Ans. (i) The products that are used in any activity and rejected after certain duration are called a waste material or waste. The wastes are generated by he natural vegetation, animal, insects and humans which are recycled and reused. Those wastes which can not be recycled, pollute the environment.

(ii) Two sources of waste are industrial waste and domestic waste.

Additional Info

Some of the other sources of waste are Agricultural waste, Commercial waste, Chemical waste, E-waste.

24. (i) What is the meaning of the 3 R's in waste management?

(ii) Give an example for each one of the above.

(iii) Mention any one way by which accumulation of waste can be hazardous for human health.

Ans. (i) Meaning of the 3R's in waste management are Reduce, Reuse and Recycling.

(ii) Example of reducing waste is to avoid use of non-biodegradable commodities like plastic bags. Example of reuse is furnishing an office with reclaimed materials instead of purchasing new chairs, tables etc. Example of Recycling- Paper recycling.

(iii) Accumulation of nuclear waste can be hazardous for human health.

25. Name the following. ***(ICSE 2018)***

(i) A city most famous for electronics and hence called 'The Electronics Capital of India'.

(ii) The location of an iron and steel industry set-up with German collaboration.

(iii) A by-product of sugar industry which is used in the manufacture of wax and shoe polish.

Ans. (i) Bangalore also known as Bengaluru is the electronic capital of India because the presence of software industries, aerospace, telecommunications and heavy industries.

(ii) Rourkela Steel Plant in Odisha is set-up by German collaboration in 1959s. It is operated by Steel Authority of India Limited (SAIL).

(iii) Sugarcane filter mud is a by-product of sugar industry which is used in the manufacture of wax and shoe polish.

Examiner's Comment

- Most of the candidates mentioned correct geographical reason for good performance of silk industry in Karnataka.
- Many candidates wrote the correct geographical reason for gain in popularity of Petrochemical products in modern times. However, some candidates wrote about petroleum products.
- Majority of the candidates wrote general factors, without relating them to the field of education.

26. What do you mean by the following terms? ***(2018)***

(i) Segregation (ii) Composting (iii) Dumping

Ans. (i) Segregation means demarcation of waste into biodegradable and non-biodegradable waste collected from residential areas, hotels, restaurants, office complexes and commercial areas for disposal.

(ii) For answer, refer to Q.20 (i) part of 2 marks questions.

(iii) For answer, refer to Q.20 (ii) part of 2 marks questions.

27. With reference to the cotton textile industry answer the following questions. ***(ICSE 2018, 2006)***

(i) Give two reasons why Mumbai is an important cotton textile industry?

(ii) Mention two more important centres of cotton textile industry in India.

Other Similar Questions

Or Give two reasons as to why Mumbai has developed into an important cotton textile Centre?

Or Why has Mumbai a large number of textile units?

Or What has made Mumbai an important centre for cotton textile production?

Ans. (i) The two reasons due to which Mumbai is an important cotton textile industry are

(a) The black cotton soil and humid climate in Mumbai are ideal for cotton.

(b) Mumbai's location as an international port and cheap Hydroelectric power easily available from Tata hydroelectric grid from Western Ghats are important reasons for the development of cotton textile industry.

(ii) Two more important centres of cotton textile industry in India are Gujarat and Tamil Nadu.

28. (i) Explain the term Sericulture.

(ii) Why is Karnataka famous for silk industry? Give two reasons.

Ans. (i) Rearing of silkworms on Mulberry leaves is known as Sericulture.

(ii) For answer, refer to Q. 22(i) part of 3 marks questions.

29. (i) Name two industries using animal fibre. Mention one important centre of production for each. ***(ICSE Specimen 2017)***

(ii) Give two problems faced by the woollen textile industry in India.

Ans. (i) Two industries which use animal fibre are the wool and silk industries. Ludhiana is famous for the woollen industry and Mysore for the silk industry.

(ii) The woollen textile industry in India faces the following problems

(a) As India is a tropical country, the market is seasonal

(b) The quality of wool produced is low, thus limiting the export market.

30. (i) Name the raw materials required by the petro-chemical industry. ***(ICSE Specimen 2017)***

(ii) Mention two products of this industry.

(iii) Give a reason why petro-chemical products are gaining importance.

Ans. (i) The raw materials required by the petro-chemical industry are petroleum, LPG and coal.

(ii) Two products of this industry are synthetic fibres and automobile fuels.

(iii) These products are gaining importance because they are used for manufacturing a large variety of articles which are cost-effective and long lasting.

31. (i) Name the two most important centres of electronic industry in India. ***(ICSE Specimen 2017)***

(ii) Name the largest and the oldest integrated iron and steel plant in the private sector in India.

(iii) What is meant by a mini steel plant? State its advantages.

Ans. (i) The two most important centres of electronic industry in India are Bengaluru and Hyderabad.

(ii) The largest and the oldest integrated iron and steel plant in the private sector is Tata Iron and Steel Company Limited at Jamshedpur.

(iii) A mini steel plant uses electric arc and induction furnaces for processing scrap iron and sponge iron to produce alloy steel, mild steel and stainless steel. Its major advantage is that it uses mostly steel scrap as raw material, which is relatively cheap.

32. What is the importance of roadways in India? Give two reasons.

Ans. Roadways are important in India because

(i) Roads link villages to urban centres, which is not always possible with railways, especially in the hilly regions of the country.

(ii) Roads provide door to door service, which is not possible with other modes of transport.

33. List some important initiatives of the Indian Government to improve the management of solid wastes.

Ans. Some important initiatives taken by the Indian Government to improve the management of solid wastes are as follows

(i) A National Waste Management Council has been set up in 1990 with the main objective of solid waste management.

(ii) A High Powered Committee under the Planning Commission has proposed a strategy for waste management ,which is being implemented.

(iii) Under the Environment Protection Act, government has formulated rules for reducing pollution, handling of hazardous wastes and controlling waste from industries.

34. Give a geographic term for each of the following. *(ICSE 2017)*

(i) Non-mulberry silk produced in Madhya Pradesh.

(ii) Rejected cane after crushing.

(iii) The rearing of silk worms to obtain silk.

Ans. (i) Non–mulberry silk produced in Madhya Pradesh–Tasar Silk

(ii) Rejected cane after crushing–Bagasse

(iii) The rearing of silk worms to obtain silk–Sericulture

35. With reference to the silk industry, answer the following. *(ICSE 2016)*

(i) Why is Karnataka the largest producer of mulberry silk?

(ii) Mention two varieties of non-Mulberry silk produced in India.

(iii) Name one silk weaving centre each in UP and in Tamil Nadu.

Ans. (i) The most important factors responsible for making Karnataka the largest producer in mulberry silk are availability of favourable climate for rearing silkworm, availability of Bombyx mori silkworm and recent introduction of new technology for handling Bombyx mori silkworm.

(ii) Non-Mulberry silk produced in India are muga, tassar and eri.

(iii) The silk weaving centre in UP is Varanasi and in Tamil Nadu it is Kanchipuram.

36. Explain briefly the meaning of the following terms.

(i) Composting (ii) Incineration *(ICSE 2016)*

(iii) Segregation

Ans. (i) For answer, refer to Q 20 (i) part of 2 marks questions.

(ii) **Incineration** It is the process of controlled high temperature oxidation of primary organic compounds that release thermal energy and produce carbon dioxide and water.

(iii) For answer, refer to Q.26 (i) part of 3 marks questions.

37. (i) State two major problems faced by the sugar industry. *(ICSE 2015)*

(ii) Name two by-products of the sugar industry.

Ans. (i) Two major problems faced by the sugar industry are

(a) **Low and Irregular Supply of Raw Material** The yield per hectare of sugarcane is very low as compared to other sugarcane producing areas in the world. This is because of irregular supply of raw material.

(b) **Fluctuation in Sugarcane Output** This happens due to the erratic nature of monsoon. It is a seasonal crop.

Additional Info

Other problems faced by the sugar industry are

- **Old and Obsolete Machinery** Low production of sugar is also because of its traditional means of production. The machinery requires to be replaced with modern machinery.
- **Small and Uneconomic Size of the Sugar Mills** Many of the sugar mills have a very small capacity of 1000 to 15000 tonnes per day.

(ii) For answer, refer to Q.12(i) of 3 marks questions.

38. (i) State one of the main problems of the silk industry. *(ICSE 2015)*

(ii) Why are synthetic fibres popular?

Ans. (i) One of the main problems of the silk industry is that it is facing tough competition from artificial silk which is cheaper and needs less maintenance.

(ii) Synthetic fibres are more durable than most natural fibres. Many synthetic fibres offer consumer-friendly functions, such as stretching, waterproofing and stain resistance.

39. Give a reason for each of the following. *(ICSE 2014)*

(i) Visakhapatnam is a leading centre for ship-building.

(ii) Mini steel plants cause less pollution than integrated steel plants.

Ans. (i) Visakhapatnam steel plant is the deepest land locked natural port and has easy availability of the necessary raw materials.

(ii) Mini steel plants use only scrap iron and sponge iron in a furnace.

40. Mention three factors that have helped the sugar industry flourish in the peninsular region rather than in the Northern regions of India. ***(ICSE 2014)***

Ans. The three factors for flourishment of sugar industry in the Peninsular region in India are

(i) Region is rich in black soil which is suitable for sugarcane cultivation.

(ii) Mills are close to the farm land.

(iii) It has a tropical climate which is best suited for growing sugarcane.

41. Give geographical reasons for the followings ***(ICSE 2013)***

(i) It is necessary to crush sugarcane within 24 hours of harvesting.

(ii) Sericulture flourished in Karnataka.

Ans. (i) If sugarcane is not crushed within 24 hours of harvesting then it will loose its sucrose content.

(ii) Karnataka has a favourable climate for rearing silkworms.

42. Mention three advantages that a mini steel plant has over an integrated steel plant. ***(ICSE 2012)***

Ans. The three advantages of mini steel plant are as follows

(i) It caters to the local needs of the market and cost of transport in their case is quite less.

(ii) This industry uses an electric arc furnace which conserves coal.

(iii) It requires small capital investment.

43. With reference to the cotton textile industry. ***(ICSE 2012)***

(i) Which is the country's most important manufacturing centre?

(ii) State two geographical reasons for its importance.

Ans. (i) Mumbai is the most important manufacturing centre in India.

(ii) The two geographical reasons are as follows

(a) Mumbai is in Maharashtra, which has a very rich black and regur soil which is best suited for cotton cultivation.

(b) The humid climate of Mumbai favours the productions of five yarns of cotton.

44. Mention two reasons for the importance of the cotton textile industry. ***(ICSE 2010)***

Ans. The importance of cotton textile industry are as follows

(i) 40% of the country's labour force depends on this.

(ii) India is the third largest exporter of cotton textile and earns foreign exchange for the nation.

45. Give geographical reasons for the followings. ***(ICSE 2010)***

(i) Karnataka is an important centre for silk.

(ii) India produces very little sugarcane though it is one of the largest producers of sugar in the world.

Ans. (i) Sericulture is the main occupation of Karnataka, it has abundant mulberry plants as well.

(ii) India produces very little sugarcane though it is one of the largest producers of sugar in the world because in India the per capita production of sugarcane is low.

CHAPTER TEST

01 Mark Questions

1. The division of dry and wet waste is called ....
   (a) composting (b) segregation
   (c) sedimentation (d) land filling
2. Mobile, laptops, chargers waste come under the category of ....
   (a) Hazardous waste (b) E- Waste
   (c) Recyclable waste (d) Liquid waste
3. The process of disposal of waste material by burying it is called. ....
   (a) landfill dumping (b) segregation
   (c) composting (d) recycling
4. Industrial locations are influenced by the availability of ....
   (a) Market (b) Labour
   (c) Raw Material (d) All of these
5. .... is an example of private sector industry.
   (a) BHEL (b) TISCO (c) SAIL (d) CIL
6. .... is also known as the electronic capital of India .
   (a) Srinagar (b) Chennai (c) Noida (d) Bengaluru

Answers

1. (b) | 2. (b) | 3. (a) | 4. (d) | 5. (b) | 6. (d)

10 Marks Questions

7. (i) Why should sewage be treated before the disposal ?
   (ii) Mention any two problems faced by the cotton textile industry in India.
   (iii) Why is Mumbai considered a hub of cotton textile units?
   (iv) Differentiate between the agro-based industry and mineral based industry.
8. (i) Why do the Iron and Steel industry constitute the backbone of modern industrial economy?
   (ii) Why the sugar industry has grown on a large scale in Maharashtra?
   (iii) What are the three main problems faced by the cotton textile in India?
   (iv) Which factors affect the development of Cotton textile industry in India?
9. (i) What do you mean by safe disposal of waste?
   (ii) What is the significance of 3 R's (Reduce, Reuse and Recycle)?
   (iii) What are biodegradable waste? Mention any 3 sources.
   (iv) What do you mean Seri-Culture? Give example.
10. (i) What is the importance of electronic Industry in current scenario?
    (ii) What do you mean by Petrochemical Industry? What are its advantage?
    (iii) (a) Why should we conserve water resources?
    (b) How are the farm waste be made useful?
    (c) How is dumping of waste harmful for environment?
    (iv) What are the problems faced by iron-steel industries in India? Give reasons.

07

Transport

TREND ANALYSIS 3 YEARS

Average No. of Questions Across all Sets

Topic	Category (Year)	2023	2020	2019
TOPIC 01 Modes of Transport	1 Mark	–	–	–
	3 Marks	–	1	–
	8 Marks	–	–	–
TOPIC 02 Major Ports in India	1 Mark	1	–	–
	3 Marks	–	2	1
	8 Marks	4	2	2

The development of an economy depends on its well knit and coordinated system of transport. The Indian Transport System comprises of **Roadways, Railways, Airways** and **Waterways**. Today, India is well linked with the rest of the world despite its varied topography and vast size. The means of transport are called the lifelines of a nation's economy.

Importance of Transport

- Transport links the backward areas to the urban cities and reduces regional industrial disparity.
- It helps in proper utilisation of natural resources lying in hills and forest.
- It protects the people during war, natural calamities and crisis.
- It helps in transportation of raw material to industries.
- It helps in the movement of goods during any calamities.

Modes of Transport

Roadways

- India has a road network of over 5.89 million km. It is the **second largest road network** in the world. Roads in India are more significant mode of transport than railways. It provides link between railway stations and other parts of the country.
- Roads in India are classified in Express Highways, National Highways, Golden Quadrilateral, District roads, Village roads, International Highways, etc.

Types of Road

In India, roads are of two types, *i.e.,* **Metalled** and **Non-metalled**. Metalled roads are made of cement and concrete. These roads are durable, weather proof and require lower maintenance compared to other roads.

Non-metalled roads can be used only during dry season. Most of the roads in villages are non-metalled road, where water logging is a common problem during rainy season.

Express Highways

These are six or eight lanes, highest class of roads with controlled access. At present, it covers around 640 km. Some of the expressways are Mumbai-Pune Expressway, (first expressway), Eastern Expressway (Mumbai), Ahmedabad-Vadodara Expressway and Delhi-Gurgaon Expressway.

National Highways

- These are highways, which connect major cities, state capitals, large industrial and tourist centres of the country. These roads carry about 65% of the freight and 80% of the traffic. The longest highway in India is NH-7, which is from **Varanasi to Kanyakumari**. India is having world's highest drivable highways connecting Manali to Leh in Ladakh, Kashmir.
- The **National Highways Authority of India** (NHAI) is the authority responsible for the development, maintenance and management of National Highways. The NHAI is undertaking the development activities and other projects on National Highways.

Some Important National Highways are

(i) **NH-1** is also called the Sher Shah Suri Marg, between Delhi and Amritsar.

(ii) **NH-2** connects Delhi and Kolkata.

(iii) **NH-3** connects Mumbai and Agra.

(iv) **NH-7** connects Varanasi and Kanyakumari.

(v) **NH-8** connects Delhi and Mumbai.

(vi) **NH-15** connects Samakhiali in Gujarat with Pathankot in Punjab.

Golden Quadrilateral

The Golden Quadrilateral is a highway network, which connects many of the major industrial, agricultural and cultural centres of India. This project is one of the largest road projects of India. The National Highway Authority of India is an authority to implement the project. The project is to be taken in following phases

Phase I

This phase comprises the connecting of Delhi, Mumbai, Chennai and Kolkata by six lanes super highways. It has the total length of approximately 5846 km.

Phase II

The North-South corridor aims to connect Srinagar to Kanyakumari.

The East-West corridor aims to connect Silchar in Assam to Porbandar in Gujarat.

Phase III

This phase mainly based on the updating of existing rational network to 4/6th lane standard. It connects state capitals with different seaports and important places of tourist interest with quadrilaterals.

Phase IV

The Government is considering widening 20000 km of highways, which will convert existing single lane highways into two lanes with paved shoulders.

Phase V

As road traffic increases over time, a number of 4 lane highways will need to be upgraded and expanded to six lanes. The current plan has taken to upgrade of about 5000 km of four-lanes road. Although, the stretches are not yet specified.

Phase VI

The World Bank is studying this project and it will be funded **Build Operate and Transfer** (BOT). It has identified Vadodara-Mumbai Expressway, Chennai-Bengaluru Expressway and Kolkata-Dhanbad Expressway to improve.

Phase VII

This phase calls for improvement to city road networks by adding ring roads to enable easier connectivity with National Highways to important cities. In this project, improvements will be made to stretches of National Highways that require additional flyovers and bypasses along the highways and increasing traffic.

Advantages of Road Transport

The advantages of road transport are as follows

(i) It gives better connectivity.

(ii) It is cheaper means of transport.

(iii) It is self-regulated means of transport, one can stop anywhere and at any time.

(iv) It facilitates door to door service.

(v) Roads are comparatively easy and cheap to construct and maintain.

(vi) It can be constructed more easily in remote areas and in difficult terrains, high altitudes and steep slopes.

(vii) Perishable goods like vegetables, fruits and milk are transported more easily and quickly by roads than by railways.

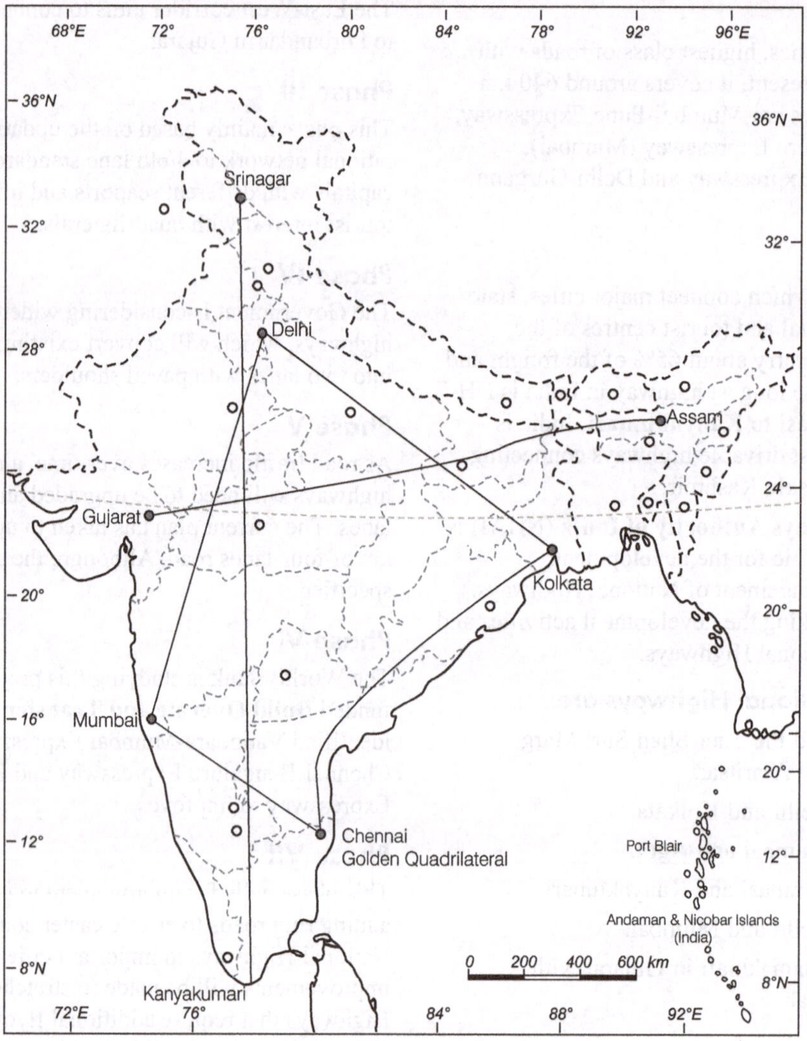

Road Projects of India

Disadvantages of Road Transport

Disadvantages of road transport are as follows

(i) The chief problem of roads is their poor maintenance. There is no stable government policy to maintain and improve the roads.

(ii) Roads are not suitable and are uncomfortable in long distance travel.

(iii) Roadside facilities like repair shop, medicine shop, telephone booths, rest houses, etc are lacking which are very essential for long distance routes.

(iv) It is more expensive than rail transport for longer distances.

(v) Increase in vehicles has led to more road accidents and air-pollution.

(vi) Heavy commodities like, coal and iron are difficult to transport by road.

Railways

- The Indian Railway Network is the **largest in Asia** and the fourth largest in the world and the main artery of the country's inland transport. It contributes to the economic growth and promotes national integration. The Indian railways transports over 110 lakh passengers and 8 lakh tonnes of goods everyday.
- It started in 1853 from (Bombay to Thane.) The railways in India made tremendous growth during pre as well as post Independence period. The entire railway management was taken over by the Central Government in 1950. In 1952, it was decided to replace existing rail networks by zones.
- Total six zones were made in 1952. Indian railways has undergone considerable improvement over the years and now is divided into **sixteen zones**. As India developed in economy its railway networks also expanded.
  Railway network in India is classified according to gauges *i.e.,* Broad, Meter and Narrow.
  1. **Broad Gauge** (Width 1.676 m) is used in most part of the country, which connects the major ports with other towns. It is accounts around 50% of total route length. In this, there is a distance of 1.676m between the two rails. More than 44776km length belongs to this. It links major cities. It has greater stability during periods of high wind and unpredictable weather.
  2. **Meter Gauge** (Width 1 m) implies, the width of the track is 1m and is mainly used in Western Rajasthan, Gujarat, Maharashtra, Karnataka. About 14987km of the railways is meter gauge.
  3. **Narrow Gauge** (Width 0.762 m) is used in mountaineous terrains of Himachal Pradesh and Western Ghats. Important narrow guage lines are Shimla-Kalka, Siliguri- Darjeeling, etc. This is confined to hilly areas. Narrow gauge covered a total of 2400 km route length in 2011.

Advantages of Railways

The advantages of railways are as follows

(i) It helps in the development of tourism in India.

(ii) It serves as the principal mode of transport of both freight and passengers.

(iii) It serves as the cheapest mode of transport for bulky products over long distances.

(iv) Railways connect the hinterland to the seaports. *e.g.,* Cotton Textile Industry in Mumbai is connected to Mumbai seaport via railways.

(v) It plays an important role in the process of economic development and urbanisation.

(vi) It promotes integration within the states, e.g., connecting Eastern states to West and Northern to South.

(vii) It forms a major employment sector in our country.

Disadvantages of Railways

- Rail tracks are very difficult to lay on irregular land such as hilly and forested areas as compared to Northern place which have dense network of railways.
- Train journey sometimes are very long and tiring, especially if we compare it with air journey.
- Trains cannot cross seas and oceans. It cannot be laid on the landscape which has loose soil base.
- Due to the electrification of trains there is an increase in the consumption of electricity and train fares.
- Lack of cleanliness and other basic facilities adds to the disadvantage of the railways.
- Rail transportation cannot provide door to door service.
- High cost is involved in construction of railway tracks.

Airways

- Air transport is the most modern means of transport, which is unmatched by its speed, time saving and long distance operation. It is very important for a large country like India.
  The beginning of the air transport was made in 1911 with a 10km air mail service between Allahabad and Naini.
- The real progress was achieved in 1920, when some aerodromes were constructed and the **Tala Sons Limited** started operating internal air services. Flying clubs were opened in Delhi, Karachi, Kolkata and Bombay in 1928.
- Air transport in India was nationalised in 1953. It connects the remote regions, where other means of transport cannot be laid *e.g.,* connecting Andaman and Nicobar to mainland India. The **Airports Authority of India** (AAI) was formed in 1st April, 1995. **Directorate General of Civil Aviation** (DGCA) is the principal regulatory body in the field of civil aviation in India.

Air traffic in India is classified in following ways

1. International Airports

International airports mainly handle airlines carrying passengers from foreign countries. These airports are available for all scheduled international operations by Indian and foreign carriers.

Five major International Airports in India are

(i) The Indira Gandhi International Airport at New Delhi.

(ii) Netaji Subhash Chandra Bose International Airport at Kolkata.

(iii) Chhatrapati Shivaji International Airport at Mumbai.

(iv) Meenam Bakkam International Airport at Chennai.

(v) Trivandrum International Airport at Thiruvananthapuram.

2. Domestic Airports

Airports, which handle domestic passengers are called domestic airports. There are 103 (23 civil aviation) domestic airports in India. Indian Airlines is the major air carrier of the country. It operates 5-7 domestic stations and 17 international stations in 14 countries.

Note The domestic airlines is now flourishing with private airlines as the Government has now ended the monopoly of Indian airlines. Some of the leading domestic private airlines are Spice Jet, Indigo, Jet Airways, etc.

3. Helicopter Services in India

Helicopter is another means of air transportation. They are smaller crafts. Helicopters do not need runway and can land and take off from helipads or open grounds.

Advantages of Helicopters

The main advantages of helicopters are as follows

(i) Helicopters are helpful during disasters. They can be used to drop food packets and medicines to the disaster affect people when they are unreachable by all communications and transport modes.

(ii) They are also helpful in rescue operations, because they can stay at one place in the air for some time.

(iii) Unaccessible areas can also be reach by helicopters such as mountain peaks, forest areas, etc.

Pawan Hans Helicopters Limited

It provides helicopter services to the petroleum sector and even to the tourists and passengers to remote areas.

Advantages of Airways

The main advantages of airways are as follows

(i) It is the fastest mode of transport.

(ii) It is most important in North-East region, where it is the only mode of transport because of the difficult terrain.

(iii) In emergency time, it is the most effective means of transport to save life.

(iv) Air travel is most indispensable for the business people, for defense, where it saves lives at the time of natural calamities like earthquake, flood, etc., where time factor is very crucial.

Disadvantages of Airways

The main disadvantages of airways are as follows

(i) This is not affordable to everyone, especially common man.

(ii) Lack of funds, reflects on the mismanagement and inefficiency of the authority as well as the Government.

(iii) The Indian Airlines is facing stiff competition from Foreign Airlines due to poor quality of service.

Waterways

- Waterways are most suitable for carrying heavy and bulky goods. India has a long coastline of 7,517 km and inland navigable waterways of 14,500 km in length, which comprises of rivers, lands, lakes and backwaters.
- It is the cheapest mode of transport. It is a fuel efficient and environment friendly mode and carries 65% of country's total foreign trade. The Northern rivers are considered more suitable for navigation as these are perennial rivers. Whereas the Peninsular or Deccan rivers are non-perennial thus, are not suitable for navigation purpose.
- Waterways can be broadly divided into two groups

  (i) Inland water transport

  (ii) Coastal shipping
- Coastal ports mainly carry the foreign trade of the countries. Inland waterways in India is controlled by **Inland Waterways Authority of India** (IWAI). Further, the **Central Water Transport Corporation** (CWTC) was constituted in 1967. It is mainly engaged in the transportation of goods by inland waterways in the Ganga, Brahmaputra, Hooghly and Sundarban regions.

Some important National Waterways are

(i) **NW-1** in Ganga river from Allahabad to Haldia (1620 km).

(ii) **NW-2** in Brahmaputra river from Sadiya to Dhubri (891 km).

(iii) **NW-3** in West Coast canal of Kerala from Kollam to Kottapuram (205 km).

(iv) **NW-4 katrinada Puducherry** stretches of the Krishan and Godavari rivers.

(v) **NW-5** Talcher Dhamra (623 km) in Odisha and West Bengal on Brahmani river.

Advantages of Waterways

The main advantages of waterways are as follows

(i) The mode of transport is cheaper as well as environment friendly.

(ii) They are most suitable for carrying heavy and bulky goods.

Disadvantage of Waterways

The disadvantages of waterways are as follows

(i) It is a slow means of transport.

(ii) It do not provide door to door services therefore it is not good for small goods transportation.

(iii) It is not operational throughout the year so during floods or when rivers dry up, transportation is not possible.

Decline in the importance of Inland Waterways

The main causes for the decrease in importance of inland waterways are as follows

(i) Water volume in the rivers is getting reduced due to diversion of river water for irrigation purposes.

(ii) Indian ports are not well connected with their hinterlands.

(iii) Most of the large rivers of the country enters the sea, through shallow sand chocked delta channels.

(iv) Expansion of roads and railways have reduced the importance and usage of inland waterways.

(v) Peninsular rivers are not ideal for navigation.

(vi) They are not perennial and water flows during monsoon or rainy season only.

(vii) Peninsular rivers flows through undulating rocky plateau region.

Major Ports in India

India has a long coastline of 7,517 km and **12 major ports** and nearly **200 minor ports**. All 12 major ports in India carry more than 95% of Indian foreign trade by volume and 70% by value. All major ports are under jurisdiction of Central Government.

Some major ports are as follows

- **On Eastern Coast** Chennai (Tamil Nadu), Eunore (Tamil Nadu), Tuticorin (Tamil Nadu), Vishakhapatnam (Andhra Pradesh), Paradip (Odisha), Kolkata (West Bengal), Haldia (West Bengal).
- **On Western Coast** Mumbai, Jawaharlal Nehru-Nhava Sheva (Maharashtra), New Mangalore (Karnataka), Marmagaon (Goa), Kochi (Kerala), Kandla (Gujarat).
- Kandla is a tidal port in Kuchchh which was developed with the objective to recover the loss of Karachi port to Pakistan during partition. Another objective to develop the port was to ease the pressure from Mumbai port. It caters the exports and imports of North-Western India.
- **Mumbai** is the biggest and oldest port of India. It is a natural port and well-sheltered harbour. Jawaharlal Nehru port was developed with a view to decongest the Mumbai port.
- New Mangalore port in Karnataka and Marmagaon port in Karnataka mainly exports iron-ore.
- Kochi port in Kerala is a natural harbour located at the enterance of a lagoon.
- Tuticorin port of Tamil Nadu is a natural port which largely handles a large variety of cargoes to Srilanka, Maldives and other neighbouring countries.
- **Vishakhapatnam** is land-locked port. It is the deepest port of India. It is often hit by cyclones during the months of October and November.

- Kolkata is an inland riverine port situated at a distance of 128 km from the coast along the bank of Hoogly river.
- Haldia port is another port of West Bengal. It is constructed as a Subsidary port to reduce the pressure from the Kolkata port.

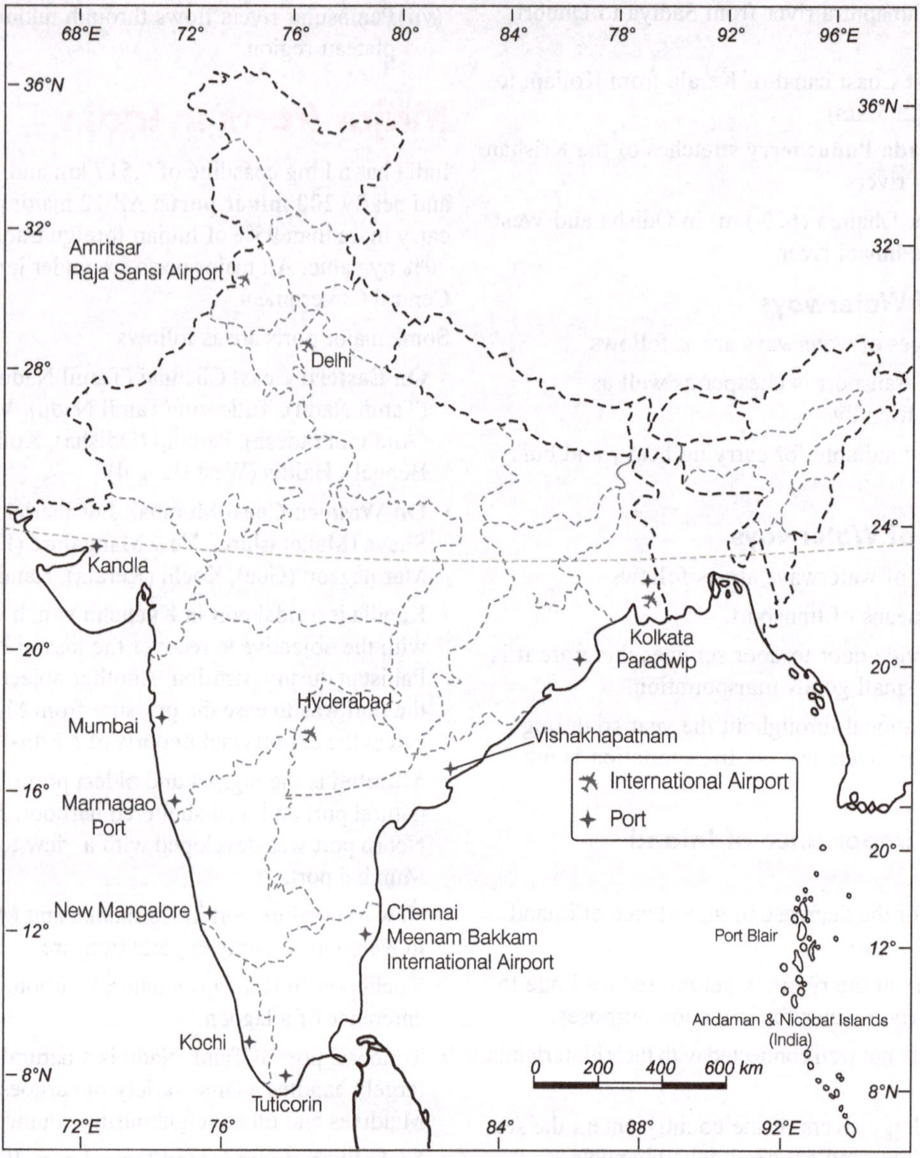

Major Ports and International Airports

PYQs Previous Years' Questions

1 Marks Questions

Multiple Choice Questions

1. ………… transport supplements the other modes of transport. *(ICSE Specimen 2023)*

(a) Airways (b) Roadways
(c) Waterways (d) Railways

Ans. (b) Roadways

2 Marks Questions

1. What is the Golden Quadrilateral? Mention two economic benefits of its. *(ICSE Specimen 2023)*

Ans. The Golden Quadrilateral, the highway network that links many India's four key cities i.e. Delhi, Mumbai, Kolkata and Chennai thus connecting the major industrial, agricultural and cultural centres of India is helping in the economic growth and national integrity of the country.

The projected economic benefits of the GQ project

(i) Faster transport networks between major cities and ports.

(ii) Smoother movement of products and people within India.

2. How is a good transport network important for India? *(ICSE Specimen 2023)*

Ans. A good transport network important for India for its economical development because India is a vast country with long distances and it has vast natural resources distributes in the whole country, transport help in link between production, distribution and consumption process. A well developed transport network brings the people closer to each other and help in strengthening the unity in divert.

3. "Though an expensive mode of transport, airways is gaining popularity in India." Explain giving two reasons.

> **HINT** *Dear students, this question simply asks you to write advantages of air transports.*

Ans. Through an expensive mode of transport airways is gaining popularity because India is a vast country where distances are large, and the terrain and the climatic conditions are so diverse and airways have following advantages

(i) It is the fastest mode of transport

(ii) It is most important in North-East region, where it is the only mode of transport because of the difficult terrain.

4. Mention two advantages of using waterways. *(ICSE Specimen Semester II 2022)*

Ans. The two advantages of waterways are

(i) The mode of transport is cheaper as well as environment friendly

(ii) They are most suitable for carrying heavy and bulky goods.

5. Mention any two advantages of using roadways.

Ans. Two advantages of roadways are *(ICSE Semester II 2022)*

(i) It provides door to door service where as the railways do not provide that.

(ii) Roads are best connecting ways from hilly areas to plains. While it is difficult to lay railway tracks in these places.

6. With reference to waterways, answer the following questions *(ICSE 2020)*

(i) Mention two advantages of inland water transport.

(ii) Why is inland water transport not well developed in India?

Ans. (i) Two advantages of inland water transport are as

(a) It is suitable for heavy and bulky goods to transport from one region to another.

(b) Rivers are the only means of transport in thick forested areas of heavy rainfall.

(ii) Inland waterway is declining in its importance due to following reasons

- Areas of water transport is restricted. It provides access to limited areas.
- It demands long travelling hours which tends to make people ill.

7. Even though all means of transport are well-developed in India, yet, road transport remains the most popular means of transport. Justify this statement. *(ICSE 2020)*

Other Similar Questions

Or Roadways are always considered more important than any other means of transportation. Give two reasons in support of the statement.

Or "Roadways are an important means of transport in India". Give two reasons to justify the statement.

Ans. Roadways are always considered as more important than any other means of transport because

(i) It is more suitable for short distance travel and it connects small villages and toward where other means of transport cannot reach.

(ii) It saves cost of transportation from one station to another station and it saves the time.

8. Transport is the backbone of a country's economy. Give two reasons to support the statement. *(ICSE Specimen 2018)*

Ans. "Transport is the backbone of a country's economy". This statement can be supported with following points.

(i) It links the backward areas to the urban areas and reduces regional industrial disparity.

(ii) It helps in utilisation of natural resources lying in hills and forest.

9. Give two ways in which rail transport is useful for the people of India. *(ICSE 2018)*

Ans. The two ways in which rail transport is useful for the people of India are

(i) It helps us in conducting various activities like business, sight seeing, pilgrimage.

(ii) It helps people to connect their family from far away and transport the goods over long distance.

10. Mention two reasons why more people use railways rather than airways. *(ICSE 2017)*

Ans. More people use railways rather than airways because

(i) the railways serve as the cheapest mode of transport.

(ii) the railways connect the hinterlands to the megacities of India.

11. Why is road transport in India considered more useful than rail transport? State two reasons in support of your reply. *(ICSE 2014)*

Ans. Road transport is more popular than rail transport because of following reasons

(i) It provides door to door service where as the railways do not provide that.

(ii) Roads are best connecting ways from hilly areas to plains. While it is difficult to lay railway tracks in these places.

12. Why is road transport favoured in the Northern plains of India? *(ICSE 2012)*

Ans. The road transport is favoured in the Northern plains of India because this region is flat and road can be easily constructed.

13. Give reasons to explain the lack of rail transport in Northern India. *(ICSE 2012)*

Ans. The Northern India is lacked by rail transport because of mountainous relief features.

3 Marks Questions

1. (i) Name the terminal stations of East-West Corridor.

(ii) Who looks after the construction and maintenance of the following? *(ICSE Specimen 2023)*

(a) National Highways

(b) Border Roads

Ans. (i) The terminal stations of East-West corridor are Silcher in Assam and Porbandar in Gujarat.

(ii) (a) The National Highways Authority of India (NHAI)

(b) Border Roads Organisation

2. (i) Why are South Indian rivers not ideal for inland water transport ? *(ICSE 2023)*

(ii) Mention two advantages of waterways.

Ans. (i) The South Indian rivers are not perennial i.e. not flowing throughout the year. So, they are not ideal for the inland water transport.

(ii) For answer, refer to Q4 of 2 marks questions.

3. Mention two advantages of using railways as means of transport. *(ICSE 2023)*

Ans. Two advantages of using railways as means of transport are

- It facilitates long distance travel and transport of bulky goods which are not easily transported through motor vehicles.
- It is a quick and more regular form of transport because it helps in the transportation of goods with speed and certainty.

4. Mention three disadvantages of waterways. *(ICSE Semester II 2022)*

Ans. Three disadvantages of waterways are as follows

- It is a slow means of transport.
- It does not provide door to door services therefore it is not good for small goods transportation.
- It is not operational throughout the year so during floods or when rivers dry up, transportation is not possible.

5. Give a reason for the following *(ICSE Semester II 2022)*

(i) Railways are not well developed in the North Eastern States of India.

(ii) Why waterways are considered as the cheapest mode of transportation? What are its benefit?

Ans. (i) Railways are not well developed in the North Eastern States of India because this is a hilly region with undulating topography and dense forest cover.

(ii) Waterways are considered cheaper mode of transport because it carries large amount of bulk goods due to its size.

- Its benefits are
- It is environment friendly, takes less maintenance.
- It can carry large no of passengers also.

6. Give a reason for each of the following. *(ICSE 2020)*

(i) Roadways is not well developed in North East India.

(ii) Railways are under the public sector.

(iii) A good network of transport is of great help for the development of the economy.

Ans. (i) Roadways is not well developed in North-East India because this region is a hilly area which has undulating topography.

(ii) Railways are managed by the public sectors of the government, as the government has a majority of the share in the railway sector. The public sector companies are involved with development and expansion of the railways.

(iii) A good network of transport is of great help for the development of the economy because it can broaden the market for goods. It can also make easy movement of raw materials, fuels, equipment, etc. to the places of production, easy.

7. (i) Give two disadvantages of airways. *(ICSE 2020)*

(ii) Why is there an increase of airway traffic in recent years?

Ans. (i) Two disadvantages of using air transport are

(a) It provides costly services.

(b) It depends greatly on weather conditions.

(ii) There is an increase of airway traffic in recent years due to economic and demographic growth and the emergence of low-cost airlines that offer holiday packages at cheaper rates.

8. Give a reason for each of the following. *(ICSE 2019)*

(i) Nearly seventy per cent of Indians do not use air transport.

(ii) A well-developed transport is important for industrial growth.

(iii) Water transport is not as popular as land transport in India.

Ans. (i) Air transport provides comfortable, but costly services. The rate of freight charges are very high in air transport. Thus, Indians mostly do not use air transport.

(ii) Good transport network helps in the development of industrialisation and urbanisation. It links the backward areas to the urban cities and reduces regional industrial disparity. It helps in transportation of raw material to industries. Thus, well developed transport is important for industrial growth.

(iii) Water transport depends on the weather conditions which obstructs its potential whereas land transport can be used in any season. Water transport is restricted to the areas having navigable rivers and oceanic modes while land transport helps to connect the remotest villages and hilly areas to towns, cities and plain areas. Thus, water transport is less popular than land transport in India.

9. (i) "The railway is an important means of transport as compared to airways." *(ICSE 2019)*

State two reasons to support the statement.

(ii) Mention one disadvantage of rail transport.

Ans. (i) For answer, refer to Q10, of 2 marks questions.

(ii) Rail tracks are very difficult to lay on irregular land such as hilly and forested areas. Train journey sometimes are very long and tiring, especially if we compare it with air journey.

Examiner's Comment

- Most of the candidates answered it correctly.
- Many candidates were unable to relate transport to industries and thus wrote vague answers.
- Most of the candidates answered it correctly.

Suggestion for Students

- Relate a well-developed transport network to growth of industries and the economy as a whole.

10. (i) State one advantage of roadways.

(ii) State one disadvantage of water transport. ***(ICSE 2018)***

Ans. (i) For answer, refer to Q 5 of 2 marks questions.

(ii) For answer, refer to Q 4 of 3 marks questions.

11. Mention three reasons why inland waterways are better developed in Northern India than in Southern India. ***(ICSE Specimen 2018)***

Ans. Inland waterways are better developed in Northern India than in Southern India, due to following reasons:

(i) The rivers in Southern India are non-perennial, thus, they are not suitable for inland waterways. On the other hand, rivers in North India like Ganga, Yamuna, Brahmaputra etc are perennial rivers and are favourable for the development of inland waterways.

(ii) Rivers of the South India flow in rocky areas hence, they are not fit for playing boats because there are waterfalls in the way.

(iii) Most of the rivers of South India have been diverted for irrigation projects.

12. State three advantages of roadways over railways. ***(ICSE Specimen 2018)***

Ans. Three advantages of roadways over railways are as following

(i) It comparatively costs less to construct road networks than railway lines.

(ii) Roads can be constructed even in irregular land and hilly regions but it is difficult to develop railway networks in such areas.

(iii) Roads provide the facility of door to door service which is very favourable and minimise the cost of loading and unloading of products and goods. It is impossible to provide door to door railway facilities.

13. Mention two advantages of waterways. ***(ICSE 2016)***

Ans. The two main advantages of waterways are as follows

(i) The mode of transport is cheaper as well as environment friendly.

(ii) They are suitable for carrying heavy and bulky goods.

14. Mention any three problems being faced by the Indian Railways. ***(ICSE 2012)***

Ans. The three important problems faced by the Indian Railways are

(i) Poor maintenance, terrorist attacks, robbery etc., have made the railway journey unsafe.

(ii) Most of the bridges were constructed long ago and maintenance is expensive and difficult.

(iii) Operating on different gauges by the railways has become very time-consuming due to which there are major delays.

CHAPTER TEST

01 Mark Questions

1. Which of the following Asian country has the largest railway network ?
   (a) Nepal
   (b) Pakistan
   (c) Bangladesh
   (d) India

2. .... is considered as the cheapest mode of transportation.
   (a) Railways (b) Roadways
   (c) Airways (d) Waterways

3. .... are durable, weather proof and require low maintenance.
   (a) Metalled roads
   (b) Sea routes
   (c) Non- metalled roads
   (d) None of the above

Answers

1. (d) | 2. (d) | 3. (a)

10 Marks Questions

4. (i) What are the advantages of using railways ?
   (ii) Mention the reason why more people use to prefer travelling via railways rather than airways in India?
   (iii) What are the benefits of using roadways over railways ? State reasons.
   (iv) What are the disadvantages of railways transportation ?

5. (i) Why are railways not well developed in North.- Eastern States of India?
   (ii) Why is air transport gaining popularity in recent times in India ?
   (iii) Why is well- developed transport is important for industrial growth?
   (iv) How does the means of transport benefits the nation as a whole?

6. (i) Why water transport is not popular as land transport in India ?
   (ii) Why are South India rivers not ideal for the inland water transport ?
   (iii) The airways are used extensively despite being an expensive mode of transport. Why?
   (iv) Mention the advantage and disadvantages of waterways.

08

Topographical Maps

A topographical map (also called 'survey sheet') presents in miniature form, a colourful vivid picture of an area as it actually existed at the time it was surveyed. It displays both the natural features of the ground like vegetation, drainage and topography and the man-made features like settlements, roads, railways, etc.

It also contains other specific information like names of towns, villages, rivers, forests, hills, etc besides symbols denoting buildings with specific functions like temples, post offices, railway stations, etc. They also contain marking of **spot heights**, which have been actually measured during the survey. These are usually the tops of hills in the area.

In India, these maps are brought out by the Survey of India Department under the Ministry of Science and Technology.

Identification of Topographical Maps

If a part of India is being depicted in the map, it can be deduced from the sheet number, which consists of a number followed by a fraction with a letter ('A' onwards up to Q, except I) in the numerator and another number in the denominator e.g. 45 D/7.

The first number indicates the serial number of the 4° (latitude) × 4° (longitude) square (India has been divided into many such squares for the purpose of survey). This square is further divided into 16 squares (they are identified by letters), which are again divided into 16 squares (they are identified by numbers 1 to 16). Thus, the 45 D/7 sheet depicts an area corresponding to 1/4° × 1/4° (or 15' × 15') of latitude and longitude.

Grid References (Four Figure)

Topographical maps of scale 1:50000 have a grid of squares marked on them, with each side of the square representing 1 km on the ground. Vertical lines of these squares are called **Eastings** (as they are numbered going towards the East or right on the map), while horizontal lines are called **Northings** (as they are numbered going towards the North or top of the map).

The South West corner of the map is considered the origin. The Eastings and Northings are called the grid. Any point on the map will be identified by a Grid Reference. These are the four figure type (giving the approximate location of any object shown). To read four figure grid references, see the examples below

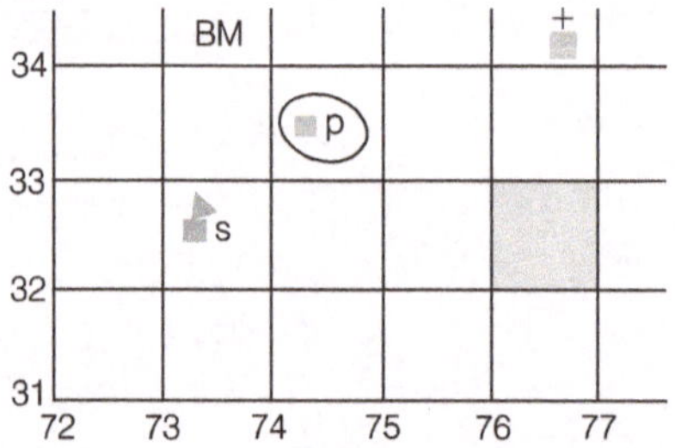

Fig. 1

In figure 1 (four figure), the school (marked as S) is in the square with its left end at the Easting marked 73 and its bottom at the Northing marked 32. Thus its four figure grid reference will be 7332, i.e., the first two numbers give the Easting and the next two give the Northing. Similarly the Post Office (marked as P) will have the grid reference 7433 and the Church will have grid reference 7634.

Six-figure Map References

To get the six-figure grid reference, you have to imagine that the four-figure square is further divided up into tenths.

In the example below, the grey box is in the four-figure grid reference square '1844', but more accurately it is 7 tenths across and 8 tenths up within that larger grid square, therefore the sixfigure map reference is '187448'.

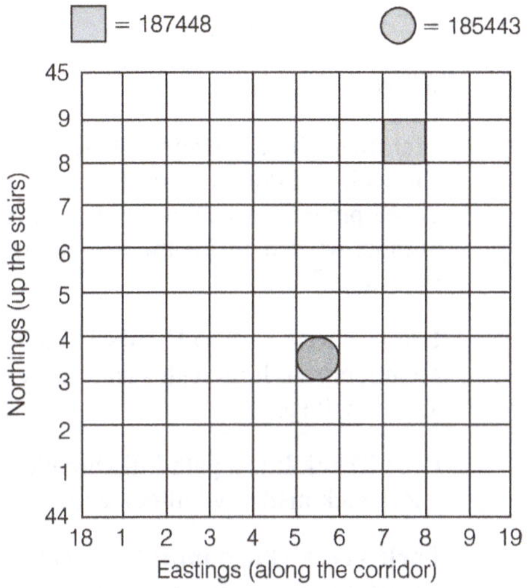

The shapes on the diagram above have the following six-figure grid references:

Grey square - 187 448, Red dot - 185 443

To be sure there is no doubt or confusion about which National Grid you're referring, when you quote the six-figure grid reference you should put the two letters of the area you are in before the numbers.

Significance of Colour

On survey sheets, each colour used has a significance. These are given below.

Colour	What it denotes	Remarks
Black	All names, heights and their numbering, latitude and longitude lines, railway lines, telephone / telegraph lines, dry streams, river banks, surveyed trees, broken ground	Surveyed trees are numbered and not allowed to be cut
Blue	Perennial rivers, ponds, lakes, tanks and other water bodies	Seasonal rivers are shown speckled
Green	All forested areas, orchards, scattered trees and scrubs	
Yellow	Cultivated areas	
White	Uncultivable land, badlands	
Brown	Contour lines and their numbering, sand hills and dunes	
Red	Grid lines (Eastings and Northings) and their numbering, roads and tracks, all buildings and settlements with specific symbols being shown for buildings with specific functions	The symbol size as well as the size and style in which its name is written decide the size of the settlement

Conventional Signs and Symbols Used in Survey Maps

Urban or Man-Made Features

Settlements

■ ■	Permanent hut
□ □	Temporary hut
	Settlement type
	**Nucleated** These settlements can be found into grouped or clustered form close to a railway station, a confluence, a mine or an industrials site.
	**Linear** Settlements which usually develop on either side of main road or along the coast with a view to provide services e.g. dhabas, hotels and shops.
	**Scattered** or **Dispersed** In these, the permanent huts are isolated or scattered. These hamlets spread over fertile farmland.

Structural Features

	Tower
	Antiquities
	Fort
	Chhatri
	Mandir (temple)
	Church
	Tomb
	Graves
	Mosque
	Idgah
PS	Police Station
....	Telegraph Lines
PO	Post Office
TO	Telegraph Office
PTO	Post and Telegraph Office (combined)
RH (forest)	Rest House
DB	Dak/Travellers Bungalow
IB (canal)	Inspection Bungalow (canal)
CG	Camping Ground
CH	Circuit House (A great house exclusively for government, officials.)

Political Boundaries

	Boundaries
	International boundaries shown by bold dash and dot. It indicates the borders between the countries.
	State boundaries (demarcated) by single dash and dot line.
—×—×	State boundaries (undemarcated)
– – –	Districts (sub-divisions) It is a series of dashes forms the border between the districts with a state.
• • • •	Teshil/taluka is represented by a series of dots.

	Boundaries
	Boundary pillars
•• ••	Forest boundary
□	Unlocated
■	Surveyed

Transport and Communication

	Roads
	Metalled (Pucca) Roads These roads shown in red double lines. Symbol of development of trade in the region. A number written beside the road shows a milestone.
====	**Unmetalled (Kutch) Roads** These roads are not tarred. It indicates an undeveloped area or village.
	Cart Track It is a path little broader than pack-track made by bullock carts.
---×---	**Pack Track (Pagdandi)** It is a path for constant use by men or animals to travel. It is shown in red broken line.
	Footpath with a Bridge It is for temporary use to cross a region. It is shown by a single line of dots in red colour.

	Railways
	Broad Gauge It is the distance between two rails i.e. 1.69 m.
	Metre Gauge 1 m distance between the rails.
	Narrow Gauge 0.7 m distance a railway line crossing a road.
	It shows railway line with a station.
	Light railway or tramway.
	Cutting with a Tunnel It is an open vertical cut in high ground to enable a road or railway to pass through.
	Level Gossing It indicates a railway line crossing a road.

Bridges	
	A bridges is a structure constructed across a road, river or railway to carry the traffic.
	A ridge without a causeway.
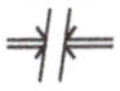	**Bridge with Piers** The bridge supported by pillars.
	**Tunnel** A passage for a railway line through a hill.
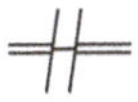	**Ford or Ferry** Ford is a shallow place where a river may be crossed wading. Ferry is a boat to carry people across a river where it is narrow.
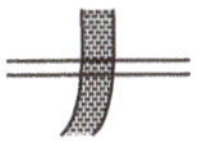	**Causeway** A road that is raised above water, marshland, sand or stream. Its presence shows that the area of scanty rainfall. It is motorable only in dry season.

Scale of a Topographical Map

The scale of a map is defined as the proportion existing between distances on the map and the actual distance on the surface of the Earth.

Thus a map drawn to the scale of 1/50000 or 1:50000 (used in Ordnance Survey Maps in India) means that 1 cm on the map represents an actual distance of 50000 cm (equal to 500 metres or ½ of a kilometre). This linear scale is used to measure the distance between two points on the map.

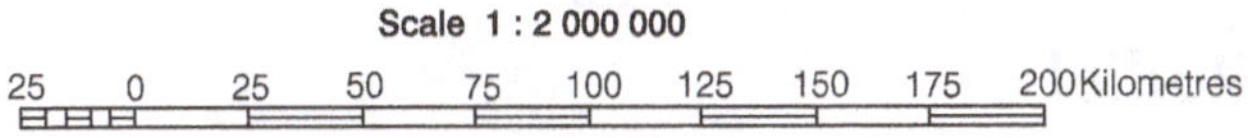

Fig. 2

Type of Scales

There are three common types of scales given

(i) **Simple Statement or Verbal Scale** It expresses the units of the map as well as the ground e.g. 1 centimetre =10 kilometres.

(ii) **The Representative Fraction (RF)** The numerical scale of a map indicates the relationship of distance measured on a map and the corresponding distance on the ground.

(iii) **Graphic (Bar) or Linear Scale** A graphic scale is a ruler printed on the map and is used to convert distances on the map to actual ground distances.

Measurement of Straight Distances

To determine straight-line distance between two points on a map, we can use a scale or a piece of paper

(i) Lay a straight-edged piece of paper or a scale on the map so that the edge of the paper or scale touches both points and extends past them. Make a tick mark on the edge of the paper at each point.

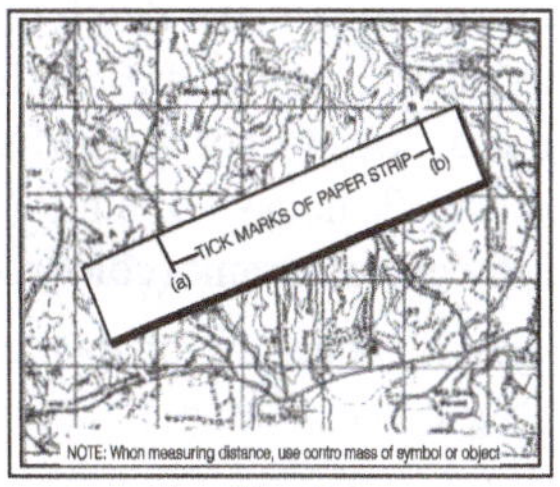

Fig. 3

(ii) To convert the map distance to ground distance, move the paper/scale down to the graphic bar scale and align the right tick mark (b) with a printed number in the primary scale so that the left tick mark (a) is in the extension scale.

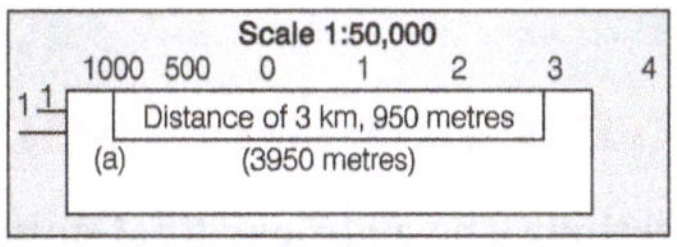

Fig. 4

(iii) Now place the divider or strip of paper on the linear scale drawn on the map. This will directly give the distance on the ground between the two point.

Interpretation of Contours and Contour Interval

A contour is a line drawn on a map joining points of equal height. The vertical difference in elevation between two contour lines is known as contour interval.

Contour is the standard method of showing relief (undulation of the terrain) on a topographical map. In ordnance maps of 1:50000, the vertical distance between two contours is usually 20 metres.

Survey Marks and their Interpretation

Spot Heights Spot heights are the actual heights of points above mean sea level, which have been fixed during surveying. These are marked by black dots with their height in metres written alongside.

Triangulated Heights Triangulated heights are fixed by using trignometrical methods and marked by black triangles 'Δ' with their height in metres written alongside.

Bench Mark Bench marks are permanent survey points having a stone or building indicating the height of that point found through accurate survey. They are marked as BM with their height mentioned, e.g. BM 224.6.

Surveyed Trees Surveyed trees are similarly marked with their heights above mean sea level.

Relative Height/Depth The relative height of a small hill (or raised portion of terrain) or the depth of a depression is marked by its height/depth along with the letter 'r' to indicate how higher or lower than the surrounding terrain the hill. Examples are 15r in case of a hill (indicated by brown dots) or 7r in case of a tank (coloured blue).

Gentle Slope In gentle slope, the change of elevation is gradual, e.g. 1:25 its gradient. Contours generally wide apart.

Steep Slope In such a slope, the land suddenly slopes up or down. The contours of this slope are drawn close to one another.

Conical Hill A conical hill rises almost uniformly from the surrounding land. A conical hill with uniform slope and narrow top is represented by concentric contour spaced almost at regular intervals.

Identification of Drainage

Marking Directions The **eight cardinal points**, e.g. North, South, East, West, North-West, South-West, North-East and South-East are used for giving the direction of flow of a river or the direction of one place from another. These are useful for indicating the flow of rivers and streams as well as the location of one town from another.

Direction of Flow To understand in which direction a river or stream is flowing, we look at the spot heights on the map and understand they are reducing, which determines that the land is sloping down. This tells us the direction of flow.

Left and Right Bank If we stand at the source of the river and look in the direction it is flowing, the left bank will be on our left and the right bank on our right. In the case of location of one town from another, we should be careful about the use of the words 'to' and 'from'.

Thus, for instance, if we want to go 'to' Mumbai 'from' Delhi, we will go SW, i.e. South-West. However if we want to go 'to' Delhi 'from' Mumbai, we will go NE, i.e. North-East.

Identification of Drainage Patterns

An area drained collectively by the network of a river and its tributaries is called a Drainage Basin. The catchment area of a river is the area drained by that particular river. In maps, it is observed that a drainage system develops a particular pattern depending on the terrain. The distinct patterns recognised are

Dendritic

This is the most common type found as it develops in a region where the underlying rock is having uniform corrosion resistance. Its interconnecting streams resemble the pattern of branches connecting to a deciduous tree (Fig. 5).

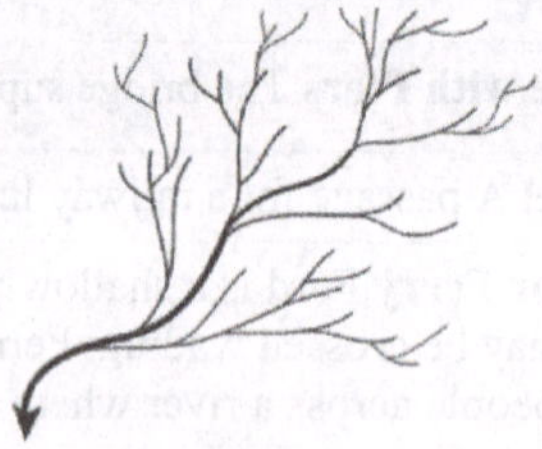

Fig. 5

Trellis

A drainage system that develops across a landscape of parallel valleys and ridges so that major tributaries flow down the valleys and join a trunk stream that cuts through the ridge; the resulting map pattern resembles a garden trellis (Fig. 6).

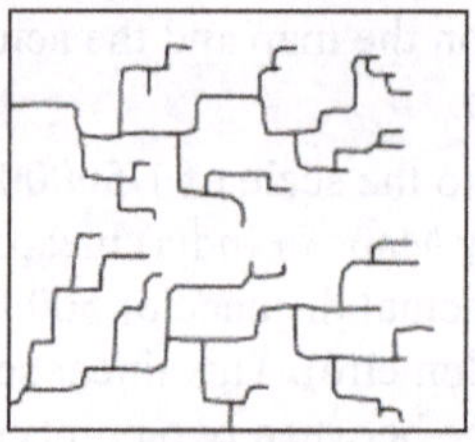

Fig. 6

Radial

This is rarely found. In this, the streams flow outward from a cone-shaped mountain, and define a pattern resembling spokes on a wheel (Fig. 7).

To determine the source of a river on the map, we find the slope of the river by the reducing spot heights mentioned above. The gradient of a river is higher in the upper reaches, thus causing vertical erosion and forming **V-shaped valleys.**

In its middle course, the river flows through flat land, where lateral erosion is dominant, causing it to change course, or meander. In its lower stage, the gradient is gentle and very little erosion occurs.

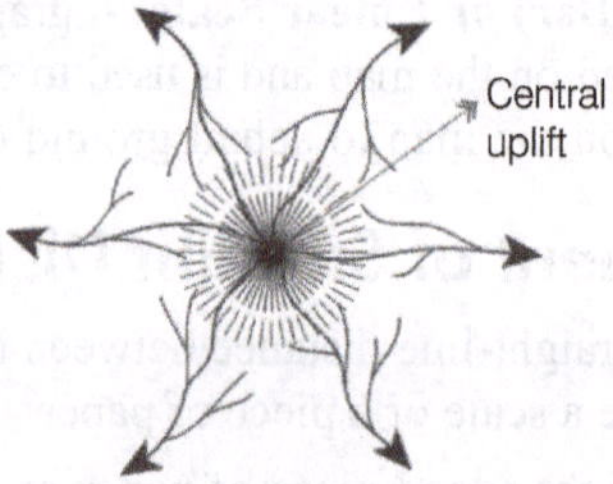

Fig. 7

Nature of Streams

A stream is a course of running water on land. Streams may vary in their width from a few centimeters to several kilometers. Some types of streams on the basis of nature are

Perennial Streams These streams have flow of water all throughout the year. Continuous rainfall during monsoons, melting of mountainous snow, etc create the supply of water continuously in the perennial rivers.

Intermittent Streams These streams have the sources of water supply only during the monsoons. There will not be any flow of water in these streams during summer.

Consequent Streams These are stream channels developed along the slope of a region as the first formed streams. Their courses are fully influenced by the slopes and natural irregularities of the area.

Subsequent Streams These streams are developed after the creation of consequent streams. They develop secondary slopes and tributaries with valleys.

Obsequent Streams These streams are tributaries that do not flow at right angles to the main stream. They even flow at opposite directions to the main stream.

Graded Streams These are streams that have reached an equilibrium between erosion and deposition. Such streams develop a smooth, concave longitudinal profiles.

Identification of Natural and Man-Made Features

- **Natural Physical Features** These include various landforms, relief features i.e. plains, plateaus, hills, mountains, waterfalls, passes etc. These are depicted by various techniques like, contour, hachures, hill shading, layer tinting/colouring, etc.
- **Man-Made or Cultural Features** These are villages, towns, types of land use, means of communication, settlement pattern, canals, bridge, etc. These are depicted by symbols called 'conventional signs'.

Types of Land Use/Land Cover

The type of vegetation is closely related to the relief of the land. In forested land (green coloured in maps), the Reserved and Protected Forests are indicated by green ribands around them. Density of the wooded area is indicated by different terms like dense forest, mixed jungle, open jungle, etc.

In the plains, most of the land which is cultivable (yellow coloured in maps) is used for agriculture. Canals, wells, tube wells and tanks indicates the availability of irrigation facilities. Perennial lined wells (blue dots in maps) show that the water table is high.

In uncultivable land, we find features like open scrub, stony waste, rock outcrop, broken ground, etc. Nothing is grown here.

Means of Transport and Communication

There are various means of transport and communication on the top sheet. This always depend on the type of relief and drainage e.g. in the plain areas there are better roads and rail connectivity available, where as in mountainous areas only roads are found, not railway tracks due to undulating topography.

There are also means of communication available like telephone lines, post offices, dak bungalow, telegraph line and other utilities/facilities like, dispensary, police chauki, etc.

Settlements and Communications Patterns

Towns and villages (called settlements) are of two types

Compact/Nucleated In a compact settlement the houses are built very close to each other and around a central point like a market. This settlement is also known as **nucleated settlement**. Various red coloured symbols are shown in clusters to indicate presence of a town, city or village.

Dispersed or Scattered These are found in remote and far away places. Only one or two buildings may be found here.

Site of Prominent Villages and/or Towns

The size of a town may be estimated by the size of the cluster and the presence of special buildings like post office, railway station etc. If the town is shown as connected by a metalled road and/or railway line with other towns, it indicates that it is well developed economically.

A larger town will also indicate the varied occupations of the residents, including business, trade, agriculture, government, public services, etc. Similarly, a large plain in yellow colour will indicate that much of the population is engaged in agriculture.

In the case of regions shown in green, the occupation of the people living nearby will be related to forestry. Areas indicating grasslands and open scrub indicate that their occupation will be related to raising of livestock.

Previous Years' Questions

1 Mark Questions

1. Refer to the image and answer the question that follow ***(ICSE Specimen Semester I 2021)***

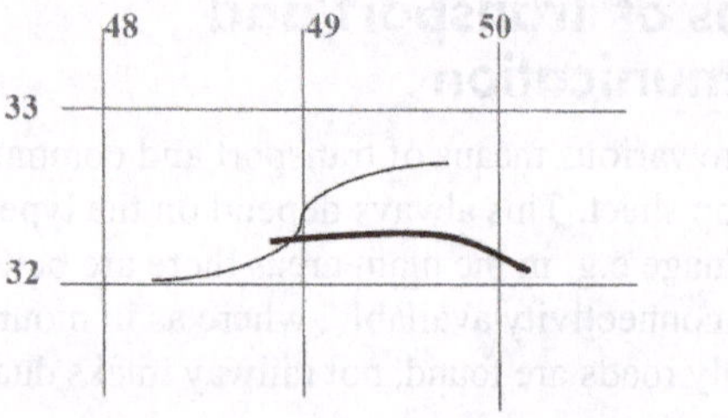

What does the black line in 4932 indicate?

(a) Open Scrub

(b) Dry land

(c) Broken land

(d) Seasonal stream

Ans. (b) Dry land

2. Refer to the image and answer the question that follow ***(ICSE Specimen Semester I 2021)***

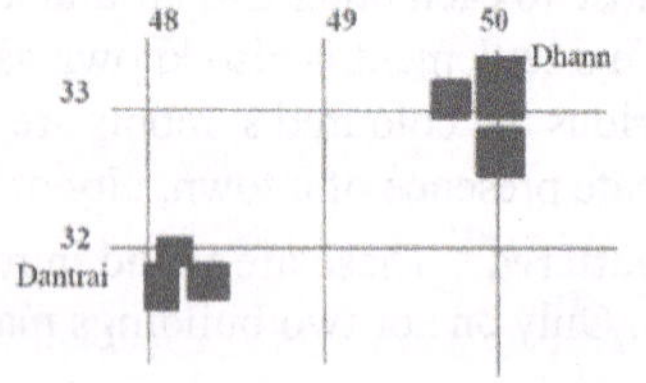

What is the direction of Dantrai from Dhann?

(a) North-East (b) North-West

(c) South-East (d) South-West

Ans. (d) South-West

3. Refer to the image and answer the question that follow ***(ICSE Specimen Semester I 2021)***

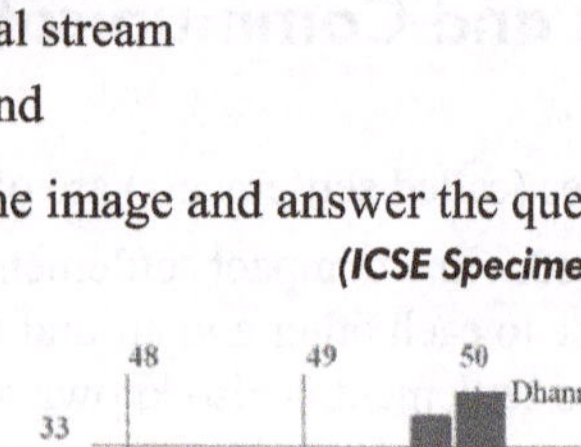

What is .277 in 4833?

(a) Spot height of 277 m (b) Spot Height of 277 cm

(c) Spot height of 277 mm (d) Spot height of 277 km

Ans. (a) Spot height of 277 m

4. Refer to the image and answer the question that follow ***(ICSE Specimen Semester I 2021)***

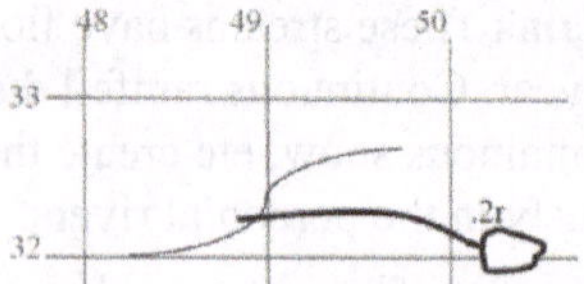

What does . 2r in 5032 indicate?

(a) The relative height of the tank is 2m

(b) The relative height of the tank is 2 cm.

(c) The relative depth of the embankment is 2 m.

(d) The relative depth of the embankment is 2cm.

Ans. (a) The relative height of the tank is 2m

5. Refer to the image and answer the question that follow

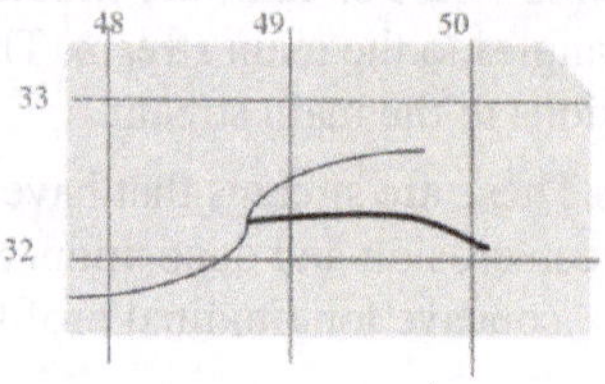

What is the main occupation of the people living in the area shown on the map extract?

(i) Mining

(ii) Agriculture

(iii) Fishing

(iv) Sheep rearing

Ans. (ii) Agriculture

6. Refer to the image and answer the question that follow ***(ICSE Specimen Semester I 2021)***

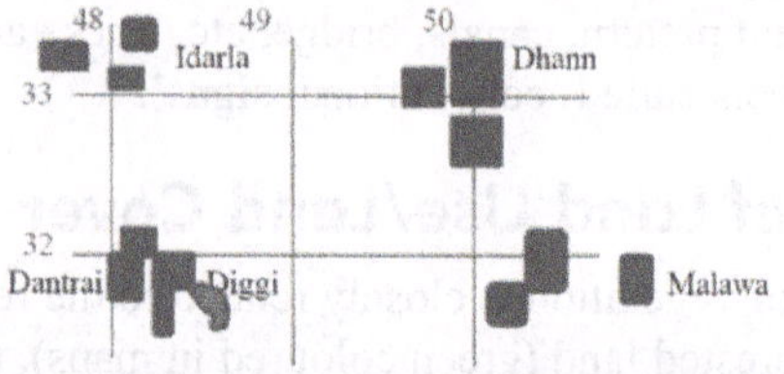

Which is the most important town in the above image?

(a) Idarla (b) Malawa

(c) Dantrai (d) Dhann

Ans. (c) Dantrai

7. Refer to the image and answer the question that follow ***(ICSE Specimen Semester I 2021)***

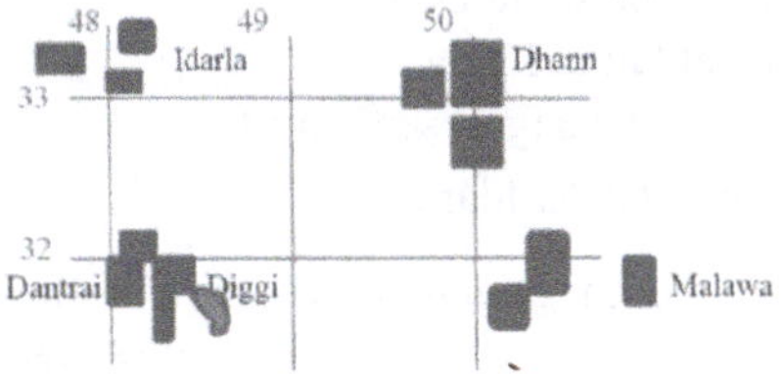

What is the black vertical line between 49 and 50 Easting?

(a) A line of latitude (b) A line of longitude
(c) An Easting (d) A Northing

Ans. (b) A line of longitude.

8. Refer to the image and answer the question that follow ***(ICSE Specimen Semester I 2021)***

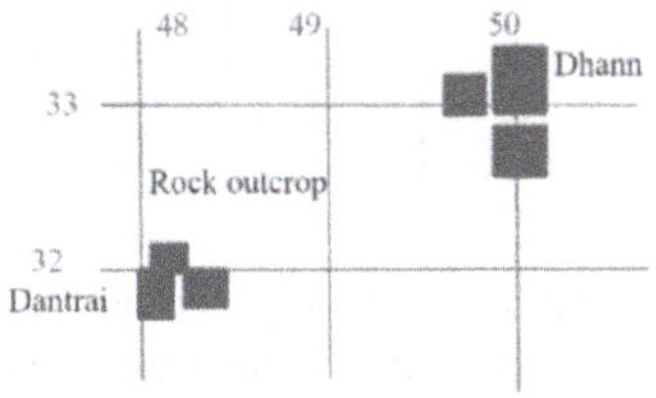

What is the four figure grid reference of rock outcrop?

(a) 4832 (b) 4933
(c) 3248 (d) 3349

Ans. (a) 4832

9. Refer to the images and answer the question that follow ***(ICSE Specimen Semester I 2021)***

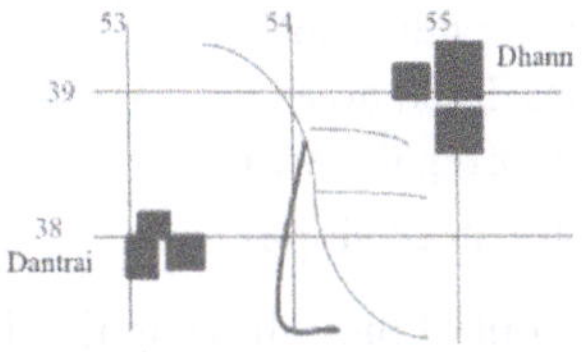

Which drainage pattern is seen in 5438?

(a) Radial. (b) Trellised
(c) Intermittent. (d) Dendritic

Ans. (b) Trellised

10. Refer to the images and answer the question that follow ***(ICSE Specimen Semester I 2021)***

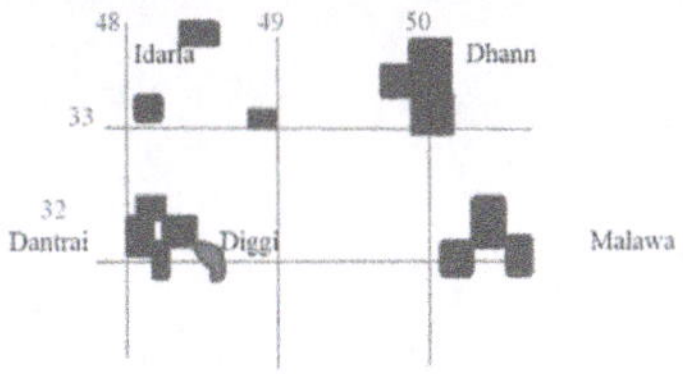

Name the settlement pattern in grid square 4833.

(a) Nucleated (b) Compact (c) Scattered (d) Isolated

Ans. (d) Isolated.

11. Refer to the image and answer the questions that follow ***(ICSE Semester I 2021)***

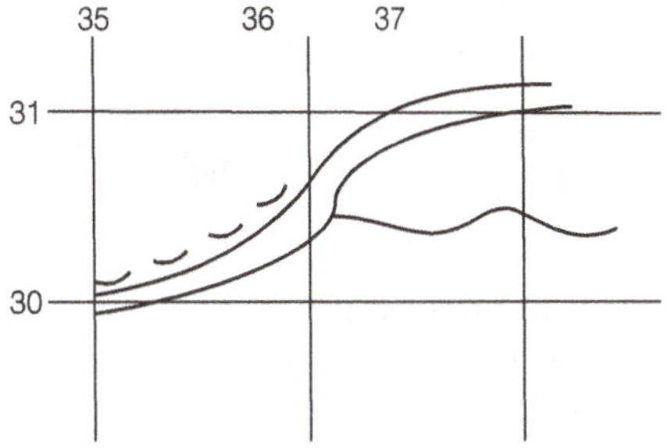

What do the black curved line in 3530 indicate?

(a) Open scrub (b) Dry land
(c) Broken ground (d) Seasonal stream

Ans. (c) Broken ground

12. Refer to the image and answer the questions that follow ***(ICSE Semester I 2021)***

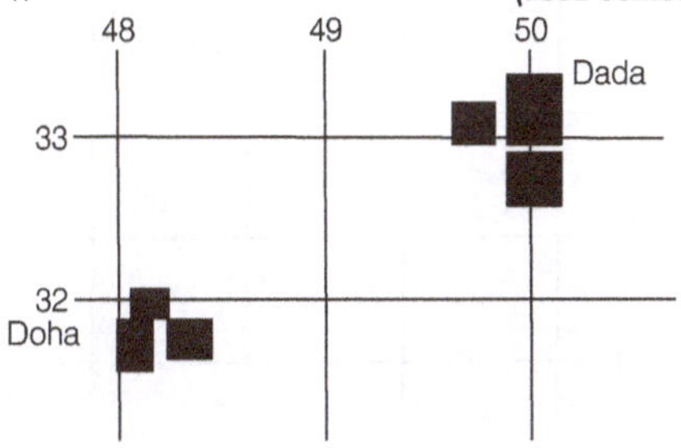

What is the direction of Dadra from Doha?

(a) North- East (b) North- West
(c) South-East (d) South- West

Ans. (a) North- East

13. Refer to the image and answer the questions that follow ***(Semester I 2021)***

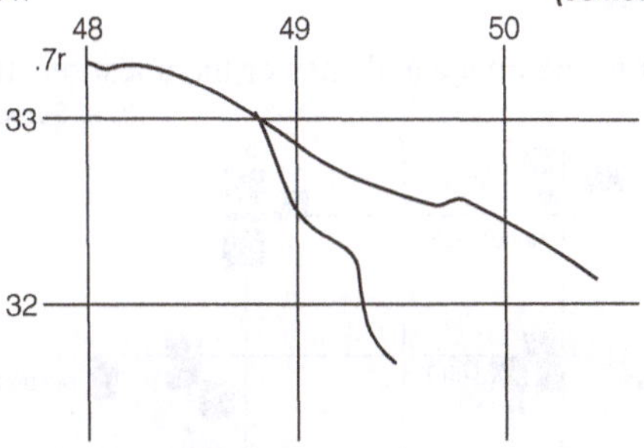

What is .7r in 4833?

(a) Relative height of 7m (b) Relative height of 7cm
(c) Relative depth of 7cm (d) Relative depth of 7m

Ans (a) Relative height of 7m

14. Refer to the image and answer the questions that follow

(ICSE Semester I 2021)

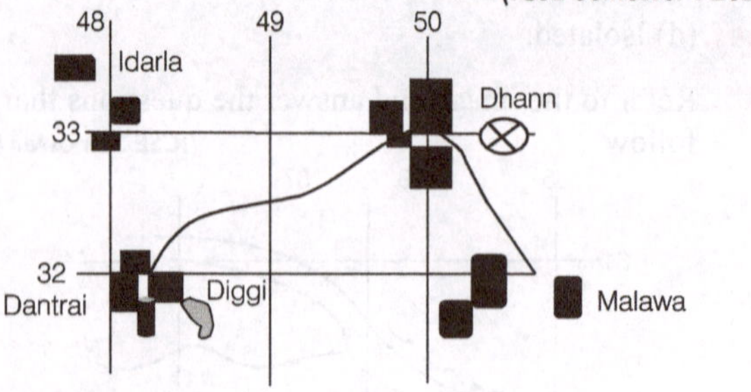

What mode of transport is used by the people of Malawa and Dantrai?

(a) Foot path
(b) Cart track
(c) Pack track
(d) Railway

Ans. (b) Cart track

15. Refer to the image and answer the question that follow

(ICSE Semester I 2021)

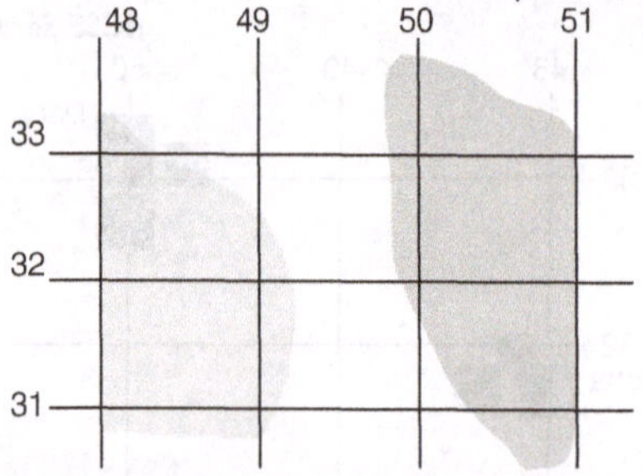

What is the main occupation of the people living in the area shown on the Eastern part?

(a) Mining
(b) Agriculture
(c) Forestry
(d) Sheep rearing

Ans. (c) Forestry

16. Refer to the image and answer the questions that follow

(ICSE Semester I 2021)

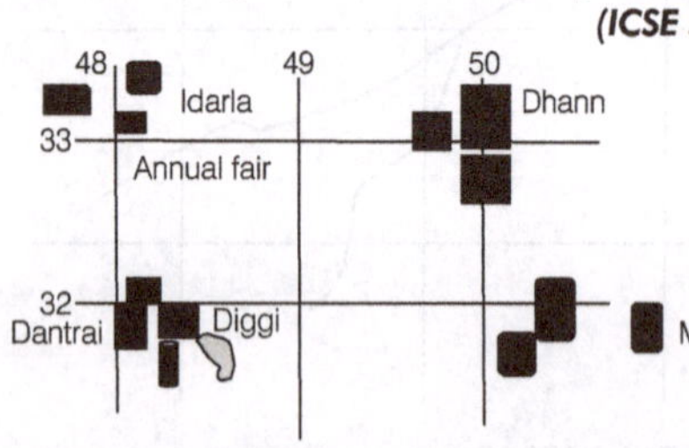

What is the social significance of Idarla?

(a) Idarla is larger than other settlements
(b) Idarla is closer to Dantrai
(c) Annual fair at Idarla
(d) Idarla is the largest settlement

Ans. (c) Annual fair at Idarla

17. Refer to the image and answer the questions that follow

(ICSE Semester I 2021)

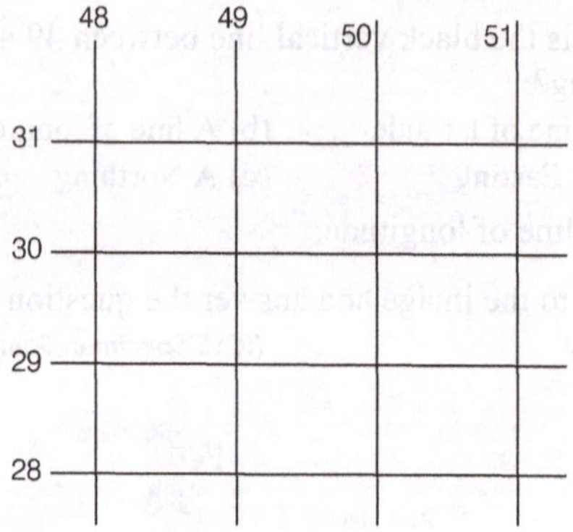

With reference to the scale given on topographical map (2cm = 1km), what is the area of the land enclosed between 48 to 50 Easting and 28 to 31 Northing?

(a) 06 sq m
(b) 06 sq km
(c) 60 sq km
(d) 60 sq m

Ans. (b) 06 sq km

18. What does nearness of contour lines indicate?

(ICSE Semester I 2021)

(a) It indicates steep slope
(b) It indicates gentle slope
(c) It indicates desert area
(d) It indicates irregular area

Ans. (a) It indicates steep slope

19. Which scale out of the following that is printed on the topographical map, is considered a special scale?

(ICSE Semester I 2021)

(a) Statement scale
(b) Representative fraction
(c) Linear scale
(d) Graphical scale

Ans. (b) Representative fraction

10 Marks Questions

1. Study the extract of the Survey of India Map Sheet No. G-13S7 and answer the following questions: *(ICSE 2023)*

(i) (a) Give the four-figure grid reference for A224.
(b) What is the contour interval used in the given map extract ?

(ii) (a) Mention two man made features seen in grid square 2706.
(b) Mention two natural features seen in grid square 2905.

(iii) (a) What do you understand by 1:50,000 printed below the map extract ?
(b) What is the pattern of drainage seen in the grid square 2505 ?

(iv) (a) What do you understand by 10r in 2709 ?
(b) What is th e compass direction of Mahudi Nani (2604) from Panswal (2909) ?

(v) Calculate the area in kilometre square of region enclosed between Easting 26 to 29 and Northing 05 to 11.

Ans. (i) (a) 2706
(b) 20 metres

(ii) (a) Two man made features seen in gird square 2706 are covered tank and lime kilns.
(b) Two natural features seen in grid square 2905 are trees and seasonal streams.

(iii) (a) 1 : 50,000 is the scale of the given map.
(b) Dendritic drainage pattern.

(iv) (a) 10r in grid square 2709 represents relative height of the area.
(b) The compass direction of Mahudi Nani (2604) from Panswal (2909) is South-West.

(v) The area in km sq of the region enclosed between Eastings 26 to 29 and Northing 05 to 11 is 18 sq. km.

2. Study the extract of the Survey of India Map sheet No. G43S10 and answer the following questions: *(ICSE Specimen 2023)*

(i) (a) Give the four figure grid reference of the settlement where Ayurvedic hospital is found.
(b) Name two man-made features in grid square 6429.

(ii) (a) What is the pattern of drainage seen in grid square 6729?
(b) What is the pattern of settlement seen in grid square 6934?

(iii) Calculate the shortest distance in kms between settlement Udwaria (6934) and Sanwara (6636).

(iv) What advantage does Representative Fraction have over Statement scale?

(v) What do you mean by the following?
(a) 3r in grid square 6933
(b) .437 in grid square 6729

Ans. (i) (a) 6533
(b) A Highway and a wall

(ii) (a) Radial drainage pattern
(b) Nucleated Settlement pattern

(iii) The shortest distance between Udwaria and Sanwara settlements is 4.5 Km.

(iv) In representative fraction (RF), the scale on the map is expressed in the numerical fraction. Its advantage is that it has universal application. Even people who live in foreign countries can find the distance on the map even if they are not familiar with the units of measurements of that country.

(v) (a) 3r in grid square 6933 represents relative height of that area in metres.
(b) .437 in grid square 6729 represents spot height of that area in metres.

3. Study the extract of the Survey of India Map sheet No. 45D/10 and answer the following questions. *(ICSE 2020)*

(a) (i) Give a six figure grid reference for the spot height .324 in northern part of the map extract.
(ii) Give a four figure grid reference for open scrub south of Dhad Talao.

(b) (i) What is the meaning of the term 'Contour interval'?
(ii) What is the contour interval of the sheet provided to you?

(c) What is the area in kilometre square of the region between 06 and 09 Eastings and 22 and 27 Northings?

(d) What is the significance of the following colours used on the survey map?
(i) Yellow colour
(ii) Green colour

(e) What is the compass direction of?
(i) Idarla (0825) from Bhamra (0420).
(ii) Dhana (0623) from Amarapura (0124).

(f) (i) Name the settlement pattern seen in the grid square 0819.
(ii) Name the drainage pattern seen in the grid square 0827.
(g) (i) Name two man made features seen in the grid square 0723.
(ii) Name two natural features seen in the grid square 0218.
(h) (i) What is the black horizontal line drawn between 18 and 19 Northings?
(ii) Name the most important settlement of the region shown on the map extract.
(i) Draw the conventional symbol for each of the following:
(i) Lined perennial well.
(ii) Seasonal tank.
(j) (i) Give one evidence to prove that the regions shown on the map extracxt receive scanty rainfall.
(ii) What is .5r in the grid square 0321?

Ans. (a) (i) 076274 (ii) 0721
(b) (i) Contour lines are imaginery lines which join places of equal heights.
(ii) 20 metre
(c) 15 sq km.
(d) (i) Yellow colour - Agricultural land
(ii) Green colour- Vegetation cover
(e) (i) North-East (ii) North-West
(f) (i) Dispersed Settlement Pattern
(ii) Dendritic Drainage Pattern
(g) (i) Settlements and agricultural land.
(ii) River and wasteland.
(h) (i) Latitude (ii) Dantrai
(i) (i)  (ii) 
(j) (i) Seasonal nature of rivers and dry tanks represent that the regions shown on the map extract receive scanty rainfall.
(ii) .5r represents relative height of the area.

4. Study the extract of the Survey of India Map sheet no. 45D/10 and answer the following questions ***(ICSE 2019)***
(a) (i) Give the six-figure grid reference for the temple that is located to the South-West of the Pithapura settlement.
(ii) Give the four-figure grid reference for a settlement where people of the region meet socially and for trade at least once in a year.
(b) (i) What is the pattern of drainage seen in the grid square 2118?
(ii) What is the pattern of settlement seen in the grid square 1923?
(c) What do each of the two numbers (281 printed in black colour and 20 printed in red colour) in the grid square 1818 indicate?
(d) (i) Name any two man-made features in grid square 2419.
(ii) Name any two natural features in grid square 2118.
(e) What is the significance of the following?
(i) Fire line in grid square 2417.
(ii) Water body found in grid square 2221.
(f) Calculate the area of the region between 16 and 19 Eastings and 18 and 22 Northings. Give your answer in kilometre square.
(g) Give a reason for each of the following.
(i) The water in some of the wells in the North-West quarter of the map is not fit for drinking.
(ii) The region near Anadra and Gulabganj has many causeways.
(h) (i) What is the main means of irrigation used by people living in the area shown on the map?
(ii) What is the main occupation of the people of the region shown on the map?
(i) Which according to you is the most important settlement? Give a reason to support your answer.
(j) Name any two means of transport used by the people living in the area shown on the map extract.

Ans. (a) (i) 202215
(ii) 1622
(b) (i) Radial drainage pattern
(ii) Nucleated settlement
(c) The number 281 represents height of that particular region in metres.
The number 20 printed in red colour represents distance stone.

(d) (i) Two man-made features in grid square 2419 are perennial lined well in blue dot and settlement by red squares.

(ii) Two natural feature in grid square 2118 are rivers and grassland.

(e) (i) Fire line is a clearing or gap made in the forest to prevent the spread of forest fires.

(ii) The water body in grid square 2221 is a reservoir which is a man-made artificial tank with embankment to store water.

(f) Area of the region $= (19-16) \times (22-18)$

$= 3 \times 4 = 12$ sq km

(g) (i) The water in some of the wells in the North-West quarter of the map is not fit for drinking because there is written brackish on the map. Brackish water is saltier than freshwater thus, is not fit for drinking.

(ii) A causeway is a road or path that is built higher than the area around it in order to cross water or wet ground. The region has many causeways because this region has many seasonal rivers which dry up in summer and occur in rainy season. The region near Gulabganj settlement also has Sipu river thus causeway is needed.

(h) (i) The main means of irrigation used by people living in the area shown on the map is perennial lined wells.

(ii) The main occupation of the people of the region shown on the map is agriculture as the region has yellow wash which depicts the agricultural activity.

(i) The most important settlement on the map is Anadra. It is because this settlement has many utilities like police chauki, dispensary, post and telegraph office, dak bungalow, metalled road and so on.

(j) The two means of transport used by the people living in the area shown on the map extract are roadways as the area has metalled roads and causeways and waterways due to presence of Sipu and Sukli, Naoj rivers.

5. Study the extract of the survey of India Map Sheet No. 45 D/7 (Eastings 91 to 01 and Northings 73 to 83) and answer the following questions. ***(ICSE Specimen 2017)***

(i) Give a six figure grid reference of

(a) Spot height 542. (b) Temple at Juvol.

(ii) (a) What is meant by the term R F?

(b) What is the total area of the given map extract in square kilometres?

(iii) Calculate the distance in kilometres along the cart track linking Juvol in grid square 9282 to Arniwada in grid square 9481.

(iv) (a) What is the direction of the main river given in the map extract?

(b) On which bank of the main river is the village Chekhla situated?

(v) (a) What is the main form of irrigation in the South-East area of the map extract?

(b) Give a reason, why the streams in grid square 9478 do not join a river.

(vi) (a) Identify the land form shown by the contours in grid square 9473.

(b) What does 4r written against the blue dot in grid square 9973 represent?

(vii) (a) In what way is the pattern of settlement in grid square 9576 different from that in grid square 9774?

(b) What difference do you notice in the pattern of drainage in grid square 9574 and the drainage pattern in grid square 9382?

(viii) (a) What is the compass direction of Antroli from Sangla ?

(b) Which is the most important settlement shown on the map extract? Give a reason for your answer.

(ix) (a) Name one man-made and one natural feature in grid square 9473.

(b) Identify the feature given in black curved lines in grid square 9679.

(x) (a) Name any two modes of transport used in the given map extract.

(b) What inference can be drawn about the general occupation of the people living in the South-East area of the map extract? Give a reason for your answer.

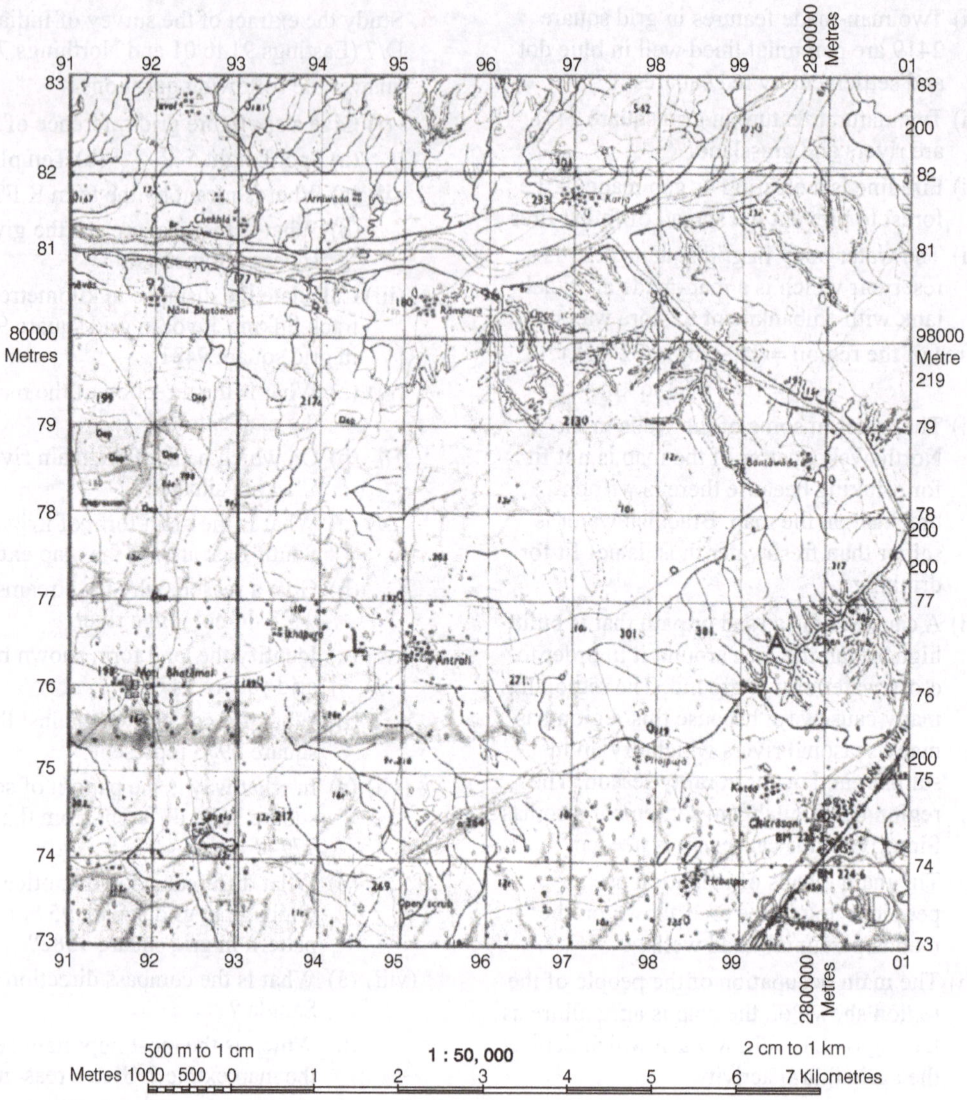

Ans. (i) (a) 976826 (b) 925827

(ii) (a) R F or Representative Fraction is the ratio between the distance measured on a map and the corresponding distance on the surface of the Earth, connecting two given points, represented in the same units.

(b) Total area of map extract = Length × Height = 20 cm × 20 cm as RF = 1/50000, this corresponds to $20 \times 0.5 \times 20 \times 0.5$ sq km = 100 sq km.

(iii) Distance on map measured by a string and scale along the cart track is 5.4 cm. This corresponds to a distance of 5.4×0.5 km = 2.7 km.

(iv) (a) The direction of the main river is from North-East to West.

(b) Village Chekhla is situated on the right bank of the main river.

(v) (a) The main form of irrigation in the South-East area are perennial lined wells, as seen by the large number of blue dots.

(b) The streams do not join any river because they seep into the sand.

(vi) (a) The landform shown by the contours denotes a conical hill, with its peak at 269 m height.

(b) This represents a lined well with a depth of 4 m below the surface.

(vii) (a) The settlement in 9576 is a nucleated settlement, while that in 9774 is a dispersed or scattered settlement.

(b) The drainage pattern in 9574 is a radial type of drainage system, while that in 9382 is a dendritic type of drainage system.

(viii) (a) Antroli is in North-East of Sangla.

(b) The most important settlement shown on the map is Chitrasani (at the South- East corner of the map) because it has a railway station, a major road passing through it and also has a post office. No other settlement in the map has any of these.

(ix) (a) The man-made feature is the temple and the natural feature is the hill with a peak of 269 m height.

(b) The black curved lines indicate a broken land.

(x) (a) Modes of transport used are metalled road and cart tracks.

(b) In the South-East, we see the land is yellow coloured and it also has many lined wells, indicating that the general occupation of the people living there is agriculture.

6. Study the extract of the survey of India map sheet No 45 D/10 and answer the following questions (Eastings 11-21, Northings 13-23). ***(ICSE Specimen 2018)***

(i) Give the four figure grid reference of the settlement of Pamera.

(ii) Give the six figure grid reference for surveyed tree North East of Bamba settlement.

(iii) What is the direct distance in kms between Malgaon and Gulabganj?

(iv) What is the difference between drainage pattern in grid square 2013 and 1422?

(v) Draw the conventional symbols for

(a) A tehsil boundary (b) A temple

(vi) What evidence from the map shows that the region receives seasonal rainfall?

(vii) What is the main occupation of the people of the region in the map extract? Give reasons for your answer.

(viii) Give a reason for each of the following.

(a) Disappearing streams in grid square 2018.

(b) Broken ground along the banks of River Sipu.

(ix) What is the area in square kms of the region enclosed within Easting 13 and 18 and Northing 17 and 21?

(x) What is the R.F. of this map? What does it mean?

Ans. (i) The four figure grid reference of the settlement of Pamera is 1622.

(ii) The six figure grid reference for surveyed tree North East of Bamba settlement is 187136.

(iii) Direct distance between Malgaon and Gulabganj is 1.5 km.

1 cm on the map represents 500m on the ground. Therefore, the distance between both the places is 3 cm on the map.

$$3 \times 500 \text{ m} = 1500 \text{ m or } 1.5 \text{ km}$$

(iv) The drainage pattern in grid square 2013 is Radial while in grid square 1422, the drainage pattern is dendritic.

(v) The conventional symbols are as follows

(i) A tehsil boundary = • • • •

(ii) A temple = 

(vi) The region receives seasonal rainfall as it mostly has non-perennial streams and dry patches of land.

(vii) The main occupation of the people of the region in the map extract is agriculture. This is seen by the presence of two rivers-River Sipu and River Nadi. The extensive yellow cover also shows the presence of agricultural land.

(viii) (a) The reason for disappearing streams in 2018 is the soil around it. The soil is porous in nature, therefore the stream water gets absorbed in the soil.

(b) Broken ground along the banks of River Sipu shows that it is a seasonal river that is formed due to alternating dry and wet season. Rapid evaporation in dry season causes weathering thereby causing broken ground along the river banks.

(ix) In a topographical map each grid square means 2 cm × 2 cm or 1 km × km as the map scale is 2 cm: 1 km. So, the area of each square is 1 sq km. To calculate the area of 13 & 18, northing 17 & 21:

Easting 13-18 = 5

Northing 17-21 = 4

$5 \times 4 = 20$ hence area

$= 20$ sq km

(x) RF or Representative Fraction expresses the proportion of map to ground numerically. It is expressed in fractions where the numerator is always I and denominator indicates the actual distance on the ground. The RF of this map is 1 / 500 which means 1 cm equals 500m.

09 Map Skills

The main objective of giving map work in the examination is to test your knowledge about the location of different features on a map of India, e.g. location of Bhakra-Nangal Dam, identification of soil type in a particular area, location of national park and so on.

Assessment for Identification

(i) Correct identification/correct name of feature (including correct spelling).

(ii) Neatness of the work.

Assessment for Location and Labelling

(i) Marking the correct location of the feature. If a river is to be drawn on the map, it should have almost the correct shape of the channel, with the source and mouth marked at the correct place on the map.

(ii) Appropriateness of symbol used, e.g. triangle or circle for a national park, a square for the location of a mineral mine, the symbol || for a dam on a river, etc.

(iii) Neatness of the work.

Types of Maps Given

(i) **India Political** This is normally given with the boundaries of states for most questions regarding identification or location and labelling.

(ii) **India Outline** This is given rarely, but is used to mark the flow of a river, area of growth of a crop, major soil type, etc.

Thematic Maps of Categories of Features

1. Mountains, Passes, Plateaus, Plains, Desert and Peaks.

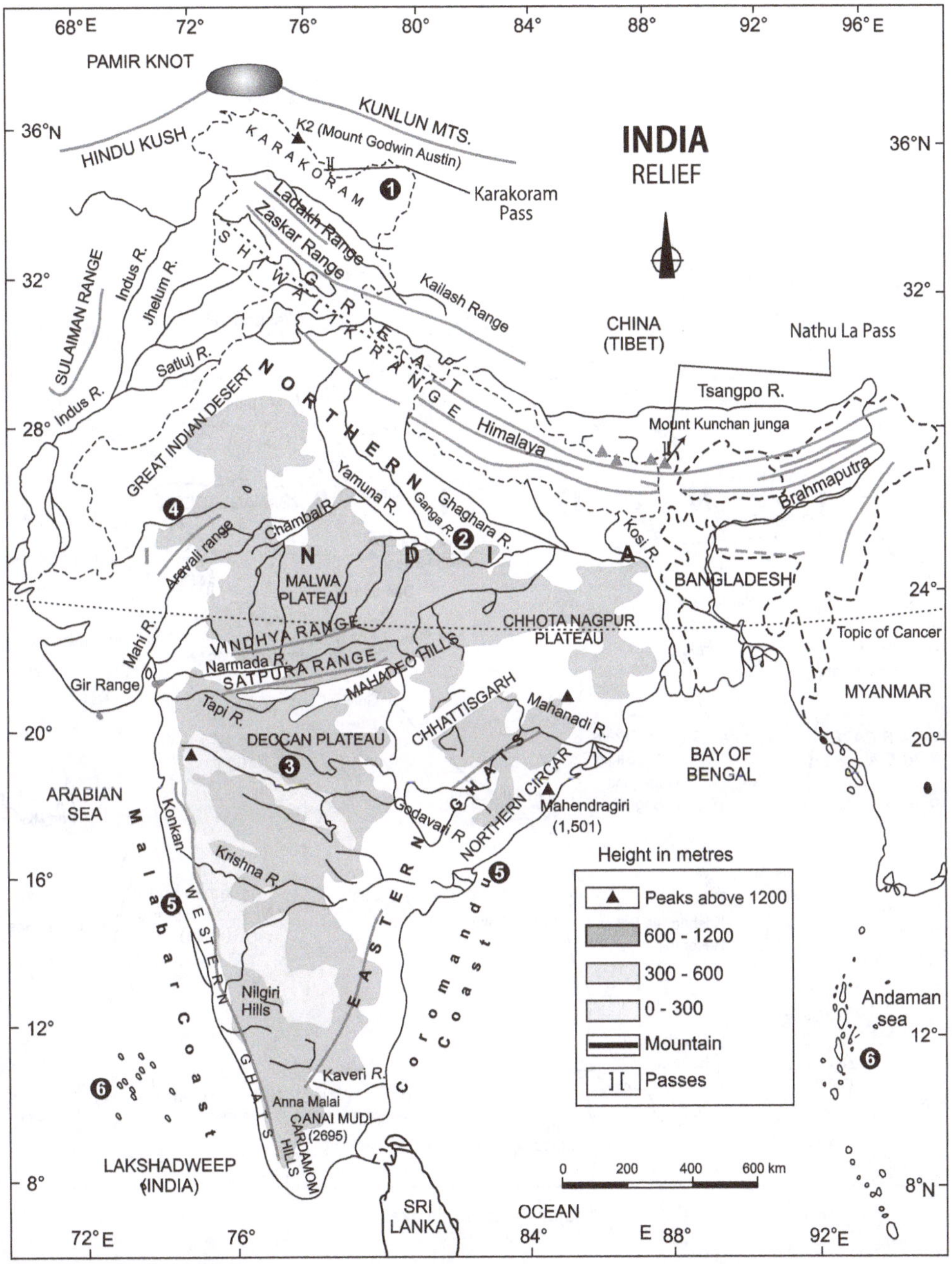

Relief

2. Rivers and Water Bodies

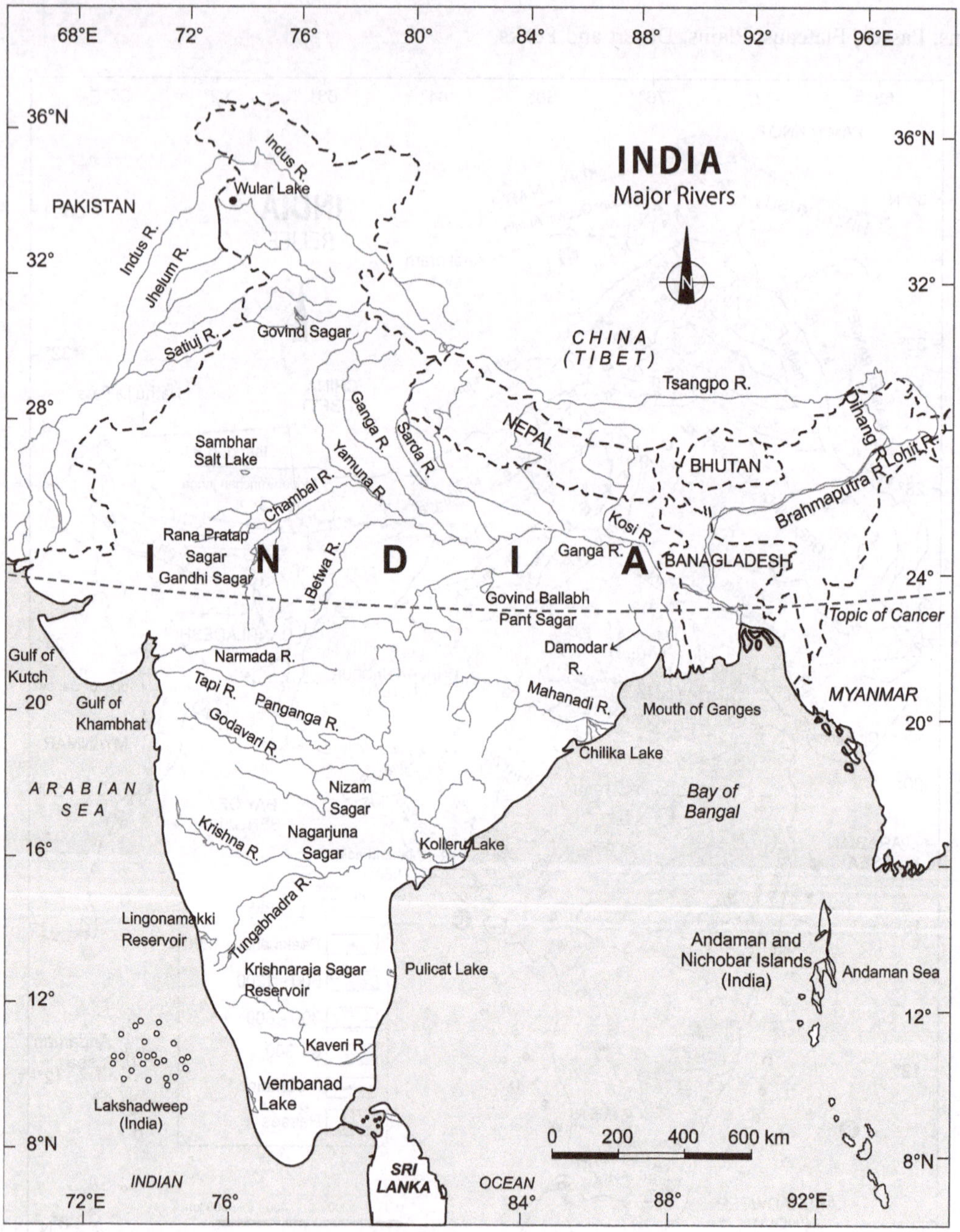

Major Rivers and Lakes

3. Latitudes and Longitudes

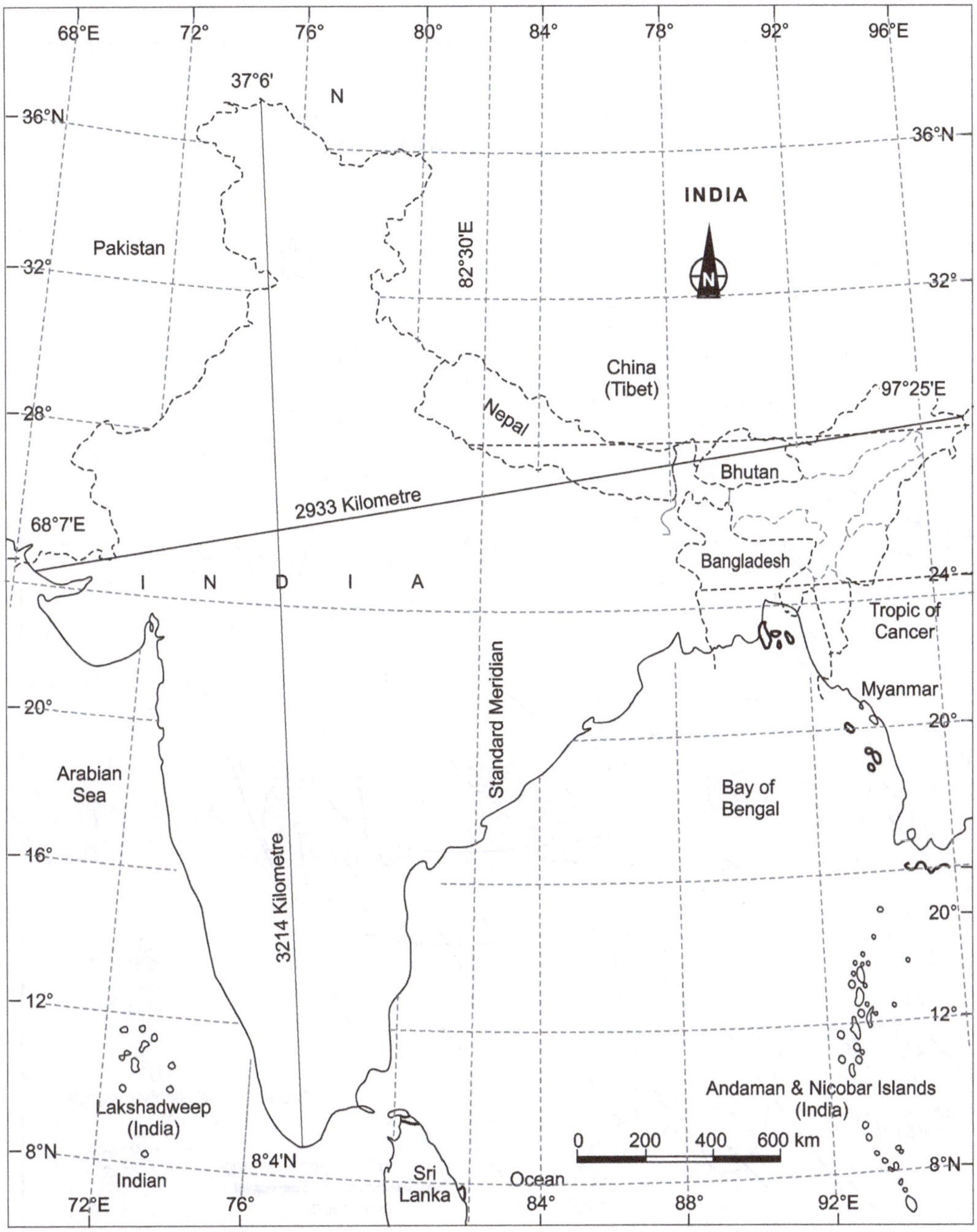

Relief

4. Direction of South-West Monsoon

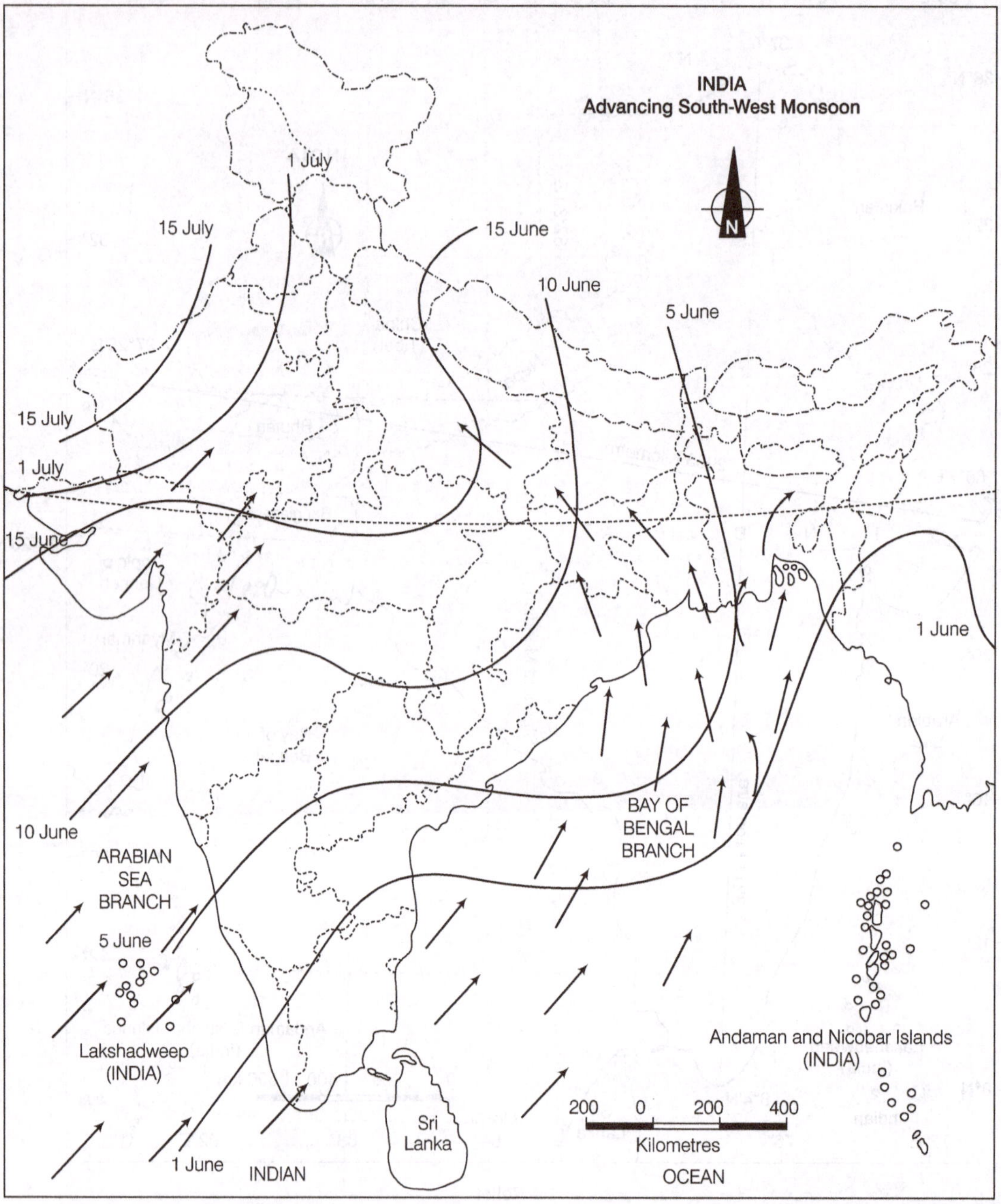

5. Direction of North-East Monsoon

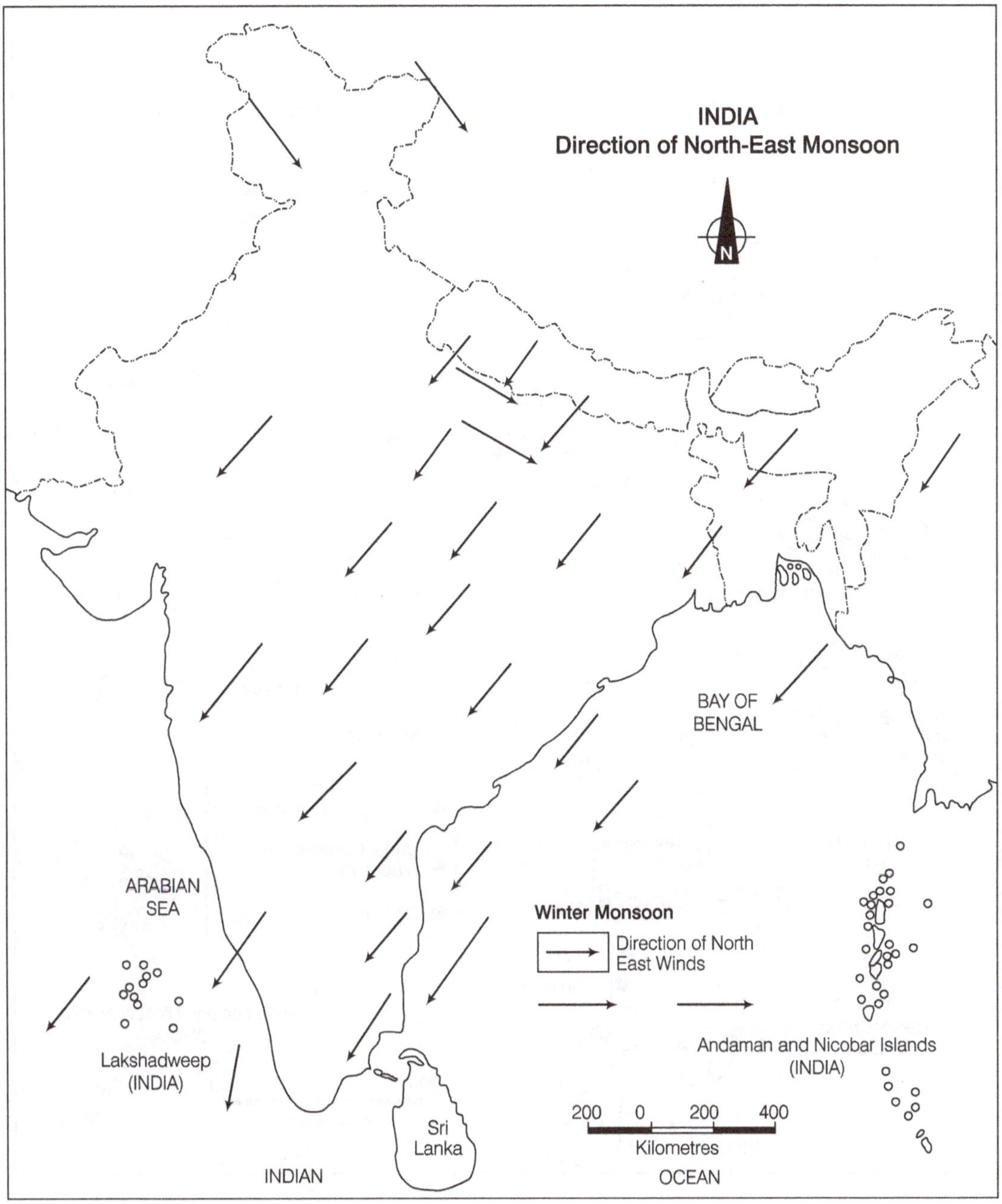

6. Minerals and Energy Sources

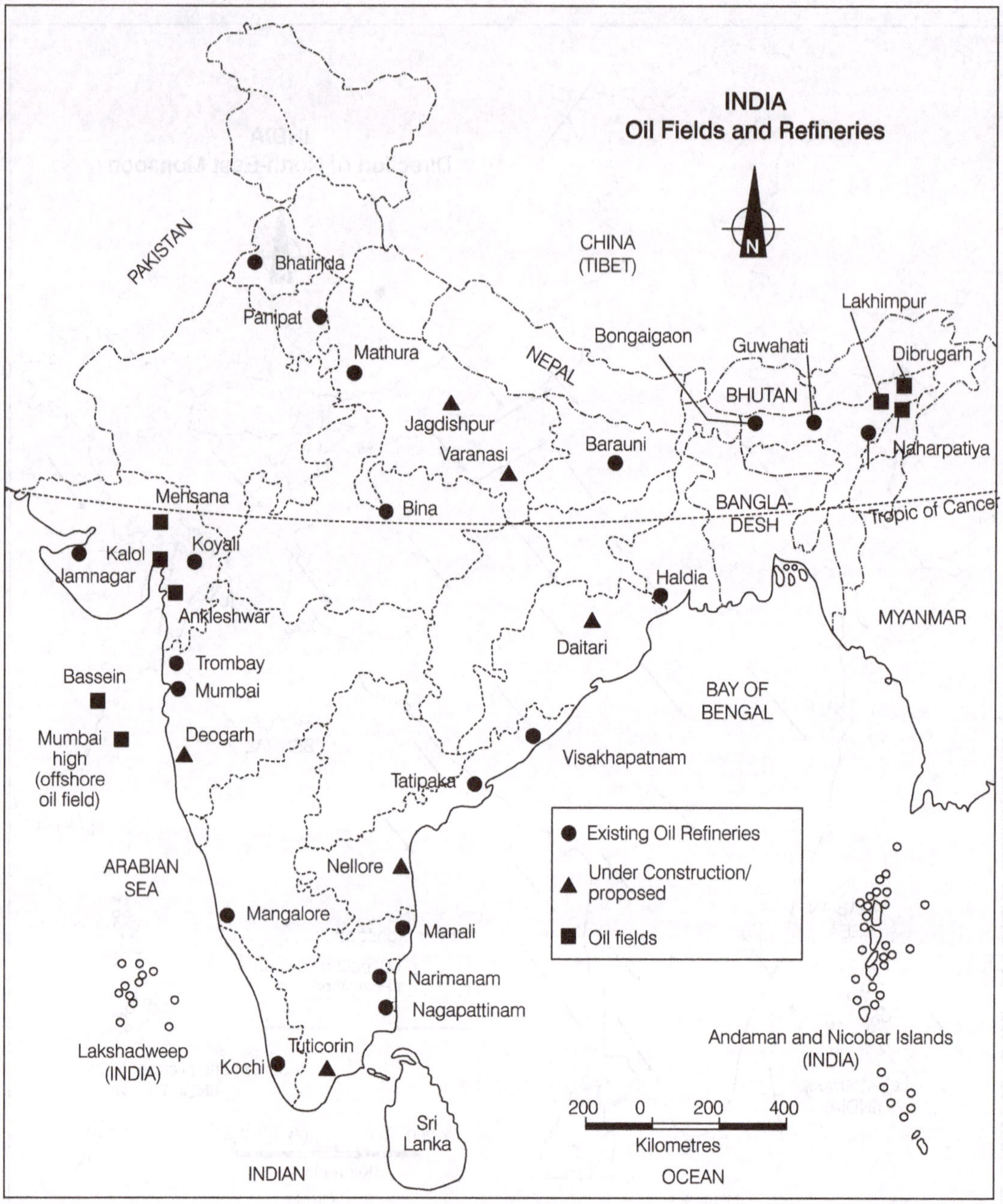

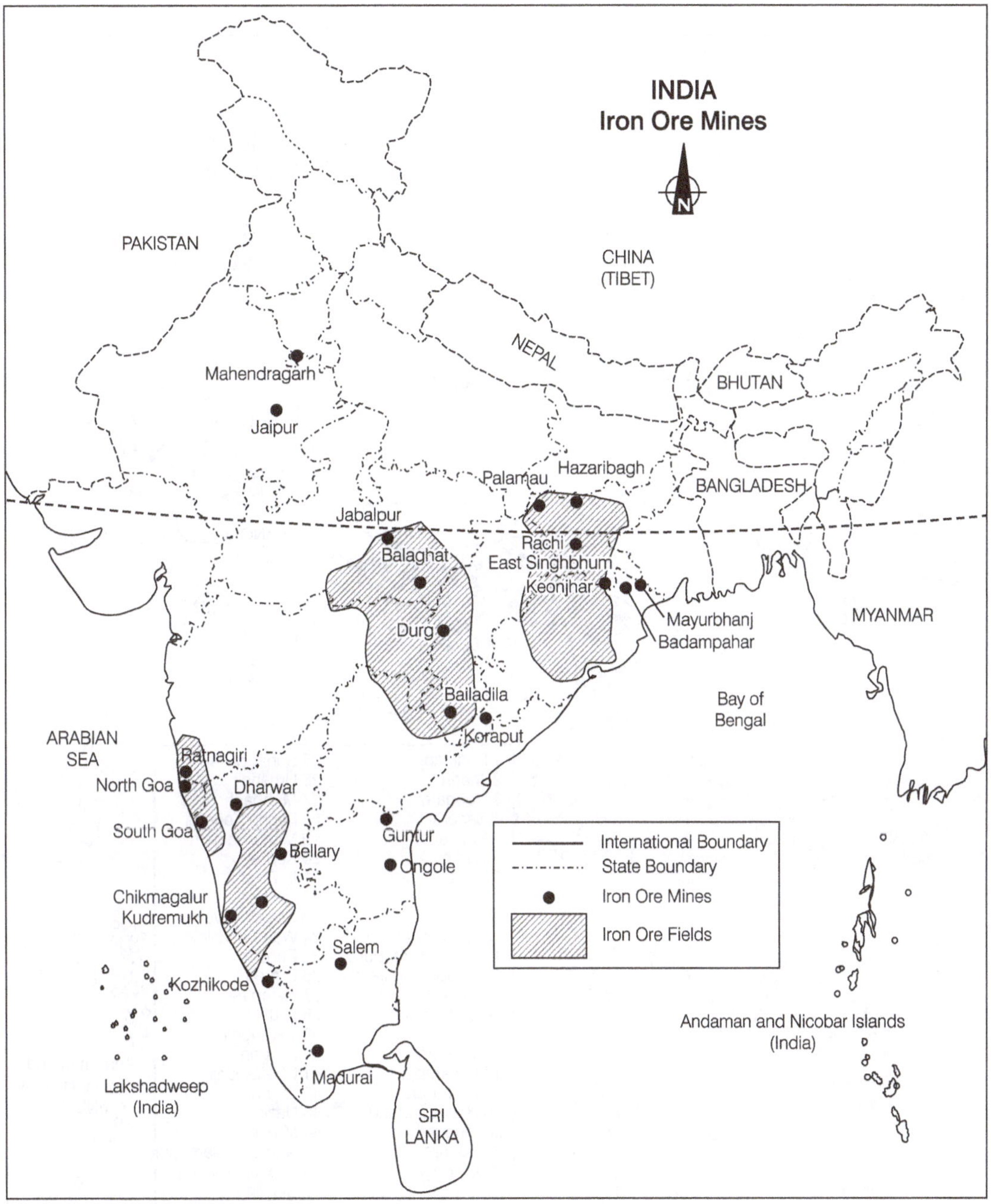
INDIA
Iron Ore Mines
N
PAKISTAN
CHINA (TIBET)
NEPAL
BHUTAN
BANGLADESH
MYANMAR
Mahendragarh
Jaipur
Palamau
Hazaribagh
Jabalpur
Balaghat
Rachi
East Singhbhum
Keonjhar
Mayurbhanj
Badampahar
Durg
Bailadila
Koraput
Bay of Bengal
ARABIAN SEA
Ratnagiri
North Goa
Dharwar
South Goa
Guntur
Bellary
Ongole
Chikmagalur
Kudremukh
Salem
Kozhikode
Madurai
Lakshadweep (India)
SRI LANKA
Andaman and Nicobar Islands (India)
International Boundary
State Boundary
Iron Ore Mines
Iron Ore Fields

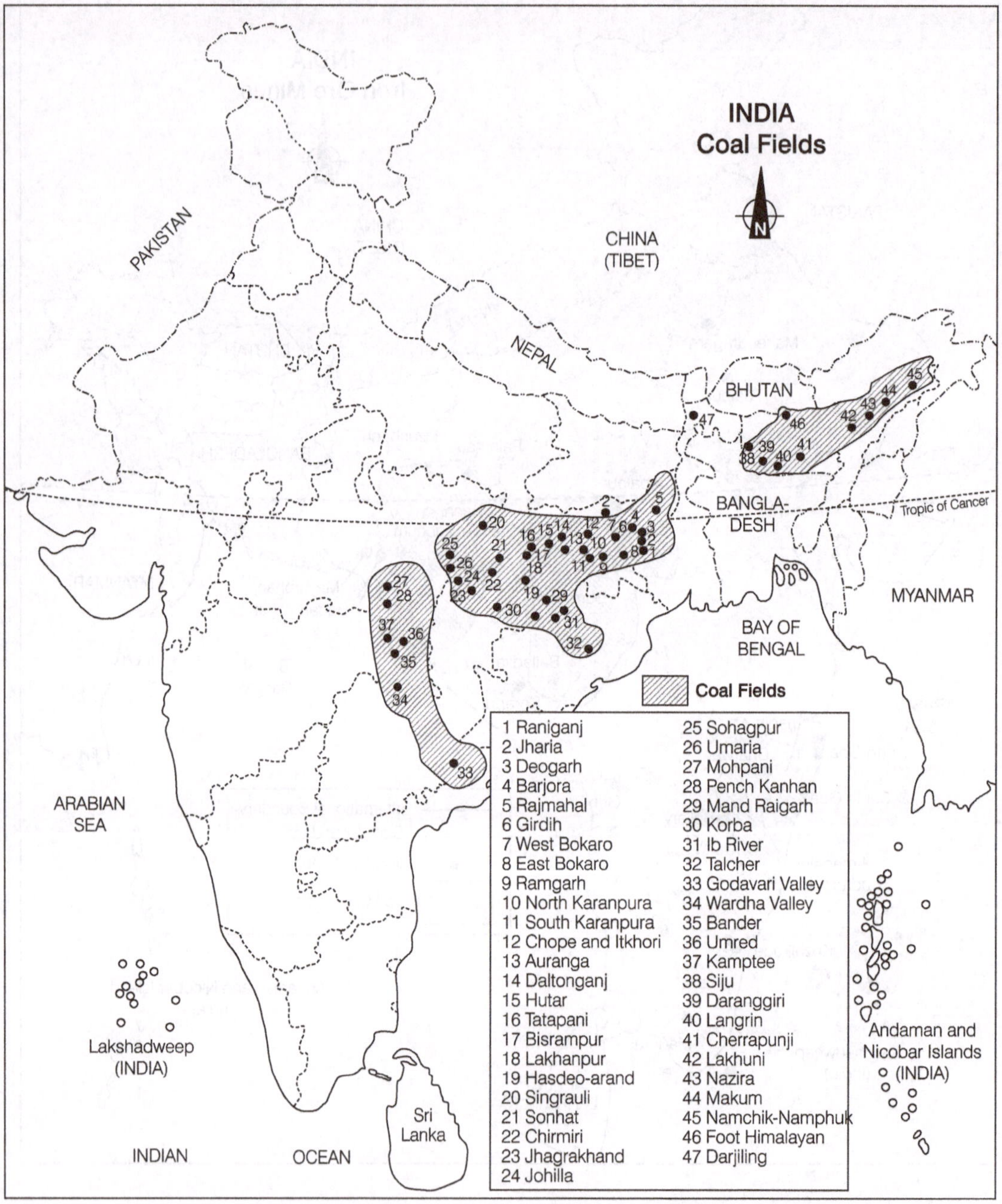
INDIA
Coal Fields
N
CHINA
(TIBET)
PAKISTAN
NEPAL
BHUTAN
BANGLA-
DESH
Tropic of Cancer
MYANMAR
BAY OF
BENGAL
ARABIAN
SEA
Coal Fields
Lakshadweep
(INDIA)
Andaman and
Nicobar Islands
(INDIA)
Sri
Lanka
INDIAN
OCEAN
1 Raniganj
2 Jharia
3 Deogarh
4 Barjora
5 Rajmahal
6 Girdih
7 West Bokaro
8 East Bokaro
9 Ramgarh
10 North Karanpura
11 South Karanpura
12 Chope and Itkhori
13 Auranga
14 Daltonganj
15 Hutar
16 Tatapani
17 Bisrampur
18 Lakhanpur
19 Hasdeo-arand
20 Singrauli
21 Sonhat
22 Chirmiri
23 Jhagrakhand
24 Johilla
25 Sohagpur
26 Umaria
27 Mohpani
28 Pench Kanhan
29 Mand Raigarh
30 Korba
31 Ib River
32 Talcher
33 Godavari Valley
34 Wardha Valley
35 Bander
36 Umred
37 Kamptee
38 Siju
39 Daranggiri
40 Langrin
41 Cherrapunji
42 Lakhuni
43 Nazira
44 Makum
45 Namchik-Namphuk
46 Foot Himalayan
47 Darjiling

7. Towns-Delhi, Mumbai, Kolkata, Chennai, Hyderabad, Bangalore (now named Bengaluru), Kochi, Allahabad, Chandigarh, Srinagar, Visakhapatnam.

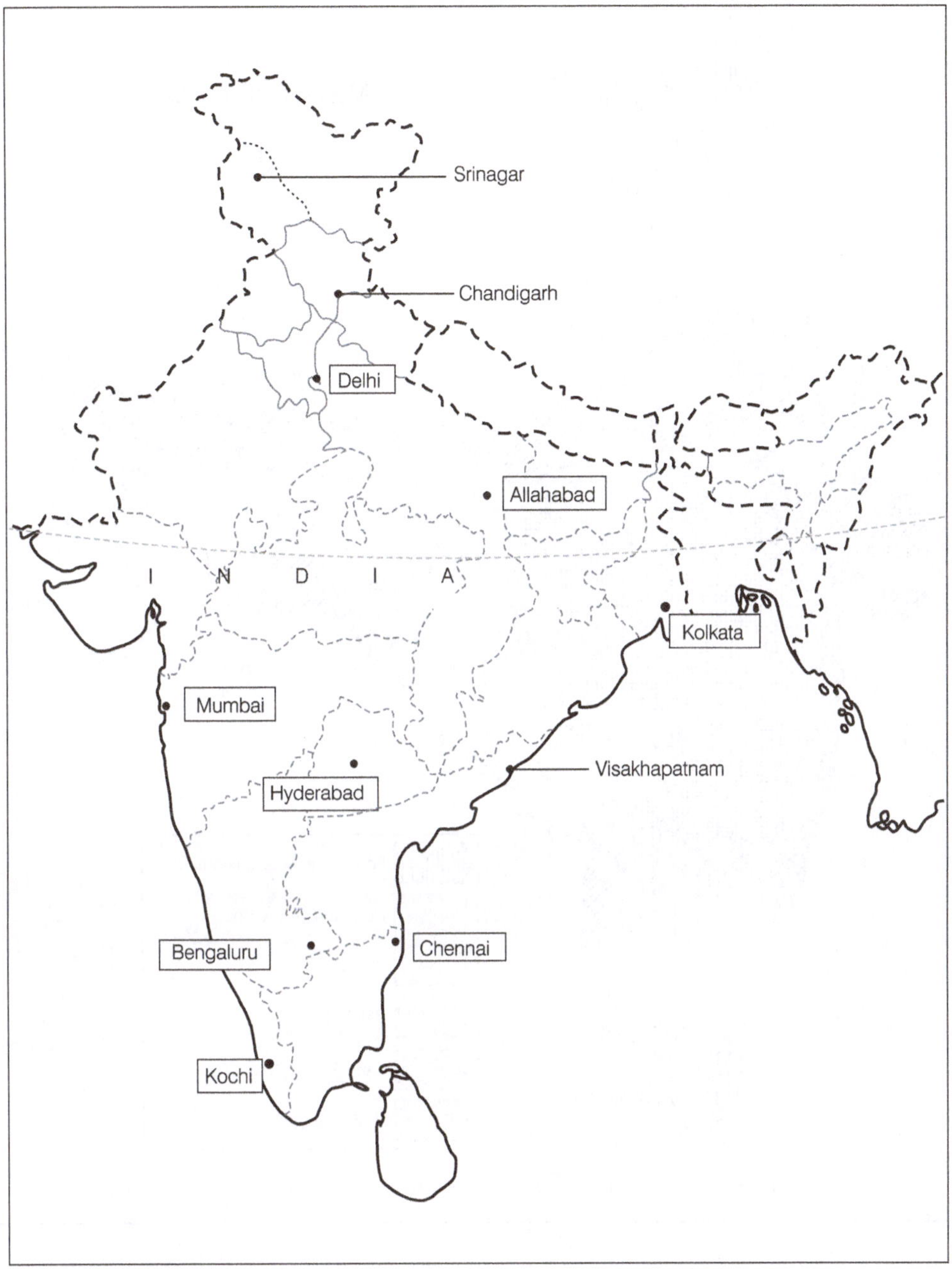

8. Major Soil Types

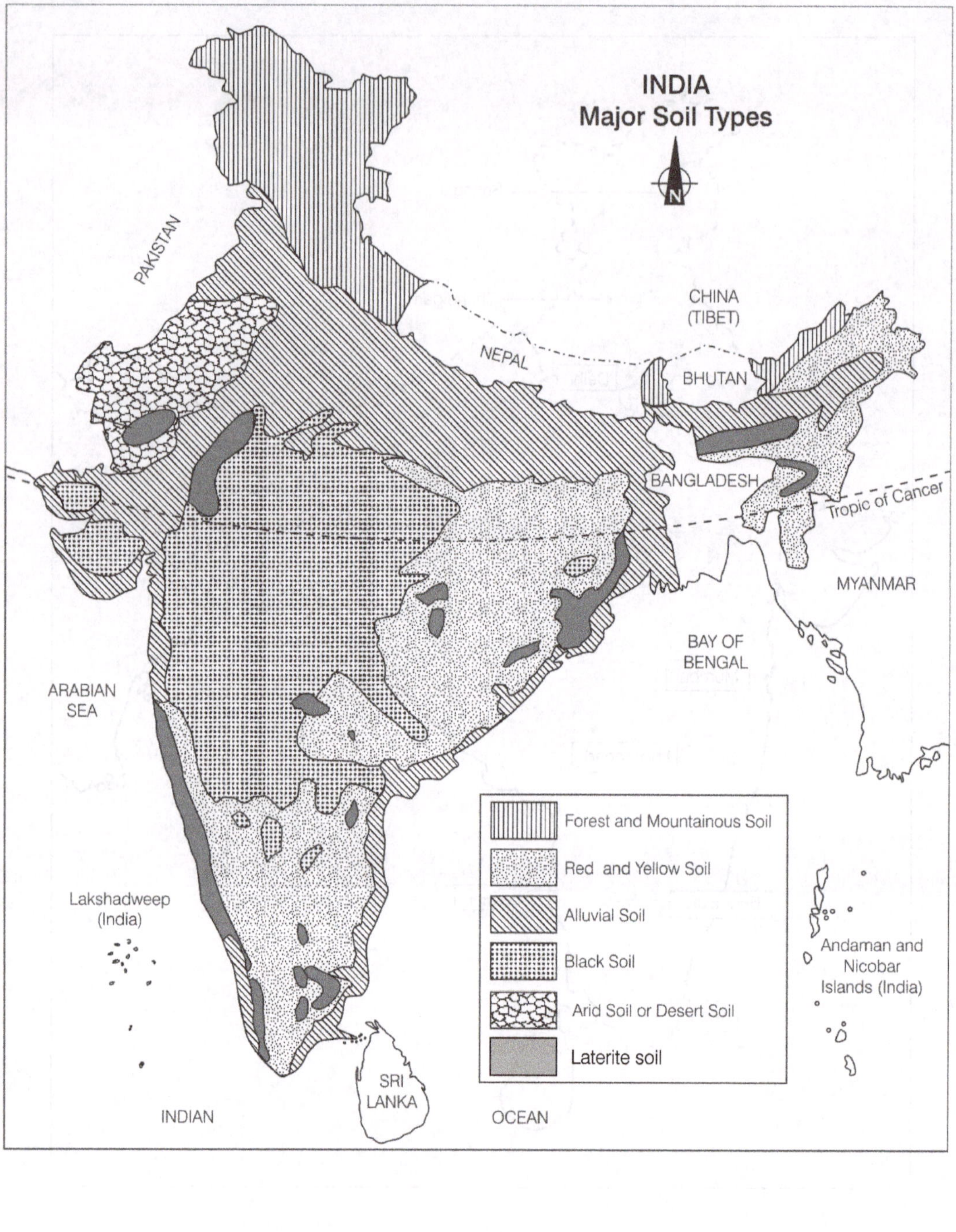

9. Population

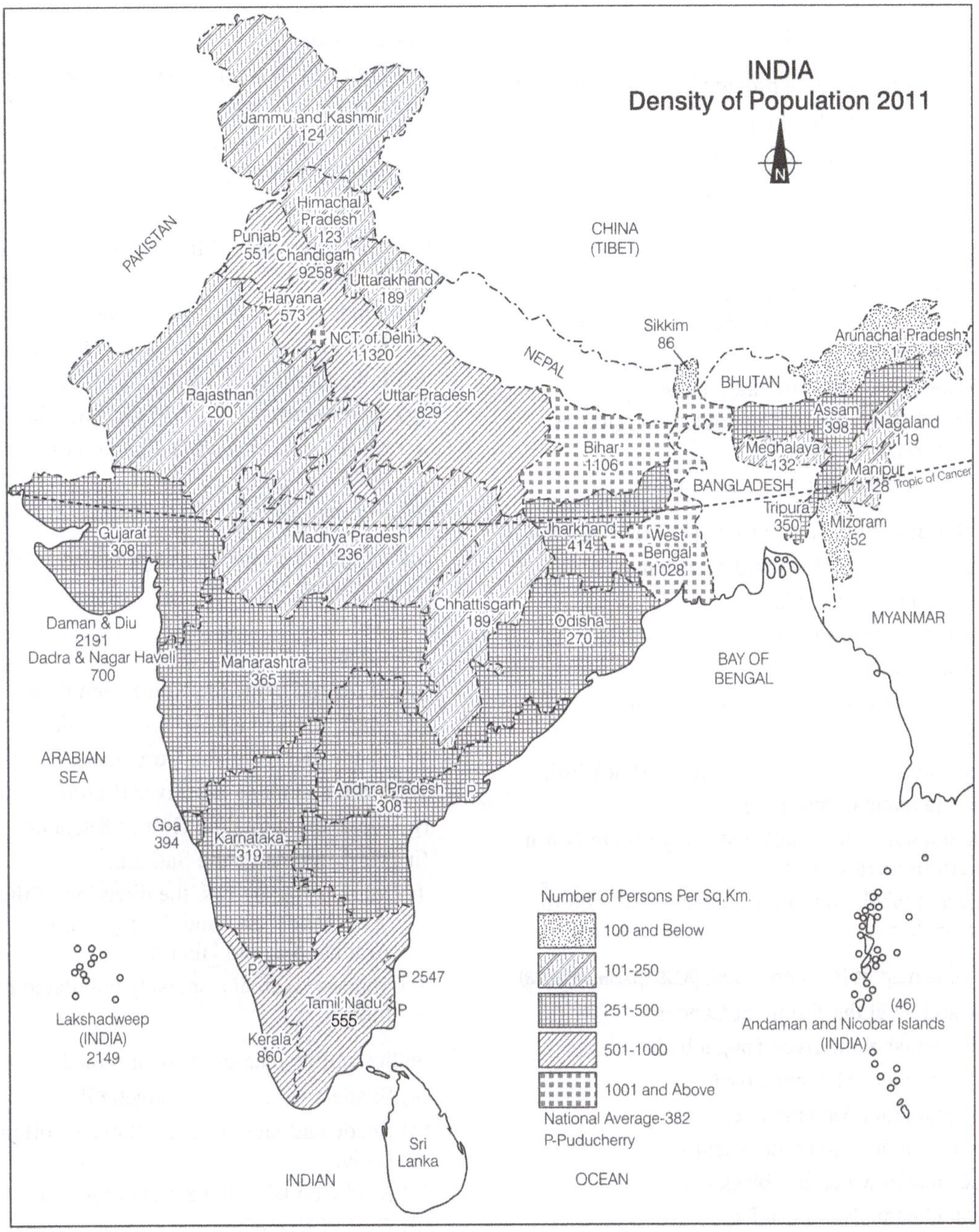

PYQs Previous Years' Questions

Map Based Questions

1. On the outline map of India provided, *(ICSE 2023)*
   (a) Mark and label the Satpura
   (b) Shade and label the Gulf of Kachchh
   (c) Mark and label the River Chambal
   (d) Mark and label Delhi.
   (e) Mark and label 80½° E longitude
   (f) Mark and label Jharia coalfield
   (g) Mark with arrows and name the South-West Monsoon winds.
   (h) Mark and label the Karakoram Pass
   (i) Shade and label a sparsely populated region in Western India
   (j) Shade an area having Alluvial soil

2. On the outline map of India provided, *(ICSE Specimen 2023)*
   (a) Mark and name the Standard Meridian of India
   (b) Mark and name Lake Chilika
   (c) Mark and name river Tungabhadra
   (d) Mark and name the Aravalli mountains
   (e) Mark and name Mount Godwin Austen
   (f) Mark and name an Offshore Oilfield
   (g) Shade and name a region covered by Black Soil
   (h) Mark and name Chandigarh
   (i) Mark and name the winds that bring rain to North Western India in winter
   (j) Shade and label a region of sparse population in Northern India

3. On the outline map of India provided, *(ICSE Specimen 2023)*
   (a) Draw and label the Tropic of Cancer.
   (b) Shade and label the river Tungabhadra.
   (c) Shade and label Malabar Coast.
   (d) Shade and label Andaman Sea.
   (e) Mark with a dot and name Kochi.
   (f) Shade an area which has black soil.
   (g) Mark and name Nathu-La Pass.
   (h) Mark and name Jharia.
   (i) Mark and label Aravalli.
   (j) Shade and label the area of sparse population in North India.

4. On the outline map of India provided, mark and name the following. *(ICSE Specimen Semester II 2022)*
   (a) Himalayas (b) River Ganga
   (c) Chennai (d) Western Ghats
   (e) Gulf of Kachchh (f) Malabar Coastal Plain
   (g) Karakoram Pass
   (h) Black soil area in Peninsular region
   (i) Standard Meridian of India
   (j) Jharia coal field

5. On the outline map of India provided, mark and name the following. *(ICSE Semester II 2022)*
   (a) Vindhya mountain (b) River Yamuna
   (c) Kolkata (d) Kanchenjunga
   (e) Lake Chilika (f) Konkan Coastal Plain
   (g) Thar Desert (h) Gulf of Khambhat
   (i) Mark with arrows the direction of N.E. Monsoon wind
   (j) Mumbai High

6. On the outline map of India provided mark and name the following. *(ICSE 2020)*
   (a) Nilgiri
   (b) Kochi
   (c) Mark and name the Karakoram Pass.
   (d) Mark and name 82½°E Longitude.
   (e) Shade and name the Coromandel Coastal Plain.
   (f) Mark and name the River Brahmaputra.
   (g) Mark and name the Gulf of Kachchh.
   (h) Mark and name the Satpura.
   (i) Mark using arrows, the direction of the South West Monsoon wind during summer over the Arabian Sea and label it.
   (j) Shade and label a sparsely populated region in India.

7. On the outline map of India provided, *(ICSE 2019)*
   (a) Shade and label the Gangetic Plain.
   (b) Shade and label an area of black soil in North India. *(Modified)*
   (c) Mark and label the Karakoram Mountains.
   (d) Gulf of Kachchh *(Modified)*
   (e) Shade and label the river Kaveri.
   (f) Mark and name Mumbai.
   (g) Mark and name the Nathu La Pass.
   (h) Mark and name one iron ore mine. *(Modified)*
   (i) Shade and name the Deccan Plateau.
   (j) Shade and label the river Jhelum.

8. On the outline map of India provided, *(ICSE 2018)*

(a) Shade and label Thar Desert.

(b) Label the river Narmada. *(ICSE 2012)*

(c) Shade and name the Wular lake.

(d) Mark and label Konkan Coast *(Modified)*

(e) Mark and name Mount Kanchenjunga.

(f) Shade and label a densely-populated region in India.

(g) Shade and label a region with red soil in India. *(ICSE 2013)*

(h) Mark with a dot and name Chennai. *(ICSE 2013)*

(i) Mark and label the Arabian Sea branch of South-West Monsoon. *(ICSE 2011)*

(j) Mark with a dot and name Singhbhum.

9. On the outline map of the India provided *(ICSE 2017)*

(a) Draw and name the Tropic of Cancer.

(b) Label the river Godavari. *(ICSE 2013, 2008)*

(c) Mark and name the Mount Godwin Austin (K2)

(d) Mark coal fields in Jharia. *(ICSE 2013)*

(e) Mark with an arrow and name the NE monsoon over the Bay of Bengal. *(ICSE 2006)*

(f) Shade and name the Gulf of Kachchh.

(g) Shade and name the coastal plain that receives rainfall in October-November.

(h) Mark with a dot and name Delhi.

(i) Shade a region with Black Cotton soil. *(ICSE 2012)*

(j) Use an arrow to point at a densely populated state in South India.

10. On the outline map of India provided, mark and name the following *(ICSE Specimen 2017)*

(a) Eastern Ghats and Western Ghats.

(b) River Chenab.

(c) Mark with arrow the direction of the Bay of Bengal branch of South-West monsoon.

(d) Shade and name an area where red soil is found extensively.

(e) The Longitude 82 ½° E.

(f) Coromandel Coast

(g) Nathu-La-Pass

(h) Mark and label the leading states for coal and iron ore

(i) Shade and name the state with highest density of population

(j) Mark with a red dot and name Allahabad

11. On the outline map of India provided, *(ICSE 2016)*

(a) Draw and number the Standard Meridian of India.

(b) Label the river Mahanadi.

(c) Mark and name Lake Chilika.

(d) Shade and name the Gulf of Khambhat. *(Modified)*

(e) Mark and name the Vindhya mountains.

(f) Shade and name a sparsely populated region in Western India.

(g) Shade a region with alluvial soil in South India.

(h) Mark and name Kolkata.

(i) Mark with arrows and name South-West monsoon winds over the Bay of Bengal.

(j) Mark and name Mumbai High.

12. On the outline map of India provided, *(ICSE 2015)*

(a) Mark and name the Nilgiri.

(b) Mark and label the Mt. Kanchenjunga. *(Modified)*

(c) Shade and label the Malabar Coastal Plains.

(d) Mark and name the river Chambal.

(e) Shade and name the Andaman Sea.

(f) Mark and name Allahabad.

(g) Mark with a single arrow and name the winds that bring monsoon rain to Kerala Coast. *(Modified)*

(h) Mark and name *Mumbai high.* *(Modified)*

(i) Mark an area with alluvial soil. *(Modified)*

(j) Mark and name the *Karakoram Pass.*

13. On the outline map of India provided, *(ICSE 2014)*

(a) Draw, name and number of the Standard Meridian.

(b) Label the river Yamuna.

(c) Shade and name the Gulf of Khambhat.

(d) Mark the name the Nathu-La Pass.

(e) Mark and name the Karakoram Range.

(f) Shade and name a sparsely populated State in North-East India.

(g) Shade a region with red soil. *(Modified)*

(h) Mark with a dot and name Kolkata. *(Modified)*

(i) Mark and name the wind that brings rain to West Bengal in summer.

(j) Print S on the iron mine in Singhbhum.

14. On the outline map of India provided, *(ICSE 2013)*

(a) Mark the name Chennai.

(b) Label the river Godavari.

(c) Shade and label the Chota Nagpur Plateau.

(d) Shade and name the Gulf of Kachchh.

(e) Mark and name the Indo-Gangetic Plains.

(f) Shade and label an area with red soil.

(g) Mark and name the winds, which bring rain to Mumbai in July and August.

(h) Mark and name the Satpura range.
(i) Mark and name the Jharia coal field.
(j) Shade and label the Northern Circar coastal region.

15. On the outline map of India provided, *(ICSE 2012)*
(a) Draw and name the Tropic of Cancer.
(b) Label the river Narmada.
(c) Shade and name Chilika lake.
(d) Mark and name the Aravalli mountains.
(e) Mark and name the Karakoram Pass.
(f) Mark and name a densely populated State in South India.
(g) Shade and name a region with Black Soil.
(h) Mark with a dot and name Bengaluru. *(Modified)*
(i) Mark and name the winds which bring rain in winter to the Coromandel Coast.
(j) Name and print O on an oilfield in North-East India.

16. On the outline map of India provided, *(ICSE 2011)*
(a) Mark and name Kochi.
(b) Label the river Krishna.
(c) Shade and label the Chota Nagpur Plateau. *(Modified)*
(d) Mark and label the Konkan Coast.
(e) Shade and label the Andaman sea. *(Modified)*
(f) Shade and label an Alluvial soil area in Peninsular India.
(g) Mark with arrows the direction of the Arabian Sea branch of South-West monsoon winds.
(h) Shade and label the Western Ghats.
(i) Mark the Jharia coal field.
(j) Shade and name a densely populated area.

17. On the outline map provided, *(ICSE 2010)*
(a) Label the river Betwa modified. *(Modified)*
(b) Label the river Chambal.
(c) Shade and label the Nilgiri hills.
(d) Mark and label the Eastern ghats.
(e) Mark and label Hyderabad.
(f) Shade and label the Great Indian Desert.
(g) Mark and name the Wular Lake. *(Modified)*
(h) Mark and label a region North of the Tropic of Cancer where tea is grown extensively.
(i) Mark and name the winds which bring rain to Mumbai in July and August.

18. On the outline map provided, *(ICSE 2009)*
(a) Label the river Kosi.
(b) Shade and label the Siwalik range.
(c) Label the river Godavari.
(d) Mark and label the Coromandel coast.
(e) Mark and label Delhi. *(Modified)*
(f) Mark and label 82.5° E Meridian.
(g) Shade and label an area of black soil. *(Modified)*
(h) Mark with a bold line and name the Western Ghats.
(i) Mark with arrows the direction of the North-East Monsoon winds. *(Modified)*

19. On the outline map of South Asia provided, *(ICSE 2008)*
(a) Label the river Sutlej.
(b) Label the river Godavari.
(c) Mark with a bold line and name the Aravalli range.
(d) Mark and label Bangalore.
(e) Shade and label an area of alluvial soil in North India.
(f) Mark and name an offshore oilfield.
(g) Mark and label the Tropic of Cancer.

20. On the outline map provided, *(ICSE 2007)*
(a) Shade and label an area of Black Soil in India.
(b) Mark and label the Konkan coast.
(c) Shade and label one region of winter rainfall in India.
(d) Label the river Yamuna.
(e) Label the river Tapti.
(f) Shade and label the Vindhya ranges.

21. On the outline map provided, *(ICSE 2006)*
(a) Shade and label the Satpura Range.
(b) Label the river Krishna.
(c) Label the river Yamuna. *(Modified)*
(d) Shade and label the Nilgiri hills. *(Modified)*
(e) Mark with arrows the direction of the North-East monsoon winds over the Bay of Bengal.
(f) Mark and label the Malabar coast.
(g) Shade and label an area of black soil in India. *(Modified)*
(h) Shade and label an area of Limestone in India.

22. On the outline map provided mark and label the following *(ICSE 2005)*
(a) 82 1/2° E longitude.
(b) River Indus.
(c) Nathu-La Pass. *(Modified)*
(d) Chilika Lake. *(Modified)*
(e) River Brahmaputra.

Answers

1.

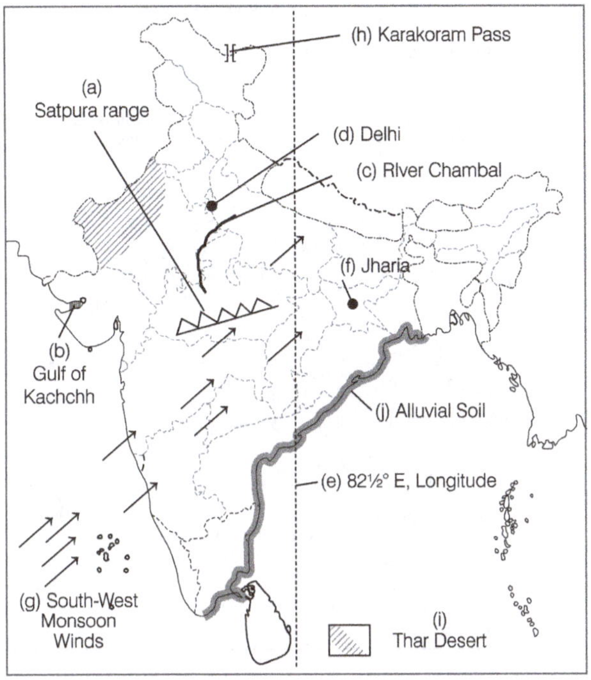

3.

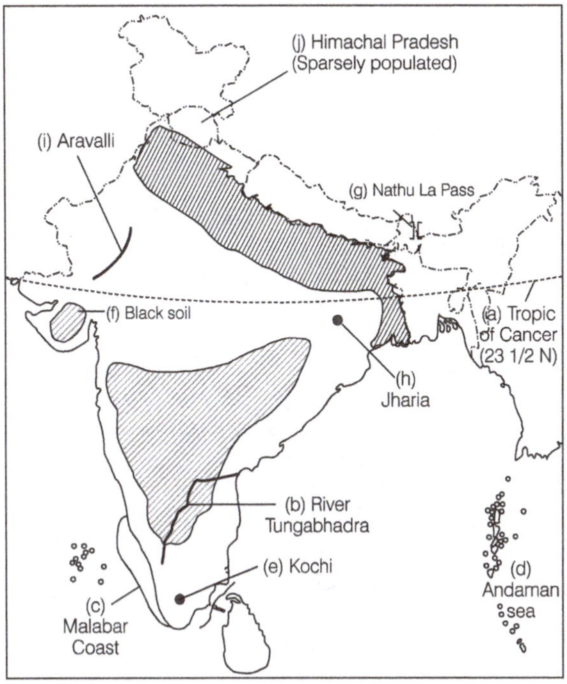

2.

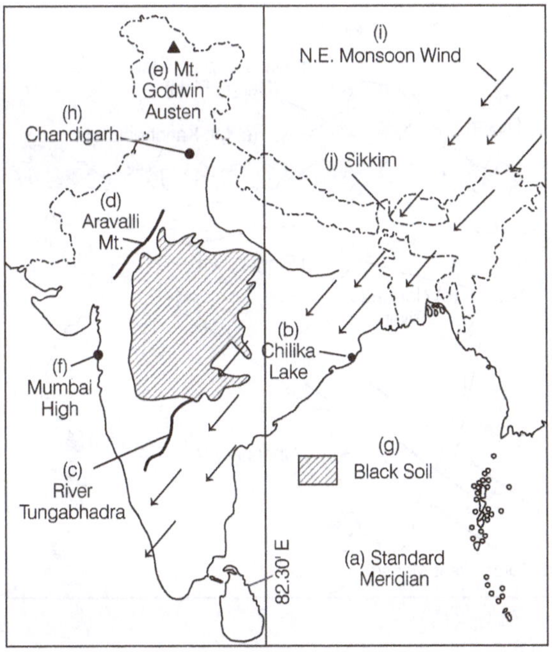

4.

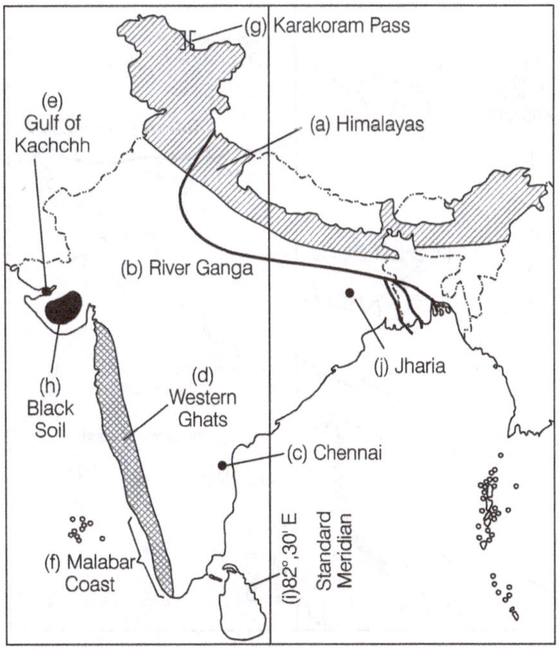

5.

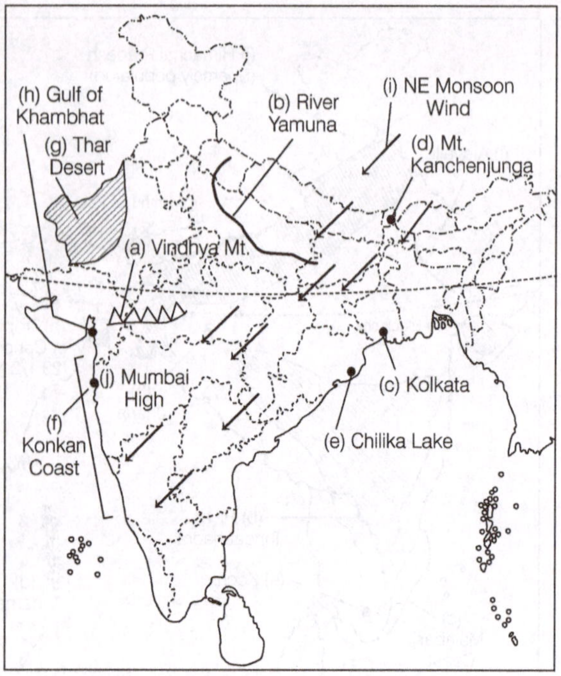

(h) Gulf of Khambhat
(g) Thar Desert
(b) River Yamuna
(i) NE Monsoon Wind
(d) Mt. Kanchenjunga
(a) Vindhya Mt.
(j) Mumbai High
(f) Konkan Coast
(c) Kolkata
(e) Chilika Lake

7.

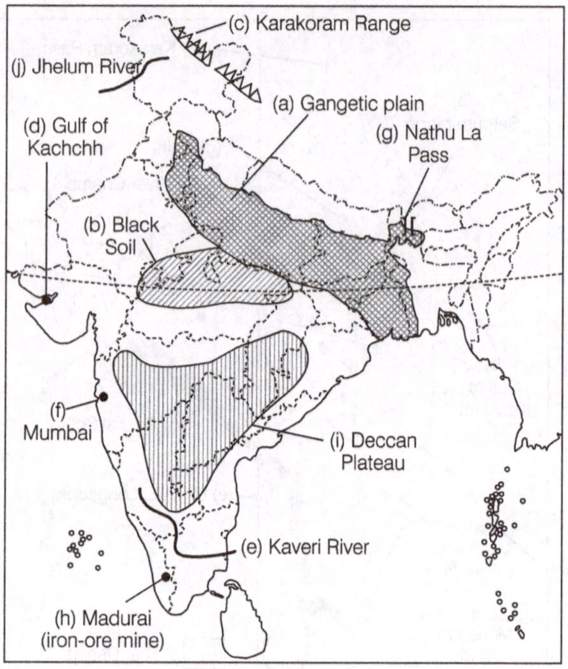

(c) Karakoram Range
(j) Jhelum River
(a) Gangetic plain
(d) Gulf of Kachchh
(g) Nathu La Pass
(b) Black Soil
(f) Mumbai
(i) Deccan Plateau
(e) Kaveri River
(h) Madurai (iron-ore mine)

6.

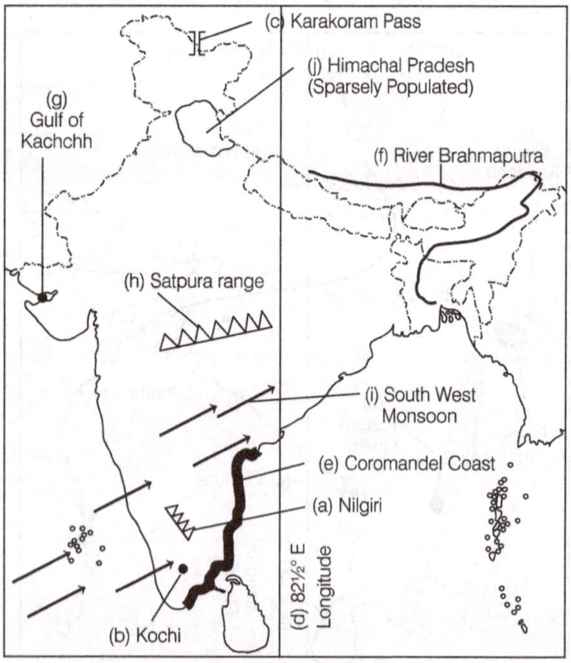

(c) Karakoram Pass
(j) Himachal Pradesh (Sparsely Populated)
(g) Gulf of Kachchh
(f) River Brahmaputra
(h) Satpura range
(i) South West Monsoon
(e) Coromandel Coast
(a) Nilgiri
(b) Kochi
(d) 82½° E Longitude

8.

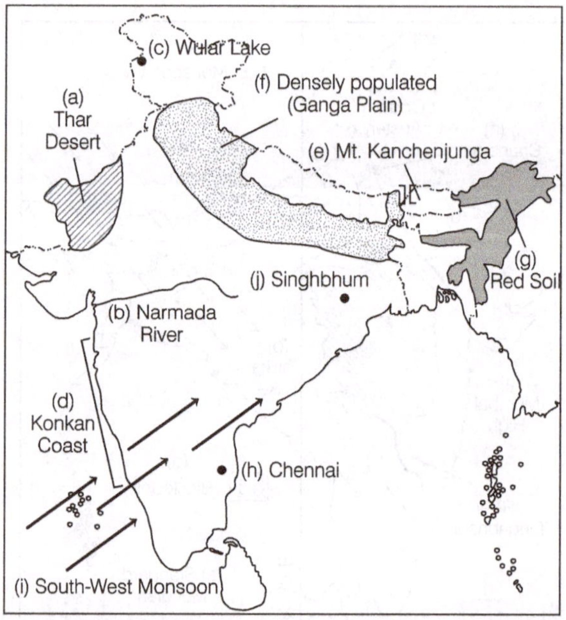

(c) Wular Lake
(a) Thar Desert
(f) Densely populated (Ganga Plain)
(e) Mt. Kanchenjunga
(g) Red Soil
(j) Singhbhum
(b) Narmada River
(d) Konkan Coast
(h) Chennai
(i) South-West Monsoon

9.

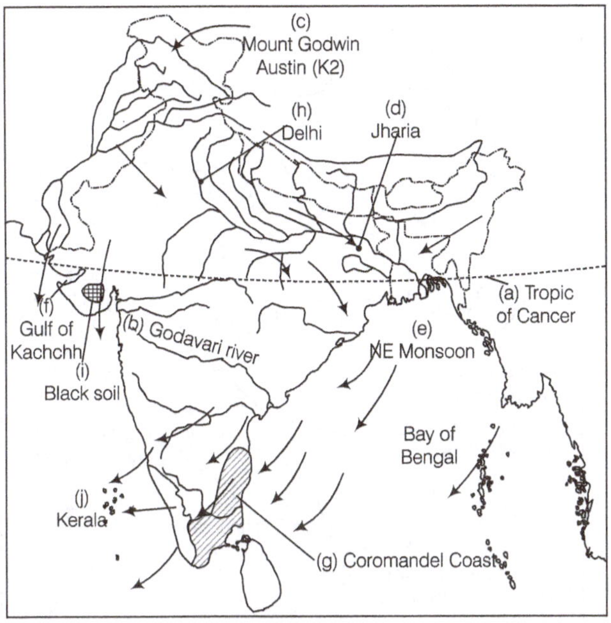
(c) Mount Godwin Austin (K2)
(h) Delhi
(d) Jharia
(a) Tropic of Cancer
(f) Gulf of Kachchh
(b) Godavari river
(e) NE Monsoon
(i) Black soil
Bay of Bengal
(j) Kerala
(g) Coromandel Coast

11.

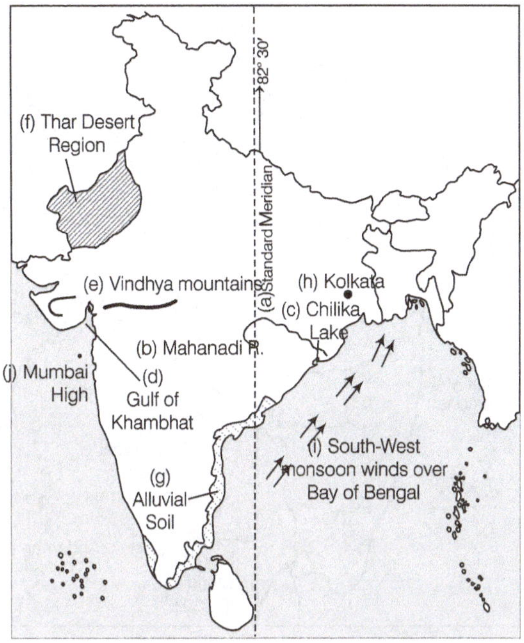
(a) Standard Meridian 82° 30'
(f) Thar Desert Region
(e) Vindhya mountains
(h) Kolkata
(c) Chilika Lake
(b) Mahanadi R.
(j) Mumbai High
(d) Gulf of Khambhat
(i) South-West monsoon winds over Bay of Bengal
(g) Alluvial Soil

10.

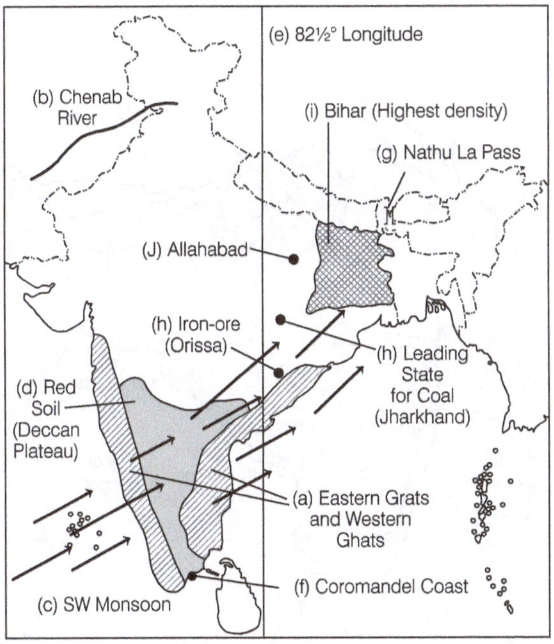
(e) 82½° Longitude
(b) Chenab River
(i) Bihar (Highest density)
(g) Nathu La Pass
(J) Allahabad
(h) Iron-ore (Orissa)
(h) Leading State for Coal (Jharkhand)
(d) Red Soil (Deccan Plateau)
(a) Eastern Grats and Western Ghats
(c) SW Monsoon
(f) Coromandel Coast

12.

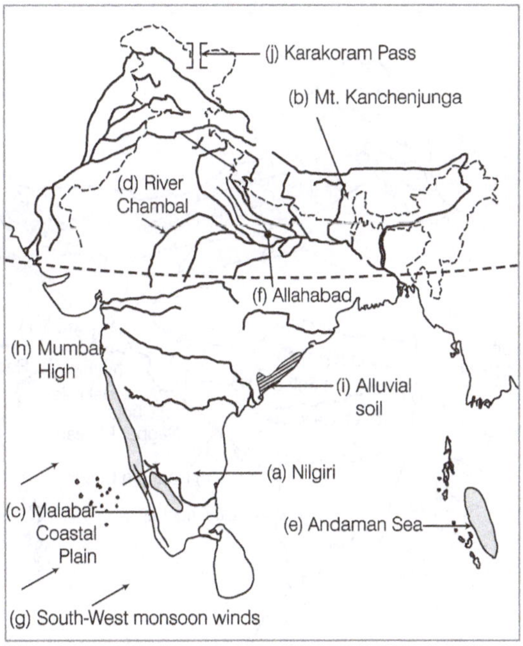
(j) Karakoram Pass
(b) Mt. Kanchenjunga
(d) River Chambal
(f) Allahabad
(h) Mumbai High
(i) Alluvial soil
(a) Nilgiri
(c) Malabar Coastal Plain
(e) Andaman Sea
(g) South-West monsoon winds

13.

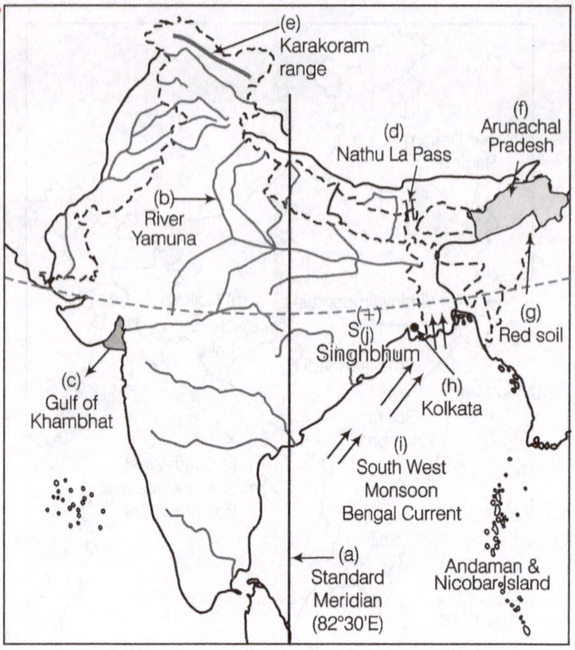
(e) Karakoram range
(f) Arunachal Pradesh
(d) Nathu La Pass
(b) River Yamuna
(g) Red soil
S(j) Singhbhum
(c) Gulf of Khambhat
(h) Kolkata
(i) South West Monsoon Bengal Current
(a) Standard Meridian (82°30'E)
Andaman & Nicobar Island

15.

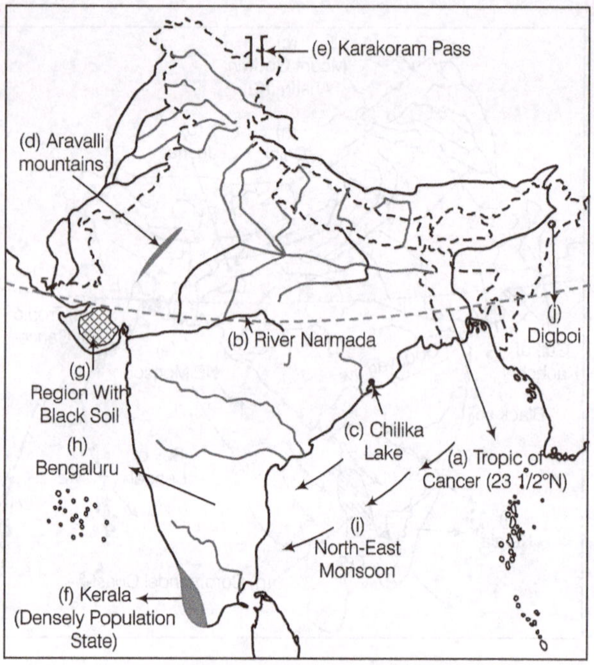
(e) Karakoram Pass
(d) Aravalli mountains
(j) Digboi
(b) River Narmada
(g) Region With Black Soil
(c) Chilika Lake
(h) Bengaluru
(a) Tropic of Cancer (23 1/2°N)
(i) North-East Monsoon
(f) Kerala (Densely Population State)

14.

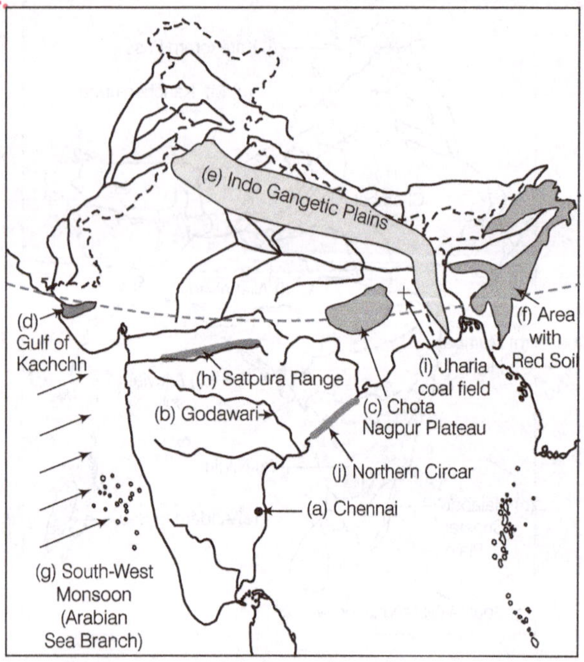
(e) Indo Gangetic Plains
(d) Gulf of Kachchh
(f) Area with Red Soil
(h) Satpura Range
(i) Jharia coal field
(c) Chota Nagpur Plateau
(b) Godawari
(j) Northern Circar
(a) Chennai
(g) South-West Monsoon (Arabian Sea Branch)

16.

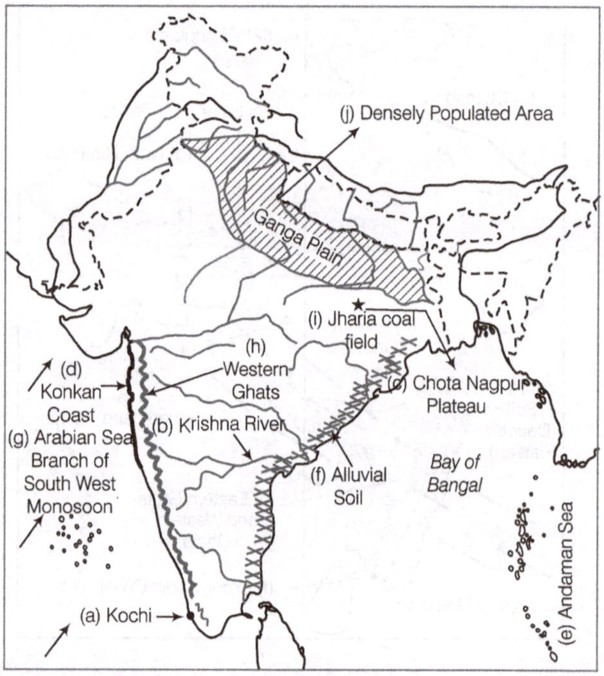
(j) Densely Populated Area
Ganga Plain
(i) Jharia coal field
(h) Western Ghats
(d) Konkan Coast
(c) Chota Nagpur Plateau
(b) Krishna River
(g) Arabian Sea Branch of South West Monosoon
(f) Alluvial Soil
Bay of Bangal
(a) Kochi
(e) Andaman Sea

17.

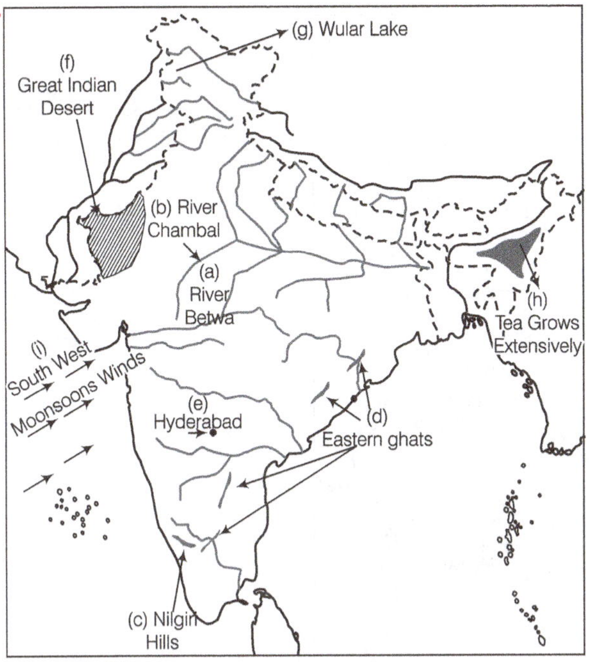
(g) Wular Lake
(f) Great Indian Desert
(b) River Chambal
(a) River Betwa
(h) Tea Grows Extensively
(i) South West Moonsoons Winds
(e) Hyderabad
(d) Eastern ghats
(c) Nilgiri Hills

19.

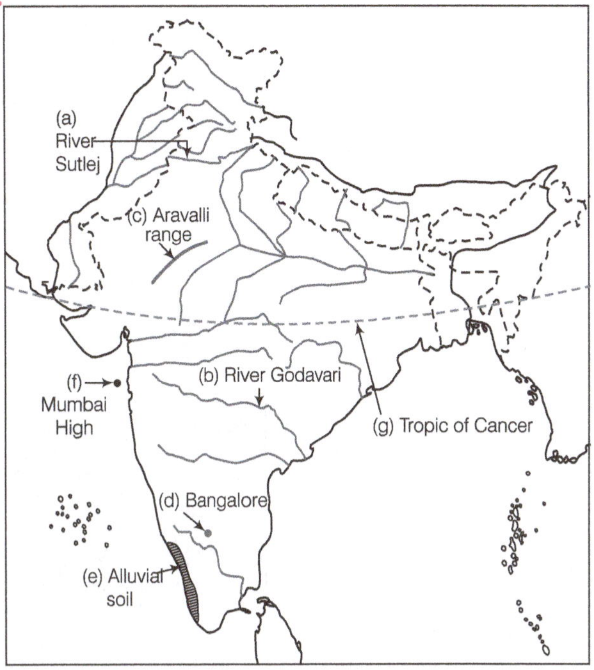
(a) River Sutlej
(c) Aravalli range
(f) Mumbai High
(b) River Godavari
(g) Tropic of Cancer
(d) Bangalore
(e) Alluvial soil

18.

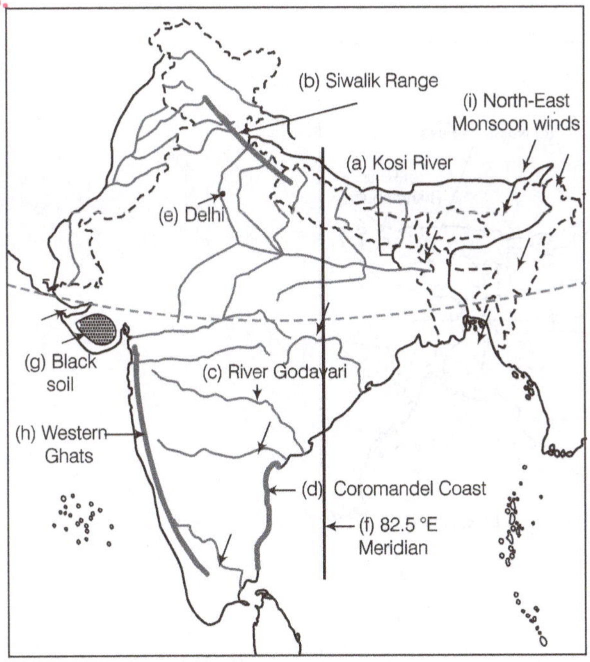
(b) Siwalik Range
(i) North-East Monsoon winds
(a) Kosi River
(e) Delhi
(g) Black soil
(c) River Godavari
(h) Western Ghats
(d) Coromandel Coast
(f) 82.5 °E Meridian

20.

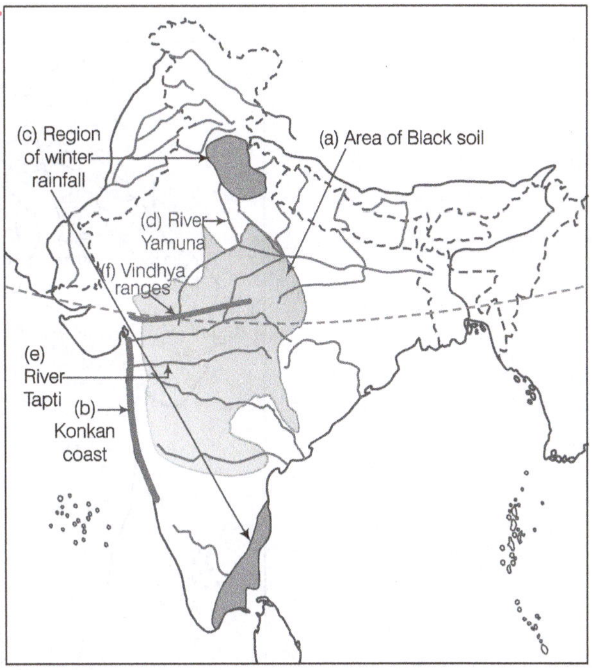
(c) Region of winter rainfall
(a) Area of Black soil
(d) River Yamuna
(f) Vindhya ranges
(e) River Tapti
(b) Konkan coast

21.

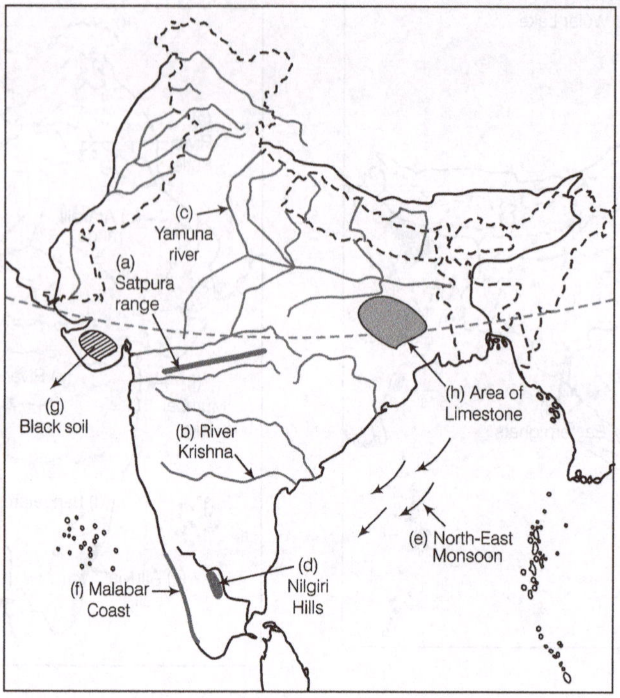
(c) Yamuna river
(a) Satpura range
(g) Black soil
(h) Area of Limestone
(b) River Krishna
(e) North-East Monsoon
(d) Nilgiri Hills
(f) Malabar Coast

22.

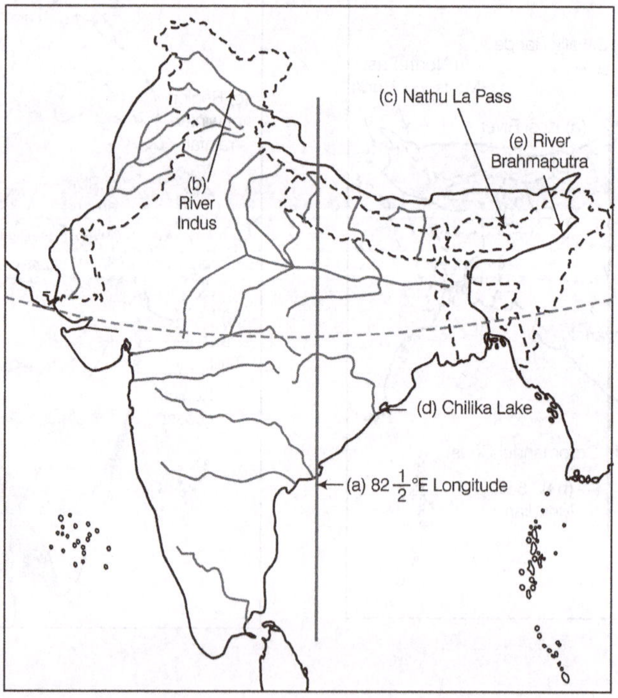
(c) Nathu La Pass
(e) River Brahmaputra
(b) River Indus
(d) Chilika Lake
(a) 82 1/2°E Longitude

ICSE

CHAPTERWISE TOPICWISE
SOLVED PAPERS

New Pattern Questions

New Pattern Questions

(Case Based Questions)

1. The Climate of India

Case Based Question

1. While talking to ANI, the Regional Head of IMD Delhi, Kuldeep Srivastava said, "Heatwave conditions in the first half of May were less severe due to Western disturbances that affected parts of North-West India. As the next Western disturbance is approaching North-West India, for the next 7 days, we are not expecting heatwave conditions there. But the temperature will be higher, up to 40°C".

   – Economic Times

   (a) How do Western disturbances influence the winter rainfall pattern in the Indian sub-continent?

   (b) Which planetary wind is responsible for Western disturbances which cause winter rainfall in Northern India?

Ans (a) Western disturbances influence the winter rainfall pattern in the Indian sub-continent by bringing moisture-laden winds from the Mediterranean region, resulting in increased rainfall during the winter season.

(b) The Westerly winds are responsible for Western disturbances which cause winter rainfall in Northern India.

2. With the El Nino phenomenon almost certain to affect the Indian monsoon this year, high hopes are pinned on the development of a positive Indian Ocean Dipole (IOD) and its ability to counterbalance the El Nino effect.

   – Indian Express

   (a) How does El Niño affect the monsoon rainfall in India?

   (b) What are the other factors that influence climate in India?

   (c) Which specific oceanic area experiences a temperature increase during El Niño?

Ans (a) El Niño leads to a decrease in monsoon rainfall in India, resulting in drought-like conditions and reduced agricultural productivity.

(b) Some other factors that influence climate in India include latitude, altitude, distance from the sea, Himalayan Mountain, Monsoon winds, Jet streams and topography.

(c) The specific oceanic area that experiences a temperature increase during El Niño is the Eastern Pacific Ocean.

2. Soils in India and Natural Vegetation of India

1. Train movement was disrupted on Itarsi-Jabalpur rail section in Madhya Pradesh on Wednesday due to soil erosion in the area following heavy rains.

   —Times of India

   (a) What is soil erosion?

   (b) Mention two steps that could be taken to prevent soil erosion caused by running water.

Ans (a) Soil erosion refers to the process of detachment and movement of topsoil or fertile soil layers by natural forces like wind and water, resulting in the loss of valuable soil resources.

(b) Two steps that could be taken to prevent soil erosion caused by running water are

Terracing Constructing terraces or steps on slopes helps to slow down the flow of water, reducing its erosive power and allowing water to infiltrate into the soil.

Contour ploughing Ploughing across the contour lines of the slope instead of up and down helps to create natural barriers to water flow, reducing the velocity of water and preventing erosion.

2. Rajasthan's new forest policy, which was released on Monday, aims to increase vegetation cover to 20% of the geographical area within the next 20 years, with focus on increasing vegetation outside forests.

   –Times of India

   (a) Which type of forest is found in Rajasthan?

   (b) How trees in this forest adapt themselves to the dry climate?

   (c) Give one reason to explain why we need to conserve our forest resources.

Ans (a) The type of forest found in Rajasthan is the tropical thorn forest, also known as the tropical desert forest.

(b) Trees in tropical desert forests adapt to the dry climate as they have long roots to reach underground water sources. They have thick, waxy leaves to reduce water loss through transpiration. They may have thorns or spines to reduce water loss and protect against herbivores.

(c) One reason to conserve forest resources is that they provide essential habitat for a wide variety of plant and animal species, supporting biodiversity and maintaining ecological balance.

3. Water Resources

1. The world's second-most populous country is running out of water. About 100 million people across India are on the front lines of a nationwide water crisis. A total of 21 major cities are poised to run out of groundwater next year, according to 2018 report by government-run think tank NITI Aayog.
   (a) Why is per capita availability of water getting decline?
   (b) Mention any two methods of recharging ground water aquifers.

Ans (a) The per capita availability of water is declining due to factors such as population growth, urbanisation, industrialisation and inefficient water management practices leading to overuse and depletion of water resources.

(b) Two methods of recharging groundwater aquifers are

Rainwater Harvesting Collecting and storing rainwater through various techniques like rooftop harvesting, recharge pits.

Artificial Recharge Constructing structures such as recharge wells, injection wells and percolation tanks that directly inject or divert surface water into the ground.

2. A new report launched Tuesday on the eve of the first major U.N. Conference on water in over 45 years says 26% of the world's population doesn't have access to safe drinking water and 46% lack access to basic sanitation. – Economic Times
   (a) What is the percentage of water on Earth?
   (b) Give two reasons for global water scarcity.
   (c) Mention two water conservation methods.

Ans (a) 71% of the Earth's surface is covered with water and the oceans hold 97% of Earth's, total water which is saline.

(b) Increasing population growth and changes in climate patterns, such as prolonged droughts and irregular rainfall, are the reasons of water scarcity.

(c) Two water conservation methods are:

Rainwater Harvesting Collecting and storing rainwater for later use.

Efficient Irrigation Practices Using methods like drip irrigation or sprinkler systems to minimise water wastage in agriculture.

4. Minerals and Energy Resources

1. The World Bank will provide USD 200 million (about ₹ 1,600 crore loan) to finance the Himachal Power Sector Development Programme to bring improvements in renewable energy integration in the state, Chief Minister said on Wednesday. – Economic Times
   (a) What are renewable energy resources?
   (b) Give two advantages that non- conventional energy sources have over conventional energy resources.

Ans (a) Renewable energy resources are sources of energy that are naturally replenished or virtually inexhaustible, such as solar energy, wind energy, hydroelectric power, biomass and geothermal energy.

(b) Non-conventional energy sources offer two significant advantages over conventional energy resources. Firstly, they are environmentally friendly, emitting fewer greenhouse gases and causing less pollution. Secondly, non-conventional energy sources are renewable and sustainable.

2. The 5.9-million-ton reserve of lithium, a crucial mineral for the manufacturing of electric vehicles and solar panels, had been discovered in Reasi district by the Geological Survey of India (GSI). – Economic Times
   (a) What type of resource is lithium?
   (b) Name some other sources of energy.
   (c) Where is country's first lithium reserve found?

Ans (a) Lithium can be described as the non-renewable mineral that makes renewable energy possible - often touted as the next oil.

(b) Some other sources of energy include fossil fuels (coal, oil and natural gas), nuclear energy, biomass energy, geothermal energy, tidal energy, hydroelectric power, etc.

(c) The country's first ever lithium reserve is found in Reasi district of Jammu and Kashmir.

5. Agriculture in India, Food and Fibre Crops of India and Cash crops of India

1. The cabinet has approved the highest ever Fair and Remunerative Price of ₹ 315/qtl for Sugarcane Farmers for sugar season 2023-24. The decision will benefit 5 crore sugarcane farmers and their dependents, as well as 5 lakh workers employed in the sugar mills and related ancillary activities," said Thakur. – Economic Times

   (a) Which Indian state is the largest producer of sugarcane?

   (b) Why the yield of sugarcane is higher in the Deccan?

Ans (a) Uttar Pradesh is the largest producer of sugarcane in India.

(b) The yield of sugarcane is higher in the Deccan region due to favourable agro-climatic conditions such as rich fertile soil, moderate rainfall and suitable temperature, which are conducive to the growth and development of sugarcane crops.

2. India's natural fibre industry is expected to grow steadily in the coming years on the back of the growing domestic and global demand for the commodity, according to Mayank Tiwari, Founder and CEO Resha Mandi, a farm-to-fashion digital marketplace for natural fibres. – The Hindu

   (a) Name the main fiber crops that are produced on a large scale in India.

   (b) State an important difference between the climatic requirements for both the crops.

   (c) Name the states that produces the largest amount of these crops.

Ans (a) The main fiber crops produced on a large scale in India include cotton and jute.

(b) An important difference in the climatic requirements for cotton and jute is that cotton requires a warm and dry climate with temperatures ranging from 21°C to 30°C, while jute thrives in a hot and humid climate with temperatures around 25°C to 35°C and heavy rainfall.

(c) The states that produce the largest amount of cotton in India are Gujarat, Maharashtra and Andhra Pradesh. West Bengal, Bihar and Assam are the major producers of jute.

6. Manufacturing Industries and Waste Management

1. The death of 11 persons from breathing toxic air resulting most probably from the illegal dumping of industrial effluents in the sewage system was an avoidable tragedy. – Economic Times

   (a) Which waste management approach would have helped to prevent the above tragedy?

   (b) What is illegal dumping?

   (c) What do you understand by landfills?

Ans (a) The implementation of proper waste management practices, such as waste treatment and disposal, would have helped to prevent the tragedy.

(b) Illegal dumping refers to the unauthorised disposal of waste materials, such as industrial effluents, into inappropriate locations such as water bodies, open land or sewage systems. It is a violation of environmental regulations and poses significant risks to public health and the environment.

(c) Landfills are designated areas where solid waste is disposed off and buried in a controlled manner. They are engineered sites with measures to prevent pollution and protect the environment.

2. Indian companies are developing the roadmap to adopt digital transformation with 54% of them implementing analytics and Artificial Intelligence (AI) for business functions, According to a survey by the professional services firm PwC India. – Economic Times

   (a) Give one reason for the growth of AI in Manufacturing industry.

   (b) Give one geographical reasons for the growth of IT industries in Bengaluru.

Ans (a) One reason for the growth of AI in the manufacturing industry is the potential to improve operational efficiency, productivity, and quality through automation and optimisation of various processes.

(b) One geographical reason for the growth of IT industries in Bengaluru is the availability of a skilled and educated workforce due to the presence of renowned educational institutions in the city, which attract and produce a pool of talented professionals.

7. Transport

1. Making a strong case for improving and promoting the use of public transport, Union Minister for Highways Nitin Gadkari said that road transport alone is responsible for 40 per cent of the air pollution in India, here on Thursday. – Economic Times

(a) State one disadvantage of road transport.

(b) Roads are always considered more important than any other means of transportation. Give reason in support of the statement.

Ans (a) One disadvantage of road transport is the vulnerability to traffic congestion, which can lead to delays, increased travel time, and inefficiencies in the transportation system, impacting the timely delivery of goods and services.

(b) Roads are often considered more important than any other means of transportation due to their extensive reach and accessibility. Unlike other modes of transportation such as railways or waterways, roads can be constructed and interconnected to even remote areas, providing connectivity

2. Prime Minister Narendra Modi flag off five Vande Bharat trains on Tuesday from Rani Kamalapati Railway Station in Bhopal. Ranchi-Patna Vande Bharat Express will be the first Vande Bharat for Jharkhand and Bihar. Enhancing connectivity between Patna and Ranchi, the train will be a boon for tourists, students and businessmen. – Economic Times

(a) Give one reason for the 'means of transportation' being called the lifelines of a nation's economy.

(b) State one advantage that railway have over other transportations.

(c) Which two cities were connected by the first-ever railway route in India?

Ans (a) One reason for the 'means of transportation' being called the lifelines of a nation's economy is that it facilitates the movement of goods and services, enables trade, promotes economic activities, and ensures the availability of essential resources, contributing to the overall economic development of a nation.

(b) One advantage that railways have over other modes of transportation is their ability to transport large quantities of goods and passengers over long distances with high efficiency.

(c) The first-ever railway route in India connected Mumbai (then Bombay) with Thane in Maharashtra.

ICSE Fully Solved

SAMPLE PAPER 01

Time : 2 hrs
Marks : 80

Geography X

General Instructions

1. Answers to this paper must be written on the paper provided separately.
2. You will not be allowed to write during the first 15 minutes. This time is to be spent in reading the question paper.
3. The time given at the head of this paper is the time allowed for writing the answers.
4. Part I is compulsory. All questions from Part I are to be attempted. A total of 5 questions are to be attempted from Part II.
5. The intended marks for questions or parts of question are given in brackets ( ).

Part - I [30 *Marks*]

Attempt all questions from this part.

1. Study the extract of the Survey of India Map Sheet No. G43S7 (Map 1 given at the end), Eastings 25-35 and Northings 89-99 and answer the following questions.

(i) (a) Give the four-figure grid reference of spot height .224 **(2)**

(b) Give the six-figure grid reference of the covered tank near Ramsida settlement.

(ii) (a) In which direction does the river in the map extract flow? **(2)**

(b) On which bank of the river, the settlement Dantiwada (2992) located?

(iii) (a) What does 14r in 3189 indicate? **(2)**

(b) How does the drainage pattern in grid square .3397 and 2698 differ?

(iv) (a) What is the general pattern of human habitation in the map extract? **(2)**

(b) What is the area in square kilometres enclosed by the vertical grid 30 to 35 and horizontal grid lines 96-99.

(v) (a) What does the black vertical line running along Easting 33 indicate? **(2)**

(b) What do you mean by 'dep' written in the South-East corner of the map? **(2)**

2. On the outline map of India provided,

(a) Shade the region under Thar Desert **(1)**

(b) Mark with the dot and name Chennai **(1)**

(c) Mark lake Chilika **(1)**

(d) Mark the river Yamuna **(1)**

(e) Shade the region of Alluvial soil in Northern plains **(1)**

(f) Draw and label the Tropic of Cancer **(1)**

(g) Mark and label Konkan Coastal Plains **(1)**

(h) Shade the region of Western Ghats **(1)**

(i) Mark with a dot and name Kolkata **(1)**

(j) Shade the region which has black soil **(1)**

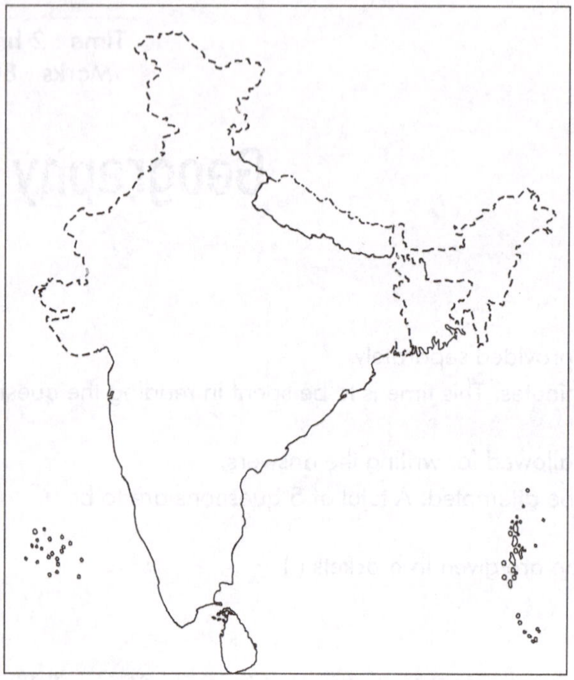

3. Choose the correct answer to the questions from the given options.

(i) **Assertion** (A) The Eastern coast of India is affected by tropical cyclones more than the Western coast.

Reason (R) Tropical cyclones originate only in the Bay of Bengal. **(1)**

(a) Both (A) and (R) are true and (R) is the correct explanation for (A).

(b) Both (A) and (R) are true, but (R) is not the correct explanation for (A).

(c) (A) is true, but (R) is false.

(d) (A) is false, but (R) is true.

(ii) Which soil type is predominantly found in the Western parts of Rajasthan and is characterised by low moisture retention? **(1)**

(a) Black soil (b) Alluvial soil

(c) Desert soil (d) Laterite soil

(iii) The forest shown in the image is located in coastal regions and is adapted to saline, waterlogged conditions with tidal influences. Identify the forest type. **(1)**

(a) Tropical Evergreen Forest

(b) Tropical Deciduous Forest

(c) Montane Forest

(d) Mangrove Forest

(iv) Which one of the following type of resource is iron ore ? **(1)**

(a) Renewable (b) Biotic

(c) Flow (d) Non-renewable

(v) Koraput : Bauxite :: Singhbhum : .... **(1)**

(a) Copper (b) Coal

(c) Iron Ore (d) Manganese

(vi) Rabi crops are harvested in the months of .... **(1)**

(a) April to June (b) July to September

(c) October to December (d) January to March

(vii) Which one of the following is a Rabi crop? **(1)**

(a) Rice (b) Gram

(c) Millet (d) Cotton

(viii) Which of the following industries manufactures telephone, computers, etc ? **(1)**

(a) Steel (b) Electronic

(c) Aluminium (d) Information Technology

(ix) Which of the following is a significant advantage of the Pradhan Mantri Gram Sadak Yojana (PMGSY)? **(1)**

(a) Enhances urban infrastructure.

(b) Provides all-weather road connectivity to unconnected villages.

(c) Develops national highways.

(d) Promotes air travel in rural areas.

(x) A city council is planning to implement a waste management strategy that focuses on reducing the volume of waste sent to landfills. Which of the following actions aligns best with this goal? **(1)**

(a) Encouraging residents to compost organic waste

(b) Increasing the number of landfill sites

(c) Collecting all types of waste together for disposal.

(d) Burning all waste materials.

Part - II [50 *Marks*]

*Attempt any **five** questions from this part.*

4. (i) On Sunday 4th, June, Pune and its surrounding region received, heavy to very heavy rains. The India IMD has predicted more rain in the next few days. The rain, IMD said was likely due to development of a cyclonic circulation over the South-East Arabian Sea. Similarly, another cyclonic circulation persists over Bay of Bengal near the coast of Myanmar. –The India Express **(2)**

(a) Name the cyclones due to which Pune and its surrounding region received heavy to very heavy rain.

(b) What are the other factors that affect climate of India?

(ii) (a) Explain why the Northern Plains do not freeze in winter despite having a continental climate.

(b) Why does the Central part of Maharashtra receive less rainfall? **(2)**

(iii) With reference to Figure A and Figure B given below, answer the questions that follow **(3)**

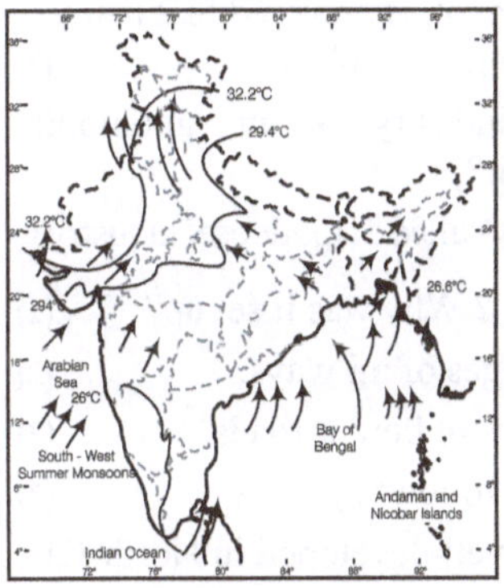

Figure A

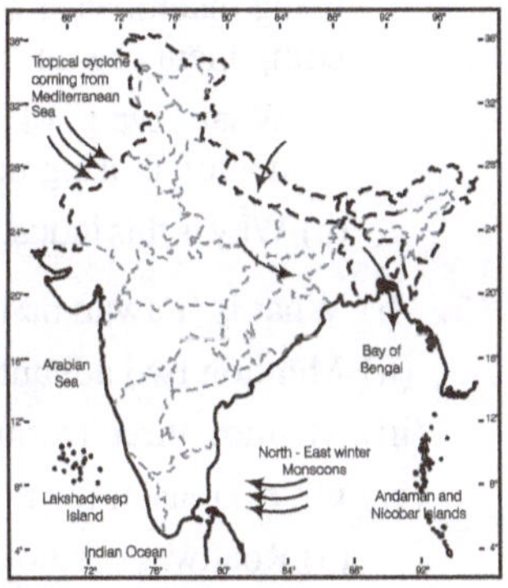

Figure B

(a) What does the image depict about the arrival of monsoon in India?

(b) How does the retreat of the monsoon differ from its arrival?

(iv) Study the climatic data of a city of India provided below and answer the questions that follow. **(3)**

Station	**Station A**	
Month	Tem. (°C)	Rainfall (cm)
Jan	16.0	3.2
Feb	18.0	5.1
Mar	21.3	8.7
Apr	23.3	24.1
May	26.1	24.2
Jun	27.8	39.2
July	27.4	54.7
Aug	27.9	42.2
Sep	26.7	35.5
Oct	25.1	13.9
Nov	21.1	1.6
Dec	17.2	1.9

(a) What is the annual range of temperature of station A?

(b) What is the total rainfall received by station A?

(c) Which are the wettest and driest months in this station?

5. (i) In the Eastern and Southern parts of the Indian Peninsula, the soil appears reddish in colour due to the presence of iron. It is generally less fertile but can support crops like millets and pulses. **(2)**

(a) Name the soil described above.

(b) Mention two characteristics of this soil.

(ii) (a) In which regions is black soil predominantly found in India? **(2)**

(b) Why is black soil also known as 'regur soil' and 'cotton soil'?

(iiii) Give a geographical reason for the following statements. **(3)**

(a) Red soil require irrigation.

(b) Laterite soil is red in colour.

(c) Afforestation prevents soil from getting eroded.

(iv) With reference to alluvial soil, answer the following questions.

(a) Name two crops that grow well in this soil. **(3)**

(b) Why is alluvial soil considered highly fertile?

(c) What are sub-categories of this soil?

6. (i) Roshan went to his village and observe that forest in his village have long roots which penetrate deep into the soil in order to get moisture. **(2)**

(a) Which type forest is found in his village?

(b) Name two trees found in this forest.

(ii) (a) Mention the names of two varieties of trees found in mountain forests along with one use of each type of tree. **(2)**

(b) What are coniferous forest? Give examples.

(iii) Mention any three main causes of deforestation. **(3)**

(iv) (a) Which is the most economically important vegetation belt of India? **(3)**

(b) Name two species of tree found in this belt with one use of each species of tree.

7. (i) What is the importance of irrigation in agriculture? Mention its different types. **(2)**

(ii) Give two reasons why inundation canals are being converted into perennial canals. **(2)**

(iii) Give one reason to explain each of the following: **(3)**

(a) Sprinkler irrigation is useful in regions with uneven land.

(b) Rainwater harvesting is promoted in urban areas.

(c) Over-irrigation can lead to waterlogging and salinity.

(iv) Why is canal irrigation very popular in North India? Give three reasons. **(3)**

8. (i) India has the fourth-largest installed capacity of wind power in the world.

— Ministry of New and Renewable Energy **(2)**

(a) Name one Indian state with high potential for wind energy generation.

(b) Mention one environmental benefit of using wind energy.

(ii) (a) What grade of iron ore is normally mined in India?

(b) Give names of two states in which iron ore is abundantly available. **(2)**

(iii) Give a reason for each of the following: **(3)**

(a) Bauxite is important for the aluminium industry.

(b) Hydel power is more suitable in hilly regions.

(c) Minerals are called non-renewable resources.

(iv)

(a) Name the renewable energy source shown in the image. **(3)**

(b) Mention one environmental advantage of using this energy source.

(c) Name one Indian state where wind energy is widely harnessed.

9. (i) Mention two geographical requirements for the growth of tea. **(2)**

(ii) What are two differences between subsistence agriculture and plantation agriculture? **(2)**

(iii) Given geographical reason for the following. **(3)**

(a) Cotton grows best in Southern part of India.

(b) Tea cultivation is done on slopes.

(c) Rice is best cultivated in flooded field.

(iv) Explain the following. **(3)**

(a) Organic Farming (b) Plantation Agriculture

(c) Crop Rotation

10. (i) What are two reasons for the jute industry being concentrated in and around West Bengal? **(2)**

(ii) Why have cotton textile industries been developed around Mumbai? Give two reasons. **(2)**

(iii) (a) Mention one reason why the sugar industry has developed in Maharashtra. **(3)**

(b) Mention any two factors due to which sugar industry is flourishing in Peninsular India.

(iv) Ravi visited an automobile manufacturing unit where different car parts were being assembled using machines and labor. He noticed that many components came from other places. **(3)**

(a) What type of industry is an automobile manufacturing unit?

(b) Why is this industry called a 'footloose' industry?

11. (i) What is 'Pawan hans'? Why was it set up? **(2)**

(ii) Mention two advantages of railways. **(2)**

(iii) Mention three features of border roads. **(3)**

(iv) Give a reason for the following. **(3)**

(a) Roadways is not well-developed in North-East India.

(b) Railways are under the pubic sector.

(c) A good network of transport is of great help for the development of the economy.

12. (i) (a) What is a natural harbour?

(b) Give an example of one such harbour in India. **(2)**

(ii) Explain why road transport is favoured in North India by giving two reasons. **(2)**

(iii) An engineering marvel in the making the world's tallest railway bridge being constructed over Chenab river in Jammu and Kashmir's Reasi district is likely to come up by December 2023.

– Hindustan Times **(3)**

(a) The Chenab bridge is part of which project?

(b) Why railways is suitable for long distance?

(c) Why it requires high cost construction and maintenance?

(iv) Give a reason for the following statements. **(3)**

(a) Composting is an eco-friendly way to manage organic waste.

(b) Reusing items is better than recycling them.

(c) Wet and dry waste should be collected separately.

Answers

1. (i) (a) 3396 (b) 31908

(ii) (a) River flows in Westward direction/from East-West.

(b) Left Bank

(iii) (a) 14r indicates that the relative height of the sand dune is 14 meters.

(b) 3397-Dendritic 2698-Trellis

(iv) (a) The general pattern of the human habitation is Nucleated.

(b) $30 - 35 = -5$

$96 - 99 = -3$

$2 \text{ cm} = 1 \text{ km}$

$\text{Area} = L \times B$

$5 \text{ km} \times 3 \text{ km} = 15 \text{ sq km}$

(v) (a) The black vertical line is the line of longitude.

(b) 'Dep' means depression found in sandy regions at the top of a mound or dune where the wind easily blows the sand away leaving a hollow.

2.

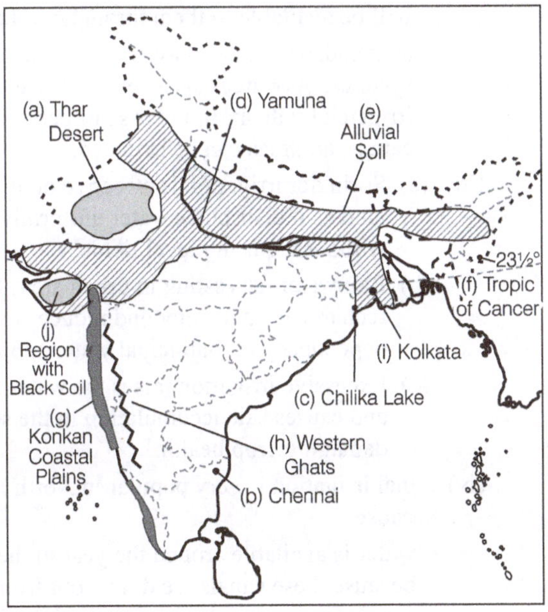

3. (i) (c) (A) is true, but (R) is false.

(ii) (c) Desert soil (iii) (d) Mangrove Forest

(iv) (d) Non-renewable

(v) (a) Copper (vi) (a) April to June

(vii) (b) Gram (viii) (b) Electronic

(ix) (b) Provides all-weather road connectivity to unconnected villages.

(x) (a) Encouraging residents to compost organic waste.

4. (i) (a) Cyclone Mocha

(b) Factors that affect the climate of India includes altitude, Western disturbances, jet streams, El-Nino, etc.

(ii) (a) The Northern Plains do not freeze in winter because the Himalayas act as a barrier to prevent the cold winds from Central Asia from entering the Indian mainland.

(b) The central part of Maharashtra lies in the rain shadow area of the Western Ghats, which are struck by the Arabian Sea branch of the South West monsoon.

(iii) (a) The image shows the onset of the South-West Monsoon, which begins in early June from the Kerala coast and gradually advances Northwards, covering the entire country by mid-July.

(b) The retreat of the monsoon begins in September from the North-Western parts of India and moves Southward. Unlike its sudden arrival, the retreat is gradual and marked by clear skies and rising temperatures.

(iv) (a) The annual range of temperature of station A is $27.9 - 16.0 = 11.9\,°C$.

(b) The total rainfall received by station $A = 254.3$ cm.

(c) The wettest month in station A is July and the driest month is November.

5. (i) (a) The soil described above is Red soil.

(b) Two characteristics of this soil are

- **Rich in iron content** The reddish colour comes from iron oxides present in the soil.
- **Low in nitrogen and humus** It requires fertilisers and irrigation for better productivity.

(ii) (a) Black soil is predominantly found in the Deccan Plateau region, covering parts of Maharashtra, Madhya Pradesh, Gujarat, Andhra Pradesh and Tamil Nadu.

(b) • It is called regur soil because of its local name in the Deccan region.

- It is also referred to as cotton soil because its properties such as moisture retention and fertility make it especially suitable for cotton cultivation.

(iii) (a) Red soil is a type of soil that develops in a warm, temperate, moist-climate and generally derived from crystalline rock that is why red soil required irrigation.

(b) Laterite soil is made up of high level of iron oxides in the form of minerals like goethite and hematite. Thus, it appears red in colour.

(c) Trees reduces the rate of erosion by protecting the soil from the impact of rain. It also bind the soil to sloping land with their roots. Thus, afforestation prevents soil from getting eroded.

(iv) (a) Two crops which grow well in alluvial soil are sugarcane and cotton.

(b) Alluvial soil is considered highly fertile because it is rich in nutrients like potash, phosphoric acid and lime.

(c) Khadar is better for agriculture because the annual floods replenish it with fresh nutrients required by the crops.

6. (i) (a) Tropical desert forests are found in Roshan's village.

(b) Timber, babool and neem trees are found in such forests.

(ii) (a) Two varieties of trees found in mountain forests are

- Silver fir, which is used for making paper, matches and packing cases.
- Chir pine, whose resin and turpentine can be extracted and used in industry.

(b) Coniferous forest is made up of conifers. Conifers are cone-bearing trees that have needle-like leaves and stay green all year long, for example, the Northern boreal forest (50°-60°N).

(iii) Main causes of deforestation are agriculture expansion, wood extraction and infrastructure expansion (road building and urbanisation).

(iv) (a) The most economically important vegetation belt of India is the deciduous monsoon forests.

(b) Two trees found here are

- Teak, whose wood is used in house construction.
- Sandalwood, which is used for making handicrafts.

7. (i) Irrigation helps to grow crops, maintain landscapes and revegetate distrurbed soil in dry areas and during times of below average rainfall. It also protect crops from frost, suppress weed growth in grain fields and present soil consolidation.

Some main types of irrigation are sprinkler irrigation, surface irrigation, drip irrigation, sub-irrigation and manual irrigation.

(ii) Inundation canals are being converted into perennial canals because

- water flows in inundation canals only when the rivers from which they are drawn are in flood. If they are converted to perennial canals, water will be available in them throughout the year.
- as inundation canals have no regulating systems, only areas at lower levels can be irrigated by them. In the case of perennial canals, all areas can be irrigated.

(iii) (a) Sprinkler irrigation is effective on uneven land as it distributes water uniformly without requiring level fields.

(b) Rainwater harvesting in urban areas helps recharge groundwater and reduce dependency on municipal water supply.

(c) Excessive irrigation raises the water table and causes salt accumulation in the soil, damaging crop health.

(iv) Canal irrigation is very popular in North India because

- water is available around the year in the canals because these canals are drawn out from rivers which are perennial, being snow-fed.

- it is easy to construct canals because the land is covered with alluvium, which is soft and easy to dig.
- a large amount of cultivated land is available, thus increasing the demand of irrigation water, which can only be met through perennial canals.

8. (i) (a) Tamil Nadu has high potential and significant wind energy generation in India.

(b) Wind energy does not emit greenhouse gases, making it an environmentally friendly power source.

(ii) (a) Haematite and Magnetite grades of iron ore are normally mined in India.

(b) Odisha and Jharkhand are two states in which iron ore is abundantly available.

(iii) (a) Bauxite is the primary ore of aluminium, containing a high percentage of aluminium oxide used to extract the metal.

(b) Hilly regions have fast-flowing rivers and steep gradients, which are ideal for generating hydel power using dams and turbines.

(c) Minerals take millions of years to form and cannot be replenished on a human timescale once extracted and used.

(iv) (a) The renewable energy source shown in the image is wind energy.

(b) Wind energy is clean and does not produce air pollution or greenhouse gases.

(c) Tamil Nadu is one of the leading states in India for wind energy production.

9. (i) Two geographical requirements for the growth of tea are

(a) It requires a hot and wet climate with temperature ranging from 25°C to 35°C and rainfall between 150 and 250 cm annually.

(b) Deep, well-drained loamy soil which is acidic in nature is most suitable to tea crop. Stagnant water is harmful to the tea plantation that is why it is grown on hill slopes.

(ii) The differences between subsistence agriculture and plantation agriculture are

- Subsistence agriculture is exclusively for personal consumption, whereas plantation agriculture is carried on for sale of the agricultural products in the market.
- Subsistence agriculture uses primitive methods with simple hand tools, whereas plantation agriculture uses modern machinery and large capital investment.

(iii) (a) Cotton is grown best in Southern part of India mainly Deccan Plateau because it has thick dark soil called regur/black soil, which is most suitable for cotton cultivation.

(b) Tea cultivation require even distribution of water without any water logging. Hill slopes provide proper drainage and prevents water logging problems.

(c) Rice is cultivated in the flooded fields to improve the growth of most varieties, to reduce vulnerability to uneven rainfall and to produce higher yield relative to dry soil by reducing pests and weeds.

(iv) (a) Organic farming is a method of farming that avoids the use of chemical fertilisers and pesticides, relying instead on natural methods like compost and crop rotation.

(b) Plantation agriculture involves the cultivation of a single cash crop on large estates for commercial sale, such as tea, coffee or rubber.

(c) Crop rotation is the practice of growing different types of crops on the same land in a planned sequence to maintain soil fertility and reduce pests.

10. (i) The two reasons are

- Proximity of the jute growing areas.
- Availability of inexpensive water transport, supported by a good network of railways, roadways and waterways to facilitate movement of raw material to the mills.

(ii) Cotton textile industries have been developed around Mumbai because of the following reasons

- The rich hinterland and black soil region help in the growth of raw cotton.
- Cheap power is available from the Tata Hydroelectric System.
- Indegenous woollens are of poor quality compared to cotton products.

(iii) (a) Sugar industry has developed in Maharashtra due to large production of sugarcane.

(b) Three factors due to which sugar industry is flourishing in Peninsular India are

- Peninsular India has the best climatic conditions for growth of the sugarcane crop. Thus, sugar extracted from this crop gives a higher yield.

(iv) (a) An automobile manufacturing unit is an assembly-based or large-scale industry.

(b) It is called a footloose industry because it is not tied to any specific location and can be set up near markets or transport hubs.

11. (i) (a) Pawan Hans Helicopters Ltd. (PHHL) was formed in 1985 to provide Helicopter support services to the petroleum sector and Oil India Ltd. in offshore exploration.

(ii) Two advantages of Railways are

- It facilitates long distance travel and transport of bulky goods.
- It is quick and more regular form of transport.

(iii) Three features of border roads are

- Border roads are the lifeline of Border areas of North and North-East part of India.
- These roads have increased the accessibility in the difficult terrain areas of India.
- These roads are constructed and maintained by Border Road Organisation (BRO).

(iv) (a) Roadways is not well-developed in North-East India because this region is a hilly area which has undulating topography.

(b) Railways are managed by the public sectors of the government, as the government has a majority of share in the railway sector. The public sector companies are involved with development and expansion of the railways.

(c) A good network of transport is of great help for the development of the economy because it can broaden the market for goods. It can also make easy movement of raw materials, fuels, equipment, etc to the places of production easy.

12. (i) (a) A natural harbour is one that occurs along a fairly indented coastline and which does not require a wall to be constructed for creating it.

(b) An example of a natural harbour in India is Mumbai.

(ii) The two reasons are

(a) North India is an agriculturally rich region. As road transport gives door-to-door service, it is the most convenient form of transport to carry agricultural inputs like fertilisers, seeds, etc and harvested crops.

(b) Most of North India is a level plain, making road construction easier and more economical.

(iii) (a) The Chenab railway bridge is part of the Udhampur-Srinagar-Baramulla Rail Link Project which provide seamless and hassle-free connectivity in Jammu and Kashmir.

(b) Railways is suitable for long distance travel as it reduce the cost of long distance travelling as compared to other modes of transport. As compared to airways, travelling through railways is easy and comfortable as one can move during his/her seat for endless amount of hours.

(c) Rail tracks are very difficult to lay on irregular terrain. Thus, high cost is involved in construction and maintenance of railway tracks.

(iv) (a) Composting is eco-friendly because it converts kitchen and garden waste into nutrient-rich manure, reducing landfill burden and improving soil health.

(b) Reusing saves more energy and resources than recycling, as it avoids the need for processing materials again.

(c) Separate collection helps in effective composting of organic waste and recycling of dry waste, making waste management more efficient.

ICSE Unsolved

SAMPLE PAPER 02

Time : 2 hrs
Marks : 80

Geography X

General Instructions

1. Answers to this paper must be written on the paper provided separately.
2. You will not be allowed to write during the first 15 minutes. This time is to be spent in reading the question paper.
3. The time given at the head of this paper is the time allowed for writing the answers.
4. Part I is compulsory. All questions from Part I are to be attempted. A total of 5 questions are to be attempted from Part II.
5. The intended marks for questions or parts of question are given in brackets ( ).

Part - I [30 *Marks*]

Attempt all questions from this part.

1. Study the extract of the Survey of India Map Sheet No. G43S10 (Map 2 given at the end) Eastings 61-71 and Northings 13-23 and answer the following questions.

(i) Give the four-figure grid reference of the
(a) hospital near Abu
(b) surveyed the 277 **(2)**

(ii) Give six figure grid reference of
(a) Gautam Maharshi Mandir
(b) Triangulated height 1327 **(2)**

(iii) (a) What is the scale of the given map extract?
(b) What does it mean? **(2)**

(iv) (a) What do you mean by 12r written in grid. 6913?
(b) Calculate the distance in km between the causeway in grid square 6213 till the end of the metalled road in grid square 6712. **(2)**

(v) What do you mean by the terms used on the map extract?
(a) Causeway (6213)
(b) Falls 15 m (6718) **(2)**

2. On the outline map of India provided,

(a) Shade the region of Gangetic plain
(b) Mark the region of Malabar coast. **(1)**
(c) Mark with a dot and name oil refinery in West Bengal. **(1)**
(d) Shade and label river Jhelum. **(1)**
(e) Mark and label the Arabian Sea branch of South-West monsoon **(1)**
(f) Mark with a dot and name, Amritsar **(1)**
(g) Mark Gulf of Khambhat **(1)**
(h) Shade and name Coromandel Coastal plain **(1)**
(i) Mark and name Mumbai **(1)**
(j) Shade and name the Deccan Plateau **(1)**

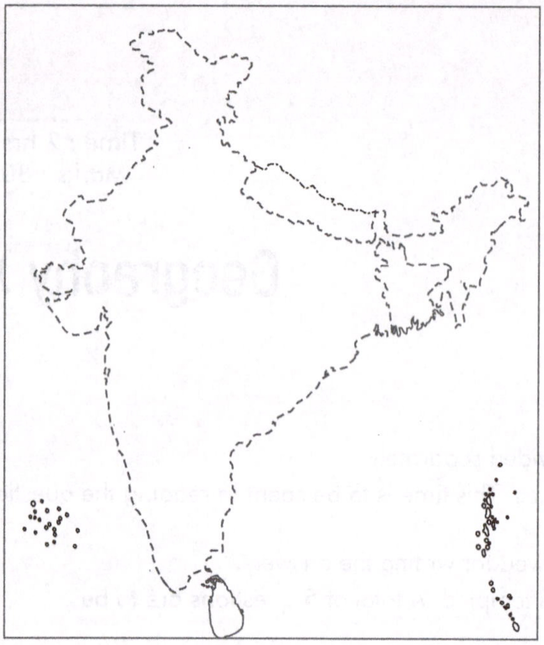

3. (i) Which port is known as the 'Gateway of India' and is the largest container port in the country? (1)

(a) Chennai Port
(b) Kolkata Port
(c) Jawaharlal Nehru Port
(d) Visakhapatnam Port

(ii) Mayurbhanj : Iron Ore :: Balaghat : .... (1)

(a) Copper (b) Manganese
(c) Bauxite (d) Coal

(iii) A manufacturing company aims to adopt a sustainable approach by minimising waste production. Which of the following strategies should they prioritise? (1)

(a) Implementing processes that reduce material usage and waste generation.
(b) Disposing of waste in nearby water bodies.
(c) Ignoring waste segregation protocols.
(d) Using non-recyclable materials for packaging.

(iv) Black soil is also known as ……… soil. (1)

(a) alluvial (b) red
(c) regur (d) khadar

(v) When running water cuts through clayey soil and makes deep channels, they lead to (1)

(a) gully erosion (b) sheet erosion
(c) deforestation (d) afforestation

(vi) The forest depicted in the image is situated in mountainous regions with cool climates and supports both coniferous and broad-leaved species. Identify the forest type. (1)

(a) Tropical Evergreen Forest
(b) Tropical Deciduous Forest
(c) Montane Forest
(d) Mangrove Forest

(vii) Which of the following industries require a low capital base ? (1)

(a) Large scale industry
(b) Small scale industry
(c) Public sector industry
(d) Private sector industry

(viii) Rice, maize , millet, ragi and pulses are examples of (1)

(a) Rabi crops (b) Kharif crops
(c) Zaid crops (d) Cash crops

(ix) Choose the correct answers to the questions from the given options. (1)

Assertion (A) The Western coast of India receives heavy rainfall during the monsoon season.

Reason (R) The Western Ghats force the moisture-laden winds of the South-West monsoon to rise, causing orographic rainfall.

(a) Both (A) and (R) are true and (R) is the correct explanation for (A).
(b) Both (A) and (R) are true, but (R) is not the correct explanation for (A).
(c) (A) is true, but (R) is false.
(d) (A) is false, but (R) is true.

(x) Which of the following is a non-conventional source of energy ? (1)

(a) Wind energy (b) Coal
(c) Petroleum (d) Natural gas

Part - II [50 *Marks*]

*Attempt any **five** questions from this part.*

4. (i) Winter season in India is marked by cool and dry conditions. **(2)**
   (a) What causes the dry winter in most parts of India?
   (b) Which region in India experiences winter rainfall and why?

   (ii) When did the following region receives most of its rainfall? **(2)**
   (a) Panaji
   (b) Visakhapatnam

   (iii) (a) What are Western disturbances and where do they originate? **(3)**
   (b) How do they affect the weather of Northern India in winter?

   (iv) Study the climatic data of two cities of India provided below and answer the questions that follow. **(3)**

Station	**Station A**		**Station A**	
Month	**Tem.** (°C)	**Rainfall** (cm)	**Tem.** (°C)	**Rainfall** (cm)
Jan	23.5	1.2	14.0	1.5
Feb	25.8	1.2	16.8	2.0
Mar	28.7	1.7	22.0	1.4
Apr	30.5	3.8	28.5	2.0
May	31.9	4.7	32.3	2.5
Jun	31.5	10.0	33.5	7.0
July	29.6	13.0	30.0	23.5
Aug	29.5	16.6	30.0	23.0
Sep	29.3	16.0	29.7	11.0
Oct	28.5	18.0	26.5	2.2
Nov	26.5	7.8	20.5	1.0
Dec	24.2	0.4	15.8	0.8

   (a) Calculate the annual range of temperature of station A. Give one reason to explain each of the following.
   (b) What is the total rainfall received by station B?
   (c) On which coast of India is station A situated? Name the rains that bring rainfall to this region.

5. (i) Define the following terms. **(2)**
   (a) Bhangar (b) Khadar

   (ii) With reference to soil types found in India, answer the following questions. **(2)**
   (a) Alluvial soil is classified into which two types?
   (b) Which soil is used to grow cashew nuts.

   (iii) (a) Name two states of India which have mostly red soil. **(3)**
   (b) What disadvantage has this soil when compared to black soil?
   (c) What crops can be grown on red soil?

   (iv) (a) What are two factors responsible for soil erosion? **(3)**
   (b) List one step that farmers can take for preventing each of these factors from eroding the soil in their fields.
   (c) Mention a problem caused by soil erosion.

6. (i) Aman went for an excursion with his friend and came across very dense forest with tall trees which also have a number of lianas (climbing plants) and epiphytes. **(2)**
   (a) Which forest type did he come across?
   (b) Mention two types of trees found in this forest.

   (ii) (a) Mention two minor products which we obtain from forests. **(2)**
   (b) What is the location of alpine forests in India? Name two trees found in these forests.

   (iii) List three important measures taken to conserve forests by the government. **(3)**

   (iv) (a) What does the uppermost branches of the trees in a forest known as? **(3)**
   (b) Name the forest which grow on the windward slope of the Western Ghats.
   (c) Name an area in India where tropical monsoon forest is found.

7. (i) What are the conditions required for the construction of tube wells? **(2)**

   (ii) What is meant by rainwater harvesting? Why is it required? **(2)**

   (iii) (a) Why Kerala has the longest rain season? **(3)**
   (b) Why Mangalore is not cold even in the month of December?

   (iv) What are three favourable factors for the development of irrigation? **(3)**

8. (i) India's growing energy demand can be met by tapping into cleaner, non-polluting energy sources." – International Energy Agency **(2)**

(a) Name one energy source that uses agricultural waste to generate power.

(b) Why is biomass energy considered environmentally-friendly?

(ii) With reference to coal, answer the following. **(2)**

(a) Name the four varieties of coal found in India.

(b) Give one use for each variety.

(iii) (a) Name two varieties of iron ore used in industry, giving one example each of where they are used.

(b) Why are many oil refineries found near to the coasts of India? **(3)**

(iv)

(a) What type of energy is being harnessed in the power system shown in the image? **(3)**

(b) Give one benefit of using this type of energy over fossil fuels.

(c) Name one Indian state that has made significant progress in solar power generation.

9. (i) What are two methods for the cultivation of rice and which method is known for its better yield? **(2)**

(ii) (a) Which state is the largest producer of sugarcane in India? **(2)**

(b) What are the climatic conditions required for cultivation of sugarcane?

(iii) Study the picture given below and answer the questions that follow. **(3)**

(a) Mention the climatic condition that is suitable for the cultivation of this crop.

(b) Name the state that produces the largest amount of this crop.

(c) In which cropping season is the crop grown in India?

(iv) After weeks of heavy rainfall, the gardeners finally began the tedious task of 'Weeding' The overgrown flower beds. **(3)**

(a) What does weeding refer to?

(b) Why weeding is important?

10. (i) Mention two reasons why Jamshedpur is a major center for the iron and steel industry. **(2)**

(ii) Why is Mumbai known as a major center for the chemical industry in India? **(2)**

(iii) (a) Name a major center for the IT industry in India. **(3)**

(b) Mention two factors responsible for the growth of this industry in that region.

(iv) Ananya read about an industry where limestone is used and it produces cement along with some dust and ash waste. **(3)**

(a) Which industry is she referring to?

(b) Name any two by-products or wastes produced in this industry.

11. (i) Why is pipeline transport becoming increasingly important in India? **(2)**

(ii) Mention two advantages of rail transport in India. **(2)**

(iii) Name the following. **(3)**

(a) The national waterway that connects Haldia to Allahabad.

(b) The organisation responsible for postal services in India.

(c) The mode of communication that provides real-time video calls across the globe.

(iv) Give a reason for the following. **(3)**

(a) Water transport is gaining popularity for transporting goods.

(b) The Himalayan region has a poor road network.

(c) The development of digital communication has changed the way people connect.

12. (i) (a) How does improper disposal of e-waste affect the environment? **(2)**

(b) What is landfill?

(ii) A school student notices old computers and mobile phones being dumped in a nearby vacant lot by some local shopkeepers.
What step should the student take to address this issue? **(2)**

(iii) Identify the correct waste management practice for each situation. **(3)**
(a) Using both sides of a sheet of paper before recycling it.
(b) Buying products with minimal packaging to avoid waste.
(c) Avoiding disposable plates and cups at a picnic.

(iv) Give reason for the following statements.
(a) Plastic waste poses a serious threat to the environment. **(3)**
(b) E-waste must be handled with care.
(c) Paper should be recycled instead of being thrown away.

Answers

2.

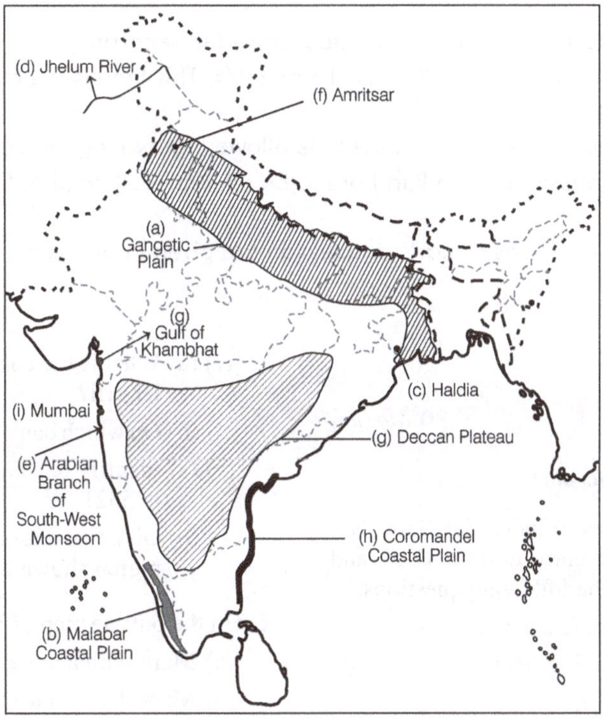

3. (i) (c) Jawaharlal Nehru Port
(ii) (b) Manganese
(iii) (a) Implementing processes that reduce material usage and waste generation.
(iv) (c) regur
(v) (a) gully erosion
(vi) (c) Montane Forest
(vii) (b) Small scale industry
(viii) (b) Kharif crops
(ix) (a) Both (A) and (R) are true and (R) is the correct explanation for (A).
(x) (a) Wind energy

ICSE Unsolved

SAMPLE PAPER 03

Time : 2 hrs
Marks : 80

Geography X

General Instructions

1. Answers to this paper must be written on the paper provided separately.
2. You will not be allowed to write during the first 15 minutes. This time is to be spent in reading the question paper.
3. The time given at the head of this paper is the time allowed for writing the answers.
4. Part I is compulsory. All questions from Part I are to be attempted. A total of 5 questions are to be attempted from Part II.
5. The intended marks for questions or parts of question are given in brackets ( ).

Part - I [30 *Marks*]

Attempt all questions from this part.

1. Study the extract of the Survey of India Map Sheet No. G43S10 (Map 3 given at the end), Easting 47-57 and Northing 13-23 and answer the following questions.

(i) Give the six-figure grid reference of

(a) Post office near Dattani settlement **(2)**

(b) Temple near Bherugarh

(ii) (a) What is the distance in kilometres along the metalled road from the Eastern edge of the map to where the East track crosses the metal road at Pipliya (5418)? **(2)**

(b) Name a feature of the relief that can be seen in grid square 5516.

(iii) (a) What does 3r in 5419 mean? **(2)**

(b) What is the drainage pattern of the grid 5213?

(iv) (a) What is the compass direction of Dolpura from Dhavli? **(2)**

(b) On which bank of river Sipu, river Sukli join it?

(v) (a) Identify one natural and one man made feature in 5321. **(2)**

(b) Give two reasons to show that the rainfall in the region shown on the map extract is seasonal. **(2)**

2. On the outline map of India provided,

(a) Mark with a dot and name Prayagraj **(1)**

(b) Mark the Nathu-La Pass **(1)**

(c) Mark and name the leading state for coal **(1)**

(d) Shade the region of Eastern Ghats **(1)**

(e) Mark the Satpura Range **(1)**

(f) Label the river Brahmaputra **(1)**

(g) Mark with a dot and name Singhbhum **(1)**

(h) Shade and label a region with red soil **(1)**

(i) Mark the Wular lake **(1)**

(j) Shade and label the river Tungabhadra **(1)**

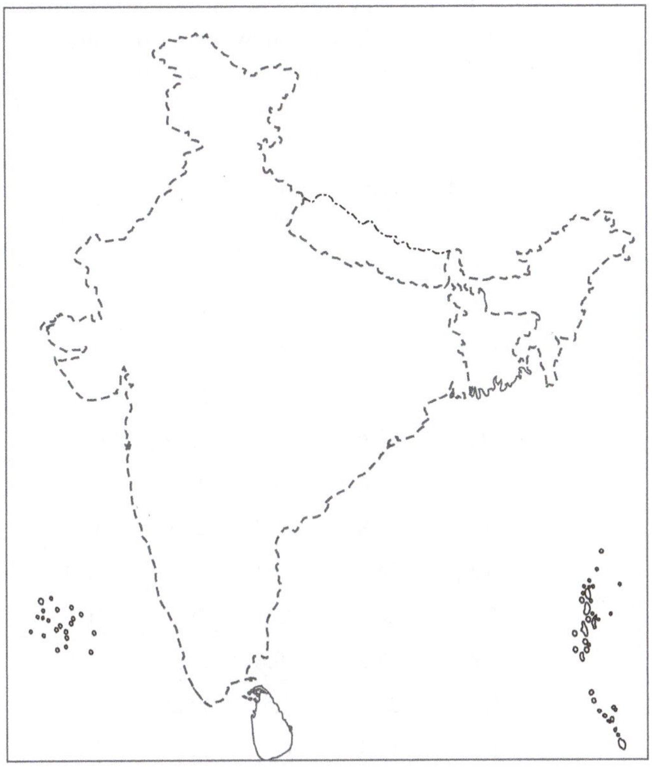

3. (i) **Assertion** (A) Rajasthan receives very little rainfall during the monsoon season. **(1)**

Reason (R) The Aravalli range runs parallel to the direction of the monsoon winds, offering no barrier.

(a) Both (A) and (R) are true and (R) is the correct explanation for (A)

(b) Both (A) and (R) are true, but (R) is not the correct explanation for (A)

(c) (A) is true, but (R) is false

(d) (A) is false, but (R) is true

(ii) Which statement is wrong regarding primitive subsistence farming ? **(1)**

(a) It is a very old type of farming method.

(b) The farming productivity is high.

(c) Slash and burn is one type of primitive subsistence farming method.

(d) It depends on monsoon and natural fertility of soil.

(iii) Rajasthan : Solar Energy :: Kerala : ? **(1)**

(a) Wind Energy (b) Thermal Energy

(c) Tidal Energy (d) Hydro Power

(iv) Minerals are deposited and accumulated in the strata of .... **(1)**

(a) sedimentary rocks (b) igneous rocks

(c) metamorphic rocks (d) None of these

(v) Which of the following industries uses bauxite as a raw material ? **(1)**

(a) Aluminium (b) Cement

(c) Jute (d) Steel

(vi) A mining company in Jharkhand needs to transport large quantities of coal to a thermal power plant in West Bengal. Which mode of transport would be the most economical? **(1)**

(a) Airway (b) Roadway

(c) Waterway (d) Railway

(vii) Rubber, tea, coffee , coconut crops come under the .... **(1)**

(a) plantation crop (b) apiculture

(c) cash crops (d) Both (a) and (c)

(viii) The wettest place on Earth- 'Mawsynram' is located in the state of .... **(1)**

(a) Meghalaya

(b) Manipur

(c) Odisha

(d) Nagaland

(ix) The image shows trees with broad leaves that shed during the dry season. These forests are widespread in central India and support diverse wildlife like tigers and elephants. Identify the forest type. **(1)**

(a) Tropical Evergreen Forest

(b) Tropical Deciduous Forest

(c) Mangrove Forest

(d) Alpine Forest

(x) Cashew nuts best grows in .... soil. **(1)**

(a) laterite (b) alluvial

(c) black (d) mountain

Part - II [50 *Marks*]

Attempt any five questions from this part.

4. Answer the following questions

(i) Every June, millions of farmers across Asia's third-largest economy wait anxiously for the monsoon rains to fall and nourish their fields, putting an end to heat waves that have become increasingly extreme as climate change accelerates. Ample rains may boost production of crops like rice, soybean, corn and sugar cane, helping to lower food prices and aiding the government's efforts to cool inflation. But abnormal monsoons can be devastating.

– The Times of India **(2)**

(a) What effects would an abnormal monsoon have?

(b) The pre-monsoon mango showers occur predominantly in which states?

(ii) What are the local summer winds in the following states known as.

(a) Kerala

(b) West Bengal **(2)**

(iii) With reference to the image below, answer the following questions: **(3)**

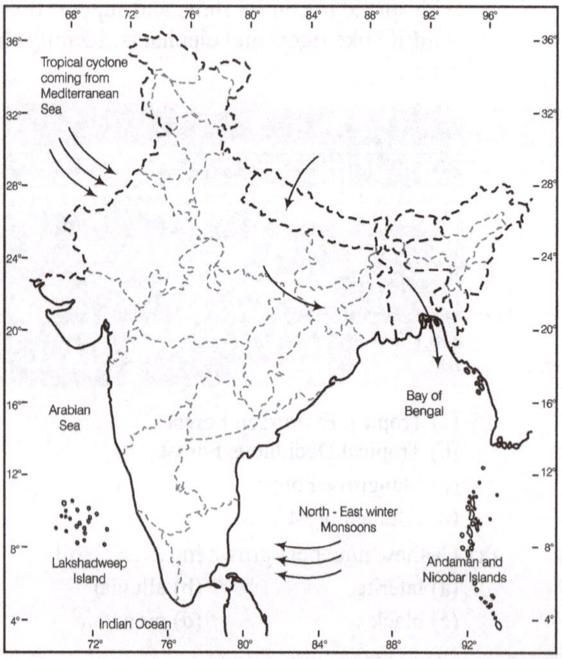

(a) What type of monsoon is depicted in the image?

(b) Why do these winds not bring much rain to most parts of India?

(iv) Study the climatic data of two cities of India provided below and answer the questions that follow. **(3)**

Station	Station A		Station B	
Month	**Tem. (°C)**	**Rainfall (cm)**	**Tem. (°C)**	**Rainfall (cm)**
Jan	19.4	0.7	21.7	0.15
Feb	21.7	2.8	23.3	0.2
Mar	26.7	3.6	27.9	0.13
Apr	29.4	4.8	31.9	0.13
May	30.6	14.5	33.9	0.99
Jun	29.4	30.2	33	9.3
July	28.9	31.8	29.8	31
Aug	28.3	32.3	28.5	20.4
Sep	28.3	25.1	29	10.6
Oct	27.2	10.6	29.4	0.89
Nov	22.8	1.8	26.2	0.36
Dec	19.4	0.4	22.7	0.1

(a) Calculate the annual range of temperature of station A.

(b) What is the total rainfall received by station B?

(c) On which coast is station A situated? Name the rains that bring rainfall to this region.

5. (i) Rajasthan is known for its arid climate and low rainfall, yet agriculture is practiced in some areas using tube wells and canals. **(2)**

(a) Which type of soil is mainly found in Rajasthan?

(b) How is farming made possible in such dry regions?

(ii) With reference to soil erosion in India, answer the following questions. **(2)**

(a) State any two natural causes of soil erosion.

(b) What is bad land?

(iii) (a) Which soil is found suitable for growing coffee in India?

(b) What type of soil is widely distributed over the Ganga-Basin? **(3)**

(c) Give the other names for black soil. Name two characteristic features of black soil.

(iv) (a) What is leaching? Give an example of a leached soil. **(3)**

(b) How are laterite soils formed?

(c) Why does laterite soil undergo leaching?

6. (i) Deepak went foe an excursion with his friend and came across a forest with the trees having height of 30-35 m with dense bushes and undergrowth of grasses. **(2)**

(a) Which type of forest did he come across?

(b) Name two varieties of trees found in this forest.

(ii) (a) Name the type of vegetation found in saline environment under tidal influence. **(2)**

(b) Name the most important tree associated with the above type of vegetation.

(iii) Why is there shrinking of forest cover in India? What precautions can be taken to reduce this shrinkage? **(3)**

(iv) (a) Under what climatic conditions do the desert and semi-desert vegetation grow? **(3)**

(b) Mention any two climatic conditions best suited for littoral type of forests.

7. (i) State the different methods of irrigation. **(2)**

(ii) State two advantages of rooftop rainwater harvesting. **(2)**

(iii) Give one reason to explain each of the following. **(3)**

(a) The Himalayan rivers are more reliable for canal irrigation than the rivers of the Peninsular Plateau.

(b) Flood irrigation is not suitable in regions with saline or alkaline soils.

(c) Drip irrigation is considered a sustainable method of irrigation.

(iv) State any three objectives of National Water Policy. **(3)**

8. (i) (a) Name two states of India where copper is found.

(b) State the uses of manganese and copper. **(2)**

(ii) With reference to iron ore answer the following. **(2)**

(a) State one advantages of using tidal energy as a renewable source of energy?

(b) What is the primary source of energy for generating tidal energy?

(iii) (a) Why is it necessary to conserve our mineral resources? **(3)**

(b) Differentiate between metallic and non-metallic mineral resources.

(iv)  **(3)**

(a) Identify the type of energy being tapped in the image above.

(b) What is the primary source of geothermal energy?

(c) Mention one location in India where geothermal energy potential exists.

9. (i) Give two natural and two man-made factors that help in the cultivation of wheat. **(2)**

(ii) (a) What kind of soil is best suited for growing rice?

(b) Name a state in India where rice is grown as a non-food crop. **(2)**

(iii) With reference to jute cultivation, answer the following. **(3)**

(a) Name a state that produces the largest quantity of jute in India.

(b) Mention any two geographical condition necessary for its growth.

(c) Which is the best method for its cultivation?

(iv) Subhas is a farmer. He told his friend that he is planning to grow Robusta. **(3)**

(a) What is Robusta?

(b) Why it is cheaper than Arabica?

10. (i) Name a few agro-based industries. **(2)**

(ii) Mention two problems of sugar industry. **(2)**

(iii) With reference to steel plants in India, answer the following. **(3)**

(a) What are integrated steel plants?

(b) Name one integrated steel plant in the public sector.

(c) From where does this plant get its requirements of iron ore and coal?

(iv) (a) What are the problems of cotton textile industry? **(3)**

(b) What are the four special features of the cotton textile industry in India?

(c) Gujarat is famous for which textile industry?

11. (i) How does a good transport network contribute to national integration? **(2)**

(ii) Mention any two advantages of rail transport in India. **(2)**

(iii) Name the following. **(3)**

(a) The longest railway route that connects the North-East to the Southern part of India.

(b) A national highway running from Srinagar in Jammu and Kashmir to Kanyakumari in Tamil Nadu.

(c) The mode of transport most suitable for transporting petroleum and natural gas.

(iv) Give a reason for each of the following. **(3)**

(a) Road transport is more suitable than railways for short-distance travel.

(b) Pipelines are considered an efficient mode of transporting petroleum and gas.

(c) Inland water transport is underdeveloped in India despite having a vast river network.

12. (i) (a) State one reason why urban areas generate more solid waste than rural areas. **(2)**

(b) What is biomedical waste?

(ii) "The greatest threat to our planet is the belief that someone else will save it." — Robert Swan

As a responsible citizen, suggest three ways in which you can promote sustainable waste management practices in your neighbourhood or school. **(2)**

(iii) With reference to the 3Rs, give a term that best describes each of the following. **(3)**

(a) Kitchen vegetable peels are converted into compost.

(b) A plastic bottle is cleaned and used for watering plants.

(c) Choosing to buy products with minimal packaging to avoid waste.

(iv) Give a reason for the following statements. **(3)**

(a) Segregation of waste at the source is essential for efficient waste management.

(b) Burning of waste in open spaces should be strictly prohibited.

(c) E-waste should be handled only by authorised recyclers.

Answers

2.

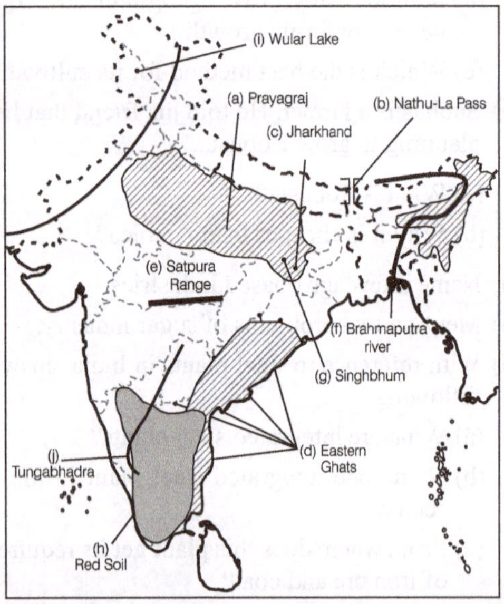

3. (i) (a) Both (A) and (R) are true and (R) is the correct explanation for (A)

(ii) (b) The farming productivity is high.

(iii) (d) Hydro Power

(iv) (a) sedimentary rocks

(v) (a) Aluminium

(vi) (d) Railway

(vii) (d) Both (a) and (c)

(viii) (a) Meghalaya

(ix) (b) Tropical Deciduous Forest

(x) (a) laterite

ICSE Fully Solved

Latest Specimen Paper

Time : 2 hrs
Marks : 80

Geography X

General Instructions

1. Answers to this Paper must be written on the paper provided separately.
2. You will not be allowed to write during the first 15 minutes. This time is to be spent in reading the question paper.
3. The time given at the head of this paper is the time allowed for writing the answers.
4. Part I is compulsory. All questions from Part I are to be attempted. A total of five questions are to be attempted from Part II.
5. The intended marks for questions or parts of questions are given in brackets [ ].

PART I

[30 Marks]

Attempt all questions from this part

1. Study the extract of the **Survey of India** Map sheet No. **G43S7** and answer the following questions.

(i) (a) Give the six-figure grid reference for .201 in the Eastern part of the map extract. **(2)**

(b) What are the brown patches in the North-East quarter of the map extract?

[Apply & Understanding]

(ii) Mohan goes on a bicycle from 02 northing to 12 northing in a straight line. If he moves at a speed of 10 kilometers per hour, how much time will he take to reach his destination? **[Apply] (2)**

(iii) (a) What is the compass direction of Rampura (2709) from Kotda (3005)? **(2)**

(b) If you are moving along the left bank of Sipu river, which settlement will you come across?

[Analyse]

(iv) (a) Ramesh returned to his native place Mahudi Moti (2404) after a gap of ten years and was happy to see the development around his village. What according to you show that the area around his village has developed? **(2)**

(b) What is the black vertical line made between the easting 25 and 26? **[Apply & Remember]**

(v) Mention two man-made and two natural features in the grid square 2508. **[Understanding] (2)**

2. On the outline map of India provided **[Recall]**

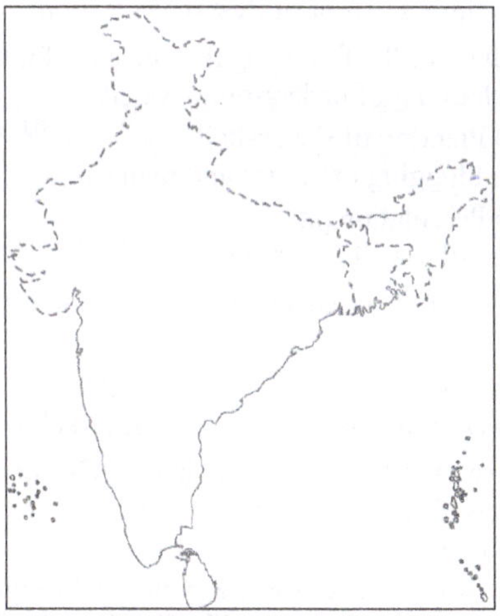

(i) Shade and label an area of alluvial soil in the North-East. **(1)**

(ii) Mark using a dot and name the commercial capital of India. **(1)**

(iii) Mark and name the highest peak of Himalayas in India. **(1)**

(iv) Shade and label Gulf of Kutch. **(1)**

(v) Mark with arrows and name the wind bringing rainfall to Punjab in winter. **(1)**

(vi) Shade and label a sparsely populated area. **(1)**

(vii) Mark and label Eastern Ghats. **(1)**

(viii) Mark and name a tributary of an important peninsular river. **(1)**

(ix) Mark and label the most important latitude passing through the country. **(1)**

(x) Mark and label Coromandel coast. **(1)**

3. Choose the correct answers to the questions from the given options. (Do not copy the question, write the correct answers only). **(10)**

(i) Himalayas have a significant impact on the climate of India as they **[Apply]**

(a) block the North-East monsoon winds
(b) causes rainfall in the Gangetic plains
(c) create a rain shadow area in the Deccan plateau
(d) cause cyclonic disturbance in the Bay of Bengal

(ii) Feel and consistency of soil is called .... of the soil. **[Remember]**

(a) profile (b) parent rock
(c) texture (d) density

(iii) Teak: Tropical Deciduous Forest **[Remember]**

(a) Mahogany: Furniture
(b) Stilted roots: Mangrove Vegetation
(c) Ebony: Tropical Rainforest
(d) Spines: Tropical Desert Vegetation

(iv) Which of the following may be used for the recharging of underground water? **[Understanding]**

(a) Planting of shelter belt
(b) Plugging of gullies and ravines
(c) Percolation pit
(d) Tube-well irrigation

(v) Which type of coal is referred to as industrial coal? **[Remember]**

(a) Peat (b) Lignite
(c) Bituminous (d) Anthracite

(vi) **Assertion** (A) During the late 1960s, there was a many-fold increase in the production of wheat in Punjab.

Reason (R) The Green Revolution brought about increased use of inputs like HYV seeds, fertilisers and pesticides. **[Analyse]**

Codes

(a) Both A and R are true and R is the correct explanation of A
(b) Both A and R are true, but R is not the correct explanation of A
(c) A is true but, R is false
(d) A is false, but R is true

(vii) Which crop is associated with Ratooning? **[Remember]**

(a) Sugarcane (b) Jute
(c) Rice (d) Cotton

(viii) Which steel plant amongst the following was set up with the collaboration with Germany? **[Remember]**

(a) Bhilai (b) Tata Steel
(c) Visakhapatnam (d) Rourkela

(ix) If you have to transport perishable goods over a long distance, which mode of transport will you use and why? **[Apply]**

(a) Air transport because it is the fastest.
(b) Road transport as it is economical.
(c) Rail transport as it is ecofriendly.
(d) Water transport as it can handle large amount of goods.

(x) Which of the following methods of disposal is best applicable for the waste depicted in the picture below? **[Apply]**

(a) Burning waste in open area
(b) Recycling waste
(c) Dumping
(d) Composting

PART II

[50 Marks]

*Attempt any **five** questions from this part.*

4. (i) India Meteorological Department (IMD) brings a ray of hope for India's agricultural sector and weather patterns in the upcoming year. After grappling with 'below normal' rains and dry conditions in 2023, the forecast suggested above-normal rainfall in certain regions, including the Southernmost parts of peninsular India, North-West India and several parts of East-Central, East and North-East India. **(2)**

– Investing.com (01.11.2023)

(a) As a student of Geography, what according to you may be the possible reason for the 'below normal' rains in 2023?

(b) During which months of the year does most of India receive major amount of its rainfall? [Analyse & Apply]

(ii) What is the source of winter rainfall in each of the following areas? (2)
(a) Punjab
(b) Tamil Nadu [Remember]

(iii) Give a reason for each of the following. (3)
(a) Kerala gets rainfall from the summer monsoons much before Uttar Pradesh.
(b) Visakhapatnam records a low annual range of temperature.
(c) Winds are mostly offshore during the cold season. [Analyse]

(iv) Study the climatic data of station X and answer the following questions. (3)

Month	**Temp** (0°C)	**Rainfall** (cm)
Jan	23.1	7.3
Feb	24.8	1.1
Mar	26.5	0.3
Apr	29.3	0.1
May	32	1.3
Jun	32.8	4.5
July	33.1	6.1
Aug	32.1	8.2
Sep	30.5	8.5
Oct	29.3	20.1
Nov	28.7	20.8
Dec	26.1	9.0

(a) What is the annual range of temperature of station X? [Apply]
(b) Which is the driest month? [Understand]
(c) Name the wind that brings maximum rainfall to this station. [Analyse]

5. (i) Nathu, a farmer in Bihar, does not get good yields as the soil he tills is coarse and has fair proportion of kankars. Motilal on the other hand, has his field closer to the river and gets better yields. (2)
(a) Identify the two soils that are being discussed in the above passage.
(b) Give a possible reason why Motilal benefits from having his field along the river banks. [Remember and Apply]

(ii) With reference to soil erosion in India answer the following questions. (2)
(a) State any two human activities that have led to soil erosion in India.
(b) Mention any two innovative agricultural techniques that can help to prevent soil erosion. [Apply]

(iii) With reference to red soil, answer the following. (3)
(a) How is it formed? [Understanding]
(b) Why is it good for dry farming? [Apply]
(c) Name any two areas where it is found. [Recall]

(iv) Give a reason for the following statements: (3)
(a) Black soil has self-ploughing property.
(b) Laterite soil is not suitable for cultivation.
(c) Alluvial soil is extensively found in the Northern Plains. [Analyse]

6. (i) Mahesh went for an excursion with his friend and came across a marshy area with trees that had stilt like roots. (2)
(a) Which natural vegetation belt did he come across? [Apply]
(b) Name an area in India where this kind of vegetation is found. [Recall]

(ii) (a) Why is Tropical Deciduous Forest commercially the most important forest belt of India? [Evaluate] (2)
(b) Why are long and deep roots a typical characteristic of desert vegetation? [Evaluate]

(iii) Give three reasons why forest conservation is the need of the hour. [Analyse] (3)

(iv) (a) Name a forest conservation method that involves the local community. (3) [Remember]
(b) Which primitive system of agriculture had led to large scale destruction of forest in the past? [Remember]
(c) Name the process which involves planting two saplings for each tree that is felled. [Remember]

7. (i) State two reasons why there is a need for irrigation in India. [Understand] (2)

(ii) Distinguish between Inundation Canals and Perennial Canals. [Analyse] (2)

(iii) (a) Name a state in India where tube wells are commonly used. (3)
(b) Give two geographical conditions that favour tube well irrigation in this state. [Analyse]

(iv) (a) What is meant by rainwater harvesting? (3)
(b) Mention any two water harvesting practices followed in India. [Understand & Remember]

8. (i) There is ample potential of setting up biogas plants in India. The National Bioenergy Programme has been recommended by the concerned Ministry, for implementation in two phases. The spread of biogas technology is a boon for Indian farmers with its direct and guaranteed benefits. *(https:/lbiogas.mnre.gov.in)* **(2)**

(a) Why do you think generation of biogas can be achieved in every household of rural India?

(b) Mention two ways in which generation of this form of energy proves to be a boon for Indian farmers. **[Analyse & Evaluate]**

(ii) With reference to Hirakud project answer the following: **(2)**

(a) On which river is it based? **[Remember & Apply]**

(b) Name an Indian state benefitted by the project.

(iii) (a) Give anyone use of iron ore. **(3)**

(b) Name the mineral used to strengthen steel.

(c) Name two Indian states where copper is found. **[Apply & Remember]**

(iv) **(3)**

(a) Identify the type of energy being harnessed in the above picture.

(b) Mention why this form of energy is preferred over fossil fuels.

(c) Why does India stand at an advantage in the production of this type of energy? **[Understand, Evaluate & Apply]**

9. (i) Mention two agricultural reforms done by the government for the betterment of the agricultural sector. **[Understand] (2)**

(ii) (a) State one point of difference between Rabi and Kharif cropping seasons**(2) [Analyse & Remember]**

(b) Name the state that is the leading producer of groundnut in India.

(iii) With reference to cultivation of pulses, answer the following. **(3)**

(a) Name a soil found suitable for the growth of pulses. **[Understand]**

(b) Name any two varieties of pulses grown in India. **[Remember]**

(c) Give a reason, why is it a popular food crop of India? **[Evaluate]**

(iv) Rohan, a farmer, hired some labourers to help him with 'GINNING'. **(3)**

(a) Name the crop grown by Rohan. **[Apply]**

(b) Mention any two climatic conditions suitable for this crop. **[Recall]**

10. (i) Mention two points of difference between small scale and large scale industry. **[Analyse] (2)**

(ii) Explain two ways in which cotton textile industry is important for India's economy. **(2) [Understand]**

(iii) With reference to petrochemical industry, answer the following. **(3)**

(a) State a reason for the growing popularity of this industry in recent times. **[Apply]**

(b) Why is it located close to oil refineries? **[Evaluate]**

(c) Name any two petrochemical products. **[Remember]**

(iv) Give one reason to explain each of the following. **(3)**

(a) Sugar production is gradually gaining importance in peninsular India.

(b) Indian silk products are becoming less popular in the international market.

(c) The importance of the iron and steel industry will never decline. **[Analyse]**

11. (i) Mention two disadvantages of using waterways. **[Understand] (2)**

(ii) The Golden Quadrilateral has contributed towards improvement of the Indian economy- Explain. **[Understand] (2)**

(iii) (a) Which rail gauge is mostly limited to hilly areas only? **(3)**

(b) Name the organisation responsible for the maintenance of the National Highways of India.

(c) Which is the Inland Waterway that connects Prayagraj to Haldia? **[Understand & Remember]**

(iv) Give a reason for each of the following. **(3)**

(a) At present times, airports are being established even in smaller towns of India.

(b) Railways are well developed in the Northern states of India.

(c) Helicopter services are crucial during emergencies. **[Analyse]**

12. (i) What is the impact of waste generation on the following? **(2)**

(a) Surface water (b) Landscape **[Understand]**

(ii) Why is dumping considered a harmful method of waste disposal? **[Analyse] (2)**

(iii) Fire broke out at the Kochi city waste treatment plant. Thick clouds of toxic smoke engulfed the city. The waste at the plant also contained plastic and biomedical wastes, both of which on combustion are extremely harmful for the general health of people.

(3) – *Economic Times, 10.03.2023*

(a) Which method of waste management would have helped in reducing health hazard in the above case? **[Analyse]**

(b) Mention one measure you can adopt in school to reduce waste. **[Apply]**

(c) State one way in which domestic waste can be made useful. **[Understand]**

(iv) (a) What are landfills? **(3)**

(b) Enumerate two advantages of composting as a method of waste disposal. **[Remember & Apply]**

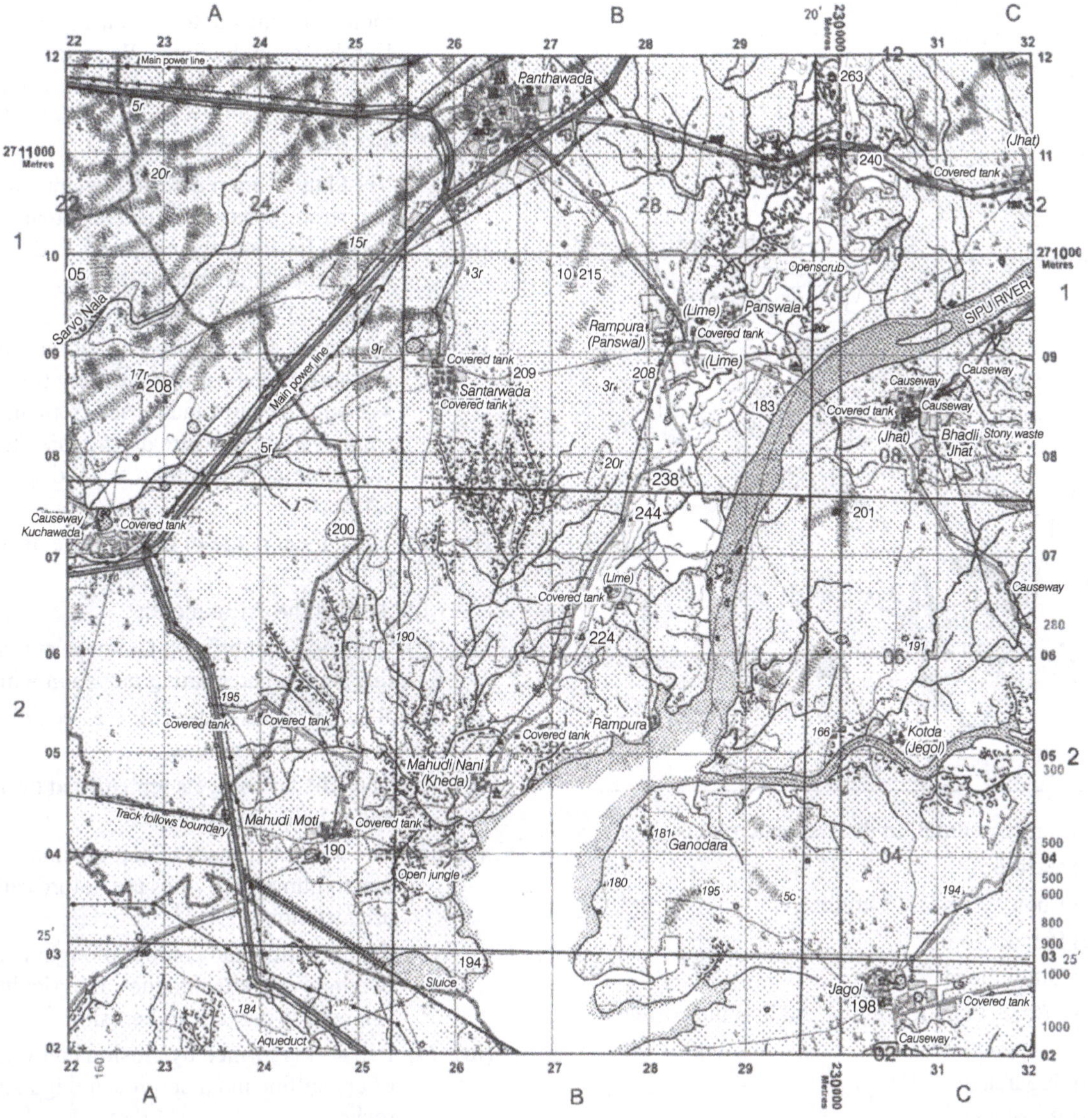

Answers

1. (i) (a) 301074 (b) Sand dunes
(ii) One hour
(iii) (a) North West (b) Jhat
(iv) (a) Powerline showing that the village now has electricity
(b) Longitude/Meridian
(v) Natural features : Sand dune, Broken Ground
Man made features : Cart track/Pack track/Permanent hut/temple

2.

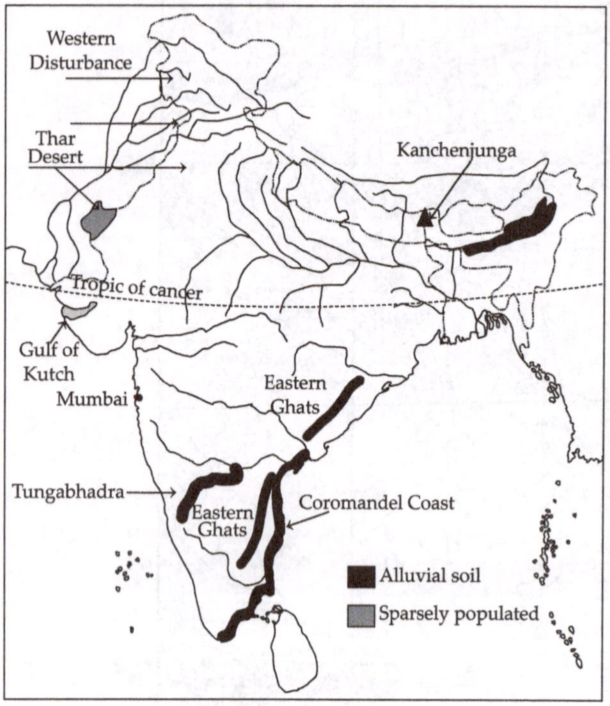

3. (i) (b) Causes rainfall in the Gangetic plains
(ii) (c) texture
(iii) (c) Ebony: Tropical Rainforest
(iv) (c) Percolation pit
(v) (c) Bituminous
(vi) (a) Both A and R are true and R is the correct explanation of A
(vii) (a) Sugarcane
(viii) (d) Rourkela
(ix) (a) Air transport because it is the fastest.
(x) (b) Recycling waste

4. (i) (a) Global warming/El Nino effects are the reason for the below normal rain in 2023.
(b) During June to September, India receives major amount of rainfall.
(ii) (a) **Punjab** Western disturbances originating in the Mediterranean region or Temperate cyclones
(b) **Tamil Nadu** North-East winter monsoon wind or retreating monsoon.
(iii) (a) Kerala gets rainfall from the summer monsoon much before Uttar Pradesh because Kerala lies in the South-West of the country where the South-West monsoon wind strikes first. The wind then advances to the North and reaches Uttar Pradesh.
(b) Visakhapatnam records a low annual range of temperature because Visakhapatnam has a coastal location and experiences the moderating influence of the sea.
(c) Winds are mostly offshore during the cold season because land loses heat fast and high pressure develops over it during the cold season. The surrounding seas remain warm and have low pressure during this time. Thus, winds blow from land to sea and are offshore.
(iv) (a) The annual range of temperature of station X is 10°C.
(b) April is the driest month.
(c) The wind that brings maximum rainfall to this station is retreating monsoon winds.

5. (i) (a) Bhangar and Khadar soil are been discussed in the above passage.
(b) The Khadar soil gets replenished every year and is hence more fertile.
(ii) (a) The possible causes of soil erosion in India due to human activities are deforestation and urbanisation.
(b) Crop rotation and contour ploughing are the two innovative techniques of agriculture that can help to prevent soil erosion.
(iii) (a) Red soil is formed by erosion and weathering of crystalline metamorphic and igneous rocks.
(b) Red soil is good for dry farming because it has a high iron content and good drainage, which helps retain moisture effectively in arid conditions.

(c) They are mostly found in parts of Odisha and Madhya Pradesh.

(iv) (a) Black soil has self-ploughing property because black soil hardens and cracks when dry which helps in aeration of the soil naturally.

(b) Laterite soil is not suitable for cultivation due to leaching, the essential minerals percolate down the soil profile making the top soil infertile.

(c) Alluvial soil is extensively found in the Northern Plains because the numerous rivers here bring large amounts of sediments and deposit them to form fertile plains.

6. (i) (a) He came across the Tidal Littoral forest.

(b) An area in India where this kind of vegetation is found is the delta of river Ganga in Sundarbans.

(ii) (a) Tropical Deciduous forests are commercially the most important forest belt in India because

(i) They supply high-quality hardwoods like teak and sal, which are crucial for furniture, construction and other industries.

(ii) They occur in pure stands making exploitation easier.

(b) Long and deep roots are typical characteristics of desert vegetation to draw water from deep underground as rainfall is scanty here.

(iii) The forest conservation is the need of the hour because

(a) **Biodiversity** Forests house 80% of terrestrial species, crucial for ecosystem balance.

(b) **Climate** Forests absorb CO_2, mitigating climate change.

(c) **Livelihoods** Forests support millions of people with food, medicine and shelter.

(iv) (a) Social forestry is the forest conservation method that involves the local community.

(b) Jhum cultivation is the primitive system of agriculture that had led to large scale destruction of the forest in the past.

(c) Reforestation is the process which involves planting two saplings for each tree that is felled.

7. (i) Irrigation is a need in India because

(a) Irrigation provides a reliable water supply, reducing reliance on unpredictable monsoon rains.

(b) It enables multiple cropping and higher crop yields, improving food security and farmers' incomes.

(ii) Inundation canals are floodwater canals that carry water only during the rainy season when the river floods.

On the other hand, perennial canals carry water all year round as they have a weir or dam at the head to regulate the flow of water.

(iii) (a) A state in India where tube wells are commonly used is Punjab.

(b) The geographical condition that favour tubewell irrigation in Punjab are

(i) **High Water Table** Punjab has a high groundwater level, making it easier and cost-effective to access water through tube wells.

(ii) **Permeable Soil** Punjab has permeable alluvial soil, which allows easy drilling and efficient water absorption for irrigation.

(iv) (a) The rainwater harvesting is collection and storage of rainwater for future use.

(b) Two water harvesting practices followed in India are

(i) **Rooftop Rainwater Harvesting** A widespread practice across India where rainwater is collected from rooftops and stored in tanks or recharge pits for various uses such as drinking, irrigation and recharging groundwater.

(ii) **Stepwells (Baolis)** These structures in Gujarat and Rajasthan designed to store rainwater and provide a water source during dry periods.

8. (i) (a) Biogas generation can be achieved in every household of rural India primarily because of the abundance of organic waste available from agricultural residues, animal dung and kitchen waste, which are essential feedstocks for biogas production.

(b) Generation of Biogas energy proves to be a boom for Indian farmers due to the following reasons

(i) **Reduced Energy Costs** Biogas generation provides a renewable and cheaper alternative to traditional fuels like firewood and LPG, saving farmers money on energy expenses.

(ii) **Improved Soil Health** The by-product of biogas production, known as bio-slurry, is a nutrient-rich organic fertiliser that enhances soil fertility and crop yields, benefiting farmers economically.

(ii) (a) River Mahanadi

(b) Odisha is benefitted by Hirakud project.

(iii) (a) Iron ore can produce steel.

(b) Manganese is used to strengthen steel.

(c) Copper is found in Madhya Pradesh and Rajasthan

(iv) (a) Solar energy is being harnessed in the above picture.

(b) It is preferred over fossil fuels because it is a clean source of energy.

(c) India stands at an advantage in the production of solar energy due to the following reasons:

- **Abundant Sunlight** India's geographical location ensures ample solar radiation.
- **Supportive Policies** Government initiatives include subsidies and incentives for solar energy.
- **Cost Efficiency** Decreasing solar technology costs make it competitive with traditional energy sources

9. (i) Two agriculture reforms done by the government for betterment of the agriculture sector are

- **Crop Diversification Policies** Introducing policies to promote diversification of crops, reducing dependency on traditional crops and enhancing resilience against climate change.
- **Integrated Watershed Management** Implementing watershed management programs to improve water efficiency in agriculture, especially in regions prone to drought or water scarcity.

(ii) (a) **Rabi Crops** is sown in October or November and harvested in February or March.

On the other hand, **Kharif crops** is sown in May or June and harvested in September or October.

(b) Gujarat is the leading producer of groundnut in India.

(iii) (a) The soil found suitable for the growth of pulses is sandy loam soil. This type of soil provides good drainage and aeration, which are beneficial for the cultivation of pulses.

(b) Moong and Masoor are the two varieties of pulses grown in India.

(c) Pulses are the most popular food crop in India because

- It is a leguminous crop
- It can help to replenish the soil naturally.

(iv) (a) Cotton is grown by Rohan.

(b) Two climatic conditions suitable for cotton cultivation are

- **Warm Climate** Cotton thrives in warm temperatures, typically between 21°C to 30 °C (70°F to 86°F), which promote optimal growth and development.
- **Moderate Rainfall** Cotton requires moderate but well-distributed rainfall during its growing season. Excessive rainfall or prolonged dry spells can adversely affect cotton yields

10. (i) The differences between small scale industries and large scale industries are

Small scale industries	Large scale industries
These require less capital investment.	These require huge capital investment.
These industries employ less labour.	These industries employ more labour.

(ii) Cotton textile industries important for India's economy because:

- It gives us valuable foreign exchange
- It generates employment

(iii) (a) One reason for the growing popularity of the petrochemical industry in recent times is its durability.

(b) It is located close to oil refineries because

- To facilitates easy availability of raw materials
- To reduce transportation costs.

(c) Two petrochemical products are
- **Ethylene** Used in the production of plastics, fibers, and other industrial chemicals.
- **Propylene** Important for making plastics, synthetic fibers and various chemical products.

(iv) (a) Sugar production is gradually gaining importance in peninsular India because sugar plantations are well planned and scientifically managed.

(b) Indian silk products are becoming less popular in the international market because of the high price of Indian silk.

(c) The importance of the iron and steel industry will never decline because it is foundational to industrialisation, infrastructure development and essential sectors like construction and manufacturing.

11. (i) Two disadvantages of using waterways are
- It is a slow means of transport
- It can be affected by weather disturbances.

(ii) The Golden Quadrilateral improved India's economy in the following ways
- It has enhanced connectivity between major cities and industrial hubs.
- It has reduced transport costs and time.
- It has boosted trade and commerce across the country.

(iii) (a) The narrow gauge is mostly limited to hilly areas only.

(b) The organisation responsible for the maintenance of the National Highways of India is the National Highways Authority of India (NHAI).

(c) The inland waterway that connects Prayagraj (formerly Allahabad) to Haldia is National Waterway 1 (NW-1).

(iv) (a) At present times airports are being established even in smaller towns of India to encourage air travel for Indians as it saves time.

(b) Railways are well developed in the Northern states of India because of flat plain land.

(c) Helicopter services are crucial during emergencies because they can easily reach remote areas fast.

12. (i) (a) The impact of waste generation on surface water is that waste can contaminate surface water sources, leading to the spread of diseases and harming aquatic life.

(b) The impact of waste generation on the landscape is that waste can spoil the aesthetics of the landscape, leading to degradation of scenic beauty and potentially reducing property values.

(ii) Dumping is considered a harmful method of disposal because it leads to soil pollution and underground water pollution.

(iii) (a) Implementing proper segregation of waste and recycling would have helped in reducing health hazards in the above case.

(b) One measure that can be adopted in school to reduce waste is to promote the use of reusable water bottles and lunch boxes instead of single-use plastic items.

(c) One way in which domestic waste can be made useful is through composting organic waste to produce nutrient-rich compost for gardening and agriculture.

(iv) (a) Landfills are large areas in the outskirts of towns and cities where wastes are deposited in the ground and covered with Earth. The waste gradually decomposes, decreases in volume and gets converted to humus.

(b) Advantages of composting as a method of which disposal are
- **Reduces Landfill Waste** Composting diverts organic waste from landfills, decreasing environmental impact.
- **Produces Nutrient-rich Compost** Composting creates a valuable soil amendment that improves soil fertility and supports sustainable agriculture.

ICSE **Fully Solved**

Time : 2 hrs
Marks : 80

Solved Paper 2024

Geography X

General Instructions

1. Answers to this Paper must be written on the answer sheet provided separately.
2. You will not be allowed to write during the first 15 minutes. This time is to be spent in reading the question paper.
3. The time given at the head of this Paper is the time allowed for writing the answers.
4. Part I is compulsory. All questions from Part I are to be attempted. A total of five questions are to be attempted from Part II.
5. The intended marks for questions or parts of questions are given in brackets ( ).

PART *[30 Marks]*

Attempt all questions from this Part.

1. Study the extract of the Survey of India Map Sheet No. G43S7 and answer the following questions.

(i) (a) Give the six-figure grid reference for spot height .522. **(2)**

(b) What is the pattern of settlement in the grid square 3591?

(ii) (a) Mention two man-made features seen in the grid square 3794. **(2)**

(b) Mention two means of transport used by the people of Nani Bhatamal in the grid square 3691.

(iii) (a) Identify the landform marked by the contours in the grid square 3896. **(2)**

(b) What is the pattern of drainage seen in the grid square 36977?

(iv) (a) What is the reason for the presence of causeway in the grid square 3695? **(2)**

(b) What is the compass direction of Khara (4097) from Karja (3994)?

(v) Calculate the area in kilometre square of the region to the South of 94 Northing. **(2)**

2. On the outline map of India provided:

(i) Mark and label the river Krishna. **(1)**

(ii) Mark and label the Eastern Ghats. **(1)**

(iii) Shade and label a densely populated area in the Southern part of India. **(1)**

(iv) Shade and label the Konkan coastal plain. **(1)**

(v) Mark with an arrow and label the direction of Western disturbance. **(1)**

(vi) Shade and label the Thar Desert. **(1)**

(vii) Shade and label the Andaman Sea. **(1)**

(viii) Mark and label the city Chennai. **(1)**

(ix) Mark and name the highest peak of Himalayas in India. **(1)**

(x) Mark and label Mumbai High. **(1)**

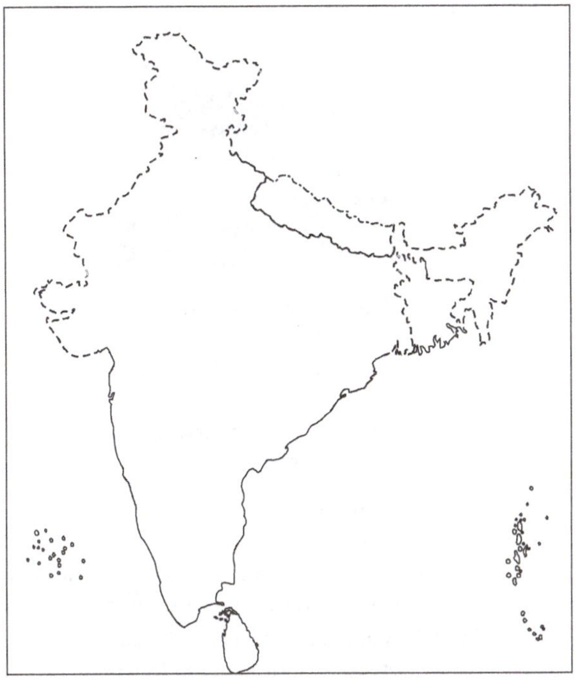

3. Choose the correct answers to the questions from the given options. **(10)**

(i) What causes snowfall in Kashmir during winter?
(a) Tropical cyclone
(b) North-East Monsoon wind
(c) South-West Monsoon wind
(d) Temperate cyclone

(ii) Which of the following helps in soil conservation?
(a) Afforestation
(b) Overgrazing
(c) Mining
(d) Shifting agriculture

(iii) Which means of irrigation can be developed with minimum expenditure?
(a) Tube well
(b) Canal
(c) Well
(d) Drip irrigation

(iv) Read the table and identify the pair that is

	Natural Vegetation Belt	Tree
P	Tropical evergreen	Babool
Q	Tropical deciduous	Teak
R	Littoral	Ebony
S	Mountain forest	Banyan

(a) P (b) Q
(c) R (d) S

(v) Bauxite is the ore of
(a) Aluminium
(b) Copper
(c) Manganese
(d) Iron

(vi) Identify the source of energy that leads to pollution.
(a) Tidal energy
(b) Wind energy
(c) Natural gas
(d) Geo-thermal energy

(vii) Which of the following is not a centre for the iron and steel industry?
(a) Bhilai
(b) Bengaluru
(c) Rourkela
(d) Visakhapatnam

(viii) Which of the following farming methods is used to grow tea on a large scale?
(a) Subsistence farming
(b) Plantation farming
(c) Mixed farming
(d) Shifting agriculture

(ix) Which of the following means of transport has best use during floods/ earthquake?
(a) Airways
(b) Railways
(c) Roadways
(d) Waterways

(x) Which of the following is a biodegradable waste?
(a) Broken glass
(b) Wastepaper
(c) Polythene
(d) Plastic bags

PART II

[50 Marks]

*Attempt any **five** questions from this part.*

4. (i) 'Himalayas act as a climatic divide'. Justify the statement giving two reasons. **(2)**

(ii) Differentiate between South-West Monsoon and Retreating Monsoon. (Any two differences) **(2)**

(iii) Give a geographical reason for the following. **(3)**
(a) Kolkata gets more rain than Delhi during rainy season.
(b) Though both are hill stations, Shimla experiences snowfall during the winters but Ooty does not.
(c) Winter monsoons bring less rain.

(iv) Study the climate data of Station X and answer the questions that follow. **(3)**

Month	Jan	Feb	Mar	Apr	May	Jun	Jul	Aug	Sep	Oct	Nov	Dec
Temp (C)	8.4	11.5	21.6	28.3	35.1	38.5	41.0	38.0	30.8	29.2	15.6	10.2
Rainfall (cms)	1.5	0.9	0.5	-	-	12.5	17.8	18.5	12.5	12.5	6.2	2.1

(a) Calculate the annual range of temperature of Station X.

(b) Name the rainiest month of the Station X.

(c) Is the Station X located in coastal area or in the continental interior?

5. (i) Why is Black soil found suitable for the production of cotton? (Any two points) **(2)**

(ii) Give one difference between each of the following. **(2)**

(a) Alluvial soil of Uttarakhand and alluvial soil of West Bengal.

(b) Transported soil and residual soil.

(iii) With reference to Laterite soil, answer the questions that follow. **(3)**

(a) How is Laterite soil formed?

(b) How can Laterite soil be made productive?

(c) Name one region where Laterite soil is found.

(iv) (a) Mention two causes of soil erosion in India. **(3)**

(b) Mention a soil conservation method suitable for hilly area.

6. (i) How is tropical monsoon forest useful for the Indian economy? (Any two points) **(2)**

(ii) Mention the climatic condition that leads to the development of tropical desert vegetation. **(2)**

(iii) Give a reason to explain each of the following. **(3)**

(a) Mountains have varied vegetation.

(b) Stilt like / aerial roots are a typical feature of littoral forest.

(c) The tropical evergreen forests do not look bare at any time of the year.

(iv) (a) How has the rising population of India resulted in the loss of forest cover? (Any one point) **(3)**

(b) Mention any two forest conservation methods that may be adopted to protect the forests.

7. (i) Mention one advantage and one disadvantage of using tank irrigation. **(2)**

(ii) (a) What is the advantage of using drip irrigation? **(2)**

(b) Why is drip irrigation not practiced on a large scale in India?

(iii) Give a reason to explain each of the following. **(3)**

(a) Sprinkler irrigation is gaining popularity in recent times.

(b) Tube well irrigation is used in Punjab.

(c) North India has more area under canal irrigation.

(iv)

(a) Name the water conservation practice shown in the above picture. **(3)**

(b) How does this system help to reduce floods?

(c) Why is water conservation necessary? (Any two reasons)

8. (i) (a) Name any three varieties of coal produced in India. **(2)**

(b) Name the variety of coal widely used in Iron and Steel Industries of India.

(ii) (a) Name the state that is the largest producer of iron ore in India. **(2)**

(b) Name any one mining area of Iron ore from the state mentioned by you.

(iii) (a) Mention two ways in which Hirakud dam has helped the people of Odisha. **(3)**

(b) Across which river is the Hirakud dam built?

(iv) Give reasons for each of the following. **(3)**

(a) Geothermal energy is not popular in India.

(b) Solar energy is gaining popularity.

(c) Petroleum is considered a harmful source of energy.

9. (i) Why is agriculture considered an important sector of Indian economy? (Any two points) **(2)**

(ii) (a) What is mixed farming?

(b) Mention any one advantage of mixed farming.

(iii) Give one reason to explain each of the following. **(3)**

(a) West Bengal is a leading producer of jute.

(b) Millets are fast becoming the popular food crops.

(c) More than two ratoon crops are not advisable for sugarcane farmers.

(iv) (a) With reference to tea cultivation, explain the term 'fine pluck'. **(3)**

(b) Name the Indian state that leads in coffee production.

(c) Why is cotton grown as a Kharif crop in India?

10. (i) (a) Based on the ownership, what type of industry is Visakhapatnam Steel Plant? **(2)**

(b) What is meant by co-operative sector industry?

(ii) Explain the following terms. **(2)**

(a) Sericulture (b) Integrated steel plant

(iii) Give one reason to explain each of the following. **(3)**

(a) Mini-Steel plants help in conservation of coal.

(b) Location of sugar industry is shifting to the Southern part of India.

(c) The electronic industry is growing at a fast rate.

(iv) (a) State two conditions that favour the location of cotton textile industry in Ahmedabad. **(3)**

(b) State any one advantage of locating iron and steel industry at Rourkela.

11. (i) Why is road transport an important means of transport in India? (Any two reasons) **(2)**

(ii) Give a reason for each of the following. **(2)**

(a) Northern plain is best suited for the development of Railways.

(b) Railways are managed completely by the Central Government.

(iii) Mention two advantages and one disadvantage of Inland water transport. **(3)**

(iv) Why has airway become more popular than other means of transport? (Any three reasons) **(3)**

12. (i) With- reference to the picture below, answer the questions that follow. **(2)**

(a) Which waste management method is depicted here?

(b) State one way in which this method may be implemented at our home.

(ii) Explain how waste accumulation can be harmful. (Any two points) **(2)**

(iii) Explain how waste generated in following sectors may be made useful. (Give one example for each) **(3)**

(a) Household (b) Industry

(c) Agriculture

(iv) (a) Give two uses of composting. **(3)**

(b) Why are landfills set up far away from the city? (Any two reasons)

Answers

1. (i) (a) 375966
   (b) Dispersed/Scatter
   (ii) (a) Chattri, Cart track, well, nets
   (b) Roadway and Waterways
   (iii) (a) Ridge (b) Radial
   (iv) (a) Cross minor stream (b) North-East
   (v) 4 Northing × 9 Easting = 36 sq km

2.

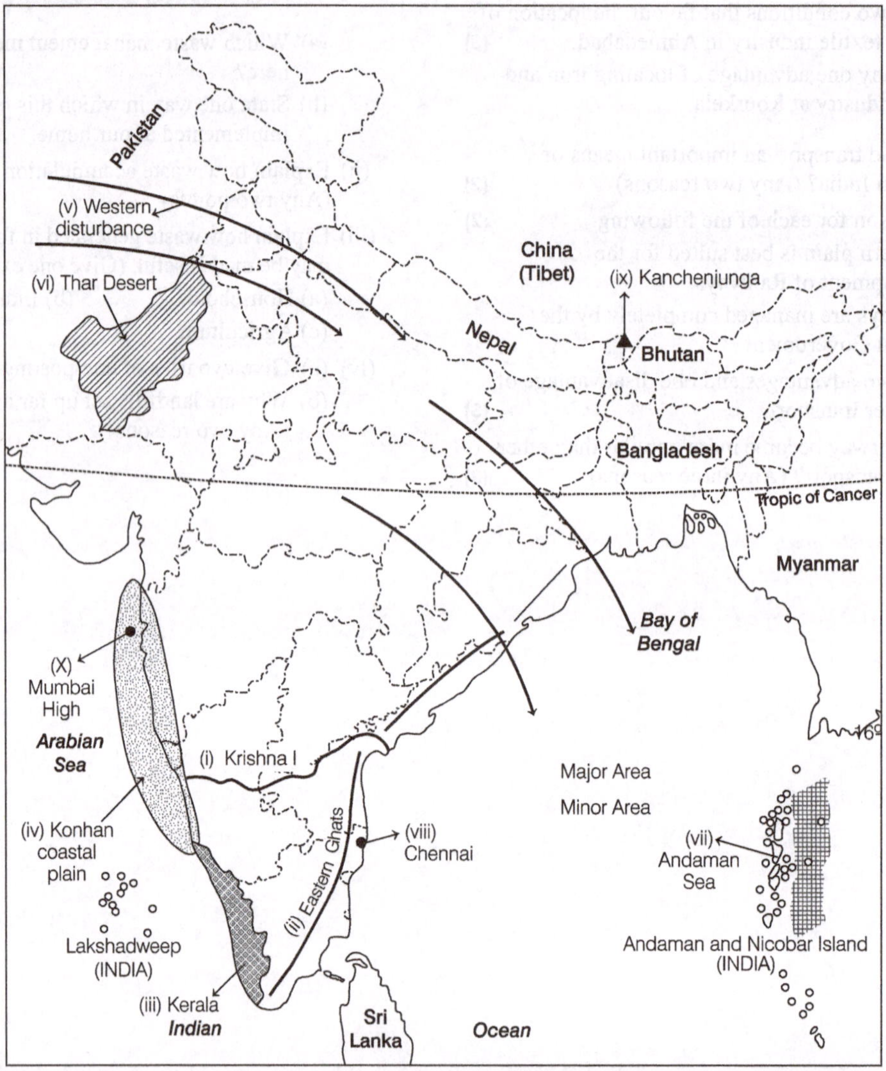

3. (i) (d) Temperate cyclone
(ii) (a) Afforestation
(iii) (d) Drip irrigation
(iv) (b) Q
(v) (a) Aluminium
(vi) (c) Natural gas
(vii) (b) Bengaluru
(viii) (b) Plantation farming
(ix) (a) Airways
(x) (b) Wastepaper

4. (i) The Himalayas act as a climatic divide due to two main reasons
(a) The Himalayan mountains act as a natural barrier against the cold winds of Central Asia and Siberia to enter India thus, preventing a severe cold climate.
(b) The Himalayas trap the rain bearing winds of South-West monsoon causing them to shed their moisture in the Indian sub-continent thus, making agriculture possible on a large scale.
(ii) The differences between South-West Monsoon and Retreating Monsoon are

South-West Monsoon	Retreating Monsoon
These winds blow from June to September.	These winds blow from October to November.
This monsoon wind covers the whole India and gives heavy rainfall.	The Eastern coast of South India receives rainfall from this wind.
Wind movement is from sea to land.	Wind movement is from land to sea.

(iii) (a) Kolkata gets more rain than Delhi during rainy season because Kolkata lies in the lower Ganga plain so it receives more rainfall from the Bay of Bengal branch of South-West monsoon but by the time, monsoon wind reach Delhi, the moisture holding capacity of the wind decreases therefore it sheds less rainfall.
(b) Though both are hill stations, Shimla experiences snowfall during the winter but Ooty does not because Shimla is located in higher elevation and close to the Himalayan range, whereas Ooty is located at a lower elevation in the Nilgiri Hills of Southern India.
(c) Winter monsoons bring less rain because during winter the direction of the prevailing winds reverse. The wind starts blowing from land towards sea. As they originate from continental interiors they carry less moisture as compared to the summer monsoon winds.
(iv) (a) The annual range of temperature is calculated through the given formula
Highest temperature- lowest temperature
41.0- 8.4= 32.6
(b) Through the observation of the given table, it is clear that August receives the maximum rainfall at 18.5 cm.
(c) Through the observation, Station X seems to be the region in the continental interior. The range of temperature varies from 8 degrees Celsius in winter to 35 degrees Celsius in summer.

5. (i) Black soil is found suitable for the production of cotton because
(a) It has excellent moisture retention capacity. It can hold water for a longer duration. This property helps in maintaining adequate soil moisture levels required for cotton cultivation.
(b) Black soil is rich in calcium carbonate, magnesium carbonate, potash and lime. These nutrients are essentials for the healthy growth of cotton plants and contribute to higher yields.
(ii) (a) Alluvial soil of Uttarakhand is relatively younger and coarser.
On the other hand, alluvial soil of West Bengal is older and more finely textured.
(b) Transported soil is found at places where they got transported by agents of erosion i.e. wind and rivers.
On the other hand, residual soil is found at places where they are formed by disintegration and weathering of rocks.
(iii) (a) Laterite soil is formed through the process of intense leaching in hot and humid tropical climates. It results from the leaching of silica and other soluble materials, leaving behind a rich concentration of iron and aluminum oxides.
(b) Laterite soil can be made productive by adding adequate amounts of manure and chemical fertilisers.

(c) Laterite soil is found in the region of Eastern and Western Ghats.

(iv) (a) The two causes of soil erosion in India are

- **Overgrazing** The continuous grazing by animals on the same piece of land without sufficient recovery periods, leads to the removals of plant cover on a large scale and become open to erosion by wind and water.
- **Deforestation** The cutting down of forests on a large scale which leaves an open and exposed landscape leads to soil erosion causing leaching and flash floods.

(b) A soil conservation method suitable for hilly area is terrace farming. In this farming method, step-like terraces are built on slopes. They prevent the soil from being washed away by running water.

6. (i) Tropical monsoon forests is useful for the Indian economy in the following ways

(a) **Biodiversity Hotspot** These forests have a rich variety of flora and fauna, attracting tourism and promoting eco-tourism, which generates revenue and employment opportunities.

(b) **Natural Resources** They provide valuable resources such as timber, medicinal plants, and non-timber forest products, supporting industries and livelihoods across the country.

(ii) The climatic condition that leads to the development of trophical desert vegetation are

- Regions having annual rainfall of 50 cm.
- Regions having average temperature between 25°C to 27°C.
- Evaporation rate is higher than precipitation due to high temperature.

(iii) (a) Mountains have diverse vegetation due to variations in altitude, climate, soil and exposure to sunlight. These factors create distinct ecological niches, protecting the evolution of different plant species adapted to specific conditions, resulting in rich biodiversity.

(b) Stilt-like/ aerial roots are a typical feature of littoral forest because this type of vegetation flourishes in wet marshy areas in river deltas, saline or other swampy areas.

(c) The tropical evergreen forests do not look bare at any time of the year because these forests have a constant supply of moisture and sunlight throughout the year, allowing vegetation to remain lush and dense. Additionally, the trees in these forests shed their leaves at different times rather than all at once, ensuring they never appear bare.

(iv) (a) The rising population of India has resulted in the loss of forest covered in the following ways

- Increasing population demand for land for housing, agriculture and infrastructure development as a result, forests are often cleared to make way for these activities, leading to the loss of forest cover.
- The growing population puts pressure on natural resources, leading to unsustainable exploitation and further degradation of forests.

(b) The two forest conservation methods to protect the forests are

- **The National Forest Policy** It was introduced in 1894 which was revised in 1952 and 1988. The main aim of this policy is protection, conservation and development of forests. It led with a programme named joint forest management which involves the local communities for protection and conservation of the nearby forest.
- **Control of Deforestation** Efforts should be made to minimise the cutting of young trees and regulate commercial deforestation. Implementing strategies like selective logging and controlled harvesting can ensure forests are utilised sustainably while preserving their ecological balance.

7. (i) One advantage of tank irrigation is that it can store abundant rainwater and it reduces the wastage of the excessive flowing water.

One disadvantage of tank irrigation is that in the absence of rainwater during the dry season, the tanks become dry and fail to provide water for irrigation.

(ii) (a) The advantage of drip irrigation is that it delivers water directly to the root zone of plants, minimising evaporation and runoff. This can save significant amounts of water compared to traditional methods like sprinklers, which can lose water to the air or leave puddles on the surface.

(b) Drip irrigation is not practiced on a large scale in India because of high initial cost. Setting up a drip irrigation system can be expensive, particularly for smallholder farmers who dominate Indian agriculture. The cost of materials, design, and installation can be a significant restriction.

(iii) (a) Sprinkler irrigation is gaining popularity in recent times due to its versatility, cost-effectiveness and its efficiency to consume water.

(b) Tube well irrigation is used in Punjab due to following reasons
- The level of water table is high in Punjab due to which tubewell irrigation is favourable.
- The soil in Punjab is soft which makes it easier to dug holes required for tubewell irrigation.

(c) North India has more area under canal irrigation because it has low level relief, deep fertile soils and perennial source of water.

(iv) (a) The water consuming practice shown in the above picture is called rooftop rainwater harvesting.

(b) Rainwater harvesting systems help reduce flooding by capturing and storing rainwater that would otherwise run off surfaces like roofs, pavements and roads, leading to floods. This stored water can then be slowly released or utilised for various purposes; this reduces water volume rushing into drainage systems during heavy rains.

(c) Water conservation is necessary due to following reasons
- Rainfall is unevenly distributed over time and space as different area receive different amounts of rainfall.
- Rapid industrialisation and urbanisation are continuously reducing the availability of water and exerting a lot of pressure on the available water resources in the country.

8. (i) (a) The three varieties of coal produced in India are
- Bituminous coal (Odisha, West Bengal, Jharkhand)
- Lignite (Tamil Nadu, Rajasthan, Kerala)
- Peat (Nilgiri mountain, Kashmir valley , swampy areas of coastal plains)

(b) The iron and steel industries in India mainly use coking coal, also known as metallurgical coal.

(ii) (a) The largest producer of iron ore in India is Odisha.

(b) A mining area of iron ore from Odisha is Gorumahisani in Mayurbhanj district.

(iii) (a) Hirakud dam has helped the people of Odisha by
- controlling the flood in Mahanadi delta
- providing about 75,000 sq km of land
- helping to generate hydro electricity.

(b) Hirakud dam is built across river Mahanadi.

(iv) (a) Geothermal energy is not popular in India because geothermal power plants and systems are expensive to build and operate.

(b) Solar energy is gaining popularity because as a tropical country India receives about 5000 trillion KWh solar energy per year that can help to produce a large amount of free energy and it is renewable and an inexhaustible source of energy.

(c) Petroleum is considered a harmful source of energy because after burning it emits large amounts of carbon dioxide and greenhouse gas which leads to global warming.

9. (i) Agriculture is considered an important sector of Indian economy because

(a) Agriculture sector provides employment to vast section of the population in our country.

(b) It provides food and food products like rice, wheat milk, etc. to human population and fodder for livestock.

(ii) (a) The practise of cultivation of crops as well as raising of animals/livestock simultaneously is popularly known as mixed farming.

(b) An advantage of mixed farming is that it gives security to the farmers because even if the crops fail they can rely on their cattle rearing for income.

(iii) (a) West Bengal is a leading producer of jute because the region has a hot and humid climate which is favourable for jute production.

(b) Millets are fast becoming the popular food crops because they contain various nutrients like iron, calcium, zinc and magnesium.

(c) More than two ratoon crops are not advisable for sugarcane farmers because it degrades the quality of the crops. The sucrose content and overall quality of sugarcane may diminish with each subsequent ratoon crop, leading to lower returns for farmers.

(iv) (a) Plucking two tender leaves and a bud or shoot together is known as fine plucking.

(b) Karnataka leads in coffee production among the states of India.

(c) Cotton is grown as a kharif crop in India because it requires a long growing season with high temperatures and adequate water availability, which coincide with the monsoon season. The warm and humid conditions during the kharif season are beneficial to cotton growth, leading to better yields.

10. (i) (a) On the basis of ownership Visakhapatnam steel plant is a public sector based industry, managed by Rashtriya Ispat Nigam.

(b) Cooperative sector industries are owned and managed on cooperatives basis by those who are producers of the raw materials required for industry. Example- dairy industry (Amul).

(ii) (a) The rearing of silkworms for the production of silk is called 'sericulture'.

(b) Integrated steel plants are the plants where all the processes of making steel such as melting of iron ore, processing of steel and shaping of metals are carried out at one place.

(iii) (a) Mini steel plants help to conserve coal due to their smaller scale and more efficient processes. These plants utilise scrap steel as a primary raw material, which reduces the dependence on coal for iron ore smelting.

(b) Location of sugar industry is shifting to the Southern part of India because the cane produced in South India has higher sucrose content which is of superior quality and gives higher yield.

(c) The electronic industry is growing at a fast rate due to advancements in technology, and increased consumer demand for electronic devices.

(iv) (a) Two conditions favouring the location of the cotton textile industry in Ahmedabad are

- **Availability of Raw Materials** Ahmedabad is close to major cotton-growing regions in Gujarat, ensuring a steady and reliable supply of raw materials for textile production.
- **Availability of Skilled Labour** The city has a skilled workforce with experience in textile manufacturing, providing a ready labour pool for the industry's needs.

(b) An advantage of locating the Iron and steel industry at Rourkela is availability of iron ore from Sundergarh and Keonjhar district.

11. (i) Road transport is an important means of transport in India because of the following reasons

(a) It is more suitable for short distance travel and it connects small villages and places where other means of transport cannot reach.

(b) It saves cost of transportation from one station to another station and it also saves the time.

(ii) (a) Northern plain is best suited for the development of railways because the land is fertile and levelled in the region.

(b) Railways are managed by the central government in India to ensure uniformity, efficiency and seamless connectivity across the country.

(iii) The two advantages of inland water transport are as follows

(a) **Cost-effective** It is often cheaper than other modes of transport for bulky and non-perishable goods, as it requires less fuel and infrastructure maintenance compared to road or rail transport.

(b) **Environmentally Friendly** Inland water transport has lower carbon emissions and pollution compared to road and air transport, making it a more sustainable option for freight transportation.

A disadvantage of inland water transport is that it may not reach all areas, limiting accessibility compared to road or rail transport, especially in regions with uneven terrain or inadequate water depth.

(iv) The three reasons due to which airways are becoming a popular means of transport in modern India are
   (a) It is the fastest means of movement from one place to the other for a vast country like India.
   (b) It has reduced the distance by minimising the travel time.
   (c) It helps to reach the large and difficult terrain places which are inaccessible through other modes of transport.

12. (i) (a) Solid waste management method is depicted here.
   (b) One way to implement solid waste management at home is by segregating waste into different bins for recyclables, organic waste and non-recyclable waste. This helps in efficient disposal and promotes recycling and composting of biodegradable waste.

(ii) Waste accumulation can be harmful in the following ways
   (a) Waste accumulation has bad impact on the quality of air around us. When we dump waste at the site and cover it with Earth then methane gas gets generated by decomposition of solid waste in landfills. This methane is not good for our atmosphere and warms up the air temperature which absorbs the Sun's heat.
   (b) The sewage waste coming from factories and industries reaches the water bodies and causes many water related diseases like diarrhea and typhoid.

(iii) Waste generated in the following sectors may be made useful in the following ways
   (a) **Household** Household waste can be made useful through composting organic waste. For example, kitchen waste can be composted to produce nutrient-rich compost, which can then be used as fertiliser for gardening or landscaping.
   (b) **Industry** Industrial waste can be made useful through recycling and reuse. For example, manufacturing waste such as scrap metal or plastic can be recycled into new products or materials, reducing the need for virgin resources and minimising environmental impact.
   (c) **Agriculture** Agricultural waste can be made useful through biomass conversion. For example, crop residues such as straw or husks can be converted into biofuels or used as feedstock for biogas production, providing renewable energy sources for agricultural operations or other purposes.

(iv) (a) Two uses of composting are
   - **Soil Amendment** Compost improves soil structure, increases soil fertility, and enhances its water retention capacity, making it an excellent organic fertiliser for gardens, lawns and agricultural fields.
   - **Waste Reduction** Composting reduces the volume of organic waste sent to landfills, thereby minimising greenhouse gas emissions and helping to alleviate environmental pollution.

   (b) Landfills are setup far away from cities due to the following reasons
   - **Public Health and Safety** Landfills can attract pests like rodents and insects, which can spread diseases. Additionally, decomposing waste can generate harmful gases and toxic liquid that can pollute the air and water near the landfill.
   - **Odour and Aesthetics** Landfills can produce unpleasant odours, which would be undesirable for residents living nearby areas.

ICSE Fully Solved

Solved Paper 2025

Time : 2 hrs
Marks : 80

Geography X

General Instructions

1. Answers to this Paper must be written on the answer sheet provided separately.
2. You will not be allowed to write during the first 15 minutes. This time is to be spent in reading the question paper.
3. The time given at the head of this Paper is the time allowed for writing the answers.
4. Part I is compulsory. All questions from Part I are to be attempted. A total of five questions are to be attempted from Part II.
5. The intended marks for questions or parts of questions are given in brackets ( ).

PART

[30 Marks]

Attempt all questions from this Part.

1. Study the extract of the Survey of India Map Sheet No. G43S10 and answer the following questions **(2)**

(i) (a) Give the six-figure grid reference for spot height. 437 in the southeastern part of the map extract.

(b) Aman, a local craftsman, wants to sell his product to a large gathering to earn money instantly.

1. Which settlement should he go to?
2. Name the month in which he should visit the settlement named by you above.

(ii) (a) On which bank of the Sukli nadi is the settlement of Pamera situated? **(2)**

(b) Identify the settlement pattern seen in the grid square 6732.

(iii) Roshan, while travelling from Sirori to Tokra, observed that the surface water sources are dry except for the reservoir near Tokra. **(2)**

(a) What according to you may be the reason for the presence of water in the reservoir in 6832 near Tokra settlement?

(b) State whether this reservoir is artificial or natural source of water.

(iv) (a) What is the direct distance between Gulabganj to Pithapura? Give your answer in kilometre. **(2)**

(b) Mention the compass direction of Pithapura from Gulabganj.

(v) (a) Name two man-made features seen in the grid square 6534. **(2)**

(b) Define contour interval.

2 On the outline map of India provided **(10)**

(i) Mark and label the Nathu-La pass.

(ii) Shade and name the coastal plain that occupies a large part of Kerala.

(iii) Mark and label Digboi.

(iv) Mark and label Chilka lake.

(v) Mark with arrows and name the wind that brings rainfall to Tamil Nadu coast during winter.

(vi) Mark and label the River Sutlej.

(vii) Mark and label the Standard Meridian of India.

(viii) Mark and label Satpura range.

(ix) Shade and label the Chota Nagpur plateau.

(x) Mark and label Visakhapatnam.

3 Choose the correct answers to the questions from the given options. **(10)**

(i) **Assertion** (A) Mumbai receives more rainfall than Pune.

Reason (R) Mumbai gets rain from Arabian Sea branch of South-West monsoon.

(a) Both (A) and (R) are true and (R) is the correct explanation for (A).

(b) Both (A) and (R) are true and (R) is not the correct explanation for (A).

(c) (A) is true and (R) is false

(d) (A) is false and (R) is true

(ii) Which of the following pairs of soils displays similar characteristics in terms of their colour and texture?

(a) Alluvial soil and laterite soil

(b) Black soil and red soil

(c) Red soil and laterite soil

(d) Alluvial soil and black soil

(iii) The type of natural vegetation shown in the picture given below is found on

(a) Tropical desert (b) Tropical deciduous

(c) Tropical evergreen (d) Littoral forest

(iv) Which of the following prevents wastage of water?

(a) Canal (b) Well

(c) Sprinkler (d) Tube well

(v) Balaghat : Manganese :: Mumbai High :

(a) Copper (b) Coal

(c) Iron Ore (d) Petroleum

(vi) A microbiological process that loosens the bark of a crop and facilitates removal of fibre from the stalk

(a) Rolling

(b) Ratooning

(c) Retting

(d) Fermentation

(vii) Which industry amongst the following has revolutionised the lifestyle of the Indian masses in recent years?

(a) Cotton Textile (b) Electronic

(c) Iron and Steel (d) Sugar

(vii) Which of the following household products is associated with the petrochemical industry?

(a) Glass bottle

(b) Wooden chopping board

(c) Kitchen knife

(d) Plastic mug

(ix) Raman, a dairy farmer in Ludhiana, supplies milk within the city on a daily basis. Which mode of transport is he most likely to use

(a) Railway

(b) Roadway

(c) Airway

(d) Waterway

(x) The collection of discarded materials and converting them into useful products ist

(a) Recycling (b) Processing

(c) Reducing (d) Composting

PART II

[50 Marks]

Attempt any five questions from this Part.

4 (i) 'Severe cyclonic storms are often formed over the Bay of Bengal during the retreating monsoon season.' **(2)**

(a) Name two states that are affected by tropical cyclones on the eastern coast of India.

(b) The temperate cyclones cause less damage than the tropical cyclones. Give any two points to support this statement.

(ii) (a) Name the local wind that causes rainfall in the states of Assam and West Bengal in the month of April. **(2)**

(b) How is this rainfall beneficial for the states mentioned above?

(iii) With reference to Figure A and Figure B given below, answer the questions that follow. **(3)**

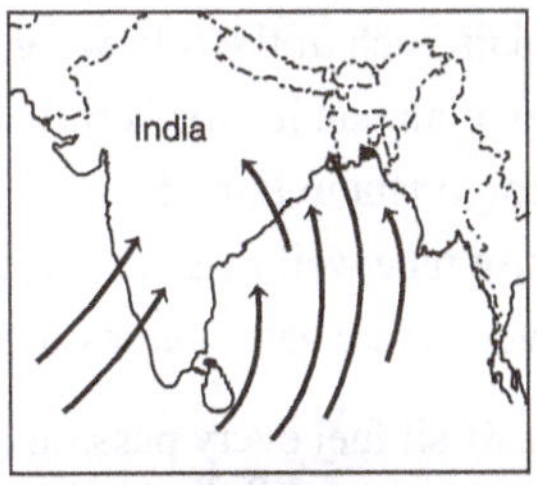

Figure A

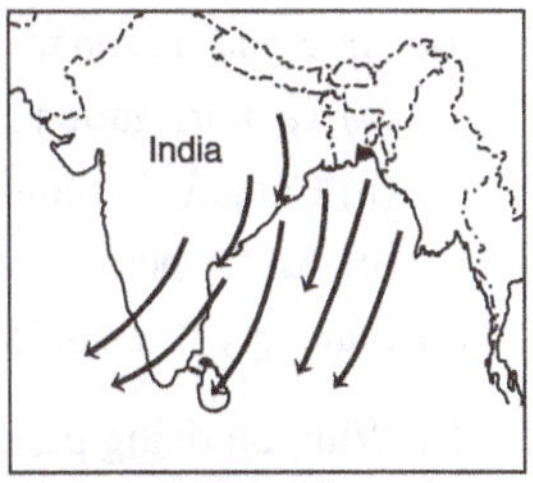

Figure B

(a) Name the winds shown by arrows in Figure A and Figure B.

(b) How is the wind shown in Figure A different from the one shown in Figure B?

(iv) Study the climate data of station X and answer the following questions **(3)**

Month	Jan	Feb	Mar	Apr	May	Jun	July	Aug	Sep	Oct	Nov	Dec
Temp (°C)	24.0	25.4	26.7	28.3	30.0	28.9	27.6	27.4	27.3	27.1	27.0	25.0
Rainfall (cm)	0.25	0.25	-	-	1.75	50.2	61.0	37.0	27.0	4.75	1.50	-

(a) What is the annual range of temperature for station X?

(b) Which is the wettest month?

(c) Name the wind which brings rainfall for station X during the rainy season.

5 (i) The Ganga Plain is known for its fertile soil, it is often referred to as the Food bowl of India. This region supports a variety of crops such as rice, wheat, pulses, jute and sugarcane. **(2)**

(a) Name the soil that is found in large parts of Ganga plain.

(b) Give two properties of this soil which helps it to produce a variety of crops.

(ii) (a) What is meant by soil erosion? **(2)**

(b) Name any two agents of soil erosion.

(iii) Give a geographical reason to explain each of the following. **(3)**

(a) Soil conservation is the need of the hour.

(b) Red soil has a poor water retention capacity.

(c) Laterite soils are infertile.

(iv) With reference to black soil of India, answer the following questions. **(3)**

(a) How is this soil formed?

(b) How is this soil able to retain moisture for a long period?

(c) Mention any two minerals present in this soil.

6 (i) India has lost 2.33 million hectares of tree cover since the year 2000. This is equivalent to a six percent decrease in tree cover during this period. *Source: The Indian Express, Date 12th April, 2024* **(2)**

(a) Mention any two causes of the decrease in the forest cover of India.

(b) Name a conservation method that may be used to help in increasing the forest cover.

(ii) Mention the climatic condition suitable for the development of tropical evergreen forest. **(2)**

(iii) State any three differences between tropical deciduous and tropical desert vegetation. **(3)**

(iv) (a) Give any two reasons for the great diversity of natural vegetation in India. **(3)**

(b) How do the forests help in maintenance of air quality?

7 (i) Mention any one advantage and any one disadvantage of well irrigation. **(2)**

(ii) Suggest any two measures to overcome scarcity of water in the metropolitan cities of India. **(2)**

(iii) Give one reason to explain each of the following **(3)**

(a) Tank irrigation is not common in Northern India.

(b) Canal irrigation is important in Punjab.

(c) All farmers do not use tube well irrigation even if the geographical condition is favourable.

(iv) State any three objectives of rainwater harvesting. **(3)**

8 (i) With the rising price of fossil fuel every passing day, it is very important to develop non-conventional energy resource. *Bulletin-Department of Non-conventional Sources of Energy* **(2)**

(a) Name a non-conventional energy source that can be harnessed by taking advantage of India's vast coastline.

(b) State one advantage of using geothermal energy.

(ii) (a) How is Biogas formed? **(2)**

(b) Mention any one advantage of Biogas over other non-conventional energy resources.

(iii) Give a reason for each of the following. **(3)**
(a) Iron ore is called a versatile mineral.
(b) Windmills set up on agricultural lands are beneficial to farmers.
(c) Coal is the most preferred source of energy in Indian industries.

(iv) **(3)**

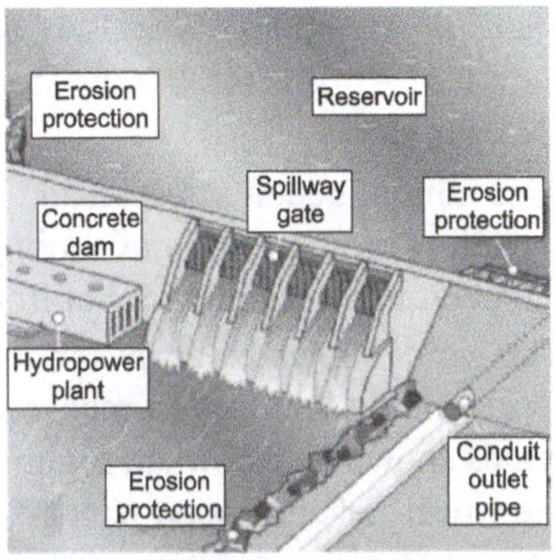

(a) Identify the type of energy being generated in the picture given above.
(b) State why this type of energy is cheaper in the long run.
(c) Name a power project associated with the generation of this energy in the Northern part of India.

9 (i) Mention two climatic conditions that favour the cultivation of groundnut. **(2)**
(ii) Give any two reasons why Maharashtra has emerged as an important sugarcane producing state. **(2)**
(iii) Give one reason to explain each of the following. **(3)**
(a) Trees are planted in between the rows of coffee plants.
(b) Cotton cultivation requires plenty of cheap labour.
(c) Hill slopes are best suited for tea cultivation.
(iv) Explain the following **(3)**
(a) Mixed farming (b) Zayad
(c) Transplantation

10 (i) State any two factors that are responsible for the growth of the cotton textile industry in Kolkata. **(2)**
(ii) 'Karnataka is the leading state for silk production in India'. **(2)**
Give any two reasons to justify the above statement.
(iii) (a) Name the Iron and Steel industry located at Chhattisgarh. **(3)**
(b) From where does the industry named by you above get its supply of the following?
1. Iron ore 2. Coal

(iv) Raghav has been given a project by his teacher in which he has to write about the by-products of an industry that is used for preparing shoe polish, carbon paper and cardboard. **(3)**
(a) Which industry will he be writing about?
(b) Name any two by-products of the industry mentioned by you.

11 (i) Why is a well-developed transport network important for India? **(2)**
(ii) Mention any two advantages of road transport. **(2)**
(iii) Name the following **(3)**
(a) The mode of transport that ensures comfortable journey, especially for elders and children.
(b) The highway connecting Silchar in Assam to Porbandar in Gujarat.
(c) The cheapest means of transport for bulky goods.
(iv) Give a reason for each of the following. **(3)**
(a) Airways are the most efficient mode of transport to connect North-East India with the rest of the country.
(b) Railways are easily developed in the Northern plains of India.
(c) Rivers of peninsular India are not ideal for inland water transport.

12 (i) (a) Give a reason for a substantial rise of E-waste in India **(2)**
(b) What is dumping?
(ii) 'You cannot protect environment unless you empower people, you inform them and help them to understand that these resources are their own, that they must protect them'. **(2)**
Wangari Maathar (recipient of Nobel Prize 2004 for Sustainable Developments)
As a responsible student how would you contribute to reduce and manage the waste generated in your surroundings. Explain by giving suitable examples.
(iii) With reference to the 3Rs, give a term that best describes each of the following. **(3)**
(a) An empty soft drink can is used as a pen stand.
(b) Old scrap papers are used to manufacture handmade paper.
(c) No food is wasted in the household.
(iv) Give a reason for the following statements. **(3)**
(a) Organic manure should replace chemical fertilisers.
(b) There should be a ban on the use of polythene and plastic products.
(c) Manual handling of waste must be avoided.

Answers

1. (i) (a) 673295

(b) 1. Malgoan or Pamera both are correct.

2. March

(ii) (a) Right bank (b) Scattered

(iii) (a) Sipu Nadi (b) Artificial

(iv) (a) 2.25 km (b) North-East

(v) (a) Settlement, Roads, Well, Temple, Post-office.

(b) **Contour Interval** A contour interval refers to the vertical distance or elevation difference between adjacent contour lines.

2.

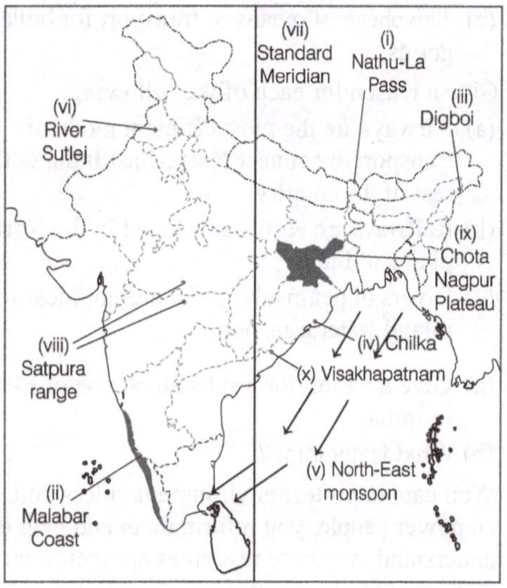

3. (i) (a) Both (A) and (R) are true and (R) is the correct explanation for (A).

(ii) (c) Red soil and laterite soil

(iii) (d) Littoral forest (iv) (c) Sprinkler

(v) (d) Petroleum (vi) (c) Retting

(vii) (b) Electronic (viii) (d) Plastic mug

(ix) (b) Roadway (x) (a) Recycling

4. (i) (a) Two states that are affected by tropical cyclones on the eastern coast of India are West Bengal and Odisha.

(b) The temperate cyclones cause less damage than the tropical cyclones due to the following reasons

- **Lower Wind Speeds** Temperate cyclones have weaker winds than tropical cyclones, causing less damage.
- **Wider Area of Influence** Temperate cyclones affect a larger area with less intensity, while tropical cyclones are more concentrated and destructive.

(ii) (a) The local wind that causes rainfall in the states of Assam and West Bengal in the month of April is the 'Norwesters' or 'Kalbaisakhi'.

(b) This rainfall benefits Assam and West Bengal by aiding crop growth and cooling down temperatures, providing relief from the heat.

(iii) (a) The winds shown by arrows in Figure A represent the South-West monsoon winds. The winds shown by arrows in Figure B represent the North-East monsoon winds.

(b) The wind shown in Figure A is different from the one shown in Figure B in the following ways

- **South-West Monsoon Winds (Figure A)** These winds blow from the Indian Ocean towards the Indian subcontinent during the summer season (June to September), bringing heavy rainfall to most parts of India.
- **North-East Monsoon Winds (Figure B)** These winds blow from the land (India) towards the Indian Ocean during the winter season (October to December), bringing rainfall mainly to the southeastern coast of India (Tamil Nadu, Andhra Pradesh, etc.).

(iv) (a) Annual range of temperature = Highest temperature – Lowest temperature

= 30.0°C (May) - 24.0°C (January)

= 6.0°C

(b) July is the wettest month.

(c) The wind that brings rainfall to station X during the rainy season is the South-West monsoon winds.

5. (i) (a) The soil found in large parts of the Ganga Plain is Alluvial soil.

(b) Two properties of alluvial soil that help in producing a variety of crops

- **High Fertility** It is rich in nutrients like potash, phosphoric acid and lime, which support the growth of crops like rice, wheat and sugarcane.

- **Good Moisture Retention** This soil has the ability to retain water, making it suitable for both rain-fed and irrigated agriculture.

(ii) (a) Soil erosion is the removal of the top fertile layer of soil by natural forces such as wind and water, leading to the loss of nutrients and reduced soil fertility.

(b) Two agents of soil erosion are wind and water.

(iii) (a) Soil conservation is the need of the hour as soil is essential for agriculture and vegetation, but erosion, deforestation, and overuse reduce its fertility. Soil conservation is necessary to prevent land degradation, maintain food security, and protect the environment.

(b) Red soil is rich in iron but has a sandy texture and lacks humus, making it less capable of retaining water. This results in quick drainage and lower moisture availability for crops.

(c) Laterite soil undergoes intense leaching due to
heavy rainfall, washing away essential nutrients. As a result, it becomes acidic and lacks fertility, making it unsuitable for most crops without proper treatment.

(iv) (a) Black soil is formed from the weathering of volcanic rocks, primarily from the Deccan Plateau region.

(b) Black soil has a high clay content, which allows it to absorb and retain moisture for a long time, even during dry seasons.

(c) Two minerals present in this soil are iron and magnesium.

6. (i) (a) Two causes of the decrease in forest cover in India

- **Deforestation for agriculture and urbanisation** Large areas of forests are cleared to make space for farming, industries, and expanding cities.
- **Illegal logging and overexploitation** Excessive cutting of trees for timber, firewood and other commercial purposes leads to forest depletion.

(b) A conservation method that may be used to help in increasing the forest cover is afforestation, i.e, planting new trees in deforested areas.

(ii) (a) The climatic condition suitable for the development of tropical evergreen forest are

- **High Temperature** The temperature remains warm and humid throughout the year, typically ranging between 25°C to 27°C.
- **Heavy Rainfall** These forests require more than 200 cm of annual rainfall, which is evenly distributed throughout the year.

(iii) Three differences between tropical deciduous and tropical desert vegetation are

Tropical Deciduous Vegetation	Tropical Desert Vegetation
Found in monsoon regions with moderate rainfall (100-200 cm).	Found in areas with extremely low rainfall (less than 25 cm), hot and dry climate.
They shed leaves in dry season to conserve water.	They have small, thorny, or wax-coated leaves to reduce water loss.
Examples-Sal, teak, and neem	Examples-cactus, acacia, and date palm

(iv) (a) Two reasons for the great diversity of natural vegetation in India are

- **Varied Climate** India has diverse climatic conditions, ranging from tropical in the South to temperate and alpine in the North. Different temperatures, rainfall patterns and humidity levels support a wide range of vegetation types.
- **Diverse Landforms** India has mountains, plateaus, plains and coastal regions, each providing unique soil types and environmental conditions that influence the growth of different plant species.

(b) The forests help in maintenance of air quality in the following ways

- **Absorption of Carbon Dioxide** Trees absorb CO_2 during photosynthesis, reducing greenhouse gases and improving air quality.
- **Release of Oxygen** Forests release oxygen (O_2), which is essential for life.

7. (i) **Advantage of Well Irrigation**
- **Low Cost and Easy to Construct** Wells can be dug at a low cost and require simple technology, making them accessible for small farmers.

Disadvantage of Well Irrigation
- **Limited Water Supply** Wells depend on groundwater, which can dry up during summers or in areas with low water tables.

(ii) Two measures to overcome water scarcity in metropolitan cities of India are
- **Rainwater Harvesting** Collecting and storing rainwater from rooftops and open spaces can help in recharging groundwater and meeting daily water needs.
- **Wastewater Recycling and Reuse** Treating and recycling wastewater for non-drinking purposes like gardening, cleaning and industrial use can reduce water wastage.

(iii) (a) Tank irrigation is not common in Northern India because of flat terrain. Northern India, especially the Indo-Gangetic Plain, has a flat landscape, making it difficult to construct tanks, which require natural depressions to store water.

(b) Canal irrigation is important in Punjab because the region has a network of perennial rivers like the Satluj, Beas, and Ravi, which provide a continuous water supply for irrigation through canals.

(c) All farmers do not use tube well irrigation even if the geographical conditions are favourable because the installation and maintenance of tube wells are expensive. Small and marginal farmers may not afford the high initial cost of setting up tube wells and the electricity or diesel expenses required to operate them.

(iv) The three objectives of rainwater harvesting are
- **Conservation of Water** To collect and store rainwater for future use, reducing dependence on groundwater and other water sources.
- **Groundwater Recharge** To replenish underground water levels by allowing rainwater to seep into the soil, preventing depletion.
- **Flood and Soil Erosion Control** To reduce surface runoff, preventing floods and soil erosion, especially in urban and hilly areas.

8. (i) (a) A non-conventional energy source that can be harnessed using India's vast coastline is Tidal Energy.

(b) Geothermal energy is a clean and sustainable source of power, producing minimal pollution and reducing dependence on fossil fuels.

(ii) (a) Biogas is formed through the anaerobic decomposition of organic waste like animal dung, plant material and kitchen waste by bacteria. This process called anaerobic digestion produces methane-rich gas, which can be used as fuel.

(b) Biogas is a continuous and reliable source of energy, unlike solar and wind energy, which depend on weather conditions.

(iii) (a) Iron ore is called a versatile mineral because it is the primary raw material for making steel, which is used in various industries like construction, transportation, machinery and infrastructure development.

(b) Windmills set up on agricultural lands are beneficial to farmers because they generate additional income for farmers through land lease payments while allowing them to continue farming activities beneath the wind turbines.

(c) Coal is the most preferred source of energy in Indian industries because it is abundantly available, affordable and provides a reliable energy source for industries like steel, cement and power generation.

(iv) (a) The type of energy being generated in the picture is Hydroelectric Energy.

(b) This type of energy is cheaper in the long run because
- It uses renewable water resources, which do not require fuel costs.
- Hydroelectric power plants have low operational and maintenance costs after initial construction. (any one point)

(c) A power project associated with the generation of this energy in Northern India is the Bhakra Nangal Hydroelectric Project on the Sutlej river.

9. (i) The two climatic conditions that favour the cultivation of groundnut are
- **Warm Temperature** Groundnut requires a warm climate with temperatures between 20°C to 30°C for proper growth.
- **Moderate Rainfall** It grows best in areas with 50-100 cm of rainfall, as excessive moisture can damage the crop.

(ii) Maharashtra has emerged as an important sugarcane-producing state due to the following reasons
- **Favourable Climate** The state has a tropical climate with hot and humid conditions, which are ideal for sugarcane cultivation. Additionally, moderate rainfall and well-distributed irrigation facilities support high yields.
- **Well-Developed Irrigation Facilities** Despite having relatively low rainfall in some regions, Maharashtra has well-developed canal and well irrigation systems, ensuring a continuous water supply for sugarcane crops.

(iii) (a) Trees are planted in between the rows of coffee plants to provide shade and protect the coffee plants from direct sunlight and strong winds, which can affect their growth and quality.

(b) Cotton cultivation requires plenty of cheap labour because most of the processes, like sowing, picking and ginning are done manually, requiring a large workforce.

(c) Hill slopes are best suited for tea cultivation because they ensure proper drainage, preventing waterlogging, which is harmful to tea plants. Additionally, the cool and humid climate of hills favours tea growth.

(iv) (a) Mixed farming is a type of agriculture where both crops and livestock are raised on the same farm.

(b) Zayad is the short cropping season between the Rabi and Kharif seasons in India, from March to June.

(c) Transplantation is the process of growing seedlings in a nursery and then shifting them to the main field for better growth.

10. (i) The growth of the cotton textile industry in Kolkata is due to the following factors
- **Availability of Cheap Labour** Kolkata has a large workforce, including migrant labourers from neighbouring states like Bihar and Odisha, which helps in keeping production costs low.
- **Well-Connected Transportation System** The city has a good network of roads, railways and a major port, making it easy to transport raw materials (cotton) and finished goods both within India and internationally.

(ii) Karnataka is the leading state for silk production in India due to the following reasons
- **Favourable Climate** Karnataka has a moderate climate with suitable temperature and humidity, which is ideal for silkworm rearing and mulberry cultivation.
- **Availability of Mulberry Leaves** The state has extensive mulberry plantations, providing a steady food supply for silkworms, essential for high-quality silk production.

(iii) (a) The Iron and Steel industry located in Chhattisgarh is the Bhilai Steel Plant.

(b) Sources of raw materials for Bhilai Steel Plant
- **Iron Ore** Sourced from the Dalli-Rajhara mines in Chhattisgarh.
- **Coal** Supplied from the Korba and Jharia coalfields.

(iv) (a) Raghav will be writing about the Sugar Industry because its by-products are used in making shoe polish, carbon paper and cardboard.

(b) Two by-products of the sugar industry are bagasse and molasses.

11. (i) A well-developed transport network is important for India because
- **Boosts Trade and Economy** Efficient transport helps in the movement of goods across the country and supports industries, agriculture and exports.
- **Enhances Connectivity** It connects remote and rural areas with cities, improving access to markets, healthcare and education.

(ii) Two advantages of road transport are

- **Door-to-Door Service** Road transport provides direct delivery of goods and passengers to their destination, reducing the need for additional handling.
- **Flexibility and Accessibility** Roads can be built in remote areas, making transport possible even in hilly and rural regions where other modes may not be available.

(iii) (a) Rail transport ensures a comfortable journey, especially for elders and children, as trains provide seating, sleeping arrangements and other facilities.

(b) The highway connecting Silchar in Assam to Porbandar in Gujarat is part of the East-West Corridor.

(c) The cheapest means of transport for bulky goods is water transport, as it is cost-effective and fuel-efficient, especially for long-distance trade.

(iv) (a) Airways are the most efficient mode of transport to connect North-East India with the rest of the country because the region has rugged terrain, dense forests and frequent floods, making road and rail transport difficult.

(b) Railways are easily developed in the Northern plains of India because the region has flat and fertile land, which makes track construction and maintenance easier compared to hilly or plateau regions.

(c) Rivers of peninsular India are not ideal for inland water transport because they are seasonal, with water levels fluctuating throughout the year. Additionally, these rivers have many waterfalls, rapids and rocky beds, making navigation difficult.

12. (i) (a) The increase in the use of electronic devices such as mobile phones, computers, televisions and home appliances, along with rapid technological advancements, has led to a substantial rise in E-waste in India.

(b) Dumping is the practice of disposing of waste materials, including industrial, household and hazardous waste, in an uncontrolled manner, often in landfills, open spaces or water bodies.

(ii) As a responsible student, I can contribute to reducing and managing waste in my surroundings through the following steps

- **Reduce Waste Generation** Use reusable items like steel water bottles, cloth bags and lunch boxes instead of plastic ones.
- **Spread Awareness** Organise cleanliness drives in school and the local community.

(iii) (a) **Reuse** Using an item again for a different purpose instead of throwing it away.

(b) **Recycle** Processing waste materials into new products to prevent waste.

(c) **Reduce** Using resources wisely to minimise waste generation.

(iv) (a) Organic manure should replace chemical fertilisers because it improves soil fertility naturally without harming beneficial microbes. Unlike chemical fertilisers, which can degrade soil quality over time, organic manure enhances soil structure and retains moisture, leading to sustainable farming.

(b) There should be a ban on the use of polythene and plastic products because they are non- biodegradable and cause severe environmental pollution. Plastic waste clogs drains, harms marine and wildlife, and releases toxic chemicals when burned, contributing to climate change.

(c) Manual handling of waste must be avoided because it poses serious health risks to workers due to exposure to harmful bacteria, toxic chemicals and sharp objects. Instead, proper waste management systems, including protective gear and mechanised waste disposal, should be implemented for safety and hygiene.